John Lee

346 901 1773

biblebasics49@gmail,com

BIBLE BASICS

FOUNDATIONS OF FAITH

Acknowledgements

All verses used in this book are from the King James Version of the Bible.

The editor would like to thank those whose help and support in this project made it possible. Special thanks to Michael Roy and Reuben Rushevsky for their significant contributions.

Compiled and edited by John Lee

Design by M-A Mignot

ISBN: 978-1-63264-119-9

Printed in China

www.compassproductionsinc.com

preface

Discovering Truth—Bible Basics outlines the basic beliefs that form the foundation for Christian faith, as set down in the Bible. It is "a declaration of those things which are most surely believed among us" (Luke 1:1), so "that thou mayest know how thou oughtest to behave thyself" (1 Timothy 3:15).

Bible Basics is intended to help new Christians become familiar with the Scriptures, and to help seasoned Christians deepen their knowledge of God's Word, find strength and direction for daily living, and share their faith with others. Pastors, counselors, parents, teachers, and mentors will also find it helpful when instructing and counseling others.

Because one of the goals for Bible Basics is to provide a basic Christian handbook that is compact enough to be carried anywhere, it was necessary to limit the in-depth studies to those topics which are most essential to understanding and growing in Christian faith. The topical index, however, provides mini-studies on over 150 topics.

Jesus said to His disciples, "If you abide in my word, you are my disciples indeed. And you shall know the truth, and the truth shall make you free" (John 8:31–32). —And that promise is also for you!

explanation

FORMAT AND CONVENTIONS

As in most Bible concordances and topical study helps, the Bible verses have not been quoted in their entirety.

Ellipses (...) indicate where words have been omitted.

Brackets [ ] are used in the following instances:

(1) When it is necessary to clarify who or what is being referred to. For example, "He prayed the third time" becomes "[Jesus] prayed the third time" (Matthew 26:44).

(2) When the meaning that the translators assigned to a certain word is not in current use. For example, "The Lord is my shepherd, I shall not want [lack]" (Psalm 23:1).

(3) When the tense or person of a verb is changed for readability. For example, "The high and lofty one that inhabiteth eternity ... dwell with him that is of a contrite and humble spirit" becomes "The high and lofty one that inhabiteth eternity ... [dwells] with him that is of a contrite and humble spirit" (Isaiah 57:15).

(4) When a Scripture passage is too lengthy or difficult to abbreviate, such as when an entire story is referred to, and a simple summary is sufficient to explain what the passage is about.

(5) When something is not stated in a verse, but is implied.

Verses of secondary importance are generally noted in a "See also" list of references, in parentheses, at the end of the section. However, if a secondary verse corresponds to a particular verse, the "See also" reference appears on the same line as that verse.

Contents at a Glance

Alphabetical Listing of Major Topics vi
Table of Contents vii
Salvation 1
Jesus Christ, the Son of God 5
The Holy Spirit 19
The Word of God 25
Prayer 32
Faith 40
Love and Forgiveness 50
Our Relationship with God 61
Fellowship 71
Witnessing 74
Giving 84
How to Find the Will of God 89
Obedience to God 100
Strength and Power 104
Protection 112
Supply 120
Trials, Temptations, and Tribulations 128
Suffering 139
Comfort 148
Healing 156
Overcoming the Devil 163
Fear Not 171
Thankfulness 178
Pride, Self-righteousness, and Humility 183
The Power of the Tongue 192
Unity 204
Discipleship 212
The Christian's Relationship to Worldly Society 218
Persecution 226
Backsliding 236
Christianity in Crisis 243
The Law of Christ 251
Creation vs. Evolution 260
The Endtime 263
Marriage and the Home 273
Children 282
Sleep 289
Old Age 292
Condensed Word Basics 298
Index 318

Alphabetical Listing of Major Topics

Backsliding 236
Children 282
Christian's Relationship to Worldly Society, The 218
Christianity in Crisis 243
Comfort 148
Creation vs. Evolution 260
Discipleship 212
Endtime, The 263
Faith 40
Fear Not 171
Fellowship 71
Giving 84
Healing 156
Holy Spirit, The 19
How to Find the Will of God 89
Jesus Christ, the Son of God 5
Law of Christ, The 251
Love and Forgiveness 50
Marriage and the Home 273
Obedience to God 100
Old Age 292
Our Relationship with God 61
Overcoming the Devil 163
Persecution 226
Power of the Tongue, The 192
Prayer 32
Pride, Self-righteousness, and Humility 183
Protection 112
Salvation 1
Sleep 289
Strength and Power 104
Suffering 139
Supply 120
Thankfulness 178
Trials, Temptations, and Tribulations 128
Unity 204
Witnessing 74
Word of God, The 25

TABLE OF CONTENTS

Topics and Subtopics — Page

SALVATION

1. All men are sinners 1
2. Salvation by grace (undeserved mercy), not works 1
3. Salvation through Jesus 1
4. Believe on Jesus 1
5. Receive Jesus 2
6. Eternal salvation 2
7. Receiving Jesus guarantees eternal life in heaven 2
8. The results of being born again 3
9. Sin brings about spiritual death; but Jesus died in our place, taking our punishment 3
10. In the Mosaic law, blood is payment for sin, but Jesus' death paid that price in full 3
11. All men are not saved sons of God in their natural state 4
12. The self-righteous refuse Jesus' salvation 4
13. New Testament examples of salvation 4

JESUS CHRIST, THE SON OF GOD

1. Jesus' Father, God 5
2. Why God sent Jesus into the world 6
3. More reasons why God sent Jesus into the world 7
4. Jesus' teachings and personal example 8
5. Jesus, the way to salvation 8
6. Jesus, the Light of the World 10
7. Jesus' life and resurrection 10
8. Eyewitness accounts in the Bible tell us that Jesus 11
9. Old Testament Messianic prophecies—fulfilled in the birth, death, and life of Jesus Christ 11
10. Jesus, the Son of God 12
11. Jesus' relationship with God 14
12. The authority and power God has given Jesus 15
13. Jesus, the Creator 17
14. Titles of Jesus 17

THE HOLY SPIRIT

1. The Holy Spirit's part in our salvation 19
2. The baptism (overflowing) of the Holy Spirit 19
3. The purpose of the Holy Spirit baptism 20
4. Gifts of the Holy Spirit 21
5. Freedom of the Holy Spirit 22
6. The Holy Spirit inspires unity of believers 23
7. Other points about the ministry of the Spirit 23
8. Obeying the Holy Spirit 23
9. The Holy Spirit in Jesus' life 24
10. Other Bible examples 24

THE WORD OF GOD

1. The Bible was written by divine inspiration 25
2. God's Word is eternally true and never fails 25
3. The Importance of God's Word 25
4. God's Word is a spiritual weapon 25
5. The Bible was written for our benefit 26
6. Keeping (obeying, heeding) the Word 26
7. What the Word does for us 27
8. What we should do with the Word 28
9. What we should not do with the Word 30
10. Beware of those who don't teach the Word 31
11. The Devil blinds men's eyes to God's Word 31
12. Stories relating to the Word 31

PRAYER

1. How to pray 32
2. Conditions to getting prayer answered 33
3. Prayer promises 33
4. Things that hinder our prayers 34
5. Private prayer and united prayer 35
6. When to pray 36
7. Wholehearted fervent prayer 37
8. Other points on prayer 38
9. Ways God answers prayer 39

FAITH

1. What is faith? 40
2. The importance of faith 40
3. The Word tells us to have faith 41
4. How to obtain faith 41
5. The rewards, blessings, and fruits of faith 43
6. Trusting in God's promises 45
7. Faith vs. natural reasoning 45
8. The power of faith 46
9. The testing of our faith 47
10. When we have faith 48
11. Lack of faith 49

LOVE AND FORGIVENESS

1. God is love, and He loves us 50
2. The first great commandment—To love God 51
3. The second great commandment—To love thy neighbour 51
4. Love one another 51
5. Real, genuine love 53
6. Real love results in good deeds 54
7. Love vs. hate 55
8. Special categories of love 56
9. Love, forgiveness, and mercy 57
10. We are to be merciful and forgiving 58
11. We must confess our sins in order to receive forgiveness 59

OUR RELATIONSHIP WITH GOD

1. We worship God by loving Him 61
2. How we show our love for God 62
3. We are to love God above all else 63
4. We are to fear and reverence God 64
5. Resting in the Lord 65
6. Drawing close and resting in the "Secret Place" 66
7. The benefits of taking quiet time with God 66
8. Hindrances to our relationship with God 67
9. Our special relationship with God 68

FELLOWSHIP

1. The Bible instructs us to fellowship 71
2. The reasons for fellowship 71
3. Holding meetings 72
4. Being "of one mind" and working together in unity 73
5. Using fellowship to witness 73

WITNESSING

1. It is the duty of Christians to witness 74
2. Why we need to witness 74
3. Don't be shy or ashamed to witness 75
4. Pointers on how to be a good witness 75
5. Use the Word in your witnessing 76
6. Keeping your witness simple 76
7. What you should preach (witness about) 77
8. Whom to witness to 77
9. A winning personal example 78
10. When to witness 79
11. Where to witness 79
12. The "fruit" Christians should bear is other Christians, new saved souls 79
13. The Holy Spirit and witnessing 80
14. Witnessing, the greatest work on earth 80
15. Reactions to the gospel 81
16. Witnessing boldly despite opposition 81
17. More verses about witnessing and testifying 82

GIVING

1. The Bible commands believers to give 84
2. God blesses us when we give 84
3. Giving to God's work 84
4. Christian duty regarding giving and sharing 85
5. Giving with the right motives 86
6. What happens when we withhold and don't give 87
7. Tithing 88
8. Other aspects of giving 88

HOW TO FIND THE WILL OF GOD

1. The prerequisite: Submit your will to God ... 89
2. The Holy Spirit guides us to find God's will ... 89
3. The first place to look for God's will is in His Word ... 89
4. God sometimes reveals His will through dreams ... 90
5. God sometimes reveals His will through visions ... 91
6. God sometimes reveals His will through prophecy and revelations ... 92
7. God sometimes reveals His will through godly counsel ... 93
8. God sometimes reveals His will by obvious circumstances ... 93
9. God sometimes reveals His will through the "witness of the Spirit" ... 95
10. God sometimes reveals His will through confirming signs ... 96
11. Sometimes God's will and plans are conditional ... 96
12. God often gives His people alternative choices ... 96
13. What to do when God does not reveal His will ... 97
14. What to do when you desperately require specific directions ... 97
15. You can count on God's leadings even when 98
16. The will of God is supreme ... 99
17. Rewards for doing God's will ... 99
18. God's will on specific subjects ... 99

OBEDIENCE TO GOD

1. Obeying God ... 100
2. If we love and know God, we will obey Him ... 100
3. Blessings for obeying God ... 100
4. Jesus' example of obedience ... 101
5. Yieldedness to God ... 102
6. Obeying God rather than ungodly men ... 102
7. Disobedience to God—How He views it ... 102
8. Various categories of disobedience ... 103

STRENGTH AND POWER

1. God's strength vs. our strength ... 104
2. Trust in God, not your own strength ... 105
3. Our weakness causes us to depend upon God ... 105

4. God can strengthen and use you 106
5. Don't trust in yourself 108
6. Power when witnessing 108
7. God's power vs. physical power 109

PROTECTION

1. Trusting in God is your only sure refuge 112
2. God will protect you because He loves you 113
3. God can protect you from 114
4. Protection from those who seek to harm you 116
5. Special protection promised in the last days 116
6. Conditions for having God's protection 116
7. Some examples of divine protection 118

SUPPLY

1. God can supply all our needs 120
2. God can do miracles to supply 120
3. Supply during famine 121
4. Conditions to God's supply 122
5. Reasons why we sometimes lack 123
6. God loves you and wants to supply 124
7. We should do our part 124
8. When God uses others to supply His workers' needs 125
9. Giving to God's work 126
10. God promises to prosper our work and businesses 126
11. God supplies our needs, not always our wants 127

TRIALS, TEMPTATIONS, AND TRIBULATIONS

1. Trials and tests are to be expected 128
2. Trials often result when things don't go our way 128
3. Why God allows trials and tests 129
4. Trials over suffering personal loss 131
5. Some Bible examples of trials and tests 132
6. Why it's worth it to endure tests and temptations 132
7. Be thankful for your trials and temptations 133
8. Helping others who are going through trials 134

9. Where temptations come from 134
10. Avoiding temptation 134
11. How to resist and overcome temptation 135
12. God will deliver you 137
13. How righteous men fell through temptation 137
14. Examples of resisting temptation 138

SUFFERING
1. Who causes suffering?—God or the Devil? 139
2. Why does God allow the righteous to suffer? 139
3. Some specific reasons that God allows suffering 140
4. Suffering because of obedience and righteousness 141
5. The benefits and good fruits of suffering 141
6. Rewards in heaven for earthly suffering 142
7. Remember, Jesus also suffered 142
8. The right attitude toward suffering 143
9. Wrong attitudes toward suffering 144
10. God comforts and strengthens us when we suffer 144
11. Deliverance from suffering 144
12. Our duty toward the suffering and afflicted 145
13. The suffering of the wicked 145
14. Much suffering is actually self-inflicted 146
15. Suffering can bring some to God 146

COMFORT
1. God will help and comfort you 148
2. How to receive God's comfort 148
3. God loves you and cares for you 150
4. God's loving hands uphold you 151
5. If you feel you're in the dark, trust in God for light 151
6. Look on the bright side 151
7. Why and how to comfort one another 152
8. When feeling abandoned, or suffering heartbreak or loss 154
9. Heavenly consolation for present suffering and sorrow 155

HEALING
1. Healing was part of Jesus' ministry 156
2. God's healing promises are still valid today 156
3. It is within God's will to heal 156
4. Nothing is too serious for God to heal 157
5. Conditions for healing 157
6. Practical steps for obtaining healing 157
7. Pray for the sick 159
8. Fight in the spirit for healing 159
9. Reasons why God allows afflictions and illnesses 159
10. Points to remember after prayer 161
11. Miraculous or natural healing? 162
12. No sickness in heaven 162

OVERCOMING THE DEVIL
1. Where did the Devil come from? 163
2. The Devil is under God's restrictions 163
3. Victory over the Devil 164
4. The spiritual warfare 165
5. The Devil's devices 166
6. The Devil is the accuser and tempter 167
7. The Devil is a destroyer 167
8. Judgement of the Devil and his demons, and his final end 168
9. Your armour and weaponry to defeat the Devil 168
10. Power, freedom, and deliverance from the Devil's darkness 169
11. Our astonishing angelic allies, the hosts of heaven 169

FEAR NOT
1. God tells us not to fear 171
2. Trusting in God overcomes fear 171
3. Some causes of fear 172
4. What fear can result in 173
5. How to have peace and freedom from fear 175
6. The fear of God 176

THANKFULNESS

1. Having a thankful, grateful attitude 178
2. Praising God 178
3. Murmuring (complaining) forbidden by God 179
4. Causes of murmuring 180
5. Why murmuring is dangerous 181
6. What to do when problems arise 181

PRIDE, SELF-RIGHTEOUSNESS, AND HUMILITY

1. What does God think about pride? 183
2. Why is it wrong for us to be proud? 183
3. Some causes of pride 185
4. Warnings against pride 185
5. Why is it wrong to think that we—in ourselves—are good and righteous? 186
6. Why is it wrong to think that we—in ourselves—are better than others? 187
7. The humbling of the proud 187
8. Why we should want to be humble 188
9. Keeping a humble attitude 189
10. Humility with one another 190
11. The solution 191
12. Special passages 191

THE POWER OF THE TONGUE

1. The power of positive speech 192
2. Silence and restrained speech 193
3. The damage an uncontrolled tongue will do 195
4. Foolish and evil speech 195
5. Controlling your tongue 196
6. Gossiping, backbiting, and slandering 197
7. The punishment for gossiping 198
8. How to avoid criticising and gossiping 198
9. Warning against judging others 199
10. What to do when others speak evil of you 200

11. Arguments and contentions 200
12. Lying, deceiving, and bearing false witness 203

UNITY
1. Unity or disunity? 204
2. How to work at keeping united 204
3. The fruits of unity 206
4. Unity of believers in Jesus 207
5. Causes of disunity 208
6. Results of disunity 209
7. How to deal with disunity 210
8. Disassociating from those who cause division 210
9. Restoration to fellowship 211
10. When contentions and disputes are necessary 211

DISCIPLESHIP
1. What is a disciple? 212
2. A disciple's job 212
3. Dedicating oneself to God 213
4. Different ministries of disciples 214
5. Discipleship and "losing your own life" 215
6. The path the disciple follows 215
7. The life of a disciple 216
8. The benefits of discipleship 217
9. Jesus' last words and prayer for His disciples 217

THE CHRISTIAN'S RELATIONSHIP TO SOCIETY
1. Christians do not belong to this world 218
2. Though in this world, we are not of it 218
3. Our attitude toward worldly values 220
4. If possible, live peaceably with others in order to win them to God 221
5. Cautions against compromising with the world 221
6. The importance of an honest, sincere example 222
7. Work and employment 223

8. The work of pastors, full-time Christian workers, and missionaries 224
9. A Christian's relationship to governments 225
10. The governments of man 225

PERSECUTION

1. Persecution promised to all followers of Jesus 226
2. Benefits of persecution 226
3. Attitude to have during persecution 227
4. Reasons why persecutors attack Christians 229
5. Persecution usually begins with verbal attacks 231
6. Persecution from family and friends 232
7. The world persecuted and rejected Jesus 232
8. Compromising, fleeing, and avoiding persecution 233
9. God will judge your persecutors 234
10. Endtime persecution 235

BACKSLIDING

1. Danger signs that lead to losing faith 236
2. God's promises of mercy to those who return to Him 238
3. Attitude for repentant prodigals to have 239
4. How to avoid losing the faith 239
5. The attitude to have toward former brethren 242

CHRISTIANITY IN CRISIS

1. Predictions of a great apostasy in the last days 243
2. Ignorance of the Word of God 243
3. Doctrines and traditions of man vs. God's Word 244
4. The dwelling place of God 245
5. The danger of complacency 246
6. Disobedience to the Great Commission 247
7. Failure to shepherd the flock 247
8. Warnings against coveting financial gain 248
9. Warnings against hypocrisy 248
10. Religious persecution 249

THE LAW OF CHRIST

1. Salvation is purely by grace, not works 251
2. What was the Mosaic law? 251
3. The Law served a purpose only for a time 252
4. Atonement (payment) for breaking the Law 253
5. The new law, the law of Christ 254
6. Now the commandment is to love God and our neighbour 255
7. Living the new law 256
8. Warnings against misusing the new law 256
9. Beware of falling into religious legalism 257
10. Trying to legalistically keep the Law is not God's will 258
11. Even under the Mosaic law, God's love and mercy prevailed 258

CREATION vs. EVOLUTION

1. God created the world, not chance evolution 260
2. God's Word created (and maintains) the universe 260
3. God's creation is proof of His existence 260
4. Jesus believed in and quoted from Genesis 260
5. The Bible and science 260
6. God, as the Creator, has ownership rights over everything 261
7. He expects and deserves reverence from His creations 261
8. God has power to control His creation 262

THE ENDTIME

1. The last days; signs of the times 263
2. How to recognise the Antichrist world government 264
3. The rise of the Antichrist 264
4. The signing of the covenant 264
5. The breaking of the covenant and stopping of the daily sacrifice (Jewish temple worship) 264
6. The great tribulation 264
7. The second coming of Jesus Christ 266
8. The resurrection and rapture 267
9. The marriage supper of the Lamb 267
10. The judgement seat of Christ 268
11. The wrath of God upon the earth 268

12. The Battle of Armageddon 269
13. The millennium 269
14. The Battle of Gog and Magog 271
15. The great white throne judgement 271
16. The new heaven and new earth 271

MARRIAGE AND THE HOME
1. Marriage 273
2. A husband's responsibility toward his wife 273
3. A wife's attributes and responsibilities 274
4. A wife's responsibility toward her husband 275
5. Spiritual ministries are not restricted to men 275
6. Harmony and marital peace 276
7. Marriage and lovemaking 277
8. Marriage vs. celibacy 278
9. Divorce, remarriage, marital infidelity, and forgiveness 278
10. Parental duties toward their children 279
11. The importance of training your children right 280
12. Parents as "good shepherds" 280

CHILDREN
1. Pregnancy 282
2. God's hand on children before birth 283
3. The Bible on "the right to life" 283
4. Childbirth 283
5. Teaching and training your children 284
6. Teaching children obedience and respect 285
7. Loving instruction balanced with discipline 286
8. The growing years 287
9. Becoming like children 288

SLEEP
1. Sleep considered a blessing 289
2. If you can't sleep, pray 289
3. Some reasons for not being able to sleep 289
4. Good reasons for missing sleep 290

5. When it is not good to sleep 290
6. Trusting God to awaken you 291

OLD AGE

1. The blessings of old age 292
2. God's help in our old age 292
3. Desiring long life 292
4. God can mightily use aged believers 294
5. Strength in old age 296
6. Cautions regarding old age 296
7. Joy in children and in grandchildren 297

SALVATION

1. ALL MEN ARE SINNERS:

Ecclesiastes 7:20	Not a just man on earth, that … sinneth not
Isaiah 64:6	All our righteousnesses are as filthy rags
Romans 3:10	There is none righteous, no not one
Romans 3:23	For all have sinned, and come short of the glory of God
James 2:10	Whoever shall offend in one point [of law], guilty of all
1 John 1:8	If we say that we have no sin, we deceive ourselves

2. SALVATION BY GRACE (UNDESERVED MERCY), NOT WORKS:

Mark 10:25–27	Who can be saved? With men it is impossible
Romans 3:20	By deeds of law shall no flesh be justified in his sight
Romans 11:6	And if by grace, then is it no more of works
Galatians 2:16	Justified by the faith of Christ and not by works of the law
Ephesians 2:8-9	For by grace are ye saved through faith, not of yourselves … not of works
2 Timothy 1:9	Saved us, not according to our works, but according to his grace
Titus 3:5	Not by works of righteousness which we have done

3. SALVATION THROUGH JESUS:

John 3:16	God … gave his only begotten Son, that whosoever believeth in him, should … have everlasting life
John 3:36	He that believeth not the Son shall not see life
John 8:24	If ye believe not that I am he, ye shall die in your sins
John 10:1	He that entereth not by the door … but climbeth up some other way … is a thief and a robber
John 10:9	I am the door: by me if any man enter in … be saved
John 14:6	I am the way, the truth, and the life: no man cometh unto the Father but by me
Acts 4:12	None other name … whereby we must be saved
1 Corinthians 3:11	For other foundation can no man lay than … Jesus Christ
1 Timothy 2:5	One mediator between God and men … Christ Jesus
1 John 5:12	He that hath not the Son of God hath not life

4. BELIEVE ON JESUS:

John 3:16	Whosoever believeth in him should not perish, but have everlasting life
John 11:25–26	I am the resurrection and the life … whosoever believeth in me shall never die
Acts 16:31	Believe on the Lord Jesus Christ, and thou shalt be saved

Romans 10:9–10	If thou shalt … believe in thine heart … thou shalt be saved
1 John 5:1	Whosoever believeth Jesus is the Christ is born of God

5. RECEIVE JESUS:

John 1:12	But as many as received him … power to become sons
Galatians 4:6	God hath sent forth the Spirit of his Son into your heart
Ephesians 3:17	That Christ may dwell in your hearts by faith
Revelation 3:20	If any man … open the door, I will come in to him

6. ETERNAL SALVATION:

A. You can never lose it:

Psalm 37:24	Though he fall, he shall not be utterly cast down: for the Lord unholdeth him with his hand
John 3:36	He that believeth on the Son … hath everlasting life
John 6:37	Him that cometh to me I will in no wise cast out
John 10:28	I give unto them eternal life; and they shall never perish, neither shall any man pluck them out of my hand
Romans 8:38–39	I am persuaded that [nothing] shall be able to separate us from the love of God ... in Christ Jesus
1 Corinthians 3:11–15	[If works are] wood, hay and stubble … shall be burned, yet he himself shall be saved
1 Corinthians 5:5	Destruction of the flesh, that the spirit may be saved
2 Timothy 2:13	Thou we believe not, yet he abideth faithful
Hebrews 13:5	I will never leave thee, nor forsake thee
1 John 5:13	Ye may know that ye have eternal life

B. But God will chasten you for wrongdoing:

Psalm 89:30–34	If they break my statutes … I will visit with the rod [but] my lovingkindness will I not utterly take away
Hebrews 12:5–8	Whom the Lord loveth he chasteneth, and scourgeth every son whom he receiveth
Revelation 3:19	As many I love, I rebuke and chasten

7. RECEIVING JESUS GUARANTEES ETERNAL LIFE IN HEAVEN:

John 11:26	Whosoever … believeth in me shall never die
John 14:2–3	In my Father's house are many mansions
Romans 6:23	The gift of God is eternal life through Jesus Christ
1 Peter 1:3–4	Incorruptible inheritance reserved in heaven for you
1 John 5:11	God hath given to us eternal life … in his Son

(See also Revelation 21:1–27; 22:1–5 for descriptions of heaven.)

8. THE RESULTS OF BEING BORN AGAIN:

A. Spiritual rebirth makes you a new creature:

Matthew 18:3	Be converted and become as little children
John 1:13	Born, not of blood, nor of the will of man, but of God
John 3:3	Except a man be born again, he cannot see the kingdom of God
Romans 12:2	Be ye transformed by the renewing of your mind
2 Corinthians 5:17	If any man be in Christ, he is a new creature
1 Peter 1:23	Born again, not of corruptible seed, but ... by the word of God

B. You will desire to work for Jesus:

Ephesians 2:10	We are his workmanship, created in Christ Jesus unto good works
Titus 2:14	[Jesus] gave himself for us [to] purify unto himself a peculiar people, zealous of good works

(See also Ephesians 4:21–24; Colossians 3:8–10; Titus 3:8; James 2:18.)

9. SIN BRINGS ABOUT SPIRITUAL DEATH; BUT JESUS DIED IN OUR PLACE, TAKING OUR PUNISHMENT:

Isaiah 59:2	Your iniquities have separated you and your God
Romans 5:8	While we were sinners, Christ died for us
Romans 6:23	The wages of [penalty for] sin is death
2 Corinthians 5:21	He hath made him [Jesus] to be sin for [in place of] us
1 John 1:9	If we confess our sins, he [will] forgive and cleanse us
1 John 2:1–2	We have an advocate ... Jesus Christ. He is the propitiation for ... the sins of the whole world

10. IN THE MOSAIC LAW, BLOOD IS PAYMENT FOR SIN, BUT JESUS' DEATH PAID THAT PRICE IN FULL:

Leviticus 17:11	It is the blood that maketh atonement for the soul
Matthew 26:28	My blood ... shed for the remission of sins
John 1:29	The Lamb of God, which taketh away sin of the world
Ephesians 1:7	We have redemption through his blood, the forgiveness of sins (See also 1 John 2:12.)
Hebrews 9:22	Without shedding of blood is no remission [of sin]
1 Peter 1:18–19	Ye were redeemed ... with the precious blood of Christ
1 John 1:7	The blood of Jesus Christ cleanseth us from all sin

11. ALL MEN ARE NOT SAVED SONS OF GOD IN THEIR NATURAL STATE:

Matthew 7:13	Wide is the gate … that leadeth to destruction, and many … go in thereat
John 3:19	Light is come into the world, and men loved darkness rather than light
John 8:44	Ye are of your father the devil
John 8:47	Ye hear [God's words] not, because ye are not of God
Ephesians 2:2–3,12	Ye were children of disobedience, children of wrath, aliens and strangers without Christ

12. THE SELF-RIGHTEOUS REFUSE JESUS' SALVATION:

(See Matthew 5:20; 9:10–13; 21:31; Luke 18:9–14; John 5:39–44; Romans 10:3; 1 John 1:9–10.)

13. NEW TESTAMENT EXAMPLES OF SALVATION:

Luke 19:1–10	[Conversion of the corrupt tax-collector, Zaccheus]
Acts 9:1–22	[Conversion of apostle Paul] (See also Acts 6:8–14; 7:57–60; 8:1–4; 26:9–11.)
Acts 10:1–8	[Conversion of Roman centurion Cornelius]
Acts 13:1–12	[Conversion of governor of Cyprus, Sergius Paulus]
Acts 16:13–34	[Conversion of the merchant Lydia and Roman jailor]

JESUS CHRIST, THE SON OF GOD

1. JESUS' FATHER, GOD:

A. God has always existed and always will:

Exodus 3:14	God said unto Moses, I AM THAT I AM
Psalm 90:2	From everlasting to everlasting, thou art God
Psalm 102:24–27	The heavens ... shall perish, but thou shalt endure ... thou art the same, and thy years shall have no end
Revelation 1:8	I am Alpha and Omega, the beginning and the ending ... which is, and which was, and which is to come, the Almighty

(See also Isaiah 41:4.)

B. God is an immortal, invisible Spirit:

John 4:24	God is a Spirit: they that worship him must worship him in spirit and in truth
1 Timothy 1:17	Unto the King eternal, immortal, invisible, the only wise God, be honour and glory

(See also 2 Corinthians 3:17; Hebrews 11:27.)

C. He fills the entire universe:

2 Chronicles 2:6	Who is able to build him an house [temple], seeing the heaven and the heaven of heavens cannot contain him?
Psalm 139:7–10	Whither shall I flee from thy presence? Thou art there
Acts 7:48–49	Heaven is my throne, and earth is my footstool
Acts 17:24–29	In him we live, and move, and have our being

(See also 1 Kings 8:27; 2 Chronicles 6:18; Isaiah 66:1.)

D. He is the only true God:

Isaiah 43:10–11	I am he: before me there was no God ... neither shall there be after me
Isaiah 44:6,8	I am the first, and the last; beside me there is no God
Isaiah 45:21–22	There is no God else beside me ... I am God, and there is none else

E. He created the world, the universe, and man:

Genesis 1:1	In the beginning God created the heaven and the earth
Genesis 1:26–27	God created man in his own image ... male and female
Genesis 2:7	God formed man of the dust of the ground

(See also Isaiah 45:18; 48:13; Acts 17:24–26.)

F. His understanding and power are infinite:

Psalm 139:4	There is not a word in my tongue, but, lo, O Lord, thou knowest it altogether
Psalm 147:5	Great is our Lord ... his understanding is infinite

Isaiah 40:13–18	All nations before him are as nothing … less than nothing, and vanity
Isaiah 40:28	There is no searching of his understanding
Romans 11:33	O the depth of … the wisdom and knowledge of God!

G. God is far beyond our limited ability to understand:

Isaiah 55:8–9	As the heavens are higher than the earth, so are … my thoughts [higher] than your thoughts

H. God has a wonderful and beautiful plan:

1 Corinthians 2:9	Neither have entered into heart of man, the [wonderful] things God hath prepared for them that love him (See also Isaiah 64:4.)

I. But our sins separate us from God:

Ecclesiastes 7:20	Not a just man on earth, that … sinneth not
Isaiah 59:2	Your iniquities have separated between you and your God
Romans 3:23	For all have sinned, and come short of the glory of God

J. God loves us and wants to save us:

Matthew 18:14	It is not the will of [God] that one … should perish
2 Peter 3:9	The Lord is … not willing that any should perish (See also Ezekiel 18:23,32; 33:11.)

2. WHY GOD SENT JESUS INTO THE WORLD:

A. God sent Jesus to show us a picture of what He is like:

2 Corinthians 4:4	Christ, who is the image of God
Colossians 1:13,15	His dear Son: who is the image [perfect picture] of the invisible God
Hebrews 1:3	The brightness of his [God's] glory, and the express [clearly communicated] image of his person

B. Through knowing Jesus, we can know God:

John 8:19	If ye had known me, ye should have known my Father
John 14:7–9	He that hath seen me hath seen the Father (See also John 12:45.)

C. God showed His love by sending His Son to earth:

John 3:16	God so loved the world, that he gave his only … Son
Romans 5:8	God commendeth his love toward us, in that … Christ [came into the world and] died for us
1 John 4:8–10	The love of God ... God sent his only begotten Son into the world, that we might live through him (See also Ephesians 2:4–7.)

D. Jesus showed God's love by dying for us:

John 10:11	I am the good shepherd: the good shepherd giveth his life for the sheep
John 15:13	Greater love hath no man than this, that a man lay down his life for his friends

E. Jesus' death paid the price for our sins, so that we can receive God's gift of salvation:

Luke 19:10	The Son of man is come to seek and to save that which was lost (See also Matthew 9:13.)
John 3:17	God sent not his Son into the world to condemn world; but that the world through him might be saved
Romans 5:6–11	We were reconciled to God by the death of his Son
1 Timothy 1:15	Christ Jesus came into the world to save sinners
1 John 3:5	He was manifested to take away our sins
1 John 4:14	The Father sent the Son to be the Saviour of the world
Revelation 5:9	Thou wast slain, and redeemed us to God by thy blood (See also 1 Corinthians 15:3; Ephesians 1:7; 2:12–18; 1 Thessalonians 5:9–10; Hebrews 9:12,14,26,28; 10:12,14; 1 John 4:9–10; Revelation 1:5.)

3. MORE REASONS WHY GOD SENT JESUS INTO THE WORLD:

A. To proclaim the truth:

John 18:37	For this cause came I into the world, that I should bear witness unto the truth

B. To destroy the power of the Devil:

Hebrews 2:14–15	That … he [Jesus] might destroy him that had the power of death, that is, the devil
1 John 3:8	For this purpose the Son of God was manifested, that he might destroy the works of the devil (See also 1 Corinthians 15:54–57.)

C. To experience humanity so that He could sympathise with us:

Hebrews 2:16–18	Made like unto his brethren … in that he himself hath suffered being tempted, he is able to succor them
Hebrews 4:15	[He was] touched with the feeling of our infirmities: Mathew 26:37 (sorrow); Luke 2:40 (growing up); Luke 4:2 (hunger); Luke 8:23 (need for sleep); Luke 9:58 (poverty); John 4:6–7 (weariness and thirst).

4. JESUS' TEACHINGS AND PERSONAL EXAMPLE:

A. Jesus taught with power and authority:

Luke 4:32	They were astonished at his doctrine: for his word was with power (See also Matthew 7:28–29.)
John 7:46	Never man spake like this man

B. Jesus' message was love:

Matthew 22:37–39	Thou shalt love the Lord … thou shalt love thy neighbour
John 13:34–35	A new commandment I give unto you, That ye love one another
John 15:12	Love one another, as I have loved you (See also John 15:17; 17:26; 1 John 3:11.)

C. Jesus was humble:

Matthew 11:29	Learn of me; for I am meek and lowly in heart
Luke 22:27	I am among you as he that serveth
John 13:3–15	[Jesus' humble example of washing His disciples' feet]
Philippians 2:5–8	[He] made himself of no reputation, and took … the form of a servant … humbled himself

D. He befriended and won sinners and outcasts:

Matthew 9:9–13	[Jesus ate with publicans and sinners]
Luke 7:36–48	[Jesus confounded a Pharisee by allowing a sinful woman to touch, wash, and kiss His feet as He was eating]
Luke 19:2–10	[Jesus ate with and forgave a despised tax collector]
Luke 23:39–43	[Jesus forgave the penitent thief dying with Him]
John 8:1–11	[Jesus forgave the woman caught in adultery]

5. JESUS, THE WAY TO SALVATION:

A. Jesus is the way to God:

John 1:29	The Lamb of God, which taketh away the sin of the world
John 14:6	I am the way, the truth, and the life: no man cometh unto the Father, but by me
Acts 4:12	Neither is there salvation in any other: for there is none other name … whereby we must be saved
1 Timothy 2:5	One mediator between God and men, Christ Jesus
1 John 5:11	God hath given to us eternal life, and this life is in his Son (See also John 8:51; 10:7–9; 17:2–3.)

B. Jesus has the power to give us eternal life:

John 5:26	As the Father hath life in himself; so hath he given to the Son to have life in himself

John 1:4	In him was life; and the life was the light of men
John 3:16	Whosoever believeth in him … have everlasting life
John 5:24	He that believeth hath everlasting life, and … is passed from death unto life
John 6:40	Every one which … believeth on him [has] everlasting life
John 6:47–48,50–51	He that believeth on me hath everlasting life. I am that bread of life … if any man eat of this bread, he shall live forever
John 10:28	I give unto them eternal life; and they shall never perish
John 11:25	I am the resurrection, and the life
John 17:2–3	This is the life eternal, that they might know … Jesus Christ
Romans 6:23	The gift of God is eternal life through Jesus Christ
Hebrews 5:9	He [Jesus] became the author of eternal salvation
1 John 5:12–13	He that hath the Son hath life … you that believe on the name of the Son of God … have eternal life

C. When we receive Jesus, God dwells in our hearts:

1 John 4:15	Whosoever shall confess that Jesus is the Son of God, God dwelleth in him, and he in God (See also John 13:20)

D. God's "sheep" will hear Jesus' voice and come to Him:

John 5:23	All men should honour the Son, even as they honour the Father
John 6:45	Every man that … learned of the Father, cometh unto me
John 8:42	If God were your Father, ye would love me [Jesus]
John 10:3,5,27	My sheep hear my voice … and they follow me

E. God loves us if we love Jesus:

John 14:21,23	He that loveth me shall be loved of my Father
John 16:27	The Father himself loveth you, because ye loved me

F. Those that hate Jesus also hate God:

John 15:23–24	He that hateth me [Jesus] hateth my Father also … now have they both seen and hated both me and my Father

G. What rejecting Jesus means:

John 3:36	He that believeth not the Son shall not see life; but the wrath of God abideth on him
John 3:18–20	He that believeth not [in Jesus] is condemned already ... this is the condemnation, that light is come into the world, and men loved darkness rather than light
John 8:24	If ye believe not that I am he, ye shall die in your sins

John 12:48	He that rejecteth me ... hath one that judgeth him: the word ... shall judge him in the last day
1 John 2:22–23	Whosoever denieth the Son ... hath not the Father

6. JESUS, THE LIGHT OF THE WORLD:

A. Jesus is the Light:

Matthew 4:16	The people which sat in darkness saw great light ... in the region and shadow of death light is sprung up
Luke 2:30–32	A light to lighten the [nations] (See also Isaiah 49:6.)
John 1:9	That was the true Light, which lighteth every man that cometh into the world
John 8:12	I am the light of the world: he that followeth me shall not walk in darkness (See also John 9:5.)
1 John 2:8	The darkness is past, and the true light now shineth (See also Acts 26:18.)

B. The Devil and evil men hate the Light:

(See 2 Corinthians 4:4; John 1:5; 3:19–21.)

7. JESUS' LIFE AND RESURRECTION:

A. The details of Jesus' life and death were recorded by eyewitnesses:

Luke 1:1–2	Those things which are most surely believed among us ... they [told] us, which were ... eyewitnesses
John 19:25–26,34–35	He [John] that saw it [Jesus' crucifixion] bare record, and his record is true: and he knoweth that he saith true
Acts 4:20	We cannot but speak the things which we have seen
Acts 10:38–39	We are witnesses of all things which he did (See also John 21:24–25; Acts 5:32; Hebrews 2:3; 1 John 1:1–3.)
2 Peter 1:16	We have not followed cunningly devised fables, when we [told of the] coming of Jesus, but were eyewitnesses

B. As was His resurrection from the dead:

Acts 1:2–3	he showed himself alive after his passion [death] by many infallible proofs, being seen of them 40 days
Acts 2:31–32	Jesus hath God raised up, whereof we all are witnesses
Acts 13:30–31	God raised him [Jesus] from the dead: and he was seen many days of them ... his witnesses
1 Corinthians 15:3–6	He rose again ... he was seen of above 500 brethren at once (See also Acts 10:40–41.)

C. Jesus' resurrection proves that He is divine:

Romans 1:3–4	Jesus Christ our Lord was ... declared to be the Son of God with power ... by the resurrection from the dead

8. EYEWITNESS ACCOUNTS IN THE BIBLE TELL US THAT JESUS ...

A. ... was crucified:

(See Matthew 27:27–50; Mark 15:15–37; Luke 23:23–49; John 19:16–30.)

B. ... was laid in a grave for three days:

(See Matthew 27:57–66; Mark 15:42–47; Luke 23:50–56; John 19:31–42; Acts 13:28–29.)

C. ... was resurrected from the dead:

(See Matthew 28:1–18; Mark 16:1–14; Luke 24:1–43; John 20–21:all; Acts 2:23–24,32; 3:14–15; 10:39–41; 13:29–31; 1 Corinthians 15:3–8; Revelation 1:18.)

D. ... was then taken up into heaven:

(See Mark 16:19; Luke 24:50–51; Acts 1:4–11.)

9. OLD TESTAMENT MESSIANIC PROPHECIES—FULFILLED IN THE BIRTH, DEATH, AND LIFE OF JESUS CHRIST:

Luke 24:44 All things ... fulfilled [in Scripture] concerning me

A. His lineage foretold:

- Abraham (Genesis 18:18—Matthew 1:1. Also compare Genesis 17:5–7 and Galatians 3:16,19; Genesis 28:13–14 and Acts 3:25–26.)
- Isaac (Genesis 17:15,19—Matthew 1:1–2)
- Jacob (Numbers 24:17—Matthew 1:2; Luke 3:34)
- The tribe of Judah (Genesis 49:10—Luke 3:33)
- Heir to the throne of David (Isaiah 9:6–7—Matthew 1:1; Acts 2:29–30)

B. His birth and childhood:

- Born in Bethlehem in Judah (Micah 5:2—Matthew 2:1–6; Luke 2:4–7; John 7:42)
- Born of a virgin (Isaiah 7:14—Matthew 1:18; Luke 1:26–35)
- Massacre of Innocents (Jeremiah 31:15—Matthew 2:16–18)
- Called out of Egypt (Hosea 11:1—Matthew 2:13–15)

C. His ministry and rejection:

- His ministry in Galilee (Isaiah 9:1–2—Matthew 4:12–16)
- An eternal priest, like Melchizedek (Psalm 110:4—Hebrews 6:20; 7:11–16; 20–26)
- His rejection by the Jews (Isaiah 53:3—Luke 17:25; 23:18; John 1:11; 5:43)
- "Rulers took counsel against him" (Psalm 2:1–2—Acts 4:25–28; 3:14–15,17) (See also Matthew 27:1; Luke 24:20; John 11:47,53.)
- His triumphal entry into Jerusalem on a donkey (Zechariah 9:9—Matthew 21:1–11; John 12:12–14)

D. His betrayal:

- Betrayed by a close friend (Psalm 41:9—Matthew 26:14–16,20–23; Mark 14:10,43–45; John 13:18)
- Sold for 30 pieces of silver, and the money then used to buy a potter's field (Zechariah 11:12–13—Matthew 26:15; 27:3–10)
- Judas' place taken by another (Psalm 109:7–8—Acts 1:15–16,20–22)

E. His persecution and crucifixion:

- False witnesses to accuse the Messiah (Psalm 27:12—Matthew 26:60–61)
- Silent when accused (Isaiah 53:7—Matthew 26:62–63; 27:12–14)
- Smitten and spat on (Isaiah 50:6—Mark 14:65; 15:19; John 18:22; 19:1–3)
- Suffered for our sins (Isaiah 53:4–5,8; Daniel 9:26—Matthew 8:16–17; Romans 4:25; 1 Corinthians 15:3)
- To die with sinners (Isaiah 53:12—Matthew 27:38; Mark 15:27–28;
- Luke 23:33)
- Hands and feet pierced—a mode of execution that the ancient Jews weren't familiar with (Psalm 22:16; Zechariah 12:10—John 19:37; 20:25–27
- Exact year of His death—AD 30—predicted (Daniel 9:25)
- Mocked while dying (Psalm 22:6–8—Matthew 27:39–44; Mark 15:29–32)
- Given gall and vinegar (Psalm 69:21—John 19:29; Matthew 27:34,48)
- His side pierced (Zechariah 12:10—John 19:34)
- Soldiers cast lots for His clothes (Psalm 22:18—Mark 15:24; John 19:24)
- Not a bone to be broken (Psalm 34:20; Exodus 12:46—John 19:33)
- Buried with the rich (Isaiah 53:9—Matthew 27:57–60)

F. His resurrection:

- His resurrection (Psalm 16:10—Matthew 28:9; Luke 24:36–48; Acts 2:23–31)
- His ascension (Psalm 68:18—Luke 24:50–51; Acts 1:9)
- Enthroned in heaven (Psalm 110:1; Psalm 2:22; Isaiah 53—Acts 2:32–35; 13:27–29)

10. JESUS, THE SON OF GOD:

A. The Old Testament states that God has a Son:

Psalm 2:7	The Lord hath said unto me, Thou art my Son
Proverbs 30:4	Who hath established all the ends of the earth? What is his name, and what is his son's name?
Daniel 3:25	I see four men … the fourth is like the Son of God

(See also Daniel 7:13–14.)

B. Jesus declared He was both the Son of God and Christ the Messiah:

Matthew 16:15–17	Thou art the Christ, the Son of … God. Jesus answered … Blessed art thou … my Father [revealed it unto you]
Matthew 26:63–64	I adjure thee … tell us whether thou be the Christ, the Son of God. Jesus saith unto him, Thou hast said
Matthew 27:43	He said, I am the Son of God (See also John 19:7.)
Mark 14:61–62	Art thou Christ, Son of the Blessed? And Jesus said, I am
John 4:25–26	Woman saith … Messias cometh, which is called Christ. Jesus saith, I that speak unto thee am he
John 9:35–38	Jesus said, Dost thou believe on the Son of God? Who is he? Jesus said, It is he that talketh with thee
John 10:33,36–38	Because I said, I am the Son of God (See also John 3:16–18,34–36; 5:19–20,25–26; 6:40; 11:4.)

C. He was declared to be both the Son of God and Christ the Messiah by others:

Matthew 16:15–17	Peter … said, Thou art the Christ, the Son of … God
Matthew 27:54	The centurion [said], Truly this was the Son of God
John 1:34	[John the Baptist:] I bear record this is the Son of God
John 1:40–41	Andrew … saith, We have found the Messias … the Christ
John 1:49	Nathanael saith unto him, Thou art the Son of God
John 6:67–69	We … are sure that thou art that Christ, the Son of God
John 11:27	[Martha] saith ... I believe that thou art the Christ, the Son of God, which should come into the world

D. Even the devils knew He was the Son of God:

(See Matthew 8:29; Luke 4:33–34,41.)

E. Jesus called God His Father:

John 5:17–18,20	Jesus ... said that God was his Father, making himself equal with God
John 8:54	My Father … of whom ye say, that he is your god (See also Luke 10:22; 22:29; John 5:22–31,36–37; 8:16,19,26–28, 38,49; 14:13; 16:28; 17:1–26; 20:17.)

F. God anointed Jesus with power:

Mark 1:27	With authority commandeth he even the unclean spirits, and they do obey him
Luke 4:16–21	Spirit of the Lord is upon me … he hath anointed me
John 3:34	God giveth not the spirit by measure unto him
Acts 10:38	God anointed Jesus … with the Holy Ghost and with power

11. JESUS' RELATIONSHIP WITH GOD:

A. Jesus' closeness to God, His Father:

John 1:18	The only begotten Son … is in the bosom of the Father
John 16:15	All things that the Father hath are mine (See also John 15:15.)

B. He was with God in His preexistence:

John 8:42	I proceeded forth and came from God … he sent me
John 17:5,24	The glory which I had with thee before the world was
2 Corinthians 8:9	Though he was rich, yet for your sakes he became poor (See also John 1:1; 13:3; 16:28; 17:8,18.)

C. God loves Jesus and is pleased with Him:

Matthew 3:16–17	This is my beloved Son, in whom I am well pleased
John 8:29	I do always those things that please him (See also Luke 9:34–35; John 15:10.)

D. Jesus is one with His Father:

John 10:30	I and my Father are one
John 10:38	The Father is in me, and I in him
John 14:9–10	He that hath seen me hath seen the Father

E. Jesus is God:

Isaiah 9:6	A child is born … and his name shall be called … the mighty God, the everlasting Father, the Prince of Peace
John 8:56–58	Before Abraham was, I am (Compare with Exodus 3:6,13–14.)
John 20:28–29	Thomas said unto him, "My Lord and my God" [Jesus then commended him for believing]
Colossians 3:11	Christ is all, and in all
1 Timothy 3:16	God was manifest in the flesh
Hebrews 1:8	Unto the Son he saith, Thy throne, O God, is for ever
Revelation 1:8,11; 22:12–13	I am Alpha and Omega, the beginning and the ending … which is, and which was … the Almighty (Compare with Isaiah 44:6.)

F. God the Father has preeminence:

John 14:28	My Father is greater than I
John 20:17	I ascend unto my Father, and your Father; and to my God, and your God (See also Ephesians 1:17.)
1 Corinthians 3:23	Ye are Christ's; and Christ is God's
1 Corinthians 11:3	The head of Christ is God
1 Corinthians 15:24–28	Then shall the Son also himself be subject unto him … that God may be all in all (See also John 15:1.)

G. Jesus' obedience to the Father:

John 4:34	To do the will of him that sent me … finish his work
John 5:19	The Son can do nothing … but what he seeth [God] do
John 5:30	I can of mine own self do nothing … I seek not mine own will, but the will of the Father
John 8:28–29	I do nothing of myself … I do always those things that please him [God]
John 12:49–50	I have not spoken of myself; but the Father … gave me a commandment, what I should say … so I speak
John 14:31	As the Father gave me commandment, even so I do
Philippians 2:6–8	[Jesus] humbled himself … obedient unto death (See also John 8:26,38,42; 14:10,24.)

H. Jesus submitted and obeyed utterly:

Matthew 26:39,42,44	He … fell on his face, and prayed, saying, O my Father … not as I will, but as thou wilt (See also Mark 14:35–36; Luke 22:41–44.)

12. THE AUTHORITY AND POWER GOD HAS GIVEN JESUS:

A. Jesus is seated on the right hand of God in heaven:

Mark 16:19	Was received into heaven, and sat on right hand of God
Luke 22:69	Hereafter shall the Son of man sit on the right hand of the power of God (See also Matthew 26:64.)
Romans 8:34	Christ … who is even at the right hand of God, who also maketh intercession for us
Ephesians 1:20	He raised him from the dead, and set him at his own right hand in the heavenly places
Hebrews 1:3	He … sat down on the right hand of the Majesty on high
Revelation 3:21	I overcame, and am set down with my Father in his throne (See also Psalm 110:1; Acts 2:32,33,34; 7:55–56; Colossians 3:1; 1 Peter 3:22.)

B. God has given all authority to Jesus:

Daniel 7:13–14	There was given him dominion, and glory and a kingdom, that all nations ... should serve him (See also Hebrews 1:8.)
Matthew 28:18	All power [authority] is given unto me in heaven and earth
John 3:35	The Father ... hath given all things into his hand
John 5:26–27	[God gave Jesus] authority to execute judgement
Ephesians 1:20–22	Set him ... far above all principality, and power, and might, and dominion ... and hath put all things under his feet
Philippians 2:9–10	At the name of Jesus every knee should bow
Colossians 2:10	[Jesus] is the head of all principality and power
1 Peter 3:22	Angels and authorities and powers ... made subject to him
Revelation 17:14	Lord of lords, and King of kings (See also 1 Timothy 6:15.) (See also Matthew 11:27; 26:53; John 3:31; Hebrews 1:4,6; Ephesians 1:10; Colossians 1:18; Revelation 1:5.)

C. Jesus is the King, and the kingdom of heaven is His:

(See Matthew 13:41; 16:28; 27:11; 25:31,34; Luke 22:29–30; John 18:33–37; Colossians 1:13.)

D. Jesus is Lord:

John 13:13	Ye call me Master and Lord: and ye say well; for so I am
Acts 2:36	God hath made that same Jesus ... both Lord and Christ
Philippians 2:11	Every tongue should confess that Jesus Christ is Lord
Revelation 19:16	King of kings, and Lord of lords (See also 1 Timothy 6:15; Revelation 17:14.)

E. God has made Him judge of the world:

Matthew 16:27	The Son of man shall come ... and then he shall reward every man according to his works
Matthew 25:31–46	The Son of man ... shall ... sit on the throne of his glory: and before him shall be gathered all nations
John 5:22	The Father ... hath committed all judgement unto the Son
Acts 10:42	Ordained of God to be the judge of [the living] and dead
Romans 2:16	God shall judge the secrets of men by Jesus Christ

F. Jesus will also sit in judgement of Christians:

Romans 14:10	We shall all stand before the judgement seat of Christ
2 Corinthians 5:10	We must all appear before the judgement seat of Christ
Revelation 2:23	I am he which searcheth the ... hearts: and I will give unto every one of you according to your works
Revelation 22:12	My reward is with me, to give every man according as his work shall be

13. JESUS, THE CREATOR:

A. God created the universe through Jesus:

Genesis 1:1	In the beginning, God created the heaven and the earth
John 1:1–3,10	In the beginning was the word [Jesus] … and all things were made by him … the world was made by him
Colossians 1:15–16	By him [Jesus] were all things created … all things were created by him, and for him
Hebrews 1:2	His Son … by whom also he made the worlds
Hebrews 1:8,10	Unto the Son he saith … Thou, Lord, in the beginning hast laid the foundation of the earth

B. Jesus upholds all matter in the universe:

Colossians 1:17	He is before all things, and by him all things consist
Hebrews 1:3	Upholding all things by the word of his power

C. All the fullness of God dwells in Jesus:

Colossians 1:19	That in him [Jesus] should all fullness dwell
Colossians 2:2–3	Christ … in whom are hid all the treasures of wisdom and knowledge
Colossians 2:9	In him [Jesus] dwelleth all the fullness of the Godhead

D. A description of Jesus' immortal resurrected body:

Revelation 1:13–17	The Son of man … eyes as a flame of fire … countenance as the sun [skin glowed like white-hot metal]

14. TITLES OF JESUS:

- Immanuel ["God with us"] (Isaiah 7:14)
- Wonderful, Counsellor, The mighty God, The everlasting Father, The Prince of Peace (Isaiah 9:6)
- The Son of man (Matthew 25:31)
- Son of the living God (Matthew 16:16)
- The bridegroom (Luke 5:34–35; John 3:29)
- The Lamb of God (John 1:29,36)
- The Messias, the Christ (John 1:41)
- Rabbi, Son of God, King of Israel (John 1:49)
- The bread of life, the living bread (John 6:35,48,51)
- The light of the world (John 8:12; 9:5)
- The door (John 10:7,9)
- The good shepherd (John 10:11)
- The resurrection and the life (John 11:25)
- Master and Lord (John 13:13)
- The way, the truth, and the life (John 14:6)
- The true vine (John 15:1)

- The Lord of glory (1 Corinthians 2:8)
- The spiritual Rock (1 Corinthians 10:4)
- The Head (Colossians 2:19)
- The blessed and only Potentate, the King of kings, and Lord of lords (1 Timothy 6:15)
- The captain of our salvation (Hebrews 2:10)
- The great high priest (Hebrews 4:14)
- The author and finisher of our faith (Hebrews 12:2)
- The great shepherd of the sheep (Hebrews 13:20)
- A living stone (1 Peter 2:4)
- A chief corner stone (1 Peter 2:6; Ephesians 2:20)
- The Shepherd and Bishop of your souls (1 Peter 2:25)
- The chief Shepherd (1 Peter 5:4)
- The faithful witness, and the first begotten of the dead, and the prince of the kings of the earth (Revelation 1:5)
- Alpha and Omega, the beginning and the ending, which is, and which was, and which is to come, the Almighty (Revelation 1:8)
- The Lion of the tribe of Judah, the Root of David (Revelation 5:5)
- Faithful and True (Revelation 19:11)
- The Word of God (Revelation 19:13)
- King Of Kings, And Lord Of Lords (Revelation 19:16)
- The root and the offspring of David, and the bright and morning star (Revelation 22:16)

THE HOLY SPIRIT

1. THE HOLY SPIRIT'S PART IN OUR SALVATION:

A. We must be born of, and made alive by, the Spirit:

John 3:5–8	Except a man be born of the Spirit, he cannot enter into the kingdom of God
John 6:63	It is the spirit that quickeneth [gives life]
John 16:8–9	[The Holy Spirit reproves and convicts men of their sin]
Titus 3:5	He saved us by the washing of regeneration, and renewing of the Holy Ghost
	(See also 2 Thessalonians 2:13; Ephesians 2:1.)

B. A measure of God's Spirit is given to us when we're saved:

2 Corinthians 1:22	Who hath sealed us, and given us the earnest [deposit] of the Spirit
Ephesians 1:13–14	After ye believed, ye were sealed with the holy Spirit
Ephesians 4:30	The holy Spirit … whereby ye are sealed unto the day of redemption

C. The Holy Spirit assures us that we are saved:

Romans 8:16	Spirit beareth witness that we are children of God
1 John 3:24	We know he abideth in us, by the Spirit
1 John 4:13	Hereby know we that … he [dwelleth] in us, because he hath given us of his Spirit

D. The Holy Spirit testifies Jesus is the truth:

John 15:26	The Spirit of truth ... shall testify of me [Jesus]
John 16:14	He [the Spirit] shall glorify me

2. THE BAPTISM (OVERFLOWING) OF THE HOLY SPIRIT:

A. Jesus gives us the Holy Spirit:

Matthew 3:11	He [Jesus] shall baptise you with the Holy Ghost
Luke 24:49	I send the promise of my Father upon you ... ye [shall] be endued [clothed] with power from on high
John 7:38–39	Out of his belly flow rivers of living water … the Spirit
John 14:16	I will pray the Father and he shall give you [a] Comforter
John 16:7	I will send him [the Comforter] unto you
Acts 2:1–4	[Spirit poured out on Christians on day of Pentecost]

B. When Christians receive the baptism of the Spirit:

Acts 8:15–17	[Samaritans baptised with the Spirit after salvation]
Acts 10:44–46	[Cornelius' household was filled with the Holy Spirit at the same time they received Jesus]
Acts 19:2	Have ye received the Holy Ghost since ye believed? They said, We have not

C. Receiving the Holy Spirit:

Luke 11:9–13	If ye know how to give good gifts ... how much more shall [God] give Holy Spirit to them that ask him?
Acts 19:1–2	Have ye received the Holy Ghost since ye believed?
1 Corinthians 6:19	Your body is the temple of the Holy Ghost (See also 1 Corinthians 3:16.)
Ephesians 5:18	Be filled with the Spirit

D. The Spirit is often received through the "laying on of hands":

Acts 8:15–17	[Peter and John laid hands on the Samaritan believers]
Acts 19:6	[Paul laid hands on the Ephesian believers]

3. THE PURPOSE OF THE HOLY SPIRIT BAPTISM:

A. The Holy Spirit anoints us with power to witness:

Micah 3:8	I am full of power by the Spirit of the Lord … to declare to Israel his sin
Luke 4:18	The Spirit of the Lord hath anointed me to preach the gospel (See also Isaiah 61:1–2.)
John 15:26	The Spirit of truth … shall testify of me [Jesus]
Acts 1:8	Ye shall receive power after that the Holy Ghost is come upon you and ye shall be witnesses unto me
Acts 4:29–31	They were filled with the Holy Ghost and spake the word of God with boldness
Acts 5:32	Ye are his witnesses, and so is also the Holy Ghost

B. The Holy Spirit transforms us into a new person:

1 Samuel 10:6	The Spirit will come upon thee, and thou shalt … be turned into another man
Psalm 51:10–13	[Creates a clean heart and a right spirit]

C. The Holy Spirit gives us a closer relationship with Jesus:

Ephesians 5:18–19	Be filled with the Spirit … singing and making melody in your heart to the Lord (See also John 14:16–18.)

D. Minding the things of the Spirit brings life and peace:

Romans 8:5–7	They that are after the Spirit mind things of the Spirit
Galatians 5:16–17	Walk in the Spirit, and ye shall not fulfil lust of the flesh

E. The Spirit brings forth virtues in our lives:

Romans 5:5	The love of God is shed in our hearts by the Holy Ghost
Romans 14:17	Righteousness and peace and joy in the Holy Ghost
Romans 15:13	Abound in hope through the power of the Holy Ghost
1 Corinthians 12:4–11	[The Spirit gives us different kinds of spiritual gifts]
Galatians 5:22–23	The fruit of the Spirit is love, joy, peace ...

F. The Holy Spirit comforts us:

John 14:16,26	The Comforter, which is the Holy Ghost
John 16:7	I will send [the Comforter] unto you
Acts 9:31	Walking in the comfort of the Holy Ghost
Romans 8:1	There is no condemnation to them which are in Christ Jesus, who walk … after the Spirit
1 Peter 4:14	If ye be reproached, happy are ye; for the Spirit of God resteth upon you

G. The Holy Spirit and prayer:

Romans 8:26–27	We know not what we should pray for … but the Spirit
Jude 1:20	Building up yourselves ... praying in the Holy Ghost

H. The Holy Spirit is the Spirit of truth:

John 16:13	When the Spirit of truth is come, he will guide you into all truth
1 John 5:6	The Spirit beareth witness, because the Spirit is truth (See also John 14:17; 15:26; 16:13.)

4. GIFTS OF THE HOLY SPIRIT:

A. The Spirit gives us wisdom and guidance:

Mark 13:11	It is not ye that speak, but the Holy Ghost
Luke 12:11–12	The Holy Ghost shall teach you ... what ye ought to say
John 14:26	Holy Ghost shall teach you all things and bring all things to your remembrance (See also 1 John 2:27.)
John 16:13	The Spirit of truth will guide you into all truth
1 Corinthians 2:9–10	God hath revealed them to us by his Spirit … yea, the deep things of God
1 Corinthians 2:12–13	We have received the Spirit that we might know the things that are freely given to us of God ... Which things also we speak ... the Holy Ghost teacheth
1 Corinthians 12:8	[The Spirit gives word of wisdom, word of knowledge]
Ephesians 1:17	May God give you the spirit of wisdom and revelation
2 Timothy 1:13–14	Hold fast sound words … keep by the Holy Ghost

B. The Holy Spirit gives us the gift of prophecy:

1 Corinthians 12:7,10	To one is given by the Spirit ... prophecy
John 16:13	Spirit of truth will show you things to come
Acts 2:17–18	I will pour out of my Spirit … your sons and your daughters shall prophesy (See also Joel 2:28–29.)
2 Peter 1:21	Prophecy came … [when] men of God spake as they were moved by the Holy Ghost

C. The Holy Spirit gives us discernment:

Isaiah 11:2–3	The Spirit of the Lord shall rest upon him ... he shall not judge after the sight of his eyes
1 Corinthians 2:12–15	[We have received the Spirit of God and can spiritually discern matters]
1 Corinthians 12:10	[Gives gift of discernment of spirits] (See also 1 John 4:1–6.)

D. The Spirit gives faith, healing, and miracles:

1 Corinthians 12:9–10	To another faith by the same Spirit; to another gifts of healing by the same Spirit; To another the working of miracles

E. The Spirit leads and restrains us:

Isaiah 30:21	[Spirit says:] This is the way; walk ye in it
Acts 8:29	[Specific directions:] The Spirit said to Philip
Acts 16:6–7	[Restrains:] The Spirit suffered [permitted] them not
Romans 8:14	As many as are led by Spirit of God are sons of God

F. The gift of tongues:

Acts 2:1–4	Spoke with other tongues as Spirit gave them utterance
1 Corinthians 12:10	To another divers kinds of tongues; to another the interpretation of tongues (See also 1 Corinthians 14:13.)
1 Corinthians 13:1	Speak with the tongues of men and of angels
1 Corinthians 14:2	He that speaketh in an unknown tongue ... in the Spirit he speaketh mysteries
1 Corinthians 14:4	He that speaketh in an unknown tongue edifieth [strengthens] himself

G. God's Spirit strengthens us:

Ephesians 3:16	Be strengthened with might by his Spirit in the inner man (See also Judges 14:6,19; 15:14–15.)

5. FREEDOM OF THE HOLY SPIRIT:

Romans 8:2	The law of the Spirit ... hath made me free from the law of sin and death
Romans 8:15	Ye have not received the spirit of bondage to fear, but the Spirit of adoption
2 Corinthians 3:17	Where the Spirit of the Lord is, there is liberty
Galatians 5:18	If ye be led of the Spirit, ye are not under the law
2 Timothy 1:7	God hath [given] us the Spirit of power, of love, and of a sound mind

6. THE HOLY SPIRIT INSPIRES UNITY OF BELIEVERS:

Acts 4:31–32	They were all filled with the Holy Ghost … and the multitude were of one heart, and of one soul
1 Corinthians 12:13	By the Spirit are we all baptised into one body
2 Corinthians 13:14	The communion of the Holy Ghost be with you all

7. OTHER POINTS ABOUT THE MINISTRY OF THE SPIRIT:

Acts 8:17–20	[The Holy Spirit cannot be bought; it's a gift]
Acts 20:28	Feed the flock … Holy Ghost hath made you overseers
Romans 8:11	He shall quicken your bodies by his Spirit that dwelleth in you

8. OBEYING THE HOLY SPIRIT:

A. The Holy Spirit is given to the obedient:

Proverbs 1:23	Turn at my reproof, I will pour out my Spirit unto you
Acts 5:32	The Holy Ghost, whom God hath given to them that obey him

B. Obey the Spirit:

Galatians 5:25	If we live in the Spirit, let us also walk in the Spirit
1 Peter 1:22	Seeing that ye obey the truth through the Spirit … see that ye love one another
Revelation 2:29	Hear what the Spirit saith unto the churches

C. We are warned to obey the Spirit and not resist it:

Romans 8:5–6	[Living according to Spirit is life and peace; being carnally minded causes death]
1 Corinthians 2:14	The natural [carnal-minded] man receiveth not the things of the Spirit, for they are foolishness unto him
Ephesians 4:29–30	Let no corrupt communication proceed out of your mouth, grieve not the Holy Spirit
1 Thessalonians 5:19	Quench not the Spirit
Hebrews 3:7–10	The Holy Ghost saith, Harden not your hearts

D. Results of resisting the Holy Spirit:

Genesis 6:3	My Spirit shall not always strive with man
Isaiah 63:10	They rebelled and vexed his Holy Spirit, therefore he … fought against them
Acts 7:51–53	Ye do always resist the Holy Ghost [resulting in them persecuting the prophets and disobeying God]
Acts 20:22–23	[Paul ignored the Spirit's warnings, resulting in his imprisonment and finally being beheaded] (See also Acts 21:10–14.)

9. THE HOLY SPIRIT IN JESUS' LIFE:

- Mary was with child of the Holy Ghost (Matthew 1:18)
- Jesus was conceived of the Holy Ghost (Matthew 1:20)
- The Holy Ghost anointed Him (Luke 3:21–22)
- Jesus' ministry began with Him being full of the Holy Ghost (Luke 4:1)
- God anointed Jesus with Holy Ghost and power (Acts 10:38)
- God gave Him the Spirit without measure (John 3:34)
- Jesus was led by the Spirit into the wilderness (Luke 4:1)
- He cast out devils by the Spirit (Matthew 12:28)
- The Spirit raised Jesus from the dead (Romans 8:11; 1 Peter 3:18)

10. OTHER BIBLE EXAMPLES:

A. Examples of being filled with the Holy Spirit:

- Bezaleel (Exodus 31:2–5)
- Saul (1 Samuel 10:6,9–10)
- David (1 Samuel 16:13)
- John the Baptist (Luke 1:15)
- Elizabeth (Luke 1:41–42)
- Zacharias (Luke 1:67)
- Simeon (Luke 2:25–26)
- Jesus (Luke 4:1)
- Christians on the day of Pentecost (Acts 2:1–4)
- Early church deacons (Acts 6:3–5,7)
- Paul (Acts 9:17)
- Barnabas (Acts 11:22–24)

B. The Spirit's anointing of power in time of need:

- Peter was anointed to preach (Acts 4:8)
- The early church [the first believers] prayed during persecution and was filled with the Holy Ghost (Acts 4:29–31)
- Stephen's witness (Acts 7:55)
- The Spirit empowered Paul to smite the sorcerer with blindness (Acts 13:9–11)
- The persecuted disciples were filled with the Holy Ghost (Acts 13:50–52)

Special chapters about the Holy Spirit: John 14, Acts 2, Romans 8

THE WORD OF GOD

1. THE BIBLE WAS WRITTEN BY DIVINE INSPIRATION:

1 Thessalonians 2:13	Ye received it not as the word of men, but as it is in truth, the word of God
2 Timothy 3:16	All scripture is given by inspiration of God
Hebrews 1:1	God … spake in time past unto the fathers by the prophets
2 Peter 1:21	Men of God spake as they were moved by the Holy Ghost

2. GOD'S WORD IS ETERNALLY TRUE AND NEVER FAILS:

1 Kings 8:56	There hath not failed one word of all his good promise
Psalm 119:89	Forever, O Lord, thy word is settled in heaven
Psalm 119:160	Every one of thy judgements endureth forever
Isaiah 40:8	The word of God shall stand forever
Isaiah 55:10–11	So shall my word be … it shall accomplish … and prosper
Matthew 24:35	Heaven and earth shall pass away, but my words [never]
John 10:35	The scripture cannot be broken [cancelled, annulled]
1 Peter 1:25	The word of the Lord endureth forever

3. THE IMPORTANCE OF GOD'S WORD:

Deuteronomy 32:46–47	Set your heart unto all the words … for it is not a vain thing for you; it is your life
Psalm 138:2	Thou [God] hast magnified thy word above all thy name

A. Jesus is the "Word made flesh":

John 1:1	In the beginning was the word … and the word was God
John 1:14	The Word [Jesus] was made flesh and dwelt among us
Revelation 19:11–13	His [Jesus'] name is called The Word of God

B. The power of the Word:

Psalm 33:6,9	By the word of the Lord were the heavens made … he spake, and it was done
John 6:63	The words that I speak, they are spirit and they are life
Romans 1:16	Gospel of Christ … is the power of God unto salvation
Hebrews 11:3	The worlds were framed by the word of God
2 Peter 3:5–7	Earth … by the word, kept in store, reserved unto fire

4. GOD'S WORD IS A SPIRITUAL WEAPON:

Jeremiah 5:14	I will make my words in thy mouth fire
Jeremiah 23:29	Is not my word like as a fire? And like a hammer?
Matthew 4:4–11	Jesus said to [Satan], It is written. [Then the devil leaves]
Ephesians 6:17	The sword of the Spirit, which is the word of God
Hebrews 4:12	Word is quick and powerful, and sharper than any twoedged sword

1 John 2:14	The word of God abideth in you, and ye have overcome the wicked one

5. THE BIBLE WAS WRITTEN FOR OUR BENEFIT:

Psalm 102:18	This shall be written for the generation to come
John 19:35	He [John] that saw it bare record … that ye might believe
John 20:31	These are written that ye might believe
Romans 15:4	Written for our learning, that we through … the scriptures might have hope
1 Corinthians 10:11	And they are written for our admonition
	(See also 1 John 5:13.)

6. KEEPING (OBEYING, HEEDING) THE WORD:

A. It's important to heed and keep the Word:

Deuteronomy 11:1	Thou shalt love the Lord thy God, and keep his … statutes, and his judgements, and his commandments, always
Hebrews 2:1	We ought to give more earnest heed to the [Word]
2 Peter 1:19	Sure word … ye do well that ye take heed

B. Obeying and keeping the Word proves we know and love Jesus:

Psalm 119:167	My soul kept thy testimonies; I love them exceedingly
John 8:31	If ye continue in my word, then are ye my disciples indeed
John 14:15	If ye love me, keep my commandments
John 14:21,23	If a man love me, he will keep my words
James 1:22–24	Be ye doers of the word, and not hearers only
1 John 2:3	Hereby we know that we know him, if we keep his commandments
1 John 5:3	This is the love of God … keep his commandments
2 John 1:6	This is love, that we walk after his commandments
Revelation 3:8	Thou … hast kept my word, and hast not denied my name

C. The benefits of keeping the Word:

Deuteronomy 7:9	The Lord … keepeth mercy with them that love him and keep his commandments
Psalm 1:2–3	In his law doth he meditate. And he shall … bring forth fruit
Psalm 37:31	Law of God is in his heart; none of his steps shall slide
Luke 8:15	They, which … having heard the word, keep it, bring forth fruit with patience

Luke 11:28	Blessed are they that hear the word of God and keep it
John 15:7	If … my words abide in you, ye shall ask what ye will, and it shall be done
John 15:10	If ye keep my commandments, ye shall abide in my love
1 John 2:5	Whoso keepeth his word, in him verily is the love of God perfected
1 John 3:24	He that keepeth his commandments dwelleth in him, and he in him (See also 1 John 2:24.)

D. The Holy Spirit will guide you in the Word:

Psalm 25:5	[Pray:] Lead me in thy truth, and teach me
John 14:26	The Holy Ghost … shall teach you, and bring all things to your remembrance
John 16:13	The Spirit … will guide you into all truth
1 John 2:27	The anointing teacheth you of all things (See also Psalm 119:18; Ezekiel 36:27.)

E. Additional verses on the importance of keeping the Word:

- Psalm 119:2,4,33–34,55,57,60,63,67,88,100,115,129,134,145–146, 167–168;
- Proverbs 3:1,21; 4:4,13,20–21; 6:20,22; 7:1–3; 19:16; 22:17–18; 28:4,7; 29:18;
- Ecclesiastes 8:5; 12:13.

7. WHAT THE WORD DOES FOR US:

A. The Word saves us and gives us spiritual rebirth:

Psalm 19:7	Law of the Lord is perfect, converting the soul
James 1:18	Of his own will begat he us with the word of truth
James 1:21	The engrafted word … is able to save your souls
1 Peter 1:23	Being born again … by the word of God
2 Peter 1:4	Precious promises: by these ye might be partakers of the divine nature

B. The Word gives us faith, truth, wisdom, and strength:

Romans 10:17	Faith cometh by hearing … the word of God
Psalm 19:7	Testimony of the Lord is sure, making wise the simple
Psalm 119:99–100	I have more understanding than all my teachers: for thy testimonies are my meditation
John 15:7	If my words abide in you, ye shall ask what ye will
John 17:17	Thy word is truth
Acts 20:32	Word of his grace, which is able to build you up
2 Timothy 3:15–17	Scriptures … are able to make thee wise

C. Meditating in the Word causes success:

Joshua 1:8	Meditate therein day and night … then shalt thou make thy way prosperous and … have good success
Psalm 1:2–3	In his law doth he meditate … whatsoever he doeth shall prosper
1 Timothy 4:15	Meditate upon these things … that thy profiting may appear to all

D. The Word guides us and is a light to our path:

Psalm 19:8	Commandment of Lord is pure, enlightening the eyes
Psalm 25:10	All the paths of the Lord are mercy and truth unto such as keep his … testimonies
Psalm 119:105	Thy word is a lamp unto my feet and light unto my path
Psalm 119:130	The entrance of thy words giveth light

E. The Word cleanses us spiritually:

Psalm 119:9	Wherewithal shall a young man cleanse his way? By taking heed … to thy word
John 15:3	Now ye are clean through the word which I have spoken
Ephesians 5:25–26	That he might sanctify and cleanse [us] with the washing of water by the word (See also John 17:17.)

F. Other things the Word does for us:

Psalm 107:20	He sent his word and healed them
Psalm 119:11	Word have I hid in mine heart, that I might not sin
Psalm 119:165	Great peace have they which love thy law
Jeremiah 15:16	Thy word was … the joy and rejoicing of mine heart
John 8:31–32	If ye continue in my word … the truth shall make you free
1 Thessalonians 2:13	Word of God … effectually worketh in you that believe
Hebrews 4:12	Word is … discerner of thoughts and intents of heart

8. WHAT WE SHOULD DO WITH THE WORD:

A. Feed on it, for it is our spiritual food:

Job 23:12	I have esteemed words more than my necessary food
Psalm 119:103	How sweet are thy words! Sweeter than honey
Jeremiah 15:16	Thy words were found, and I did eat them
Matthew 4:4	Man shall not live by bread alone, but by … word
1 Peter 2:2	As newborn babes, desire the sincere milk of the word

B. Teach the Word to our children:

Deuteronomy 6:7	And thou shalt teach them diligently unto thy children
Deuteronomy 11:19	And ye shall teach [the word unto] thy children
Psalm 78:1–8	They should make them known unto their children
2 Timothy 3:15	From a child thou hast known the holy scriptures

C. Teach "milk" to babes, and "meat" to the mature:

John 16:12	I have many things to say … ye cannot bear them now
1 Corinthians 3:1–2	I have fed you with milk, and not with meat
Hebrews 5:13–14	Every one that useth milk … is a babe. But strong meat belongeth to them that are [mature]
Hebrews 6:1–3	Leaving the principles of the doctrine … let us go on
2 Timothy 2:15	A workman … rightly dividing the word of truth

D. Love the Word and let it dwell in our hearts:

Deuteronomy 6:6–7	These words … shall be in thine heart
Deuteronomy 11:18	Lay up these my words in your heart and in your soul
Psalm 40:8	I delight to do thy will … thy law is within my heart
Psalm 119:20	My soul breaketh for the longing that it hath unto thy judgements [word]
Psalm 119: 40	Behold, I have longed after thy precepts
Psalm 119:47–48	I will delight myself in thy commandments, which I have loved (See also Psalm 119:113,140,159,163.)
Psalm 119:72	Law of thy mouth better than thousands of gold
Psalm 119:97	O how I love thy law! It is my meditation all the day
Psalm 119:127	I love thy commandments above gold
Psalm 119:131	I panted … I longed for thy commandments
Psalm 119:162	I rejoice at thy word, as one that findeth great spoil
Colossians 3:16	Let the word of Christ dwell in you richly
1 Timothy 4:15	Meditate upon these things, give thyself wholly (See also Isaiah 51:7.)

E. Study the Word and "search the Scriptures":

John 5:39	Search the scriptures … they testify of me
Acts 17:11	Received the word with all readiness of mind, and searched the scriptures daily
1 Timothy 4:16	Take heed … unto the doctrine; continue in them
2 Timothy 2:15	Study to shew thyself approved unto God … rightly dividing the word of truth

F. Answer questions and witness with the Word:

Psalm 119:42	So shall I have wherewith to answer him
Proverbs 22:20–21	Answer words of truth to them that send unto thee
Philippians 2:15–16	Shine as lights … holding forth the word of life
Titus 1:9	By sound doctrine to convince gainsayers
1 Peter 3:15	Be ready always to give an answer to every man
1 Peter 4:11	If any speak, let him speak as the oracles of God

G. Teach and preach the Word:

Psalm 68:11	Great was company of them that published it
Jeremiah 23:28	He that hath my word, let him speak [it] faithfully

Habakkuk 2:2	Write the vision, and make it plain
Matthew 28:20	Teaching them to observe all things … I have commanded
Acts 8:25	They testified and preached the word of the Lord
Acts 18:11	Continued … teaching the word of God among them
1 Corinthians 2:4,13	Not with enticing words of man's wisdom
2 Timothy 4:2	Preach the word … reprove, rebuke, exhort
	(See also John 12:49; 14:10,24; 17:8.)

9. WHAT WE SHOULD NOT DO WITH THE WORD:

A. We shouldn't read it skeptically or doubtfully:

Hebrews 4:2	Word did not profit … not mixed with faith in them that heard

B. We shouldn't err by being ignorant of the Word:

Matthew 22:29	Ye do err, not knowing the scriptures
	(See also Matthew 12:3; 19:4; 21:42; John 20:9; Acts 13:27.)

C. We shouldn't "wrest" or twist the Scriptures:

2 Corinthians 2:17	Not as many which corrupt the word of God
2 Corinthians 4:2	Not … handing the word of God deceitfully
2 Peter 3:14–17	They that are unlearned and unstable wrest … scriptures

D. We shouldn't argue over minor, controversial doctrines:

Romans 14:1	Him that is weak in the faith, receive ye, but not to doubtful disputations
2 Timothy 2:14–17	They that are unlearned and unstable wrest … scriptures
Titus 3:9	Avoid foolish questions and strivings about the law

E. We shouldn't harden our heart and despise the Word:

2 Chronicles 36:16	But they mocked the messengers of God and despised his words
Proverbs 13:13	Whoso despiseth the word shall be destroyed
Isaiah 5:24	They cast away the law … and despised the word
Zechariah 7:12–13	They made their hearts as stone, lest they should hear the words the Lord sent

F. The fate of those who despise the Word:

2 Chronicles 36:16	They … despised his words … until the wrath of the Lord arose
Psalm 50:17,21	Thou castest my words behind thee … I will reprove thee
Isaiah 5:24	Their root shall be as rottenness … because they despised the word

Hosea 4:6	My people are destroyed for lack of knowledge: because thou hast rejected knowledge, I will reject thee
Zechariah 7:11–12	They refused to hearken … therefore came a great wrath
Luke 16:31	If they hear not [the word], they will not be persuaded, though one rose from the dead
John 12:48	He that receiveth not my words … the word … shall judge him in the last day
	(See also Amos 2:4; Zechariah 7:12; 2 Peter 2:21; Jeremiah 36:all.)

10. BEWARE OF THOSE WHO DON'T TEACH THE WORD:

Isaiah 8:20	If they speak not according to this word, it is because there is no light in them
Romans 16:17	Mark them which cause divisions … contrary to doctrine
Galatians 1:8–9	If any preach any other gospel … let him be accursed
1 Timothy 4:1–2	Some shall depart from the faith … speaking lies
1 Timothy 6:3–5	If any man teach otherwise, and consent not to wholesome words … he is proud, knowing nothing
Titus 1:10–11	Unruly and vain talkers … teaching things which they ought not … whose mouths must be stopped
Hebrews 13:9	Be not carried about with diverse and strange doctrines
2 Peter 2:1–2	False teachers … shall bring in damnable heresies
	(See also 2 Timothy 4:3–4; Acts 20:29–30.)

11. THE DEVIL BLINDS MEN'S EYES TO GOD'S WORD:

Luke 8:12	They hear, then cometh the devil and taketh away the word
2 Corinthians 4:4	The god of this world hath blinded the minds of them
	(See also John 8:43,47; 1 John 2:11.)

12. STORIES RELATING TO THE WORD:

Matthew 4:3–11	[Jesus, tempted by the Devil, quotes the Word]
Matthew 7:21–27	[The parable of the house on the rock and the one on the sand]
Matthew 13:1–13	[The parable of the sower] (See also Mark 4:1–20; Luke 8:4–15.)

Special chapter about God's Word: Psalm 119—King David's beautiful tribute to the Word

PRAYER

1. HOW TO PRAY:

Luke 11:1–4	Lord, teach us to pray … when ye pray, say, Our Father which art in heaven (See also Matthew 6:9–13.)

A. Praise and thank God before petitioning Him:

Psalm 95:2	Let us come before his presence with thanksgiving
Psalm 100:4	Enter into his gates with thanksgiving, and into his courts with praise: be thankful … and bless his name
Philippians 4:6	With thanksgiving let your requests be made known

B. If you have the gift of tongues, pray and praise in it:

1 Corinthians 14:2,4	He that speaketh in an unknown tongue speaketh … unto God [and] edifieth himself
1 Corinthians 14:39	Forbid not to speak with tongues
Ephesians 6:18	Praying always with … supplication in the Spirit
Jude 1:20	Building up your … faith, praying in the Holy Ghost

C. Be specific and ask for what you need:

1 Kings 3:5,9–10	[God told Solomon:] Ask what I shall give thee
Matthew 7:7–8	Ask, and it shall be given you; seek, and ye shall find
Matthew 21:22	Whatsoever ye ask in prayer … ye shall receive
John 16:24	Ask, and ye shall receive, that your joy may be full
Philippians 4:6	Let your requests be made known unto God
James 4:2	Ye have not, because ye ask not

D. Pray to the Father in Jesus' name:

John 14:13–14	Whatsoever ye shall ask in my name, that will I do
John 16:23	Whatsoever ye … ask Father in my name, he will give (See also John 15:16; 16:26; Ephesians 2:18.)

E. Prayer also includes you listening to God:

Genesis 24:63	Isaac went out to meditate in the field at eventide
Numbers 9:8	Stand still, and I will hear what the Lord will command
1 Samuel 3:9–10	If he call thee … say, "Speak, Lord; for thy servant heareth"
Psalm 4:3–4	Lord will hear … commune with your heart … and be still
Psalm 46:10	Be still, and know that I am God (See also Ecclesiastes 5:1; Zephaniah 1:7; Zechariah 2:13.)

F. Listen by meditating on God's Word:

Joshua 1:8	Thou shalt meditate therein [the Law] day and night
Psalm 1:2	In his law doth he meditate day and night
Psalm 119:148	[Before] the night watches … I meditate in thy word
1 Timothy 4:15	Meditate on these things; give thyself wholly to them

G. Be diligent in prayer:

Isaiah 64:7	There is none that calleth upon thy name, that stirreth himself to take hold of thee
Daniel 9:13	All this evil is come upon us: yet made we not our prayer
Jonah 1:6	What meanest thou, O sleeper? Arise, call upon thy God
Luke 18:1	Men ought always to pray, and not to faint
Luke 22:46	Why sleep ye? Rise and pray

2. CONDITIONS TO GETTING PRAYER ANSWERED:

A. Pray in faith:

Matthew 21:21–22	Have faith ... doubt not ... whatsoever ye shall ask in prayer, believing, ye shall receive
Mark 11:24	When ye pray, believe that ye receive and ye shall have
Romans 4:21	Being fully persuaded that, what he had promised, he was able also to perform
Hebrews 11:6	He that cometh to God must believe that he is
James 1:5–7	Let him ask in faith, nothing wavering

(See also Matthew 17:18–20; Luke 7:1–10.)

B. Obey God and do His will:

John 9:31	If any man ... doeth God's will, him he heareth
John 15:7	If ye abide in me, and my words abide in you, ye shall ask what ye will, and it shall be done unto you
1 John 3:22	We ask, we receive, because we keep his commandments

(See also Isaiah 58:6–9.)

C. Pray according to God's will:

Psalm 143:10	Teach me to do thy will; for thou art my God
Matthew 6:10	Thy will be done in earth, as it is in heaven
Luke 22:42	Nevertheless not my will, but thine [God's], be done
John 5:30	[Jesus]: I seek not mine own will, but [God's] will
1 John 5:14	If we ask anything according to his will, he heareth

D. Pray humbly:

Daniel 9:18	We do not present our supplications [because of] our righteousnesses, but for thy great mercies
Luke 18:10–14	The publican [said], God be merciful to me a sinner
James 4:6	God resisteth the proud, but giveth grace to the humble

3. PRAYER PROMISES:

2 Peter 1:4	Are given unto us exceeding great and precious promises

A. Remind God of His promises when praying:

Genesis 32:6–12	Jacob was greatly afraid and distressed [and prayed, reminding God of His promises of protection]
Nehemiah 1:4–11	[Nehemiah prayed:] Remember … the word that thou commandest thy servant Moses

B. Some promises to claim in prayer:

Psalm 37:4–5	Delight thyself in the Lord: and he shall give thee desires
Psalm 81:10	Open thy mouth wide, and I will fill it
Isaiah 65:24	Before they call, I will answer; and while they are yet speaking, I will hear
Jeremiah 33:3	Call unto me, and I will answer thee and shew thee great and mighty things
John 15:7	Ask what ye will, and it shall be done unto you
John 15:16	Whatsoever ye ask in my name … [God will] give it

C. God promises to hear prayer:

2 Samuel 22:7	In my distress I called … he did hear my voice
Psalm 34:15,17	The righteous cry, and the Lord heareth
Psalm 72:12	He shall deliver the needy when he crieth
Psalm 91:15	He shall call upon me, and I will answer him

D. God's blessings for those who seek Him:

2 Chronicles 26:5	As long as he sought the Lord, God made him to prosper
2 Chronicles 31:21	He [sought God] with all his heart, and prospered

4. THINGS THAT HINDER OUR PRAYERS:

A. Disobedience:

Deuteronomy 1:43–45	Ye would not hear, but rebelled against [the word] of the Lord … the Lord would not hearken to your voice
Deuteronomy 3:23–27	[Moses' request to enter Canaan denied] (See also Numbers 20:12.)
1 Samuel 28:5–6	When Saul enquired of the Lord, the Lord answered him not (See the reason in 1 Samuel 28:15–19.)
Isaiah 1:15	When ye make many prayers, I will not hear
Micah 3:4	Then shall they cry unto the Lord, but he will not hear … they have behaved themselves ill

(See also 1 Samuel 13:8–14; 14:37; Hosea 5:6.)

B. Disbelief:

Job 9:16	If I called, and he answered me; yet would I not believe he had hearkened unto my voice

Matthew 17:19–20	Why could not we cast him out? Because of your unbelief
Hebrews 11:6	Without faith it is impossible to please him: for he that cometh to God must believe that he is

C. Unconfessed sin:

Psalm 68:18–19	If I regard iniquity in my heart, Lord will not hear
Isaiah 59:1–2	Your sins have hid his face … that he will not hear
James 5:16	Confess your faults … and pray one for another

D. Doubts:

Proverbs 1:24–28	Then shall they call upon me, but I will not answer
Proverbs 28:9	He that turneth ear … his prayer shall be abomination
Zechariah 7:12–13	Therefore … they cried, and I would not hear
James 1:5–7	Let not that man [who doubts] think he shall receive anything of the Lord

E. Resentment:

Mark 11:25	When ye stand praying, forgive, if ye have ought

F. Selfish motives:

Deuteronomy 23:4–5	They hired against thee Balaam … curse thee. [But] the Lord would not hearken unto Balaam
James 4:3	Ye ask, and receive not, because ye ask amiss, that ye may consume it upon your lusts

G. Pride:

Matthew 6:5–6	Not be as hypocrites [who] love to pray [publicly]
Luke 18:10–14	God, I thank thee, that I am not as other men are

H. Don't pray long, repetitive prayers:

Ecclesiastes 5:2	God is in heaven … let thy words be few
Matthew 6:7–8	When ye pray, use not vain repetitions
Matthew 23:14	Woe unto you [who] for a pretence make long prayer
Joshua 7:6,10	[God told Joshua to stop praying and get up]

I. What happens when we don't pray:

James 4:2	Ye have not, because ye ask not (See also Isaiah 64:7.)

5. PRIVATE PRAYER AND UNITED PRAYER:

A. Private prayer:

Matthew 6:6	When thou prayest, enter into thy closet … in secret
Mark 1:35	He … departed into a solitary place, and there prayed
Mark 6:46	He sent them away, he departed to a mountain to pray
Luke 5:16	He withdrew himself into the wilderness, and prayed

B. United prayer:

Matthew 18:19–20	Where two or three are gathered together in my name
Acts 1:13–15	These all [120 people] continued with one accord in prayer … in an upper room
Acts 4:23–31	[After a beating, Peter and John held a prayer meeting]
Acts 12:12	House of Mary … many were gathered together praying

C. "Watching" in prayer:

1 Samuel 15:11	It grieved Samuel; and he cried unto the Lord all night
Matthew 26:40–41	Could ye not watch with me one hour? Watch and pray
Luke 6:12	He [Jesus] continued all night in prayer to God
Acts 12:5	Peter was kept in prison … prayer was made without ceasing of the church unto God for him
Ephesians 6:18	Praying always … and watching thereunto

6. WHEN TO PRAY:

A. Be in a continual attitude of prayer:

1 Chronicles 16:11	Seek the Lord … seek his face continually
Proverbs 3:6	In all thy ways acknowledge him, and he shall direct
Luke 18:1	Men ought always to pray
Luke 21:36	Watch ye therefore, and pray always
1 Thessalonians 5:17	Pray without ceasing (See also Ephesians 6:18.)

B. Pray in time of special need:

Psalm 27:8	When thou saidst, "Seek ye my face"
Psalm 50:15	Call upon me in the day of trouble
Psalm 107:19	They cry unto the Lord in their trouble, and he saveth
Hebrews 4:16	Let us come boldly unto the throne of grace that we may … find … help in time of need
James 5:13	Is any among you afflicted? Let him pray (See also 2 Chronicles 14:11–12; Psalm 34:4,6.)

C. Pray in the morning:

Psalm 5:3	In the morning will I direct my prayer unto thee
Psalm 63:1	O God, thou art my God; early will I seek thee
Psalm 119:147	I [rose before] the dawning of the morning, and cried
Proverbs 8:17	Those that seek me early shall find me
Mark 1:35	In the morning, rising up before day, he … prayed

D. Pray in the evening:

Genesis 24:63	Isaac went out to meditate in the field at eventide
Psalm 55:17	Evening, and morning, and at noon, will I pray
Daniel 6:10	Daniel … kneeled three times a day, and prayed
Mark 6:46–47	[Jesus] departed to mountain to pray … even was come

E. Pray at night:

Psalm 42:8	In the night his song shall be with me, and my prayer
Psalm 63:5–6	When I ... meditate on thee in the night watches
Isaiah 26:9	With my soul have I desired thee in the night
Lamentations 2:19	Arise, cry out in the night … pour out thine heart like water before the face of the Lord
Luke 6:12	[Jesus] continued all night in prayer to God
Acts 16:25	At midnight Paul and Silas prayed, and sang praises
	(See also Psalm 4:4; 119:55,62.)

7. WHOLEHEARTED FERVENT PRAYER:

A. Stir yourself up; call on God wholeheartedly:

1 Samuel 15:11,16	It grieved Samuel; and he cried unto the Lord all night
Isaiah 64:7	None ... stirreth up himself to take hold of thee
Jeremiah 29:13	Ye shall seek me, and find me, when ye search for me with all your heart (See also Deuteronomy 4:29.)
Lamentations 2:19	Arise, cry out … poor out thine heart like water
Luke 22:44	Being in an agony, he [Jesus] prayed more earnestly
Hebrews 4:16	Let us therefore come boldly … in time of need
Hebrews 5:7	[Jesus] offered up prayers … with strong crying and tears
James 5:16	Effectual fervent prayer … availeth much
	(See also Psalm 61:1–2; 119:10.)

B. Pray fervently for others:

Romans 15:30–31	Strive together with me in our prayers to God
Colossians 4:12	Epaphrus … always labouring fervently for you in prayers

C. Don't give up; be persistent:

Genesis 18:23–32	[Abraham repeatedly asks God to spare Sodom for the sake of the righteous. God agrees, if there are 10]
Genesis 32:24–28	[Jacob refuses to let angel go until he blesses him]
Luke 11:5–10	Because of his importunity [insistence] he will give
Luke 18:1–8	[Widow and unjust judge] Lest by her continual coming
Romans 12:12	Continuing instant [steadfast, persevering] in prayer
Ephesians 6:18	Praying always … watching thereunto with perseverance
James 5:16–18	The effectual, fervent prayer of a righteous man (See also 1 Kings 18:2,41–45.)

D. Challenge God to keep His Word and answer prayer:

2 Kings 2:14	[Elisha challenges:] "Where is the God of Elijah?"
Isaiah 45:11	Concerning the work of my hands command ye me
	(See also Exodus 32:11–14.)

E. Sometimes you can change God's mind through prayer:

Genesis 19:17–21	I will not overthrow this city [Zoar], for the which thou hast spoken
Exodus 32:9–14	Moses besought the Lord … and the Lord repented of the evil which he [had] thought to do
2 Kings 20:1–6	[King Hezekiah was told he would die, but when he prayed, God changed His mind and healed him]
Amos 7:1–6	The Lord repented for this: This also shall not be
Jonah 3:4–10	[Nineveh repented, so God spared it]

F. Praying repeatedly:

1 Kings 18:42–43	Elijah [prayed] seven times
Matthew 26:44	[Jesus] prayed the third time, saying the same words

G. Fasting and prayer:

Ezra 8:23	So we fasted and besought our God for this: and he was intreated of us
Joel 2:12	Turn ye to me with all your heart, and with fasting
Matthew 17:21	This kind goeth not out but by prayer and fasting (See also Deuteronomy 9:9,18; Acts 13:2–3; 1 Corinthians 7:5.)

8. OTHER POINTS ON PRAYER:

A. Jesus prays for us:

Romans 8:34	Christ … who is at the right hand of God … maketh intercession for us
Hebrews 7:25	He ever liveth to make intercession for [us] (See also Luke 22:32; John 17:9.)

B. The Holy Spirit prays for us:

Romans 8:26–27	[The Spirit] maketh intercession for the saints

C. Be thankful to God for answering prayer:

Psalm 116:1–2,7	I love the Lord, because he hath heard my [prayers] (See also Psalm 30:1–4; 66:16–17,19–20.)

D. Prayer is precious:

Psalm 141:2	Let my prayer be set before thee as incense
Proverbs 15:8	The prayer of the upright is his delight
Revelation 5:8	Golden vials full of odours are the prayers of saints (See also Revelation 8:3.)

E. Give thanks before eating:

1 Samuel 9:13	People will not eat till he … bless the sacrifice
Matthew 14:19	Looking up to heaven, he blessed and brake … the loaves

Matthew 26:26	Jesus took bread, and blessed it, and brake it, and gave
Mark 8:6	He [Jesus] took the seven loaves, and gave thanks
Acts 27:35	He [Paul] took bread, and gave thanks to God
1 Timothy 4:3–5	[Food] sanctified by prayer

9. WAYS GOD ANSWERS PRAYER:

A. The answer can surpass the request:

1 Kings 3:7–14	[Solomon prayed for wisdom and God granted him much more]
Acts 12:1–16	[Church prayed for Peter, but they were surprised at his miraculous release from prison]
Ephesians 3:20	Able to do exceeding abundantly above all that we ask

B. The answer can be delayed (which tests our faith):

Job 30:20	[Job's prayer not answered immediately]
Psalm 40:1	I waited patiently for the Lord, and he … heard my cry
Jeremiah 42:4,7	[Jeremiah's prayer answered 10 days after he prayed]
Lamentations 3:25–26	The Lord is good unto them that wait for him, to the soul that seeketh him (See also Psalm 62:1.)
Daniel 10:2,12–13	[The answer to Daniel's prayer was delayed for 21 days]
Luke 16:7–8	[Answer] his elect … though he bear long with them
Hebrews 10:36	Patience … after ye have done will of God, receive
Revelation 6:10–11	How long, O Lord? [Answer:] Rest yet a little season

C. The answer can be different from the request:

Deuteronomy 3:23–27	[Moses allowed to view the promised land, not enter]
John 11:1–3,6	[Jesus is asked to heal Lazarus, but lets him die, then resurrects him] (See also John 11:14–15,32,37,43–45.)
2 Corinthians 12:7–9	[Paul prays for healing; instead is given grace to bear his affliction] (See also 2 Kings 5:9–13.)

D. Beware about insisting that God grant your request:

Psalm 106:15	He gave them their request; but sent leanness into their soul (See also 1 Samuel 8:4–22; 12:1,13,16–19, about when the Israelites asked God for a king.)

FAITH

1. WHAT IS FAITH?

A. Faith is believing God:

2 Corinthians 4:18	We look not at the things which are seen, but at the things which are not seen … which are eternal
2 Corinthians 5:7	We walk by faith, not by sight
Hebrews 11:27	By faith he … endured, as seeing him who is invisible (See also Romans 8:24.)

B. Faith is a real thing:

2 Timothy 1:5	The unfeigned faith that is in thee
Hebrews 11:1	Faith is the substance of things hoped for, the evidence of things not seen

2. THE IMPORTANCE OF FAITH:

A. We are saved by faith:

John 3:16	Whosoever believeth in Him [Jesus] should … have everlasting life
John 3:36	He that believeth on the Son hath everlasting life
Luke 7:47–50	Thy sins are forgiven. Thy faith hath saved thee
Acts 10:43	Whoever believeth in him … receive remission of sins
Acts 16:31	Believe on ... Jesus Christ, and thou shalt be saved
Romans 5:1	Being justified by faith, we have peace with God
Galatians 3:26	Ye are all children of God by faith in Christ Jesus
Ephesians 2:8–9	For by grace are ye saved through faith
Ephesians 3:17	That Christ may dwell in your hearts by faith (See also 1 Peter 1:9.)

B. We must live by faith:

Galatians 2:20	Life which I live, I live by the faith of [Jesus]
Hebrews 10:38	The just shall live by faith (See also Romans 1:17.)
1 John 5:4	This is the victory that overcometh the world, even our faith

C. We cannot please God without faith:

Romans 14:23	Whatsoever is not of faith is sin
Hebrews 11:6	Without faith it is impossible to please him [God]

D. Faith gives us the strength to keep going:

Psalm 27:13	I had fainted, unless I had believed to see the goodness
Romans 11:20	Thou standest by faith
2 Corinthians 4:16–18	We faint not … while we look not at things which are seen, but at things which are not seen

3. THE WORD TELLS US TO HAVE FAITH:

A. In God and Jesus:

2 Chronicles 20:20	Believe in the Lord your God
Mark 11:22	Jesus saith unto them, Have faith in God
John 6:28–29	Believe on him [Jesus] whom he [God] hath sent
John 14:1	Ye believe in God, believe also in me
1 John 3:23	His commandment, that we should believe on Jesus (See also Acts 20:21.)

B. We are to trust God:

Psalm 37:5	Commit thy way unto the Lord; trust also in him
Proverbs 3:5–6	Trust in the Lord with all thine heart
Jeremiah 17:7	Blessed is the man that trusteth in the Lord, and whose hope the Lord is

C. Have faith in the Word, God's promises to us:

Mark 1:15	Believe the gospel
2 Peter 1:19	We have a … sure word of prophecy; whereunto ye do well that ye take heed (See also 2 Peter 3:2.) (See also Acts 15:7.)

4. HOW TO OBTAIN FAITH:

A. Faith is a gift from God:

Romans 12:3	God hath dealt to every man the measure of faith
1 Corinthians 12:7,9	To another [is given] faith by the same Spirit
Galatians 5:22	The fruit of the Spirit is … faith
Ephesians 6:23	Peace be to brethren … and love with faith, from God
Hebrews 12:2	Jesus, the author and finisher of our faith

B. Pray for it:

Mark 9:24	Lord, I believe; help thou mine unbelief
Luke 17:5	[They] said unto the Lord, Increase our faith

C. Read the Word:

John 20:30–31	These are written that ye might believe
Acts 15:7	Hear the word of the gospel and believe
Romans 10:17	Faith cometh by hearing … the word of God
Romans 15:4	Written … that we through … Scriptures might have hope

D. The Word nourishes and builds up our faith:

Acts 20:32	The word of his grace, which is able to build you up
1 Timothy 4:6	Thou shalt be … nourished up in the words of faith

E. Read the Word in a receptive, believing spirit:

Luke 8:15	They … which in an honest and good heart, having heard the word, keep it, and bring forth fruit
Hebrews 4:2	The word … did not profit them, not being mixed with faith in them that heard it
Hebrews 11:13	[Past saints died in faith believing and embracing the promises of the word]

F. Listen to testimonies of faith:

1 Kings 5:1–5	[The Hebrew maid's witness inspires Naaman's faith]
John 4:28–30,39	Many of the Samaritans … believed on him [Jesus] for the saying of the woman, which testified
John 17:20	Them which believe on me through their word

(See also 2 Peter 1:16,19.)

G. Miracles glorify God's power and often inspire faith:

Acts 4:4	[After the lame man was miraculously healed,] many of them which heard the word believed … 5,000 men
Acts 8:5–6,14	[The Samaritans believed Philip and received the word] seeing the miracles which he did
Acts 9:36–42	[Many believed in the Lord when Peter raised the dead]

(See also 1 Kings 18:30–39; 2 Kings 5:9–17.)

H. Faith grows:

2 Thessalonians 1:3	We thank God for you … your faith groweth exceedingly

I. Becoming strengthened and steadfast in the faith:

Acts 14:22	Confirming the souls of the disciples, and exhorting them to continue in the faith
1 Corinthians 16:13	Watch ye, stand fast in the faith … be strong
Colossians 1:23	Continue in the faith, grounded and settled, and be not moved away from the hope of the gospel
Colossians 2:6–7	Rooted and built up in him, stablished in the faith

J. We should have faith when we pray:

Matthew 21:21–22	Have faith, and doubt not … whatsoever ye shall ask in prayer, believing, ye shall receive
Mark 11:24	What things soever ye desire, when ye pray, believe that ye receive them
Romans 4:21	Being fully persuaded that, what he had promised, he was able also to perform
Hebrews 10:22	Let us draw near … in full assurance of faith
James 1:5–6	Ask of God … ask in faith, nothing wavering

5. THE REWARDS, BLESSINGS, AND FRUITS OF FAITH:

Hebrews 11:6	He is a rewarder of them that diligently seek him

A. Access to God:

Romans 5:2	We have access by faith into this grace
Ephesians 3:11–12	We have access … by the faith of him

B. God's love:

Psalm 32:10	He that trusteth in the Lord, mercy shall compass him
John 16:27	The Father loveth you, because ye … have believed

C. Righteousness and purity:

Genesis 15:6	He [Abraham] believed in the Lord; and he counted it to him for righteousness (See also Romans 4:1–5.)
Acts 15:9	Purifying their hearts by faith
Romans 4:8–9	Faith was reckoned to Abraham for righteousness
Romans 9:30	The righteousness which is of faith
Philippians 3:9	That which is through the faith of Christ, the righteousness which is of God by faith

D. The Holy Spirit:

John 7:38–39	He that believeth on me [Jesus] out of his belly shall flow rivers of living water … the Spirit
Galatians 3:14	We … receive the promise of the Spirit through faith

E. Protection against the devil's attacks and lies:

Ephesians 6:16	Shield of faith … quench all the fiery darts
1 Thessalonians 5:8	Putting on the breastplate of faith and love

F. Rewards in heaven:

John 14:1–3	Believe in me … I go to prepare a [mansion] for you
Hebrews 11:13,16	These all died in faith … he [God] hath prepared for them a city

G. Conviction to share our faith:

2 Corinthians 4:13	Having spirit of faith … we believe, and therefore speak

H. Spiritual strength:

Psalm 27:13	I had fainted, unless I had believed to see
Psalm 31:24	He shall strengthen your heart, ye that hope in the Lord
Isaiah 26:4	Trust ye in the Lord … for in the Lord is … strength
Isaiah 30:15	In confidence shall be your strength
1 John 5:4	This is the victory that overcometh the world … faith

I. Stability:

2 Chronicles 20:20	Believe in the Lord … so shall ye be established
Psalm 125:1	They that trust in the Lord … cannot be removed

J. Joy:

Psalm 33:21	Our heart shall rejoice in him, because we have trusted in his holy name
Psalm 146:5	Happy is he … whose hope is in the Lord his God
Proverbs 16:20	Whoso trusteth in the Lord, happy is he
Acts 16:34	He … rejoiced, believing in God
1 Peter 1:8	Ye see him not, yet believing, ye rejoice with joy

K. Understanding:

Hebrews 11:3	Through faith we understand that the worlds were framed by the word of God

L. Protection:

Psalm 5:11	[They] put their trust in thee … thou defendest them
Psalm 115:1	Trust in the Lord: he is their help and their shield
Proverbs 29:25	Whoso putteth his trust in the Lord shall be safe
Proverbs 30:5	[God] is a shield unto them that put trust in him
Jeremiah 39:17–18	I will surely deliver thee … because thou hast put thy trust in me
Hebrews 11:31	By faith the harlot Rahab perished not with them that believed not (See also Joshua 2:1–22; 6:17,22–25.)

M. Provision:

Psalm 33:18–19	Them that hope in his mercy … keep alive in famine
Psalm 37:3	Trust in the Lord … so shalt thou dwell in the land, and verily thou shalt be fed
Jeremiah 17:7–8	Blessed is the man that trusteth in the Lord … he shall not [worry] in drought, [nor] cease from yielding fruit
Malachi 3:10	Prove me herewith, if I will not open you the windows of heaven, and pour you out a blessing

N. Healing:

Psalm 42:11	Hope thou in God … who is the health of my countenance
Mark 5:25–29,34	If I … touch his [Jesus'] clothes, I shall be whole. [Jesus said:] Thy faith hath made thee whole
Mark 10:51–52	Go thy way; thy faith hath made thee whole
Luke 8:49–50	Fear not: believe only, and she shall be made whole
James 5:14–15	Prayer of faith shall save the sick … Lord shall raise him

O. Desires of our heart:

Psalm 37:4–5	Trust in the Lord … and he shall give desires of thin heart

P. Resurrection from the dead:

John 11:25–26	He that believeth in me, though he were dead, yet shall he live (See also 1 Corinthians 15:12–20.)

6. TRUSTING IN GOD'S PROMISES:

A. We trust in God's promises because we trust Him:

Matthew 8:5–10	The centurion said, Lord … speak the word only
Luke 5:4–5	We have toiled all the night, and taken nothing: nevertheless at thy word I will let down the net
2 Timothy 1:12	I know whom I believed, and am persuaded he is able
Hebrews 10:23	Hold fast the profession of our faith without wavering; for he is faithful that promised
Hebrews 11:11	[Childless Sara] judged him faithful who had promised

(See also 2 Chronicles 6:14–15.)

B. We trust that He is able to fulfil His promises:

Romans 4:20–24	Being fully persuaded that, what he had promised, he was able also to perform
2 Corinthians 1:20	All the promises of God in him [Jesus] are yea, and amen
Ephesians 3:20	He is able to do exceeding … above all that we ask

C. God is able to do anything:

Jeremiah 32:17	Ah Lord God! There is nothing too hard for thee
Jeremiah 32:27	I am the Lord … is there anything too hard for me?
Matthew 19:26	With God all things are possible
Luke 1:37	With God nothing shall be impossible
Romans 4:17	God … calleth those things which be not as though they were

D. We trust Him because He has not failed in the past:

1 Kings 8:56	There hath not failed one word of his good promise

(See also 2 Chronicles 6:15.)

E. We know He will not go back on His Word:

Numbers 23:19	Hath he said, and shall he not do it? Or hath he spoken, and shall he not make it good?
Psalm 119:49	Remember the word … upon which though hath caused me to hope
Hebrews 6:18	It [is] impossible for God to lie

7. FAITH VS. NATURAL REASONING:

1 Samuel 16:7	The Lord seeth not as man seeth; man looketh on the outward appearance … Lord looketh on the heart
Psalm 118:8	It is better to trust in the Lord than … in man
Proverbs 3:5–6	Trust in the Lord; and lean not unto thine own understanding
Isaiah 11:3	He shall not judge [according to] the sight of his eyes
Isaiah 55:8–9	Neither are your ways my ways, saith the Lord

Jeremiah 17:5	Cursed be the man that trusteth in man [and not in God]
John 20:29	Blessed are they that have not seen, and yet … believed
1 Corinthians 1:21	The world by wisdom knew not God
1 Corinthians 2:5	Your faith should not stand in the wisdom of men, but in the power of God
1 Corinthians 2:14	The natural man receiveth not the things of the Spirit
2 Corinthians 5:7	For we walk by faith, not by sight

8. THE POWER OF FAITH:

A. Genuine believing faith has tremendous power:

Mark 9:23	If thou canst believe, all things are possible
Luke 7:50	Thy faith hath saved thee [woman who touched His hem]
Luke 18:42	Receive thy sight: thy faith hath saved thee
John 14:12	He that believeth on me … greater works … shall he do
Acts 6:8	Stephen, full of faith … did great wonders and miracles
James 5:15	The prayer of faith shall save the sick

B. "Faith as a grain of mustard seed":

Matthew 17:20	Say unto this mountain, Remove hence to yonder place
Matthew 21:21–22	Ye shall not only do this which is done to fig tree
Mark 11:22–23	Have faith in God … say unto mountain, Be removed
Luke 17:6	Say unto this sycamine tree, Be thou plucked up

C. Faith trusts God to do miracles:

Numbers 13:26–30	[Caleb had faith to conquer the promised land]
Joshua 14:6,12	[Caleb had the faith to drive out the giants]
1 Samuel 17:37	[David said:] The Lord will deliver me [from Goliath]
Luke 18:27	Things … impossible with men are possible with God
Hebrews 11:11	Through faith, Sarah received strength to conceive … when she was past age
Hebrews 11:29–30	By faith they passed through the Red Sea ... By faith the walls of Jericho fell down
Hebrews 11:33–35	Through faith … stopped the mouths of lions … women received their dead raised to life again...

D. Answers to prayer depend on our faith; God can do anything, but we need to believe:

Matthew 8:13	As thou hast believed, so be it done unto thee
Matthew 9:27–30	Believe ye that I am able to do this? They said, Yea. [Jesus said:] According to your faith be it unto you
Matthew 17:19–20	Why could not we cast him out? Because of unbelief
Matthew 21:21–22	If ye have faith, and doubt not … ye shall receive

E. Believing, expectant faith will be rewarded:

Matthew 15:28	Great is thy faith: be it unto thee even as thou wilt
Mark 5:22–23	[Jairus said:] Come … that she may be healed (See also 5:35–36,41–42.)
Mark 9:23	All things are possible to him that believeth
Mark 11:23	Whosoever … shall not doubt in his heart, but shall believe … he shall have whatsoever he saith
Luke 1:45	Blessed is she that believed: for there shall be a performance of those things which were told her
John 11:40	If thou wouldest believe, thou shouldest see the glory of God

F. Persevering faith:

Matthew 15:22–28	A woman … cried to him, Have mercy on me … he answered not a word [but she continued insisting until He did]
Mark 10:46–52	[Blind Bartimaeus continued crying out to Jesus until Jesus granted his request for healing]

G. Faith and patience:

Romans 8:25	If we hope for that we see not, then do we with patience wait for it
Hebrews 6:12	Who through faith and patience inherit the promises
Hebrews 6:15	After he patiently endured … obtained the promise
Hebrews 10:35–36	Cast not away your confidence. After ye have done the will of God … receive the promise
James 1:3	The trying of your faith worketh patience

9. THE TESTING OF OUR FAITH:

Job 23:10	When he hath tried me, I shall come forth as gold
1 Peter 1:6–7	Trial of your faith … more precious than gold

A. God tests our faith:

Genesis 22:1–18	[God tested Abraham to see if he was willing to offer Isaac as a sacrifice] (See also Hebrews 11:17–19.)
Joshua 6:2–5	[He had Israelites merely walk around the walls of Jericho]
Judges 7:2–7	[He had Gideon drastically reduce the size of his army]
John 11:39–40	Take ye away the stone ... Lord, by this time he stinketh
Acts 5:17–20	[Just released from prison, the apostles are commanded to go preach publicly again] (See also Deuteronomy 8:2.)

B. He allows the Devil and wicked men to test saints' faith:

Daniel 3:14–27	[Shadrach, Meshach, and Abednego:] God … will deliver us … but if not … we will not serve thy gods

Matthew 4:1–11	[The Devil tempted Jesus:] If thou be the Son of God, cast thyself down
Hebrews 11:35–38	[Saints were] stoned, sawn asunder, tempted, slain

10. WHEN WE HAVE FAITH ...

A. We will continue to trust God, even when things look hopeless:

Job 13:15	[Job, having lost his wealth, family, and health, said:] Though he slay me, yet will I trust in him
Daniel 3:16–18	Our God whom we serve is able to deliver us from the burning fiery furnace ... and out of thine hand, O king
Matthew 8:24,26	There arose a great tempest ... the ship was covered with waves, [but Jesus chided His disciples for fearing]
John 11:21–22	[Four days after Lazarus died, Mary said:] I know, that even now, whatsoever thou wilt ask ... God will give it
Acts 27:18–25	All hope ... was taken away. [But Paul said:] I believe God, that it shall be even as it was told me
Acts 28:3–6	[Paul calmly shook off a poisonous snake that had just bitten him]
Romans 4:18	Who against hope believed in hope, that he [Abraham] might [receive the promise]
Romans 4:20	He staggered not at promise of God through unbelief

(See also 2 Chronicles 32:7,8; Isaiah 26:3; Jonah 2:1–9; Acts 9:36–38.)

B. We will not be unduly shaken or alarmed at bad news:

Psalm 112:7	He shall not be afraid of evil tidings: his heart is fixed [steadfast], trusting in the Lord

C. We will not fret or be anxious:

Psalm 37:7	Rest in the Lord, and wait patiently for him: fret not
Isaiah 28:16	He that believeth shall not make haste

D. Trust, obey, and put your faith into action.—Your deeds and words will show your faith:

Psalm 116:10	I believed, therefore have I spoken
Matthew 8:5–8,13	[The centurion believed Jesus' word, returned home] and his servant was healed in the selfsame hour
Matthew 12:10,13	[Jesus tells man with withered had:] stretch forth thine hand. And he [did]; and it was restored whole
Mark 7:25–30	[Syrophenician woman believed Jesus, went to her home and found her daughter well]
Luke 17:11–19	[Ten lepers:] As they went, they were cleansed [healed]
John 4:46–53	Go thy way; thy son liveth. And the man believed the word ... and he went his way
John 11:39–41	Take ye away the stone. They took away the stone

	[and Jesus raised Lazarus from the dead]
Hebrews 11:7	By faith Noah, moved … prepared an ark
James 2:21–26	As the body without the spirit is dead, so faith without works is dead also
	(See also Joshua 6:1–16,20; Judges 7:7,16–22; 1 Kings 17:9–16; 2 Kings 3:9–11,16–20; 4:1–6; Hebrews 11:8,17,23.)

E. Declarations of faith, followed by victorious action:

Judges 7:15–22	Arise; for the Lord hath delivered [them] into your hand
1 Samuel 14:6–16	There is no restraint to the Lord to save by many or few
1 Samuel 17:32–50	The Lord … will deliver me out of the hand of this Philistine

11. LACK OF FAITH:

A. Warnings not to doubt or lose faith:

Matthew 14:31	O thou of little faith, wherefore didst thou doubt?
Luke 12:29–30	Neither be ye of doubtful mind
John 20:27	Be not faithless, but believing
Hebrews 3:12	Take heed … lest there be in any of you an evil heart of unbelief, in departing from the living God
Hebrews 4:11	Lest any man fall after the same example of unbelief
Hebrews 10:35	Cast not away therefore your confidence

B. The consequences of not having faith:

Isaiah 7:9	If ye will not believe, ye shall not be established
Matthew 13:58	Did not many mighty works because of their unbelief
John 3:36	He that believeth not the Son shall not see life
Romans 14:23	For whatsoever is not of faith is sin
1 Timothy 1:19	Faith … which some having put away, made shipwreck
Hebrews 3:18–19	They should not enter in [and receive God's promises] because of unbelief
Hebrews 11:6	Without faith it is impossible to please him [God]
James 1:6–7	Ask in faith, nothing wavering … he that wavereth … shall receive [nothing] of the Lord

C. Faith or doubt?—To do or not to do:

Matthew 9:29	According to your faith be it unto you
Romans 14:5	Let every man be fully persuaded in his own mind
Romans 14:22–23	Hast thou faith? Happy is he that condemneth not himself in that thing which he alloweth. And he that doubteth is damned if he eat, because he eateth not of faith: for whatsoever is not of faith is sin

Special chapter about faith: Hebrews 11—"The Faith Chapter" or "Faith's Hall of Fame"

LOVE AND FORGIVENESS

1. GOD IS LOVE, AND HE LOVES US:

1 John 4:8	God is love

A. God's love for us:

Jeremiah 31:3	I have loved thee with an everlasting love: therefore with lovingkindness have I drawn thee
Romans 8:38–39	For I am persuaded, that [nothing] shall be able to separate us from the love of God
Ephesians 2:4–6	God … for his great love wherewith he loved us … hath raised us up
1 John 3:1	What manner of love the Father hath bestowed upon us
1 John 4:10	Love, not that we loved God, but that he loved us

(See also Zephaniah 3:17.)

B. How God showed us His love:

John 3:16	God so loved the world, that he gave his only … Son
Romans 5:7–8	God commendeth his love toward us, in that, while we were yet sinners, Christ died for us
1 John 4:9	In this was manifested the love of God … God sent his only begotten Son into the world, that we might live through him

C. Jesus' love for us:

John 10:11	I am the good shepherd: the good shepherd giveth his life for the sheep
John 15:13	Greater love hath no man … that [he] lay down his life
2 Corinthians 8:9	Though he [Jesus] was rich, yet for your sakes he became poor, that ye … might be rich
Ephesians 3:19	Know the love of Christ, which passeth knowledge
Revelation 1:5	Jesus Christ … loved us, and washed us from our sins in his own blood

D. Dwelling and abiding in God's love:

John 14:21	He that loveth shall be loved of my Father, and I will love him, and will manifest myself to him
John 14:23	If a man love me … my Father will love him, and we will come unto him, and make our abode with him
John 17:26	That the love … may be in them, and I in them
1 John 2:5	Whoso keepeth his [Jesus'] word, in him verily is the love of God perfected
1 John 4:19	We love him, because he first loved us
Jude 1:21	Keep yourselves in the love of God

2. THE FIRST GREAT COMMANDMENT—TO LOVE GOD:

Deuteronomy 6:5	Thou shalt love the Lord thy God with all thine heart, and with all thy soul, and with all thy might
Deuteronomy 10:12	What doth the Lord … require of thee, but to … love him … with all thy heart and with all thy soul
Deuteronomy 30:20	Love … God, and … cleave unto him: for he is thy life
Joshua 22:5	Take diligent heed to … love the Lord your God … and to cleave unto him
Joshua 23:11	Take good heed therefore unto yourselves, that ye love the Lord
Matthew 22:37–38	Thou shalt love the Lord thy God with all thy heart … This is the first and great commandment

(See also Deuteronomy 30:6; Mark 12:30.)

3. THE SECOND GREAT COMMANDMENT—TO LOVE THY NEIGHBOUR:

Leviticus 19:18	Thou shalt love thy neighbour as thyself
Matthew 22:39	And the second [commandment] is like unto it [the first]. Thou shalt love thy neighbour as thyself
John 13:34	Love one another; as I have loved you
John 15:12	This is my commandment, That ye love one another, as I have loved you
John 15:17	These things I command you, that ye love one another
1 John 3:11	For this is the message that ye heard from the beginning, that we should love one another
1 John 3:23	His commandment, That we should … love one another

4. LOVE ONE ANOTHER:

A. God loves us so we should love one another:

John 13:34	As I have loved you … ye [ought to] love one another
Ephesians 5:2	Walk in love [one to another], as Christ also hath loved us, and hath given himself for us
1 John 4:7	Beloved, let us love one another: for love is of God
1 John 4:11	If God so loved us, we ought also to love one another
1 John 5:1	Every one that loveth him that begat loveth him also that is begotten of him

B. God gives us love to love others:

Romans 5:5	The love of God is shed abroad in our hearts by the Holy Ghost which is given unto us
Galatians 5:22	The fruit of the Spirit is love … longsuffering
1 Thessalonians 3:12	And the Lord make you to increase and abound in love one toward another, and toward all men
1 Thessalonians 4:9	Ye yourselves are taught of God to love one another

2 Thessalonians 3:5	The Lord direct your hearts into the love of God
2 Timothy 1:7	God hath not given us the spirit of fear; but of ... love (See also Ephesians 6:23.)

C. To love is the greatest law of God:

Mark 12:33	To love [God] ... and to love his neighbour as himself, is more than all ... burnt offerings and sacrifices
Luke 10:25,27–28	To inherit eternal life ... love ... God with all thy heart ... thy neighbour as thyself ... this do, and thou shalt live
Galatians 5:14	All the law is fulfilled in ... this; Thou shalt love thy neighbour as thyself

D. Love is the most important virtue:

1 Corinthians 13:2	Though I have faith ... and have not love, I am nothing
1 Corinthians 13:13	Faith, hope, love ... the greatest of these is love
Galatians 5:6	Faith ... worketh by love.
Ephesians 3:17	[Be] rooted and grounded in love
Ephesians 3:19	The love of Christ ... passeth knowledge
Revelation 2:3–4	For my name's sake hast laboured ... [but] I have somewhat against thee ... thou hast left thy first love (See also Ephesians 1:15–16; Colossians 1:3–4; Philemon 1:5.)

E. Love one another fervently:

1 Thessalonians 3:12	Increase and abound in love one toward another
1 Peter 4:8	Above all things have fervent love among yourselves
1 Peter 1:22	Love one another with a pure heart fervently

F. Love sincerely and genuinely:

Judges 16:15	How canst thou say, I love thee, when thine heart is not with me?
Romans 12:9	Let love be without dissimulation
Philippians 1:9–10	That your love may abound yet more and more ... that ye may be sincere and without offence
1 Peter 1:22	Obeying the truth ... unto unfeigned love of the brethren (See also 2 Corinthians 6:6; 8:8.)

G. The benefits that loving others brings us:

John 13:35	By this shall all men know that ye are my disciples, if ye have love one to another
2 Corinthians 13:11	Live in peace; and the God of love and peace shall be with you
Ephesians 3:17–19	Ye, being rooted and grounded in love ... might be filled with all the fulness of God
1 John 2:10	He that loveth his brother abideth in the light

1 John 3:14	We know that we have passed from death unto life, because we love the brethren
1 John 4:7	Every one that loveth is born of God, and knoweth God
1 John 4:12	If we love one another, God dwelleth in us, and his love is perfected in us (See also 1 John 2:15.)
1 John 4:16	God is love; and he that dwelleth in love dwelleth in God, and God in him

5. REAL, GENUINE LOVE:

A. Whatever you do, do it in love:

1 Corinthians 16:14	Let all your things be done with charity
2 Corinthians 5:14	For the love of Christ constraineth [compels] us

B. The qualities that genuine love will have:

1 Corinthians 8:1	Love edifieth [builds up, strengthens]
1 Corinthians 13:4–6	Charity [love] envieth not; charity vaunteth [exalts] not itself, is not puffed up [proud], doth not behave itself unseemly, seeketh not her own, is not easily provoked, thinketh no evil; rejoiceth not in iniquity, but rejoiceth in the truth
Colossians 3:14	Love … is the bond of perfectness
1 John 4:18	There is no fear in love … love casteth out fear

C. Genuine love results in unity of believers:

Colossians 2:2	That their hearts might be … knit together in love (See also 1 Samuel 18:1; Ephesians 4:15–16; Philippians 2:1–2.)

D. Real love will not give up or fail:

Song of Solomon 8:7	Many waters [troubles] cannot quench love … drown it
1 Corinthians 13:4	Charity [love] suffereth long
1 Corinthians 13:7–8	Beareth all things, believeth all things, hopeth all things, endureth all things. Charity [love] never faileth
Hebrews 13:1	Let brotherly love continue

E. Love is not pushy:

Romans 12:10	With brotherly love; in honour preferring one another
Philemon 1:8–9	Though I might be much bold … to [command, impose upon] thee … yet for love's sake I rather beseech thee

F. Love is considerate of others' weaknesses:

Romans 14:21	It is good [not to do] any thing whereby thy brother stumbleth, or is offended, or is made weak
Romans 15:1–2	We … ought to bear the infirmities of the weak ... Let every one of us please his neighbour for his good

Galatians 5:13	By love serve one another
Ephesians 4:2	With longsuffering, forbearing one another in love

G. Love will not hurt or do wrong to others:

Romans 13:9–10	Love worketh no ill to his neighbour

H. If we have love, we will be kind and courteous:

1 Corinthians 13:4	Love suffereth long, and is kind
Ephesians 4:15	Speaking the truth in love [not inconsiderately blunt]
Ephesians 4:32	Be ye kind … tenderhearted, forgiving one another
1 Peter 3:8	[Have] compassion one of another, love as brethren, be pitiful, be courteous

6. REAL LOVE RESULTS IN GOOD DEEDS:

A. Putting love into action:

Matthew 14:14	Jesus … was moved with compassion toward them, and he healed their sick
Matthew 25:35	I was an hungered … I was thirsty, and ye gave
Luke 6:31	As ye would that men should do to you, do ye also to them
Luke 10:30–35	[The good Samaritan took loving action and helped]
Galatians 6:10	Let us do good [deeds] unto all men, especially unto them who are of the household of faith
1 John 3:18	Let us not love in word [only] … but in deed and in truth
2 John 1:6	This is love, that we walk after his commandments

B. Sacrificial love, giving our lives for others:

John 15:13	Greater love hath no man than this, that a man lay down his life for his friends
Acts 15:25–26	Barnabas and Paul … hazarded their lives for the name of Jesus (See also Acts 20:24.)
Philippians 2:30	For the work of Christ he was nigh unto death
1 John 3:16	He [Jesus] laid down his life for us: and we ought to lay down our lives for the brethren

C. Be concerned about others' welfare:

1 Corinthians 13:5	[Love] seeketh not her own
Philippians 2:4	Look not every man on his own things, but every man also on the things of others
1 Thessalonians 4:9	But as touching brotherly love … love one another

D. Selfishness shows a lack of love:

James 4:17	To him that knoweth to do good, and doeth it not, to him it is sin
1 John 3:17	Whoso … seeth his brother have need, and shutteth up his … compassion … how dwelleth the love of God in him?

E. Doing good to our brethren is doing it to Jesus:

Matthew 25:35–40	Inasmuch as ye have done it unto one of the least of these my brethren, ye have done it unto me
Hebrews 6:10	Love, which ye have showed toward his name, in that ye have ministered to the saints (See also Ephesians 6:5–8; Colossians 3:22–24.)

F. Failing to do good to our brethren is failing to do it to Jesus:

Matthew 25:41–45	Inasmuch as ye did it not to one of the least of these, ye did it not to me

7. LOVE VS. HATE:

A. We do not truly love God if we don't love our fellow man:

Titus 3:3–5	[Before we were saved] we … [lived] in malice and envy, hateful, and hating one another
James 3:9–12	Bless we God … and … curse we men. My brethren, these things ought not so to be (See also James 3:14; 1 John 3:17.)
1 John 4:20–21	He that loveth not his brother whom he hath seen, how can he love God whom he hath not seen? And this commandment have we from him, That he who loveth God love his brother also (See also Matthew 5:23–24.)

B. We are commanded not to be hateful:

Leviticus 19:17–18	Thou shalt not hate thy brother in thine heart … but thou shalt love thy neighbour as thyself

C. When we don't love one another:

1 John 2:9,11	He that … hateth his brother, is in darkness … blinded
1 John 3:10	He that loveth not his brother … is not of God
1 John 3:14–15	He that loveth not his brother abideth in death. Whosoever hateth his brother is a murderer
1 John 4:8	He that loveth not knoweth not God; for God is love
1 John 4:20	If a man say, I love God, and hateth his brother, he is a liar

D. The bad fruit of hatred:

Genesis 37:4	They hated him, and could not speak peaceably unto him
Proverbs 10:12	Hatred stirreth up strifes
1 John 3:15	Whosoever hateth his brother is a murderer (See also Genesis 4:3–8; Proverbs 26:26; Ezekiel 5:15.)

8. SPECIAL CATEGORIES OF LOVE:

A. We are to love all men:

Matthew 5:46–47	If ye [only] love them which love you … what do ye more than others? (See also Luke 6:32–33.)
1 Thessalonians 3:12	Increase and abound in love … toward all men
Hebrews 12:14	Follow peace with all men

B. We are especially to love brothers and sisters in faith:

John 13:35	By this shall all men know that ye are my disciples, if ye have love one to another
Galatians 6:10	Especially unto them who are of the household of faith
1 Peter 2:17	Honour all men. Love the brotherhood (See also Hebrews 13:1; 1 Peter 4:8. Also compare Titus 3:15; 2 John 1:1; 3 John 1:1, regarding "loving in the faith.")

C. Examples of unusually great love and/or admiration:

1 Samuel 18:1	The soul of Jonathan was knit with the soul of David, [he] loved him as his own soul. (See also 20:17.)
2 Samuel 1:26	[David declared his deep love for Jonathan]
Mark 10:17–21	[Jesus was moved with love for the rich young ruler]
John 11:3,5	[Jesus' special love for Mary, Martha, and Lazarus]
John 13:23	[Jesus had a special love for the apostle John] (See also John 19:26; 21:7,20.)
1 Thessalonians 5:13	Esteem them very highly in love for their [good] work's sake

D. We are even to demonstrate God's love to our foes:

Proverbs 25:21–22	If thine enemy be hungry, give him bread … and if he be thirsty, give him water … and the Lord shall reward thee
Matthew 5:43–47	Love your enemies, bless them that curse you, do good … that ye may be the children of your Father
Luke 6:27–30	Love your enemies, do good to them which hate you, bless them that curse you, and pray for them
Luke 6:32–35	If ye love them which love you, what thank have ye? Sinners also love those that love them
Luke 10:30–37	A Samaritan [despised by the Jews] … when he saw him [a wounded Jew], he had compassion on him

9. LOVE, FORGIVENESS, AND MERCY:

A. To love means to be forgiving:

Proverbs 10:12	Love covereth all sins.
1 Peter 4:8	Love shall cover the multitude of sins

B. God is merciful to us:

Numbers 14:18–19	The Lord is longsuffering, and of great mercy, forgiving iniquity and transgression ... Pardon … the iniquity of this people according unto the greatness of thy mercy
Psalm 103:8	The Lord is merciful and gracious, slow to anger, and plenteous in mercy
Psalm 103:10–11	He hath not dealt with us after our sins … great is his mercy toward them that fear him.
Isaiah 63:7	The great goodness … he hath bestowed on them according to his mercies, and … multitude of his lovingkindnesses
Lamentations 3:22–23	It is of the Lord's mercies that we are not consumed, because his compassions fail not … new every morning (See also 2 Samuel 24:14; Psalm 25:6; 36:7; 40:11; 69:16; 103:2–4; 119:149; Isaiah 54:7–8; Jeremiah 9:24.)

C. God loves mercy more than justice and retribution:

Proverbs 16:6	By mercy and truth iniquity is purged
Micah 7:18	God … pardoneth iniquity … he delighteth in mercy
Matthew 9:13	I will have [desire] mercy, and not sacrifice (See also Hosea 6:6.)
Romans 5:20	Where sin abounded, grace did much more abound
James 2:13	Mercy rejoiceth against judgement

D. He often refrains from justly punishing us:

Exodus 32:14	The Lord repented of the evil which he thought to do unto his people.
Psalm 103:9–10	He hath not dealt with us after our sins; nor rewarded us according to our iniquities
Psalm 130:3–4	If thou … shouldest mark iniquities, O Lord, who shall stand? But there is forgiveness with thee
2 Samuel 24:16	The Lord repented him of the evil, and said to the angel that destroyed the people … stay now thine hand (See also Genesis 18:20,23–26; Jonah 1:1–2; 3:10; 4:11.)

E. God mercifully forgives our sins:

Psalm 103:12	As far as the east is from the west, so far hath he removed our transgressions from us

Isaiah 1:18	Though your sins be as scarlet, they shall be as white as snow … as wool
Isaiah 43:25	I, even I, am he that blotteth out thy transgressions
Isaiah 44:22	I have blotted out, as a thick cloud … thy sins
Micah 7:19	He will have compassion upon us … and cast all their sins into the depths of the sea
Hebrews 8:12	I will be merciful … and their sins … remember no more

(See also Psalm 32:1–2; Isaiah 38:17.)

F. God is especially merciful to those who love and fear Him:

Exodus 20:6	Showing mercy unto … them that love me, and keep my commandments
Deuteronomy 7:9	God … keepeth covenant and mercy with them that love him
Psalm 103:11	As the heaven is high above the earth, so great is his mercy toward them that fear him
Psalm 103:13	Like as a father pitieth his children, so the Lord pitieth them that fear him
Psalm 103:17	The mercy of the Lord is from everlasting to everlasting upon them that fear him
Luke 7:47–48	Her [many] sins … are forgiven; for she loved much
Acts 26:18	Turn them from darkness to light … that they may receive forgiveness of sins

10. WE ARE TO BE MERCIFUL AND FORGIVING:

Micah 6:8	What doth the Lord require of thee, but to … love mercy

A. We should forgive others as God has forgiven us:

Matthew 18:33	Shouldest not thou also have had compassion on thy fellowservant, even as I had pity on thee?
Luke 6:36	Be ye … merciful, as your father is also merciful
Ephesians 4:32	Forgiving one another, even as God … hath forgiven you
Colossians 3:13	Forbearing one another, and forgiving one another … even as Christ forgave you, so also do ye

B. Have longsuffering and keep forgiving:

Proverbs 17:9	He that covereth [passes over] a transgression seeketh love
Matthew 18:21–22	Lord, how oft shall my brother sin against me, and I forgive him? … Until seventy times seven [times]
Luke 17:4	If he trespass against thee seven times in a day, and seven times … repent; thou shalt forgive him

C. Make mercy a rule in your heart:

Proverbs 3:3–4	Let not mercy and truth forsake thee … write them upon the table of thine heart

D. Forgive sincerely; don't harbour grudges or hatred:

Leviticus 19:17–18	Thou shalt not … bear any grudge … but thou shalt love
Matthew 18:35	From your hearts forgive … every one his brother
Ephesians 4:31–32	Let all bitterness … be put away from you with all malice: forgive one another (See also Hebrews 12:15.)
James 5:9	Grudge not against another, brethren

E. God shows mercy to us if we are merciful and forgiving:

Psalm 18:25	With the merciful thou wilt show thyself merciful
Matthew 5:7	Blessed are the merciful: for they shall obtain mercy
Matthew 6:12	Forgive us our debts, as we forgive our debtors
Matthew 6:14	If ye forgive men their trespasses, your heavenly Father will also forgive you
Mark 11:25	Forgive, if ye have ought against any: that your Father … may forgive you your trespasses
Luke 6:37	Condemn not, and ye shall not be condemned: forgive, and ye shall be forgiven

F. But woe to the unmerciful:

Matthew 6:15	If ye forgive not men their trespasses, neither will [God] forgive your trespasses. (See also Mark 11:26.)
Matthew 18:23–35	So … shall [God] do also unto you, if ye … forgive not every one his brother their trespasses
James 2:13	He shall have judgement without mercy, that hath showed no mercy

G. The self-righteous feel they don't sin and don't need forgiveness; therefore they are unloving and unforgiving to others:

Luke 7:47	To whom little is forgiven, the same loveth little
Luke 15:25–30	[The faithful older brother was angry that his father forgave the penitent Prodigal Son]
Luke 18:9	Certain trusted in themselves that they were righteous, and [therefore] despised others

11. WE MUST CONFESS OUR SINS IN ORDER TO RECEIVE FORGIVENESS:

Psalm 32:5	I acknowledged my sin unto thee … and thou forgavest
Psalm 86:5	Thou, Lord, art good, and ready to forgive; and plenteous in mercy unto all them that call upon thee
Acts 3:19	Repent ye … that your sins may be blotted out

2 Corinthians 2:6–8	[After punishment] ye ought to forgive him, and comfort him, lest [he] be swallowed up with overmuch sorrow
1 John 1:9	If we confess our sins, he is faithful and just to forgive

OUR RELATIONSHIP WITH GOD

Includes dedication, devotion, and loving and reverencing God

1. WE WORSHIP GOD BY LOVING HIM:

A. We are to love God with all our heart:

Deuteronomy 6:5	Thou shalt love the Lord thy God with all thine heart, and with all thy soul, and with all thy might
Deuteronomy 10:12	What doth the Lord ... require of thee, but to ... to love him ... with all thy heart and with all thy soul
Matthew 22:37–38	Love the Lord thy God with all thy heart, and with all thy soul, and with all thy mind. This is the first and great commandment
	(See also Deuteronomy 30:6,20; Joshua 22:5; 23:11.)

B. Our souls should thirst for God:

Psalm 42:1–2	As the hart panteth after the water brooks, so panteth my soul after thee, O God. My soul thirsteth for God
Psalm 63:1	My soul thirsteth for thee ... in a dry and thirsty land
	(See also Psalm 143:6; Matthew 5:6; John 4:10,14.)

C. We should greatly desire Him:

Psalm 16:8	I have set the Lord always before me ... at my right hand
Psalm 27:4	One thing have I desired ... that will I seek after; that I may ... behold the beauty of the Lord
Psalm 63:8	My soul followeth hard after thee
Psalm 84:2	My soul longeth, yea, even fainteth for the courts of the Lord
Isaiah 26:9	With my soul have I desired thee in the night

D. We are to desire Him above all else:

Psalm 73:25	Whom have I in heaven but thee? and there is none upon earth that I desire beside thee
Isaiah 26:8	The desire of our soul is to thy name

E. We are to worship Jesus as we worship God:

John 5:23	All men should honour the Son, even as ... the Father
Philippians 2:9–11	At the name of Jesus every knee should bow ... every tongue should confess that Jesus Christ is Lord
Colossians 1:18	[He] is the beginning, the firstborn from the dead; that in all things he might have the preeminence
1 John 5:1	Every one that loveth him [God] that begat loveth him [Jesus] also that is begotten of him

F. Why we love and worship Jesus:

1 John 3:16	Hereby perceive we the love of God, because he [Jesus] laid down his life for us
1 John 4:19	We love him, because he first loved us
Revelation 5:8–13	Worthy is the Lamb that was slain to receive … honour, and glory, and blessing (See also 1 John 2:23; 4:15.)

2. HOW WE SHOW OUR LOVE FOR GOD:

A. By loving and obeying His Word:

Deuteronomy 11:1	Thou shalt love the Lord thy God, and keep his … statutes, and his judgements, and his commandments, always
Job 23:12	I have esteemed [God's] words ... more than my necessary food
Psalm 119:20	My soul breaketh for the longing that it hath unto thy judgements [word] at all times. (See also Psalm 119:40.)
Psalm 119:131	I … panted: for I longed for thy commandments
John 14:21	He that [keepeth] my commandments … he it is that loveth me
1 John 3:22	We keep his commandments, and do those things that are pleasing in his sight
1 John 5:3	This is the love of God, that we keep his commandments
2 John 1:6	This is love, that we walk after his commandments (See also Psalm 119:47–48,97,113,127,140,159,163,167.)

B. By worshipping Him in prayer:

Psalm 18:1,3	I will love thee, O Lord … I will call upon the Lord
Psalm 63:1–4	Thou art my God; early will I seek thee … to see thy power and thy glory
Psalm 91:14–15	Because he hath set his love upon me … he shall call upon me, and I will answer him
Psalm 116:1–2	I love the Lord … therefore will I call upon him

C. By loving one another:

Matthew 25:40	Inasmuch as ye have done it unto one of the least of these my brethren, ye have done it unto me
1 John 4:20–21	Commandment … he who loveth God love his brother also

D. By listening to His voice:

1 Samuel 3:9–10	If he call thee … say "Speak, Lord; for they servant heareth"
Psalm 143:8	Cause me to hear they lovingkindness

Isaiah 50:5 — The Lord hath opened mine ear, and I was not rebellious

E. By obeying, following, and serving Him:

Deuteronomy 10:12–13	What doth the Lord thy God require of thee, but to … serve [him] … keep the commandments of the Lord
Joshua 24:14	Fear the Lord, and serve him in sincerity and truth
1 Samuel 12:24	Fear the Lord, and serve him in truth with all your heart
John 10:27	My sheep hear my voice … and they follow me
John 12:26	Follow me; where I am, there shall also my servant be
John 15:10	If ye keep my commandments, ye shall abide in my love
Ephesians 6:7	Doing service, as to the Lord, and not to men
Hebrews 12:28	Serve God acceptably with reverence and godly fear

F. By self-sacrifice and giving our lives in love:

Matthew 10:38	He that taketh not his cross, and followeth after me, is not worthy of me
John 10:17	My father [doth] love me, because I lay down my life
1 Corinthians 15:31	I die daily (See also 2 Corinthians 11:22–28.)
Galatians 2:20	I am crucified with Christ
Philippians 3:7–8	I count all things but loss … that I may win Christ
Revelation 12:11	They counted not their lives unto the death

G. By honouring and obeying Him more than men:

Acts 5:29 — We ought to obey God rather than men (See also Acts 4:19.)

H. By giving to Him and supporting His work:

Proverbs 3:9 — Honour the Lord with … the firstfruits of all thine increase (See also Leviticus 27:30; 1 Corinthians 9:6–11.)

3. WE ARE TO LOVE GOD ABOVE ALL ELSE:

Matthew 22:37 — Love … God with all thy heart … soul and … mind

A. We are not to love—or put—anything before Him:

Exodus 20:3 — Thou shalt have no other gods before me (See also Psalm 96:4.)

B. God is jealous of our love:

Exodus 20:3,5 — Thou shalt not … serve [other gods]: for I the Lord thy God am a jealous God (See also Exodus 34:14; Deuteronomy 32:16,21; Isaiah 42:8; 1 Corinthians 10:22.)

C. We are to love God even more than our loved ones:

Genesis 22:12 — Now I know that thou fearest God, seeing thou hast not withheld thy son, thine only son from me.

Matthew 10:37	He that loveth father or mother … [or] son or daughter more than me is not worthy of me (See also Luke 14:26.)

D. We are to love God more than we care about ourselves:

Matthew 4:4	Not live by bread alone, but by every word … of God
Matthew 6:24–33	No man can serve two masters: for either he will hate the one, and love the other … Ye cannot serve God and mammon ... Seek ye first the kingdom of God, and his righteousness (See also Psalm 84:10–11.)

E. Our focus should be on heavenly things, rather than on things of the earth:

Matthew 6:20–21	Lay up for yourselves treasures in heaven … for where your treasure is, there will your heart be also
Luke 12:15	A man's life consisteth not in abundance of things
Colossians 3:1–2	Seek those things which are above, where Christ sitteth on the right hand of God. Set … affection on things above, not on things on the earth (See also Hebrews 10:34.)

F. We mustn't even put God's service above loving Him:

Luke 10:38–42	[The story of Martha busy serving, while Mary listened to Jesus]
Luke 11:42	Ye tithe … [but] pass over judgement and the love of God
Revelation 2:3–5	For my name's sake hast laboured … nevertheless … thou hast left thy first love … thou art fallen

4. WE ARE TO FEAR AND REVERENCE GOD:

A. Fearing God:

Deuteronomy 10:12	What doth the Lord thy God require of thee, but to fear the Lord thy God
2 Kings 17:35–36	The Lord … him shall ye fear, and him shall ye worship
Ecclesiastes 12:13	Fear God, and keep his commandments
Isaiah 8:12–13	Let [God] be your fear, and let him be your dread
Luke 12:4–5	Be not afraid of [men] … I will forewarn you whom ye shall fear: Fear [God] … yea, I say, Fear him (See also Matthew 10:28.)

B. Fearing (reverencing) God is healthy:

Psalm 19:9	The fear of the Lord is clean (Compare with Proverbs 29:25.)

C. The benefits of fearing God:

Psalm 111:10	The fear of the Lord is the beginning of wisdom (See also Proverbs 9:10.)

Proverbs 1:7	The fear of the Lord is the beginning of knowledge
Proverbs 14:26–27	In the fear of the Lord is strong confidence ... The fear of the Lord is a fountain of life, to depart from the snares of death
Proverbs 16:6	By the fear of the Lord men depart from evil

D. God's blessings on us for fearing Him:

Psalm 25:12	He that feareth the Lord … shall he teach in the way
Psalm 31:19	How great is thy goodness … for them that fear thee
Psalm 103:13	The Lord pitieth [has compassion on] them that fear him
Psalm 147:11	The Lord taketh pleasure in them that fear him
Luke 1:50	His mercy is on them that fear him
Acts 10:35	He that feareth him … is accepted with him

5. RESTING IN THE LORD:

A. The Bible instructs us to "rest in the Lord":

Psalm 37:7	Rest in the Lord, and wait patiently for him
Hebrews 4:3	We which have believed do enter into rest
Hebrews 4:9	There remaineth therefore a rest to the people of God

B. Take time to sit at Jesus' feet:

Luke 10:38–42	Mary … sat at Jesus' feet and heard his word. But Martha was cumbered … serving. Mary hath chosen the good part

C. Cast your burdens and worries on God:

Psalm 55:22	Cast thy burden upon the Lord, and he shall sustain thee
Matthew 11:28–30	Come unto me, all ye that labour and are heavy laden, and I will give you rest … unto your souls
1 Peter 5:7	Casting all your care upon him; for he careth for you

D. Quietly meditate on God's power:

Genesis 24:63	Isaac went out to meditate in the field at the eventide
Job 37:14	Stand still, and consider the wondrous works of God
Psalm 46:10	Be still, and know that I am God
1 Thessalonians 4:11	Study to be quiet

E. Be humble before Him:

1 Kings 3:7	[King Solomon prayed to God] I am but a little child
Isaiah 57:15	The high and lofty one that inhabiteth eternity … I dwell … with him also that is of a contrite and humble spirit

Micah 6:8	What doth the Lord require of thee, but to … walk humbly with thy God?

6. DRAWING CLOSE AND RESTING IN THE "SECRET PLACE":

Hebrews 4:11	Let us labour … to enter into that rest
James 4:8	Draw nigh to God, and he will draw nigh to you

A. The "secret place" of God's presence:

Psalm 17:8	Hide me under the shadow of thy wings
Psalm 31:19–20	Thou shalt hide them in the secret of thy presence
Psalm 61:4	I will trust in the covert [hiding place] of thy wings
Psalm 91:1	He that dwelleth in the secret place of the most High shall abide under the shadow of the Almighty
	(See also Psalm 27:5; 32:7; 119:114.)

B. Rest in "the shadow of His wings":

Deuteronomy 32:11–12	As an eagle stirreth up her nest, fluttereth over her young ... so the Lord [watches over His people]
Psalm 57:1	My soul trusteth in thee … in the shadow of thy wings
Psalm 91:4	He shall cover thee with his feathers, and under his wings shalt thou trust
Matthew 23:37	[Jesus longs to gather us to Him] even as a hen gathereth her chickens under her wings (See also Luke 13:34.)
	(See also Psalm 36:7; 63:7; Ruth 2:12.)

7. THE BENEFITS OF TAKING QUIET TIME WITH GOD:

A. God heals and restores our souls:

Psalm 23:2–3	He leadeth me beside the still waters. He restoreth my soul
Malachi 4:2	Unto you that fear my name shall the Sun of righteousness [Jesus] arise with healing in his wings
2 Corinthians 4:16	We faint not; but though our outward man perish, yet the inward man is renewed day by day (See also Ephesians 4:23.)

B. He gives us joy:

Psalm 5:11	Let all those that put their trust in thee rejoice … let them also that love thy name be joyful in thee
Psalm 16:11	In thy presence is fulness of joy
Psalm 40:16	Let all those that seek thee rejoice and be glad in thee
Psalm 51:12	Restore unto me the joy of thy salvation
	(See also Nehemiah 8:10; 1 Peter 1:8.)

C. He gives us spiritual strength:

Judges 5:31	Let them that love him be as the sun when he goeth forth in his might
Isaiah 30:7	Their strength is to sit still
Isaiah 30:15	In quietness and in confidence shall be your strength
Isaiah 40:29–31	They that wait upon the Lord shall renew their strength; they shall mount up with wings as eagles ... and not be weary
Isaiah 41:1	Keep silence before me ... renew their strength
Daniel 11:32	The people that do know their God shall be strong
Ephesians 3:16	That he would grant you ... to be strengthened with might by his Spirit in the inner man (See also Psalm 138:3.)
Colossians 1:9,11	Strengthened with all might, according to his ... powerD. He gives us rest in the Spirit:

D. He gives us rest in the Spirit:

Exodus 33:14	My presence shall go with thee, and I will give thee rest
1 Kings 8:56	The Lord ... hath given rest unto his people
Matthew 11:28–30	Come unto me ... I will give you rest ... unto your souls

E. When we take time to love Him, He loves us:

Proverbs 8:17	I love them that love me
John 14:21,23	He that loveth me [Jesus] shall be loved of my Father
John 16:27	The Father ... loveth you, because ye have loved me

F. Other benefits of loving God:

Deuteronomy 30:16	Love the Lord ... walk in his ways ... that thou mayest live ... and the Lord shall bless thee
Psalm 91:14	Because he hath set his love upon me, therefore will I deliver him: I will set him on high, because he hath known my name
Psalm 119:132	Be merciful ... unto those that love thy name
Psalm 145:20	The Lord preserveth all them that love him
Proverbs 8:21	I may cause those that love me to inherit substance
1 Corinthians 8:3	If any man love God, the same is known of him.
Ephesians 6:24	Grace be with all them that love our Lord Jesus Christ in sincerity
James 1:12	The crown of life, which the Lord hath promised to them that love him (See also 2 Timothy 4:8.)

(See also Deuteronomy 11:13–15,22–23; Psalm 36:10.)

8. HINDRANCES TO OUR RELATIONSHIP WITH GOD:

A. Being "too busy" to take time with Him:

Isaiah 26:12	This is the refreshing wherewith ye may cause the weary to rest: yet they would not hear

Matthew 23:37	How often would I have gathered [thee] as a hen gathereth her chickens under her wings, and ye would not
Luke 10:39–40	Mary sat at Jesus feet, and heard his word. But Martha was encumbered about with much serving
John 5:40	Ye will not come to me, that ye might have life

B. Becoming caught up with the world and its cares:

Matthew 13:22	The care of this world, and the deceitfulness of riches, choke the word (See also Luke 8:14.)
2 Timothy 2:4	[To please God, don't become entangled with the affairs of this life]
1 John 2:15	If any man love the world, the love of the Father is not in him

C. Cooling off and losing our "first love":

Jeremiah 2:2–5	The kindness of thy youth, the love … when thou wentest after me … [now] gone far from me … become vain?
Matthew 24:12	The love of many shall wax [grow] cold
Revelation 2:4–5	I have somewhat against thee, because thou hast left thy first love

D. Doubting God's love:

Malachi 1:2	I have loved you, saith the Lord. Yet ye say, Wherein hast thou loved us?

E. Harbouring unrepented sin in our hearts:

Psalm 66:18	If I regard iniquity in my heart, the Lord will not hear me
Isaiah 59:2	Your iniquities have separated between you and your God

F. Being too full of our own thoughts:

Isaiah 65:2	I have spread out my hands all the day unto a rebellious people, which walketh … after their own thoughts (See also Psalm 10:4; 119:113; Isaiah 55:7.)

9. OUR SPECIAL RELATIONSHIP WITH GOD:

A. Obedient believers are a blessed and chosen people:

Exodus 19:5	If ye will obey my voice … ye shall be a peculiar treasure unto me above all people
Deuteronomy 7:6	God hath chosen thee to be a special people unto himself, above all people … upon the face of the earth
Deuteronomy 14:2	Thou art an holy people … a peculiar [special] people
Isaiah 43:4	Thou wast precious in my sight … and I have loved thee
Matthew 22:14	Many are called, but few are chosen

John 15:16	I have chosen you, and ordained you
1 Peter 2:9	Ye are a chosen generation, a royal priesthood, an holy nation, a peculiar [special] people (See also Ephesians 1:4; Revelation 17:14.)

B. Jesus bought us; we belong to Him:

1 Corinthians 3:23	Ye are Christ's
1 Corinthians 6:20	Ye are bought with a price … your body and your spirit … are God's (See also 1 Corinthians 7:23.)
Revelation 5:9	Thou wast slain, and hast redeemed us … by thy blood
1 Peter 1:18–19	Ye were … redeemed … with the precious blood of Christ (See also Matthew 20:28; Luke 10:45; Galatians 3:13; 1 Timothy 2:5–6.)

C. Instead of making us slaves, He adopted us as children and heirs:

Matthew 12:50	Whosoever shall do the will of my Father … the same is my brother, and sister, and mother
Romans 8:14–17	Ye have received the Spirit of adoption, whereby we cry, Abba, Father ... If children, then … heirs of God, and joint-heirs with Christ
Galatians 4:5–7	To redeem [us] … that we might receive the adoption of sons. And because ye are sons, God hath sent forth the Spirit of his Son into your hearts, crying, Abba, Father ... Thou art no more a servant, but a son and … an heir (See also Ephesians 1:5–7.)

D. We are spiritually married to God:

Isaiah 54:5	Thy Maker is thine husband; the Lord of hosts
Isaiah 62:5	As the bridegroom rejoiceth over the bride, so shall thy God rejoice over thee
Jeremiah 3:14	Turn … for I am married unto you
Hosea 2:19–20	I will betroth thee unto me for ever
Romans 7:4	Ye should be married to another, even to [Jesus]
2 Corinthians 11:2	I have espoused you to one husband, that I may present you as a chaste virgin to Christ
Revelation 19:7–9	The marriage of the Lamb [Jesus] is come, and his wife, [the church] hath made herself ready (See also Ezekiel 16:8; Ephesians 5:28–32.)

E. We live and abide in Him, and He lives in us:

John 14:23	We will come unto him, and make our abode with him.
John 15:1–5	[We are to abide in Jesus as a branch joined to a vine]
John 17:26	That the love … may be in them, and I in them
2 Corinthians 5:17	If any man be in Christ, he is a new creature

2 Corinthians 6:16	I will dwell in them, and walk in them; and … be their God
1 John 4:13	Hereby know we that we dwell in him, and he in us
1 John 4:16	He that dwelleth in love dwelleth in God, and God in him
	(See also Acts 17:28.)

F. We are Jesus' body:

Ephesians 1:22–23	[Jesus is] the head over all things to the church, which is his body
Ephesians 5:30	We are members of his body, of his flesh, and of his bones.
Colossians 1:18	He is the head of the body, the church
	(See also 1 Corinthians 12:12–27.)

G. We are God's temple:

1 Corinthians 6:19	Your body is the temple of the Holy Ghost which is in you
2 Corinthians 6:16	Ye are the temple of the living God
Ephesians 2:19–22	An holy temple … ye also are builded together for an habitation of God
Hebrews 3:6	Christ as a son over his own house; whose house are we

H. Jesus is our shepherd, we are His sheep:

Psalm 23:1–4	The Lord is my shepherd … he leadeth me
Psalm 95:7	He is our God; and we are … the sheep of his hand
Psalm 100:3	We are his people, and the sheep of his pasture
John 10:1–29	I am the good shepherd (See also Hebrews 13:20.)
	(See also Psalm 78:52; 79:13; Isaiah 40:11; Matthew 25:32–33; John 21:15–17.)

I. He loved and rescued us when we were lost and gone astray:

1 Peter 2:25	Ye were as sheep going astray; but are now returned unto the Shepherd … of your souls
	(See also Isaiah 53:6; Ezekiel 34:1–12; Matthew 9:36; Luke 15:3–7; John 10:11.)

FELLOWSHIP

"The assembling of ourselves together." (Hebrews 10:25)

1. THE BIBLE INSTRUCTS US TO FELLOWSHIP:

A. The importance of fellowship:

Psalm 133:1–3	How good … for brethren to dwell together in unity
Matthew 18:19–20	Where two or three are gathered … there am I in the midst of them
Hebrews 10:25	Not forsaking the assembling of ourselves together …
1 John 1:7	If we walk in the light … have fellowship one with another (See also Psalm 119:63; 1 John 1:3.)

B. We are one body in Jesus:

Romans 12:5	So we, being many, are one body in Christ, and every one members one of another. (See also 1 Corinthians 12:12–28.)

C. There is strength in united fellowship:

Ecclesiastes 4:9–10	Two are better than one … if they fall, the one will lift up
Ecclesiastes 4:12	A threefold cord is not quickly broken.
Acts 28:15	The brethren … came to meet us as far as Appii forum … whom when Paul saw, he thanked God, and took courage

D. It's hard to be without fellowship:

Ecclesiastes 4:10	Woe to him that is alone when he falleth; for he hath not another to help
2 Timothy 4:16	At my first answer no man stood with me

2. THE REASONS FOR FELLOWSHIP:

A. Edification and inspiration:

Acts 2:42	They continued stedfastly in … doctrine and fellowship
1 Corinthians 14:3–4	[Prophesying and doctrine edify the church]
1 Corinthians 14:26	When ye come together … let all things be … edifying

B. Reading the Word together:

Acts 15:30–31	Gathered the multitude together, they delivered the epistle
1 Timothy 4:13	Give attendance to reading, to exhortation, to doctrine.
Hebrews 8:1–4,8	The people gathered themselves together … Ezra read (See also Acts 16:4; Colossians 4:16; 1 Thessalonians 5:27.)

C. Exhortation and instruction:

Acts 15:32	Exhorted the brethren with many words, and confirmed them
Acts 20:7	When the disciples came together … Paul preached

Hebrews 10:25	Assembling of ourselves together … exhorting one another
	(See also Acts 11:22–23; 15:36,41.)

D. Gathering for special prayer:

1 Timothy 4:14	The gift … which was given thee … with the laying on of the hands of the presbytery.
James 5:14	Call for the elders of the church; and … pray over him

E. United prayer:

Acts 1:13–15	[120 disciples gathered to pray in the upper room]
Acts 12:5,12	House … where many were gathered together praying

F. Having communion:

Acts 20:7	The disciples came together to break bread

G. Meeting to discuss important matters:

Acts 15:2,4	[Went] unto the apostles and elders about this question.
Acts 20:17–18	He called the elders of the church. And when they were come
Acts 21:17–19	All the elders were present … [Paul] declared

H. Making a point to seek fellowship:

(See also Acts 21:3–4; 27:2–3; 28:13–14.)

3. HOLDING MEETINGS:

A. Everyone can contribute something:

1 Corinthians 14:26	When ye come together … one of you hath a psalm, a doctrine, a tongue, a revelation, an interpretation

B. Be united and orderly during fellowship meetings:

Acts 4:32	The multitude of them that believed were of one heart and of one soul
1 Corinthians 14:33,40	In all churches of the saints. Let all things be done decently and in order.
	(See also 1 Corinthians 11:17–34; 14:23–31; James 2:2–4.)

C. United singing during fellowship:

Ezra 3:11	They sang together … praising and giving thanks
Matthew 26:30	And when they had sung an hymn, they went out
Hebrews 2:12	In the midst of the church will I sing praise

D. End meetings with prayer:

Acts 20:36	When he had thus spoken, he … prayed with them all.
Acts 21:5–6	We departed … and we kneeled down … and prayed

E. Fellowshipping together constantly:

Acts 2:46	Continuing daily with one accord … from house to house

4. BEING "OF ONE MIND" AND WORKING TOGETHER IN UNITY:

1 Corinthians 1:10	No divisions among you … be perfectly joined together
1 Corinthians 12:25	Should be no schism in the body … have the same care
Philippians 2:2	Be likeminded … being of one accord, of one mind. (See also Galatians 2:9; 1 Peter 3:8.)

5. USING FELLOWSHIP TO WITNESS:

Matthew 9:9–13	Why eateth your Master with publicans and sinners? … I am not come to call the righteous, but sinners to repentance.
1 Corinthians 10:27,31	If any … that believe not bid you to a feast, and ye be disposed to go … do all to the glory of God

WITNESSING

1. IT IS THE DUTY OF CHRISTIANS TO WITNESS:

A. Jesus gave "the Great Commission" to all His disciples:

Matthew 4:19	Follow me, and I will make you fishers of men
Matthew 28:19–20	Go ye therefore, and teach all nations
Mark 13:10	The gospel ... must be published among all nations
Mark 16:15	Go ye into all the world, and preach the gospel
Luke 24:47	Repentance and remission of sins should be preached in his name among all nations
John 15:16	Ordained you, that ye should go and bring forth fruit (See also Matthew 24:14.)
Acts 1:8	Ye shall be witnesses ... unto the uttermost part of the earth

B. Jesus sends us as His labourers and witnesses:

Isaiah 6:8	Whom shall I send? ... Here am I; send me
Matthew 9:37–38	Labourers are few; Pray ... the Lord ... that he will send forth labourers into his harvest
Luke 9:2	[Jesus] sent them to preach ... the kingdom of God
John 20:21	As my Father hath sent me, even so send I you
Romans 10:14–15	How shall they hear without a preacher? And how shall they preach, except they be sent?
2 Corinthians 5:20	We are ambassadors for Christ

2. WHY WE NEED TO WITNESS:

A. To share what we believe in:

Psalm 107:2	Let the redeemed [saved] of the Lord say so
John 3:11	We speak that we do know, and testify that we have seen
Acts 4:20	We ... speak the things which we have seen and heard
2 Corinthians 4:13	I believed, and therefore have I spoken (See also Psalm 116:10.)

B. To save souls from death:

Proverbs 14:25	A true witness delivereth souls
Acts 26:18	To open their eyes, and to turn them ... from the power of Satan unto God
James 5:20	He which converteth the sinner ... save a soul from death

C. If we don't, we and they will suffer:

Ezekiel 3:17–19	Nor speakest to warn the wicked ... his blood will I require at thine hand (See also Acts 20:26–27.)
Mark 8:38	Of him shall the Son of Man be ashamed when he cometh
Luke 12:8–9	He that denieth me before men shall be denied

1 Corinthians 9:16	Woe is unto me, if I preach not the gospel
2 Corinthians 4:3	But if our gospel be hid, it is hid to them that are lost (See also Jeremiah 8:20; Jonah 1:1–17.)

3. DON'T BE SHY OR ASHAMED TO WITNESS:

Psalm 119:46	I will speak of thy testimonies ... and will not be ashamed
Isaiah 40:9	Lift up thy voice with strength ... be not afraid
Isaiah 62:6	Ye that make mention of the Lord, keep not silence
Matthew 5:14–16	Ye are the light of the world ... cannot be hid ... Let your light so shine before men (See also Mark 4:21; Luke 8:16.)
Mark 8:38	Whosoever shall be ashamed of me and my words ... of him shall the Son of Man be ashamed
Acts 18:9	Be not afraid, but speak, and hold not thy peace
Romans 1:16	I am not ashamed of the gospel of Christ
Ephesians 6:18–20	[Pray] I may speak boldly, as I ought to speak
1 Thessalonians 2:2	We were bold ... to speak unto you the gospel of God
2 Timothy 1:8	Be not thou therefore ashamed of the testimony of our Lord (See also Jeremiah 1:6–9.)

4. POINTERS ON HOW TO BE A GOOD WITNESS:

- Ask questions: He that answereth a matter before he heareth it, it is folly (Proverbs 18:13)
- Listen: Let every man be swift to hear, slow to speak (James 1:19)
- Get them to speak their heart: Draw it out (Proverbs 20:5)
- Ask what they believe: Believest thou the prophets? (Acts 26:27)
- Find points of agreement: Your own poets have said (Acts 17:23–28)
- Be adaptable: I am made all things to all men, that I might by all means save some (1 Corinthians 9:19–22)
- Give your personal testimony (Acts 26:1–20)
- Illustrate your point: [Jesus] taught them many things by parables (Mark 4:2)
- Use current events: Pilate; tower of Siloam falling (Luke 13:1–5)
- Patiently explain: And with many other words did he exhort (Acts 2:40)
- Have a broken heart: He was moved with compassion on [the lost sheep] (Matthew 9:36)
- Speak in love, or it's just empty words, like sounding brass or a tinkling cymbal (1 Corinthians 13:1)
- Music has spiritual power: Example of David playing the harp for King Saul (1 Samuel 16:23)
- Be zealous and determined: Compel them to come in (Luke 14:23)
- Bring them to a decision: How long halt ye between two opinions? (1 Kings 18:21) (See also Joshua 24:15; Hebrew 3:7–8; 2 Corinthians 6:2.)

5. USE THE WORD IN YOUR WITNESSING:

A. The Word is powerful and convinces people:

2 Chronicles 17:9	[They] had the book of the law of the Lord with them, and went about … and taught the people
Luke 8:5,11	Sower sowed seed … the seed is the word of God
John 4:41–42	Many more believed because of his own word … Now we believe, not because of [the woman's] saying
John 5:39	Search the scriptures … they testify of me [Jesus]
John 20:31	These are written, that ye might believe that Jesus is the Christ.
Acts 17:2–3	Paul … reasoned with them out of the scriptures
Acts 18:28	He mightily convinced … showing by the scriptures
Titus 1:9	[The] word … sound doctrine … convince the gainsayers

B. Familiarity with Scripture is important to witnessing:

Psalm 119:42	Wherewith to answer him … for I trust in thy word.
Proverbs 22:17–21	Answer the words of truth to them that send unto thee
Malachi 2:6	The law of truth was in his mouth … and did turn many away from iniquity.
Matthew 12:34–35	A good man out of the good treasure of the heart bringeth forth good things
Acts 13:32–35	[Quote the Word] As it is also written in the second psalm
2 Timothy 4:2	Preach the word … exhort with all … doctrine
1 Peter 3:15	Be ready always to give an answer to every man

6. KEEPING YOUR WITNESS SIMPLE:

John 12:32	If I [Jesus] be lifted up … will draw all men unto me
1 Corinthians 1:17	Preach the gospel: not with wisdom of words
1 Corinthians 2:1–2	[I] came not with excellency of speech or of wisdom
1 Corinthians 2:4	My preaching was not with enticing words of man's wisdom
1 Corinthians 14:9	Except ye utter … words easy to be understood, how shall it be known what is spoken?
2 Corinthians 1:12	In simplicity and godly sincerity, not with fleshly wisdom
2 Corinthians 3:12	We use great plainness of speech

7. WHAT YOU SHOULD PREACH (WITNESS ABOUT):

A. Preach the gospel; preach Jesus:

Matthew 28:19–20	Teaching ... all things whatsoever I have commanded you
Mark 16:15	Preach the gospel [good news of salvation in Jesus]
Luke 9:2	[Jesus] sent them to preach the kingdom of God
John 3:16	[That they may have eternal life by believing in Jesus]
Acts 4:2	They taught ... the resurrection from the dead
Acts 5:42	They ceased not to teach and preach Jesus Christ
Acts 13:32–35	[Jesus fulfilled old Messianic prophecies]
Acts 13:38	Through [Jesus] is preached ... forgiveness of sins
Acts 20:21	Testifying ... repentance toward God, and faith toward Jesus
Romans 5:8	God commendeth his love toward us ... while we were yet sinners, Christ died for us
1 Corinthians 1:23	We preach Christ crucified
1 Corinthians 15:3–4	I delivered unto you ... that Christ died for our sins ... He was buried, and ... rose again [from the dead]
2 Corinthians 4:5	We preach not ourselves, but Christ Jesus the Lord
2 Corinthians 5:20	We pray you ... be ye reconciled to God
1 Timothy 1:15	Christ Jesus came into the world to save sinners
1 John 4:14	[We] testify that the Father sent the Son to be the saviour

(See also Acts 10:42; 24:25; Ephesians 3:8.)

B. What not to talk about:

1 Corinthians 3:2	Not with meat [strong doctrine] ... ye were not able to bear it
1 Thessalonians 2:3–6	Our exhortation was not of deceit ... nor in guile ... neither at any time used we flattering words
2 Timothy 2:23	Foolish and unlearned questions avoid
Titus 3:9	Avoid foolish questions ... and contentions, and strivings
Hebrews 5:14	Strong meat [doctrine] belongeth to [the mature]

8. WHOM TO WITNESS TO:

A. Jesus commanded us to witness to the whole world:

Isaiah 61:1	Preach good tidings unto the meek
Ezekiel 2:7	[Give everyone a chance, even the rebellious]
Ezekiel 3:17–18	Warn the wicked from his wicked way
Matthew 11:5	The poor have the gospel preached to them
Matthew 28:19	Go ye therefore, and teach all nations
Mark 5:19	Go home to thy friends and tell them
Mark 16:15	Preach the gospel to every creature [person]
Luke 8:39	Return to thine own house, and shew how great things

Acts 17:18–21	[To curious philosophers and intellectuals]
Acts 22:21	Unto the Gentiles [people of many nations]
Acts 26:22	Witnessing both to small and great
Acts 28:28	Salvation of God is sent unto the Gentiles
Romans 15:20–21	I strived to preach … [to] they that have not heard

B. Whom not to witness to:

Proverbs 14:7	Go from the presence of a foolish man
Proverbs 23:9	Speak not in the ears of a fool: for he will despise
Matthew 7:6	Give not that which is holy unto the dogs, neither cast ye your pearls before swine
Matthew 9:13	I am not come to call the righteous, but sinners
Matthew 10:14	Whosoever shall not … hear your words … depart
Acts 13:45–46	[Don't continue witnessing to unreceptive rejecters]
Acts 18:6	When they opposed themselves, and blasphemed … [he] said … I will go
Titus 3:10–11	Heretic after the first and second admonition reject

9. A WINNING PERSONAL EXAMPLE:

A. Our personal example is part of our witness:

Matthew 5:16	Let your light so shine … they may see your good works
John 13:35	By this shall all men know that ye are my disciples, if ye have love one to another
2 Corinthians 3:2	Ye are our epistle [letter] … known and read of all men
Philippians 2:15–16	Be blameless and harmless … shine as lights in the world; Holding forth the word of life
1 Timothy 4:12	Be thou an example of the believers
Titus 2:7–8	In all things showing thyself a pattern of good works
1 Peter 3:1–2	[Unbelieving spouses to be won by believer's example]

(See also 1 Timothy 5:14.)

B. The believer's sample of happiness is appealing:

Psalm 51:12–13	Restore unto me the joy of thy salvation … and sinners shall be converted unto thee

C. Win souls with love, not by arguing:

1 Thessalonians 1:7–8	We were gentle … affectionately desirous of you
2 Timothy 2:23–24	The servant of the Lord must not strive; but be gentle

(See also 1 Corinthians 13:1–2,8.)

D. Our personal example must back up our witness:

John 13:15	I [Jesus] have given you an example, that ye should do as I

Romans 2:21–24	Thou therefore which teachest another, teachest thou not thyself? thou that preachest a man should not … dost thou?

(See also 1 Corinthians 11:1; 1 Timothy 6:1; Titus 2:4–5.)

10. WHEN TO WITNESS:

A. We are to constantly witness:

Ecclesiastes 11:6	In the morning sow thy seed, and in the evening
John 4:35	Look on the fields; for they are white already to harvest
Acts 5:42	Daily in the temple, and in every house, they ceased not
2 Timothy 4:2	In season, out of season [even when not convenient]
1 Peter 3:15	Be ready always to give an answer to every man

(See also Acts 20:31.)

B. Pray for God to "open up" witnessing opportunities:

Colossians 4:3	Praying … that God would open unto us a door of utterance, to speak the mystery of Christ

C. Wait until it's God's time to witness to certain people:

Matthew 10:5–7	Go not into the way of the Gentiles [but later, He said to go into all the world (Mark 16:15)]
Acts 16:6–7	[Paul] forbidden … to preach … in Asia [but did with great success a few years later (Acts 19:1,10)]

11. WHERE TO WITNESS:

- In your own house (Acts 28:30–31)
- In every house (Acts 5:42)
- From house to house (Acts 20:20)
- In schools and lecture halls (Acts 19:9–10)
- In church (Hebrews 2:12)
- In marketplaces (Acts 17:17)
- In neighbourhoods of different ethnic groups (John 4:1–42)
- In the streets, lanes, highways, hedges (Luke 14:21,23)
- All over the city (Luke 8:39)
- In cars [chariots] (Acts 8:29–35)
- On boats (Acts 27:22–25)
- In prison (Philippians 1:12–13)
- In court (Matthew 10:18–20)
- In the wilderness (Matthew 3:1–2)
- Everywhere (Acts 8:4)

12. THE "FRUIT" CHRISTIANS SHOULD BEAR IS OTHER CHRISTIANS, NEW SAVED SOULS:

Proverbs 11:30	He that winneth souls is wise
Mark 4:14	The sower [witness] soweth the word

Luke 8:5–15	[The parable of the sower] (See also Matthew 13:3–8,18–23; Mark 4:2–8,14–20.)
Luke 8:11	The seed is the word of God [which we sow in hearts]
John 12:24	But if it die [to self] it bringeth forth much fruit
John 15:5	He that abideth in me … bringeth forth much fruit
John 15:8	Herein is [God] glorified, that ye bear much fruit
Romans 7:4	Married to [Jesus] … bring forth fruit unto God

13. THE HOLY SPIRIT AND WITNESSING:

A. The Holy Spirit anoints us to witness about Jesus:

Isaiah 61:1	Spirit of the Lord GOD is upon me … anointed me to preach
Acts 1:8	Ye shall receive power, after that the Holy Ghost is come upon you: and ye shall be witnesses unto me
Acts 4:29–31	They were all filled with the Holy Ghost, and they spake the word of God with boldness
1 Thessalonians 1:5	Our gospel came … in power, and in the Holy Ghost (See also Colossians 1:27–29.)

B. Only God and His Holy Spirit can really win people:

Zechariah 4:6	Not by might, nor by power, but by my spirit
Matthew 10:20	It is not ye that speak, but the Spirit … which speaketh in you
John 6:44	No man can come to me, except the Father … draw him
John 15:5	Without me ye can do nothing
1 Corinthians 3:6–7	I have planted … but God gave the increase

14. WITNESSING, THE GREATEST WORK ON EARTH:

A. Witnessing is a job worth giving all for:

Matthew 4:19–22	Follow me, and I will make you fishers of men. And they … left their nets (See also Luke 5:9–11.)
Mark 8:35	Lose his life for my sake and the gospel's
Mark 10:29	[Leave house, family, wife, lands for gospel's sake]

B. Heavenly reward for witnessing:

Proverbs 11:30	He that winneth souls is wise.
Daniel 12:3	They that be wise shall shine … and they that turn many to righteousness as the stars
Luke 12:8	Him shall the Son of Man confess before the angels
1 Corinthians 3:8	Every man shall receive … reward according to his own labour
1 Corinthians 9:16–17	If I preach [the gospel] willingly, I have a reward

15. REACTIONS TO THE GOSPEL:

A. The receptive believe the Word:

Jonah 3:1–9	[Jonah preached in Nineveh, and entire city repented]
John 4:39–42	[Samaritans at Sychar received Jesus and believed]
Acts 8:5–6,8,14	[Samaritans] with one accord gave heed … Samaria received the word of God
Acts 16:14	Lydia … whose heart the Lord opened … she [listened]
Acts 16:32–34	They spake unto him the word … [he] rejoiced, believing

B. The unreceptive reject the Word:

Luke 8:5,12	Devil taketh away the word, lest they believe
1 Corinthians 1:18	Preaching … is to them that perish foolishness
2 Corinthians 4:4	The god of this world hath blinded the minds of [unbelieving]

(See also Jeremiah 36.)

C. Unpopularity and persecution because of witnessing:

Luke 6:22	Men shall cast out your name as evil for [Jesus'] sake
John 7:7	The world … hateth [me] because I testify [it is] evil
Acts 16:20–21	These men, being Jews, do exceedingly trouble our city, And teach customs, which are not lawful

D. Our witness a testimony against the unrepentant:

Matthew 10:18	Brought before … kings … for a testimony against them
Mark 6:11	Shake off dust … for a testimony against them
John 12:48	The word that I have spoken … shall judge him

16. WITNESSING BOLDLY DESPITE OPPOSITION:

A. Neither threats, persecution, nor martyrdom should stop us:

Luke 21:12–15	They shall … persecute you … I will give you … wisdom
Acts 4:29,31,33	Behold their threatenings … spake the word with boldness
Acts 14:1–3	Long time therefore abode they speaking boldly in the Lord
Acts 20:24	None of these things move me, neither count I my life dear
1 Thessalonians 2:2	Even after that we had suffered … we were bold in our God to speak
Revelation 6:9	Them that were slain for the word of God, and for the testimony
Revelation 12:11	And they overcame him by … the word … loved not their lives
Revelation 20:4	Them that were beheaded for the witness of Jesus

B. We should find ways of sharing our faith even when it is forbidden:

Amos 7:12–15	[Evil priest said:] Prophesy not again any more at Bethel … the Lord said unto [Amos], Go, prophesy
Matthew 10:16	Be ye therefore wise as serpents, and harmless as doves
Luke 10:3	I send you forth as lambs among wolves: be wise
Acts 4:17–20	We cannot but speak the things which we have seen and heard
Acts 5:27–29	We ought to obey God rather than men
Acts 5:40–42	Commanded that they should not speak … [but] they ceased not

17. MORE VERSES ABOUT WITNESSING AND TESTIFYING:

A. From the Old Testament:

- I will publish the name of the Lord (Deuteronomy 32:3)
- Make known his deeds among the people (1 Chronicles 16:8)
- Declare among the people his doings (Psalm 9:11)
- I give thanks unto thee among the heathen (Psalm 18:49)
- Publish … tell of all thy wondrous works (Psalm 26:7)
- I will declare what he hath done for my soul (Psalm 66:16)
- My mouth shall show forth … thy salvation all the day (Psalm 71:15)
- With my mouth will I make know thy faithfulness to all (Psalm 89:1)
- Declare his … wonders among all people (Psalm 96:3)
- Say among the heathen that the Lord reigneth (Psalm 96:10)
- So shall I talk of thy wondrous works (Psalm 119:27)
- I will speak of glorious honour of thy majesty (Psalm 145:4–7)
- Make known to the sons of men his mighty acts (Psalm 145:11–12)
- Ye are my witnesses, saith the Lord (Isaiah 43:10)
- How beautiful upon the mountains are the feet of him that bringeth good tidings, that publisheth peace (Isaiah 52:7)

B. From the New Testament:

- They went forth, and preached everywhere (Mark 16:20)
- Preaching and showing glad tiding of the kingdom of God (Luke 8:1)
- Many believed on him for the saying of the woman (John 4:39)
- Lovest thou me? Feed my sheep (John 21:17)
- Go, speak to the people … all the words of this life (Acts 5:20)
- And we are his witnesses of these things (Acts 5:32)
- He commanded us to preach unto the people, and to testify (Acts 10:42)
- Word of the Lord published throughout all the region (Acts 13:49)
- Being fervent in spirit, he spake and taught diligently (Acts 18:25)
- Thou shalt be his witness unto all men (Acts 22:15)
- How beautiful are the feet of them that preach the gospel (Romans 10:15)

- The things which thou hast heard … commit to faithful men, who shall … teach others (2 Timothy 2:2)
- Preach the Word, be instant in season, out of season (2 Timothy 4:2)

GIVING

1. THE BIBLE COMMANDS BELIEVERS TO GIVE:

Deuteronomy 15:7–8	Thou shalt not harden thine heart, nor shut thine hand ... thou shalt open thine hand wide
Proverbs 3:27–28	Withhold not good from them to whom it is due ... Say not … to morrow I will give; when thou hast it by thee
Matthew 5:42	Give to him that asketh thee, and … would borrow
Luke 3:11	He that hath two coats … impart to him that hath none
Romans 12:13	Distributing to the necessity of saints; given to hospitality

2. GOD BLESSES US WHEN WE GIVE:

Matthew 6:4	Thy Father which seeth in secret himself shall reward thee openly

A. Spiritual blessings:

Proverbs 11:25	The liberal soul … shall be watered also himself
Proverbs 13:7	[He] maketh himself poor [gives], yet hath great riches
Proverbs 14:21	He that hath mercy on the poor, happy is he.
Mark 10:21	Give to the poor and thou shalt have treasure in heaven
Acts 20:35	It is more blessed to give than to receive

B. Material blessings:

Deuteronomy 15:10	For this thing the Lord thy God shall bless thee in all thy works
Proverbs 11:24	There is that scattereth, and yet increaseth
Isaiah 58:10–11	If thou draw out thy soul to the hungry… the Lord shall … satisfy thy soul in drought
Luke 6:38	Give and it shall be given you; good measure…With the same measure ye mete it shall be measured again

3. GIVING TO GOD'S WORK:

A. When we give, we are giving to Jesus:

Matthew 25:40	Inasmuch as ye have done it unto one of the least of these my brethren, ye have done it unto me.

B. When we give to God's work, we are investing:

Proverbs 19:17	He that hath pity upon the poor lendeth unto the Lord; … he [will] pay him again
Luke 10:30–37	Whatsoever thou spendest … when I come, I will repay
Philippians 4:17	Not because I desire a gift: but I desire fruit that may abound to your account

C. God will pay us back for sacrificial giving:

Proverbs 22:9	He … shall be blessed; for he giveth … to the poor
Proverbs 28:27	He that giveth unto the poor shall not lack

Ecclesiastes 11:1	Cast thy bread upon the waters: for thou shalt find it
2 Corinthians 9:6	He which soweth bountifully shall reap also bountifully

4. CHRISTIAN DUTY REGARDING GIVING AND SHARING:

2 Corinthians 8:4–5,7	As ye abound in every thing, in faith … in your love to us, see that ye abound in this grace [giving] also
Hebrews 13:16	To do good and to communicate [share with others] forget not

A. Believers are to support Christian workers and missionaries:

Romans 15:27	Their debtors they are … their duty is also to minister unto them in carnal things.
1 Corinthians 9:6–11	If we have sown unto you spiritual things … we shall reap your carnal things
Galatians 6:6	Let him that is taught … [share materially] unto him that teacheth
1 Timothy 5:17–18	They who labour in the word … the labourer is worthy of his reward [wages]

(See also 3 John 1:7–8.)

B. Believers are also expected to help needy fellow Christians:

Romans 15:26	Pleased them … to make a certain contribution for the poor saints
Galatians 6:10	Do good unto … them who are of the household of faith
Philippians 4:15–16	[Paul said] Concerning giving and receiving … ye sent once and again unto my necessity

(See also 1 Corinthians 16:1; 2 Corinthians 9:12.)

C. Everyone should give according to their ability:

Deuteronomy 16:17	Every man shall give as he is able, according to the blessing of the Lord … which he hath given thee
Acts 11:29	The disciples, every man according to his ability, determined to send relief unto the brethren
1 Corinthians 16:2	Let every one of you lay by him in store [set aside to give], as God hath prospered him
2 Corinthians 8:12	It is accepted according to that a man hath, and not according to that he hath not

D. Wealthy Christians are especially enjoined to give:

Luke 8:3	Joanna, wife of Chuza, Herod's steward, and many others ministered unto [Jesus] of their substance
2 Corinthians 8:14–15	Your abundance may be a supply for their want
1 Timothy 6:17–19	Charge them that are rich … that they … ready to distribute, willing to communicate [share]

(See also examples in 2 Timothy 1:16–18; Philemon 1:7.)

E. The church should redistribute gifts among the needy:

Acts 2:44–45	[They] parted them to all men, as every man had need
Acts 4:34–35	Distribution was made unto every man according as he had need
Acts 6:1	[The early church had a "daily ministration" to widows]
1 Timothy 5:4,16	[Church's duty to "relieve them that are widows"]

F. Even poor believers are encouraged to give:

1 Kings 17:9–16	[Poor widow of Zarephath gave sacrificially, and God blessed her with unending supply of food in famine]
Mark 12:43–44	Poor widow hath cast more in … For they did cast in of their abundance; but she of her want cast in all
2 Corinthians 8:1–4	In … their deep poverty … they were willing … praying us that we would receive the gift

5. GIVING WITH THE RIGHT MOTIVES:

A. Give cheerfully:

2 Corinthians 9:7	Not grudgingly … for God loveth a cheerful giver
Deuteronomy 15:10	Thou shalt surely give him, and thine heart shall not be grieved
Exodus 25:2	Bring me an offering: of every man that giveth it willingly with his heart ye shall take my offering
Exodus 35:21	Every one whose heart stirred him up, and … spirit made willing … brought the Lord's offering to the work
1 Chronicles 29:9	People rejoiced … because with perfect heart they offered willingly to the Lord
Hebrews 10:34	[Ye] took joyfully the spoiling of your goods

B. Give generously:

Proverbs 21:26	The righteous giveth and spareth not

C. Give till it hurts; not just what we can spare:

2 Samuel 24:24	Neither will I offer burnt offerings unto the Lord my God of that which doth cost me nothing
Luke 21:4	All these have of their abundance cast in … but she of her penury hath cast in all the living that she had

D. Give with pure motives:

1 Corinthians 13:3	Though I bestow all my goods to feed the poor … and have not charity, it profiteth me nothing
Matthew 5:24	Leave there thy gift before the altar … first be reconciled
Matthew 6:1–3	Do not your alms before men … otherwise ye have no reward of your Father ... The hypocrites [give alms] … that they may have glory of men … They have their reward ... When thou doest alms, let not thy left hand know what thy right hand doeth
Luke 6:34–35	Lend, hope for nothing again

6. WHAT HAPPENS WHEN WE WITHHOLD AND DON'T GIVE:

A. It puts extra strain on others:

Philippians 2:30	He was nigh unto death … to supply your lack of service

B. God may hold back on blessing us:

Proverbs 11:24	There is that withholdeth … but it tendeth to poverty
Proverbs 13:7	There is that maketh himself rich, yet hath nothing
Proverbs 28:27	He that hideth his eyes shall have many a curse

C. It shows we lack Christian love:

James 2:15–16	If a brother or sister be naked, and destitute of daily food, And … ye give them not … what doth it profit?
1 John 3:17–18	Whoso hath … and seeth his brother have need [and doesn't give] … how dwelleth the love of God in him?

D. The results of giving stingily or dishonestly:

Malachi 1:7–10	Ye offer polluted bread … I have no pleasure in you neither will I accept an offering at your hand
Malachi 1:13–14	Ye brought … torn, lame, and sick; should I accept this?
2 Corinthians 9:6	He which soweth sparingly shall reap also sparingly

(See also Malachi 1:8; Acts 5:1–2,9–10.)

E. Beware of covetousness and greed:

Proverbs 28:16	He that hateth covetousness shall prolong his days
Ecclesiastes 5:10	He that loveth silver shall not be satisfied with silver
Luke 12:15	Beware of covetousness: a man's life consisteth not in … things
1 Timothy 6:10	The love of money is the root of all evil
James 5:1–5	Your gold and silver is cankered; and the rust of them shall be a witness against you

(See also Ecclesiastes 5:13,15; Acts 5:1–10.)

7. TITHING:

A. Giving 10% of our income to God's work:

Leviticus 27:30	All the tithe of the land … is the Lord's: it is holy
Numbers 18:21	I have given the children of Levi all the tenth … for their service which they serve
Numbers 18:24	The tithes … which they offer … unto the Lord, I have given to the Levites [God's workers]
Deuteronomy 14:22	Thou shalt truly tithe all the increase [profit] (See also Deuteronomy 12:19; Nehemiah 10:37–39.)

B. God will bless us for tithing:

Deuteronomy 14:28–29	Thou shalt bring forth all the tithe … that the Lord may bless thee in all the work of thine hand
Proverbs 3:9–10	Honour the Lord with … all thine increase: So shall thy barns be filled with plenty
Malachai 3:10	Bring ye all the tithes … and prove me … if I will not open you the windows of heaven, and pour you out a blessing
Malachai 3:8–11	[God grants protection and freedom from curses]

C. Setting aside our tithe on a frequent basis:

1 Corinthians 16:2	Upon the first day of the week let every one of you lay by him in store, as God hath prospered him

D. Believers are encouraged to give extra (above their tithe) for special projects:

Exodus 35:5	Take … an offering unto the Lord: whosoever is of a willing heart, let him bring it (See also 35:21–22.)
2 Kings 12:4–5,9–12	[Freewill offerings encouraged for the work of God]

8. OTHER ASPECTS OF GIVING:

A. Gifts can help obtain a man's favour or forgiveness:

Proverbs 19:6	Every man is a friend to him that giveth gifts
Proverbs 21:14	A gift in secret pacifieth anger (See also Proverbs 17:23.)

B. When not to accept gifts:

Exodus 23:8	Take no gift [with "strings" attached] for the gift blindeth the wise, and perverteth the … righteous.
Numbers 22:18	If Balak would give me his house full of silver and gold, I cannot go beyond the word of the Lord
1 Kings 13:7–10	[Young prophet refused gifts from disobedient king]
2 Kings 5:15–16	[Elisha refused Naaman's money, but Gehazi coveted it—5:20–27] Is it a time to receive money? (On bribes, see also Deuteronomy 16:19; Proverbs 29:4; Ecclesiastes 7:7.)

HOW TO FIND THE WILL OF GOD

1. THE PREREQUISITE: SUBMIT YOUR WILL TO GOD:

A. Seek God's will, not your own:

Luke 22:42	Not my will, but thine, be done
John 5:30	I seek not mine own will, but the will of the Father
John 6:38	I came … not to do mine own will, but the will of [God]

B. Seek and trust God:

Psalm 37:5	Commit thy way unto the Lord; trust also in him
Psalm 143:10	[Pray] Teach me to do thy will … lead me
Proverbs 3:6	In all thy ways acknowledge him, and he shall direct
Colossians 1:9	Pray … that ye might be filled with the knowledge of his will

C. Sincerely desire to do God's will:

Psalm 40:8	I delight to do thy will, O my God
Matthew 6:10	Thy will be done in earth, as it is in heaven
John 4:34	My meat is to do the will of [God] that sent me
Ephesians 6:6	Doing the will of God from the heart

D. As you obey Him, He will reveal His will to you:

Hosea 6:3	Then shall we know, if we follow on to know the Lord
Mark 4:24–25	Unto you that hear shall more be given
John 7:17	If any man will do his will, he shall know
Romans 12:1–2	Present your bodies a living sacrifice, holy … that ye may prove what is that good … and perfect, will of God

2. THE HOLY SPIRIT GUIDES US TO FIND GOD'S WILL:

John 16:13–14	The Spirit … will guide you into all truth … and show you
1 Corinthians 2:11	The things of God knoweth no man, but the Spirit of God
James 1:5	If any of you lack wisdom, let him ask of God (See also Philippians 3:15.)
1 John 2:27	The same anointing teacheth you of all things

3. THE FIRST PLACE TO LOOK FOR GOD'S WILL IS IN HIS WORD:

A. The Bible is His written, revealed will:

Psalm 119:105	Thy word is a lamp unto my feet, and a light unto my path
Romans 2:18	Knowest his will … being instructed out of the law
2 Timothy 3:16	All scripture is given by … God … for instruction (See also Deuteronomy 29:29; Psalm 119:128; John 5:39; Acts 17:11; 1 Timothy 3:14–15.)

B. Warning against not obeying the Word:

Proverbs 28:9	He that turneth away his ear from hearing the law

Isaiah 8:20	If they speak not according to this word … no light

C. Beware of interpreting it as you please:

2 Peter 1:20	No … scripture is of any private interpretation
2 Peter 3:16	Unlearned … wrest … scriptures, unto their own destruction
Isaiah 28:10	For precept must be upon precept … line upon line, here a little, and there a little (See also Luke 10:25–26.)

D. Read and study the Word carefully:

Nehemiah 8:8	They read in … the law of God distinctly, and gave the sense, and caused them to understand
Matthew 9:13	Go ye and learn what that [scripture] meaneth
2 Timothy 2:15	Study … rightly dividing the word of truth

E. When a verse speaks specifically, directly to you:

Psalm 103:20	Ye … that do his commandments, hearkening unto the voice of his word
Psalm 119:130	The entrance of thy words … giveth understanding
Psalm 119:133	Order my steps in thy word
Proverbs 6:22–23	When thou goest, [the Word] shall lead thee … and when thou awakest, it shall talk with thee
Luke 24:32	Did not our heart burn within us … while [Jesus] opened to us the scriptures?
Acts 2:37	When they heard this, they were pricked in their heart

F. Pray and ask God to help you understand:

Psalm 119:18	Open thou mine eyes, that I may behold wondrous things out of thy law
Psalm 119:34–35	Give me understanding, and I shall keep thy law
Proverbs 2:3–11	If thou … liftest up thy voice for understanding … seekest … Then shalt thou … find knowledge
Luke 24:45	Then opened [Jesus] their understanding, that they might understand the scriptures

G. Ask mature Christians to explain difficult passages to you:

Acts 8:30–35	How can I [understand], except some man should guide me? ... I pray thee, of whom speaketh the prophet this? of himself, or of some other man?

4. GOD SOMETIMES REVEALS HIS WILL THROUGH DREAMS:

A. Revelatory dreams given to His people:

Numbers 12:6	I the Lord … will speak unto him in a dream.

Job 33:15–17	In a dream … [God] sealeth their instruction
Jeremiah 23:28	The prophet that hath a dream, let him tell
Joel 2:28	Your old men shall dream dreams (See also Acts 2:17.)

B. Old Testament examples:

- God gave Abraham a prophetic message in a dream (Genesis 15:12–16)
- God's warning dream to Abimelech, the Philistine king (Genesis 20:2–7)
- God promised Jacob that He was with him (Genesis 28:10–16)
- Jacob's dream warned him to depart (Genesis 31:10–13)
- Laban warned not to harm Jacob (Genesis 31:22–24)
- Joseph's two prophetic dreams (Genesis 37:5–9)
- Prophetic dreams of Pharaoh's baker and butler (Genesis 40:1–13,16–22)
- Pharaoh's dream of coming famine (Genesis 41:17–32)
- Israel instructed to go to Egypt (Genesis 46:1–4)
- Gideon encouraged to do God's will by hearing dream of barleycake (Judges 7:9–15)
- Solomon's dream (1 Kings 3:5–15)
- Eliphaz's dream (Job 4:12–21)
- Nebuchadnezzar's dream of coming world kingdoms (Daniel 2:1,28–29,31–45)
- The description of the dream and its interpretation was given to Daniel (Daniel 2:16–19)
- Daniel's dream of coming world kingdoms (Daniel 7:1–28)

C. New Testament examples:

- Joseph's four dreams of instruction and warning (Matthew 1:20–21; 2:13,19–20,22)
- Wise men warned in a dream (Matthew 2:12)
- Pilate's wife's warning dream concerning Jesus (Matthew 27:19)

D. Caution regarding determining God's will by dreams:

Ecclesiastes 5:3	A dream [can come] through the multitude of business
Ecclesiastes 5:7	In the multitude of dreams … there are also divers vanities
Jeremiah 23:25–27	I have dreamed … deceit of their own heart
Jeremiah 23:32	I am against them that prophesy false dreams
Jeremiah 29:8	Neither hearken to your dreams which ye cause to be dreamed

5. GOD SOMETIMES REVEALS HIS WILL THROUGH VISIONS:

A. A vision is when God flashes a picture in your mind's eye:

Numbers 12:6	I the Lord will make myself known unto him in a vision
Numbers 24:4	Falling into a trance, but having his eyes open
Ezekiel 1:1	The heavens were opened, and I saw visions of God

Hosea 12:10	I [God] have multiplied visions [to instruct people]
Joel 2:28	I will pour out my spirit … young men shall see visions
Acts 10:9–11	Peter … fell into a trance, And saw heaven opened

B. Some Old Testament examples:

- Abraham received prophecy in a vision (Genesis 15:1–5)
- Micaiah's vision of the defeat of Israel and of the council around God's throne (1 Kings 22:17–36)
- Ezekiel's visions (Ezekiel 1:1–4; 8:1–2; 10:1)
- Daniel's visions of future events (Daniel 8:1–2; 10:4–7)
- Zechariah's visions (Zechariah 1:7–8)

C. New Testament examples:

- Archangel Gabriel appeared and prophesied to Zacharias (Luke 1:11–13,22)
- Paul's vision of Jesus (Acts 9:1–7; 26:13–19)
- God instructed Ananias in a vision (Acts 9:10–11)
- Paul's vision of Ananias (Acts 9:12)
- An angel instructed Cornelius (Acts 10:1–6)
- God instructed Peter with vision of unclean animals (Acts 10:9–16)
- Paul's vision of a Macedonian man (Acts 16:9)
- God encouraged Paul in a vision (Acts 18:9–10)

D. Beware of false visions:

Jeremiah 14:14	They prophesy unto you a false vision … the deceit of their heart
Jeremiah 23:16	They speak a vision of their own heart, and not out of the mouth of the Lord.
Lamentations 2:14	Thy prophets have seen vain and foolish things

6. GOD SOMETIMES REVEALS HIS WILL THROUGH PROPHECY AND REVELATIONS:

A. Prophecy: God speaking through you, or to your heart:

1 Kings 19:12	[God spoke to Elijah in] a still small voice
Jeremiah 1:9	Behold, I have put my words in thy mouth
Ezekiel 3:10–11	All my words that I shall speak unto thee receive in thine heart, and hear with thine ears
Ezekiel 3:27	I will open thy mouth, and thou shalt say unto them
Luke 2:26	It was revealed unto [Simeon] by the Holy Ghost
Acts 2:17	In the last days … your sons and your daughters shall prophesy
Acts 10:19–20	While Peter thought … the Spirit said unto him
Acts 13:1–2	There were … certain prophets … the Holy Ghost said

1 Corinthians 12:28	And God hath set some [prophets] in the church (See also Acts 8:26; 1 Corinthians 14:31; Ephesians 3:3,5.)

B. Warnings about false prophecy:

Deuteronomy 13:1–3	[Don't heed prophets which try to turn you astray]
Deuteronomy 18:22	If the thing follow not, nor come to pass … the prophet hath spoken it presumptuously
Jeremiah 23:21	I have not spoken to them, yet they prophesied
Jeremiah 23:26	They are prophets of the deceit of their own heart
Ezekiel 13:6–7	Ye say, The Lord saith it; albeit I have not spoken
Galatians 1:8	Though we, or an angel … preach any other gospel … let him be accursed. (See also Matthew 24:4–5,11,23–26)

7. GOD SOMETIMES REVEALS HIS WILL THROUGH GODLY COUNSEL:

A. Counselling with others who know God and His Word well:

Exodus 18:25–26	Able men … judged the people
Deuteronomy 17:8–11	If there arise a matter too hard for thee in judgement … matters of controversy … come unto the … judge
Proverbs 11:14	In the multitude of counsellors there is safety
Proverbs 15:22	In the multitude of counsellors [purposes] are established
Proverbs 20:18	Every purpose is established by counsel
2 Corinthians 13:1	In the mouth of two or three witnesses shall every word be established (See also Acts 11:22–23; 15:22,32.)

B. Coming to a reasonable agreement:

Acts 15:25	It seemed good unto us, being assembled with one accord
Acts 15:28	For it seemed good to the Holy Ghost, and to us

C. Warnings about not seeking (or not heeding) godly counsel:

Proverbs 15:22	Without counsel purposes are disappointed
2 Chronicles 10:1–15	And Rehoboam … forsook the counsel which the [wiser] old men gave him, and took counsel with the young men
Acts 27:9–15,21,41	[The sailors rejected Paul's counsel, based their decisions on natural reasoning (27:12–13), and were shipwrecked]

D. Be willing to change plans if God leads otherwise:

2 Samuel 7:1–13	[Nathan agreed to David's plan to build a temple, but changed his mind after God showed him otherwise]

8. GOD SOMETIMES REVEALS HIS WILL BY OBVIOUS CIRCUMSTANCES:

A. God often sets up circumstances to show His will:

2 Samuel 5:22–25	[God gave David a specific sign as to when to rise and attack the Philistines]
Mark 14:12–16	Go into the city and there shall meet you a man bearing a pitcher … follow him (See also Luke 22:7–13.)

B. Sometimes circumstances indicate God's leading:

Luke 10:8–9	Into whatsoever city ye enter, and they receive you, eat (See also Matthew 10:11.)
1 Corinthians 16:9	A great door and effectual is opened unto me
2 Corinthians 2:12	When I came to Troas … a door was opened unto me of the Lord
Revelation 3:8	I have set before thee an open door … for thou … hast kept my word
Luke 10:8–9	Into whatsoever city ye enter, and they receive you, eat (See also Matthew 10:11.)

C. Examples of obvious circumstances:

Acts 8:30–35	[Ethiopian eunuch requested an explanation of Isaiah 53]
Acts 13:7	Sergius Paulus, [governor of Cyprus] called for Barnabas and Saul, and desired to hear the word of God
Acts 13:14–16	If ye have any word of exhortation for the people, say on
Acts 17:18–22	May we know what this new doctrine … is?
John 2:1–11	There was a marriage … Jesus was called, and his disciples [His miracle there caused many to believe]

D. Gauging circumstances and conditions, and acting accordingly:

1 Kings 17:1–9	[When the brook Cherith dried, Elijah knew it was time to move on, and God told him where to go]
Matthew 12:14–15	Pharisees … held a council … how they might destroy him
Luke 10:10	In whatsoever city they receive you not, go your ways (See also Matthew 10:14.)
John 7:1	He would not walk in Jewry, because the Jews sought to kill him
John 11:53–54	Jesus therefore walked no more openly among the Jews, but went
Acts 8:1,4	[God uses persecution and adverse circumstances to make you obey if you won't otherwise] (See also Acts 1:8.)
Acts 14:5–6	There was an assault … they were ware of it, and fled
Acts 20:3,6	[About to sail to Syria, Paul learned of an ambush and travelled another route instead]
Acts 27:9–10	When sailing was now dangerous … Paul admonished them
Acts 27:12–15	[Warning regarding wrongly judging conditions]

E. Circumstances are not always an indication of God's will:

Exodus 14:9–16	[The Red Sea seemed to be an impassable closed door]
2 Kings 7:1–2,18	If the Lord would make windows in heaven [to provide food], might this thing be? … And it came to pass
Ecclesiastes 11:4	He that regardeth the clouds shall not reap
Jeremiah 1:6–7	[Youthful Jeremiah knew the elders might not listen to him, but was commanded to prophesy anyway]
Matthew 14:15–21	This is a desert … and the time is now [late]; send the multitude away [But Jesus fed them miraculously]
Matthew 15:32–38	Whence should we have so much bread [to feed them]?

F. Have faith and don't "look at the waves" and conditions:

Matthew 14:30–31	When [Peter] saw the wind boisterous, he was afraid … Jesus … said unto him, Wherefore didst thou doubt?
Mark 2:2–5	When they could not come nigh to him for the [crowds] they [broke up] the roof … and let down the bed
Luke 5:5	Master we have toiled all night, and have taken nothing: nevertheless at thy word I will
Luke 8:49–50	Thy daughter is dead; trouble not the Master. [Jesus] answered … Fear not: believe only
John 11:39–40	By this time he stinketh … Jesus saith … If thou wouldest believe, thou shouldest see the glory of God
2 Corinthians 5:7	For we walk by faith, not by sight
Hebrews 11:23–27	By faith Moses [obeyed God] … not fearing the … king

9. GOD SOMETIMES REVEALS HIS WILL THROUGH THE "WITNESS OF THE SPIRIT":

A. Sometimes God leads by giving a strong desire:

Psalm 37:4	Delight thyself also in the Lord; and he shall give thee the desires of thine heart.
Proverbs 16:1	The preparations of the heart in man … from the Lord
Proverbs 21:1	The king's heart is in the hand of the Lord … he turneth it whithersoever he will
Judges 14:1–4	[Samson desired a Philistine woman] It was of the Lord

B. Beware about insisting on something you want:

Numbers 22:12–22,32	[Balaam—greedy for gain—went with wicked king Balak's messengers]
2 Kings 5:15–16,20–27	[Elisha refused to accept gifts from Naaman, but Gehazi covetously took some and was struck leprous]
Psalm 106:14–15	He gave them their request; but sent leanness into their soul
Acts 21:4,10–14,27,33	[Paul determined to go to Jerusalem despite the Holy Spirit's warning, and was imprisoned]
James 4:3	Ye ask amiss, that ye may consume it upon your lusts

10. GOD SOMETIMES REVEALS HIS WILL THROUGH CONFIRMING SIGNS:

A. Setting a condition for a specific confirming sign:

Genesis 24:14	[Abraham's servant set a specific requirement to let him know who was to be Isaac's wife]
Judges 6:36–40	[Gideon and the "sign" of the wet and dry fleeces]
1 Samuel 14:8–10	But if they say thus … this shall be a sign unto us

B. Requiring a "sign" often indicates unbelief:

Matthew 12:39	An evil and adulterous generation seeketh after a sign
John 4:48	Except ye see signs and wonders, ye will not believe

11. SOMETIMES GOD'S WILL AND PLANS ARE CONDITIONAL:

A. What God does often depends upon man's actions and reactions:

1 Kings 21:17–29	[Judgement delayed because Ahab repented]
2 Chronicles 7:13–14	[If the people repented, God's judgements turned away]
2 Chronicles 34:24–28	[Judgement delayed because Josiah repented]
Jeremiah 26:2–3,13	Turn every man from his evil way, that I may repent me of the evil, which I purpose to do unto them
Matthew 10:13	If the house be worthy, let your peace come upon it
Hebrews 4:6	Some must enter therein, and they to whom it was first preached entered not in because of unbelief (See also Hebrews 3:10–12,18–19.)

B. Examples of God changing His mind:

Exodus 32:9–14	Moses besought the Lord … and the Lord repented of the evil which He thought to do (See also Genesis 19:17–21; 2 Kings 20:1–6; Amos 7:1–6; Jonah 3:4–10.)

12. GOD OFTEN GIVES HIS PEOPLE ALTERNATIVE CHOICES:

A. He lets us choose within the boundary of His overall will:

1 Samuel 10:7	Do as occasion serve thee; for God is with thee.
2 Samuel 24:11–15	[David allowed to choose his punishment]
1 Kings 3:5,9–10	[Solomon told to ask God for whatever he wanted]
1 Corinthians 7:36	Let him do what he will, he sinneth not
1 Corinthians 10:27	If any … bid you to a feast, and ye be disposed to go

B. Our plans should be subject to the will of God:

James 4:13–15	Ye ought to say, If the Lord will, we shall
Acts 18:21	I will return again unto you, if God will
Romans 1:10	Making request, if … I might have a prosperous journey by the will of God to come unto you. (See also 1 Corinthians 4:19; 1 Corinthians 16:7; Hebrews 6:3.)

C. Be sure you're right before going ahead:

Romans 14:23	For whatsoever is not of faith is sin

D. Lovingly consider the effects of your actions on others:

Romans 14:15	If thy brother be grieved … walkest thou not charitably
1 Corinthians 8:9	Lest … this liberty of yours become a stumblingblock
1 Corinthians 8:13	If meat make my brother to offend, I will eat no flesh

13. WHAT TO DO WHEN GOD DOES NOT REVEAL HIS WILL:

A. God sometimes conceals His will from the unyielded and disobedient:

1 Samuel 28:6,15–16	[When rebellious Saul prayed and enquired of the Lord, He didn't answer him]
1 Kings 22:5–7,19–23	[God sent a lying spirit to deceive wicked King Ahab and hide His true plans from him]
Jeremiah 4:10	Thou hast greatly deceived this people … saying, Ye shall have peace; whereas the sword [comes]
Micah 3:4,6–7	He will not hear them … there is no answer of God
Luke 10:21	Thou hast hid these things from the [worldly] wise
2 Thessalonians 2:10–12	Because they received not the love of the truth … God shall send them strong delusion (See also Isaiah 66:4.)

B. How not to try to find God's will:

[Avoid divination, séances, and all occult-related mediums: See Leviticus 20:6; Deuteronomy 18:10–11,14; 2 Kings 21:6; 1 Chronicles 10:13–14; Isaiah 8:19; Ezekiel 21:21; Daniel 2:27–28.]

14. WHAT TO DO WHEN YOU DESPERATELY REQUIRE SPECIFIC DIRECTIONS:

Psalm 73:24	Thou shalt guide me with thy counsel (See also Psalm 16:7.)
Proverbs 4:11	I have taught thee … I have led thee in right paths

A. God promises to tell you exactly where to go:

Psalm 32:8	I will instruct thee and teach thee in the way which thou shalt go: I will guide thee with mine eye
Psalm 37:23	The steps of a good man are ordered by the Lord
Isaiah 30:21	And thine ears shall hear a word behind thee, saying, This is the way, walk ye in it

B. You must depend upon God to lead you:

Jeremiah 10:23	The way of man is not in himself: it is not in man that walketh to direct his steps
Psalm 25:4–5	Show me thy ways, O Lord; teach me thy paths
Psalm 31:3	For thy name's sake lead me, and guide me
Proverbs 4:26	Ponder the path of thy feet, and let all thy ways be established

C. God sends His angels to guide you:

Exodus 23:20	I send an Angel before thee, to keep thee in the way, and to bring thee into the place which I have prepared
Exodus 32:34	Go … mine Angel shall go before thee (See also Genesis 24:7.)

D. You must seek and pray for His leading:

Psalm 25:4	Show me thy ways, O Lord; teach me thy paths
Psalm 143:8	Cause me to know the way wherein I should walk; for I lift up my soul unto thee
Proverbs 3:5–6	In all thy ways acknowledge him, and he shall direct thy paths

E. Let God lead, even if you don't know where you're going:

Hebrews 11:8	Abraham, when he was called to go out … obeyed; and he went out, not knowing whither he went (See also Genesis 12:1.)

15. YOU CAN COUNT ON GOD'S LEADINGS EVEN WHEN …

A. You're discouraged and at wits' end:

Psalm 23:4	Though I walk through the valley of the shadow of death … thou art with me
Psalm 142:3	My spirit was overwhelmed … thou knewest my path

B. You feel lost:

Isaiah 42:16	I will bring the blind by a way that they knew not; I will lead them in paths that they have not known

C. You desperately need guidance in time of danger:

2 Kings 6:8–12	[Elisha warned the king of Israel of the enemies' plans]
Psalm 27:11	Teach me thy way … lead me in a plain path, because of mine enemies
Psalm 78:43–52	[Though Egypt suffered plagues, God] made his own people to go forth like sheep, and guided them

D. You need a place to stay or eat:

Psalm 107:6–7	They cried unto the Lord … and he led them forth by the right way … to a city of habitation.
Mark 14:12–16	Go into the city and there shall meet you a man bearing a pitcher of water, follow him (See also Luke 22:9–13.)

E. You're in a faraway, strange land:

Psalm 139:9–10	In the uttermost parts of the sea; Even there shall thy hand lead me

16. THE WILL OF GOD IS SUPREME:

A. God is omnipotent and does whatever He wills:

Psalm 75:6–7	God is the judge: he putteth down one, and setteth up another.
Daniel 4:17	The most High ruleth in the kingdom of men
Daniel 4:35	He doeth according to his will in the army of heaven
Acts 5:38–39	If this counsel … be of God, ye cannot overthrow it
Romans 9:15–18	Not of him that willeth … but of God that showeth mercy
Ephesians 1:11	[God] worketh all things after the counsel of his own will

B. Even seeming bad things happen only by God's will:

Job 2:3–6	[In order to test and purge Job] the Lord said unto Satan, He is in thine hand
Acts 2:23	[Jesus] delivered by the … foreknowledge of God
1 Peter 4:19	Let them that suffer according to the will of God commit the keeping of their souls to him

(See also Acts 4:28.)

17. REWARDS FOR DOING GOD'S WILL:

Matthew 7:21	He that doeth the will of my Father [shall enter the kingdom]
Matthew 12:50	Whosoever shall do the will of [God] is my brother
John 9:31	If any man … doeth [God's] will, him he heareth
John 15:14	Ye are my friends, if ye do whatsoever I command you
Hebrews 10:36	After ye have done the will of God … receive the promise
1 John 2:17	He that doeth the will of God abideth for ever
1 John 5:14	If we ask any thing according to his will, he heareth us

18. GOD'S WILL ON SPECIFIC SUBJECTS:

A. God's will regarding salvation:

(See Matthew 18:14; John 1:13; 6:39–40; Ephesians 1:5; 1 Timothy 2:4; James 1:18; 2 Peter 3:9.)

B. Verses on different aspects of God's will in a Christian's life:

(See 1 Corinthians 12:11; Galatians 1:4; Ephesians 5:17; 1 Thessalonians 4:3; Hebrews 2:4; 10:10; 1 Peter 2:15; 3:17; 4:2,19.)

C. The will of God is the path of life:

(See Psalm 16:11; 23:3; 25:10; Proverbs 2:8,13,20; 4:11,18; 12:28; Micah 4:2.)

OBEDIENCE TO GOD

1. OBEYING GOD:

A. Obedience to God is our duty:

Deuteronomy 13:4	Walk after the Lord … and keep his commandments, and obey his voice, and ye shall serve him
Deuteronomy 27:9–10	Thou art become the people of the Lord … therefore obey the voice of the Lord
Ecclesiastes 12:13	Keep his commandments: for this is the whole duty of man
Jeremiah 11:7	I earnestly protested … saying, Obey my voice
John 2:5	Whatsoever [Jesus] saith unto you, do it
	(See also Luke 17:10.)

B. Obey wholeheartedly:

Deuteronomy 26:16	The Lord … hath commanded thee to do these statutes … keep and do them with all thine heart, and with all thy soul
Psalm 119:34	I shall keep thy law … with my whole heart
Romans 6:17	Ye have obeyed from the heart that form of doctrine
	(See also Psalm 119:69.)

C. Obey in all things:

Deuteronomy 5:32	Observe to do therefore as the Lord … commanded you: ye shall not turn aside to the right hand or to the left
2 Kings 22:2	And he did that which was right in the sight of the Lord … and turned not aside to the right hand or to the left
	(See also 2 Corinthians 2:9.)

2. IF WE LOVE AND KNOW GOD, WE WILL OBEY HIM:

John 14:15,21	If ye love me, keep my commandments (See also 14:23.)
1 John 2:3–4	We know him, if we keep his commandments. He that saith, I know him, and keepeth not his commandments, is a liar
1 John 3:24	He that keepeth his commandments dwelleth in him
2 John 1:6	This is love, that we walk after his commandments

3. BLESSINGS FOR OBEYING GOD:

Deuteronomy 11:26–27	I set before you this day a blessing … if ye obey the commandments of the Lord
Joshua 1:8	Meditate therein [the Word] … observe to do according to all that is written therein … then thou shalt have good success

A. Souls are saved:

Romans 5:19	By the obedience of one shall many be made righteous
1 Timothy 4:16	Heed … the doctrine … in doing this thou shalt both save thyself, and them that hear thee

B. Spiritual blessings:

Exodus 19:5	If ye will obey my voice … ye shall be a peculiar treasure unto me above all people
Jeremiah 7:23	Obey my voice, and I will be your God, and ye shall be my people
John 13:17	If ye know these things, happy are ye if ye do them
John 15:10	If ye keep my commandments, ye shall abide in my love
John 15:14	Ye are my friends, if ye do whatsoever I command you
Acts 5:32	Holy Ghost … given to them that obey [God]
1 Peter 1:22	Ye have purified your souls in obeying the truth (See also James 1:25.)

C. Material blessings:

Deuteronomy 28:2	All these blessing shall come on thee, and overtake thee, if thou shalt hearken unto the Lord
Deuteronomy 32:46–47	Set your hearts unto all the words … and through this ye shall prolong your days in the land
Job 36:11	If they obey and serve him, they shall spend their days in prosperity, and their years in pleasures
Isaiah 1:19	If ye be willing and obedient, ye shall eat the good of the land
Jeremiah 38:20	Obey … voice of the Lord: so it shall be well unto thee, and thy soul shall live
Hebrews 11:8	Abraham, when he was called to go into a place which he should after receive for an inheritance, obeyed (See also Deuteronomy 28:1–14; Jeremiah 35:18–19.)

D. Protection:

Exodus 23:22	If thou shall obey and do all that I speak; then I will be an enemy unto thine enemies
Leviticus 25:18	Do my statutes … and shall dwell in the land in safety

4. JESUS' EXAMPLE OF OBEDIENCE:

Luke 22:42	Nevertheless not my will, but thine, be done. (See also Matthew 26:39,42.)
John 5:30	I seek not mine own will, but the will of the Father
John 14:31	As the Father gave me commandment, even so I do
Philippians 2:7–8	[Jesus] took upon him the form of a servant … and became obedient unto death

Hebrews 5:8	Though he were a Son, yet learned he obedience

5. YIELDEDNESS TO GOD:

A. Let God have His way in your life:

Job 1:21	Lord gave, and … hath taken away; blessed be the name of the Lord
Isaiah 64:8	Lord … we are the clay, and thou our potter
Matthew 6:10	Thy kingdom come. Thy will be done
John 3:30	He must increase, but I must decrease.
Romans 12:1	Present your bodies a living sacrifice … unto God
James 4:7	Submit yourselves therefore to God
	(See also Matthew 26:39; Luke 1:38; Romans 6:13,16.)

B. Submit your plans to God:

Hebrews 6:3	This will we do, if God permit
James 4:15	Ye ought to say, If the Lord will, we shall … do this

C. Obeying God even when it hurts:

Genesis 22:2,12	Take now thy … only son Isaac, whom thou lovest, and … offer him there for a burnt offering (See also Hebrews 11:17–19.)
Jeremiah 42:6	Whether it be good, or whether it be evil [hard to do], we will obey the voice of the Lord our God
Matthew 26:38–54	[Jesus agonised in prayer, knowing the cost, but then yielded to God's will] (See also Luke 22:44; John 18:11.)

D. Yield to God and pray for His leading:

Psalm 27:11	Teach me thy way, O Lord, and lead me in a plain path
Psalm 139:23–24	Search me, O God, and know my heart … know my thoughts … lead me in the way everlasting
Psalm 143:10	Teach me to do thy will; for thou art my God … lead me

6. OBEYING GOD RATHER THAN UNGODLY MEN:

Acts 4:13–20	Whether it be right in the sight of God to hearken unto you more than unto God, judge ye
Acts 5:29	We ought to obey God rather than men
	(See also 1 Samuel 22:17; 1 Kings 18:3,13; Ezra 4:21; 5:1–5; Daniel 3:1–25; 6:1–13; Hebrews 11:23.)

7. DISOBEDIENCE TO GOD—HOW HE VIEWS IT:

Jeremiah 18:10	If [they] obey not … then I will repent of the good, wherewith I said I would benefit them
Matthew 7:26–27	Heareth these sayings of mine, and doeth them not … a foolish man, which built his house upon the sand

James 1:23–24	A hearer of the word, and not a doer, he is like unto a man beholding his natural face … and straightway forgetteth

8. VARIOUS CATEGORIES OF DISOBEDIENCE:

A. Merely "agreeing" is not enough:

Ezekiel 33:30–33	They sit before thee as my people, and they hear thy words, but they will not do them
Matthew 21:28–31	He answered and said, I go, sir: and went not
Matthew 23:2–3	Do not ye after their works: for they say, and do not
Luke 6:46	Why call ye me, Lord, Lord, and do not the things I say?
Titus 1:16	They profess that they know God; but in works they deny him, being … disobedient

(See also Jeremiah 42:1–22; 43:1–4.)

B. "Good works" not a substitute for obedience:

1 Samuel 15:22	Hath the Lord as great delight in burnt offerings and sacrifices, as in obeying … to obey is better than sacrifice
Luke 11:42	Ye tithe … and pass over judgement and the love of God: these ought ye to have done, and not to leave the other undone

C. Halfhearted obedience:

2 Chronicles 25:2	And he did that which was right in the sight of the Lord, but not with a perfect heart
Jeremiah 3:10	Judah hath not turned unto me with her whole heart, but feignedly
Acts 5:1–11	[Ananias and Sapphira pretended to give all, but kept back part of the money from the sale of their land]

STRENGTH AND POWER

1. GOD'S STRENGTH VS. OUR STRENGTH:

A. God is infinitely more powerful than weak man:

Psalm 8:3–4	When I consider thy heavens … the moon and the stars, which thou hast [made] … what is man?
Isaiah 40:15,17,22	All nations before him are as nothing … as a drop of a bucket … less than nothing
Daniel 4:35	All the inhabitants of the earth are reputed as nothing, none can stay his hand
1 Corinthians 1:25	[Even] the weakness of God is stronger than men (See also 2 Chronicles 20:6; Psalm 89:6.)

B. An honest view of man and his strength:

Job 8:9	We know nothing … our days upon earth are a shadow
Job 14:1–2	Man … is of few days … he cometh forth like a flower, and is cut down (See also Job 7:1.)
Job 25:6	Man is a worm
Psalm 39:5–6	Every man at his best state is altogether vanity
Psalm 78:39	He remembered that they were but flesh; a wind that passeth away (See also Isaiah 2:22; James 4:14–15.)
Psalm 103:14	He knoweth our frame … remembereth that we are dust. (See also Genesis 18:27; Isaiah 29:5–6.)
Psalm 144:3–4	What is man? Man is vanity: his days are as a shadow (See also 1 Chronicles 29:15; Psalm 62:9; 90:10; Ecclesiastes 6:12.)
Isaiah 40:6–8	All flesh is grass … the grass withereth (See also Psalm 90:5–6; 103:15–16; James 1:10–11; 1 Peter 1:24–25.)
Isaiah 40:22	The inhabitants thereof are as grasshoppers (See also Job 4:18,20; Romans 7:18.)

C. God is able to do absolutely anything:

Job 42:2	I know that thou canst do everything
Psalm 62:11	Power belongeth unto God
Jeremiah 32:27	I am the Lord, the God of all flesh: is there any thing too hard for me? (See also Genesis 18:14.)
Matthew 19:26	With men this is impossible; but with God all things are possible
Matthew 28:18	All power is given unto me in heaven and in earth

D. God has total power:

Job 12:10	In [His] hand is the soul of every living thing, and the breath of all mankind (See also Daniel 5:23.)
Job 12:13–25	With him is strength … he increaseth the nations, and destroyeth them (See also Psalm 75:6–7; 107:33–40.)
Psalm 115:3	God hath done whatsoever he hath pleased

Isaiah 43:13	There is none that can deliver out of my hand
Isaiah 64:8	We are the clay, and thou our potter; we all are the work of thy hand. (See also Isaiah 45:9.)
	(See also 1 Chronicles 29:12; 2 Chronicles 20:6; Job 9:4; Psalm 104:29–30; Isaiah 40:23,25.)

2. TRUST IN GOD, NOT YOUR OWN STRENGTH:

A. Let God strengthen you with His strength:

2 Chronicles 20:12	We have no might against this great company … neither know we what to do: our eyes are upon thee
Psalm 20:7–8	Some trust in chariots, and some in horses: but we will remember the name of the Lord our God
Psalm 84:5	Blessed is the man whose strength is in thee
Psalm 105:4	Seek the Lord, and his strength: seek his face evermore
Isaiah 26:4	Trust ye in the Lord, in the Lord is everlasting strength
2 Corinthians 3:4–5	not ... that we are sufficient of ourselves … but our sufficiency is of God
Ephesians 6:10	Be strong in the Lord, and in the power of his might
Philippians 3:3	We worship God … and have no confidence in the flesh
	(See also Exodus 15:2; 2 Samuel 22:33; Psalm 27:1; 68:28,35; 118:8; 147:10–11.)

B. He can do what you can't do:

1 Samuel 2:9	By [his own] strength shall no man prevail
Psalm 60:11	Give us help from trouble: vain is the help of man
Psalm 127:1	Except the Lord build the house, they labour in vain that build it
Zechariah 4:6	Not by [your own] might, nor by power, but by my spirit
John 15:5	Without me ye can do nothing
	(See also Job 9:19; Psalm 33:16–17.)

3. OUR WEAKNESS CAUSES US TO DEPEND UPON GOD:

A. God's strength is manifest in our weakness:

Psalm 8:2	Out of the mouth of babes … hast thou ordained strength
Psalm 37:39	The Lord … is their strength in the time of trouble
Psalm 73:26	My flesh and my heart faileth: but God is [my] strength
Isaiah 25:4	Thou [art] a strength to … the needy in his distress
Isaiah 40:29	He giveth power to the faint; and to them that have no might he increaseth strength
Isaiah 41:10	I will strengthen thee; yea, I will help thee
2 Corinthians 1:8–9	We were pressed out of measure, above strength … but we [do] not trust in ourselves, but in God

2 Corinthians 4:7	We have this treasure in earthen vessels, that the … power may be of God, and not of us
2 Corinthians 12:9–10	[God's] strength is made perfect in [our] weakness … when I am weak, then am I strong
2 Corinthians 13:4	We are weak in him, but we shall live … by the power of God
Hebrews 11:34	[Bible saints] out of weakness were made strong

(See also Psalm 94:17–18.)

B. When you have no other help, He'll strengthen you:

Psalm 72:12	He shall deliver the needy when he crieth; the poor also, and him that hath no helper
Luke 22:43,45	[Jesus' disciples slept, but] an angel [came] from heaven, strengthening him
2 Timothy 4:16–17	No man stood with me, but all men forsook me … the Lord stood with me, and strengthened me

(See also Psalm 27:10.)

C. He will give strength day by day to keep you going:

Deuteronomy 33:25	As thy days, so shall thy strength be
Matthew 6:34	Take no thought for the morrow … sufficient unto the day is the evil thereof

D. When you have only a little strength, God will help you:

Psalm 37:24	Though he fall … the Lord upholdeth him with his hand
Isaiah 35:4	Say to them that are of a fearful heart, "Be strong"
Daniel 11:34	When they fall, they shall be holpen with a little help
Revelation 3:8	Thou hast a little strength, and hast kept my word

4. GOD CAN STRENGTHEN AND USE YOU:

A. How to receive God's power:

Joshua 1:5–9	Only be thou strong and very courageous … observe the [word] … then thou shalt have good success
2 Chronicles 16:9	The Lord [shews] himself strong in the behalf of them whose heart is perfect toward him
Nehemiah 8:10	The joy of the Lord is your strength
Psalm 138:3	When I cried thou … strengthenedst me with strength
Isaiah 27:5	Let him take hold of my strength
Isaiah 30:15	In quietness and in confidence shall be your strength
Isaiah 40:31	They that wait upon the Lord shall renew their strength
Daniel 11:32	People that do know their God shall be strong, and do exploits
Micah 3:8	I am full of power by the spirit of the Lord … and of might
Acts 1:8	Ye shall receive power, after that the Holy Ghost is come

	upon you
Ephesians 3:16	Strengthened with might by his Spirit in the inner man
1 John 2:14	Ye are strong [because] the word of God abideth in you

B. He strengthens you with His power:

Psalm 18:29–34	It is God that girdeth me with strength
Psalm 68:28	Thy God hath commanded thy strength
Psalm 68:35	God … giveth strength and power unto his people
Psalm 71:16	I will go in the strength of the Lord God
Psalm 80:17	Let thy hand be upon the man … whom thou madest strong for thyself
Psalm 84:5,7	Blessed is the man whose strength is in thee … they go from strength to strength
Matthew 10:1,8	He gave [His disciples] power against unclean spirits
Philippians 4:13	I can do all things through Christ which strengtheneth me
Colossians 1:11	Strengthened with all might [by] his glorious power

(See also Judges 14:6,19; 15:14–15; Psalm 8:2; Luke 10:19.)

C. Praise God for strengthening you:

Psalm 28:7–8	The Lord is my strength … I am helped … with my song will I praise him

D. Give God the glory for working through you:

Isaiah 10:13,15	[Proud] saith, "By [my] strength … I have done it." Shall the ax boast itself against him that heweth?
Jeremiah 9:23–24	Let not … the mighty man glory in his might … but glory in this, that he knoweth me
Acts 12:21–23	The angel of the Lord smote [Herod], because he gave not God the glory
Philippians 2:13	For it is God which worketh in you
1 Peter 4:11	Let him do it as of the ability which God giveth: that God in all things may be glorified

E. Sometimes God Himself wants to do the whole thing:

Exodus 14:13–14	Stand still, and see the salvation of the Lord … Lord shall fight for you, and ye shall hold your peace
Judges 7:all	[Gideon and his 300 men fight the battle God's way]
2 Chronicles 20:15–17	Be not afraid nor dismayed … the battle is not yours, but God's ... Ye shall not need to fight in this battle: stand ye still, and see the salvation of the Lord
Nehemiah 4:20	Our God shall fight for us
Psalm 18:17	He delivered me from my strong enemy … for they were too strong for me
Isaiah 30:7	Their strength is to sit still

5. DON'T TRUST IN YOURSELF:

A. Warnings against trusting in your own strength:

Psalm 52:5–7	God shall destroy … the man that made not God his strength
Psalm 118:8–9	It is better to trust in the Lord than … in man
Psalm 146:3	Put not your trust in princes, nor in … men, in whom there is no help
Jeremiah 9:23–24	Let not … the mighty man glory in his might … but glory … that he knoweth me, that I am the Lord
Jeremiah 17:5	Cursed be the man that trusteth in man, and maketh flesh his arm, and whose heart departeth from the Lord
John 15:4–5	Without me ye can do nothing

(See also Isaiah 31:3.)

B. What can happen when you rely on your own strength and plans:

2 Chronicles 26:16	When he was strong, his heart was lifted up to his destruction: for he transgressed against the Lord
Hosea 10:13	Ye have reaped iniquity … because thou didst trust in thy way, in the multitude of thy mighty men
1 Corinthians 10:12	Him that thinketh he standeth take heed lest he fall

(See also 1 Samuel 15:1–28; 28:4–25; 31:1–8.)

C. Lack of strength is often due to sin:

Leviticus 26:27,36–37	I will send a faintness into [your] hearts … and ye shall have no power to stand before your enemies
Joshua 7:12	[They] could not stand before their enemies … because they were accursed
Judges 2:13–15	They forsook the Lord … [His] anger was against Israel … they could not stand before their enemies
Psalm 31:10	My strength faileth because of mine iniquity

(See also Amos 2:13–15.)

6. POWER WHEN WITNESSING:

A. Power comes from the Holy Spirit:

Micah 3:8	I am full of power by the spirit of the Lord … to declare to Israel his sin
John 6:63	It is the spirit that quickeneth; the flesh profiteth nothing
Acts 1:8	Ye shall receive power [when] the Holy Ghost is come upon you: and ye shall be witnesses
Acts 4:8,13	Peter, filled with the Holy Ghost … they saw the boldness of Peter
Acts 4:31,33	They were all filled with the Holy Ghost … and with great power gave the apostles witness

1 Thessalonians 1:5	For our gospel came unto you … in power
2 Timothy 1:7	God hath not given us the spirit of fear; but of power

B. No man can stand against the power of God's Spirit:

Jeremiah 5:14	I will make my words in thy mouth fire, and this people wood
Luke 21:15	For I will give you a mouth … which all your adversaries shall not be able to gainsay [dispute] nor resist
Acts 6:10	They were not able to resist the wisdom and the spirit by which he [Stephen] spake
2 Corinthians 10:4	The weapons of our warfare are … mighty through God to the pulling down of strong holds

C. It has to be by God's power:

1 Corinthians 1:18	The preaching of the cross … is the power of God
1 Corinthians 2:4–5	My preaching was … in … the Spirit and power: That your faith should … stand … in the power of God
1 Corinthians 4:20	The kingdom of God is not in word, but in power (See also Luke 4:14.)

D. God can use you even when you're weak:

Galatians 4:13–14	[Paul witnessed to and won the Galatians even though suffering infirmity in the flesh]

E. God can take over and powerfully use you:

Exodus 4:10–12	I am not eloquent … I am slow of speech. The Lord said, "I will be with thy mouth, and teach thee"
Jeremiah 1:6–9	I cannot speak. Lord said, "Whatsoever I command thee … speak. I have put my words in thy mouth"
Matthew 10:20	For it is not ye that speak, but the Spirit … which speaketh in you (See also Mark 13:11; Luke 12:12.)
Acts 4:13	They … perceived [Peter and John] were … ignorant men … and they took knowledge … that they had been with Jesus (See also 1 Samuel 10:6.)

7. GOD'S POWER VS. PHYSICAL POWER:

A. For your spiritual battles, defending the faith:

2 Corinthians 10:3–5	We do not war after [in] the flesh: For the weapons of our warfare are not carnal, but mighty through God
Jude 1:3	Ye should earnestly contend for the faith (See also 1 Corinthians 10:11.)

B. If you must physically defend your loved ones or country:

Luke 11:21	When a strong man armed keepeth his palace, his goods are in peace
John 10:11	The good shepherd giveth his life for the sheep

C. Physical might is no match for the power of God:

1 Samuel 17:45	Thou [Goliath] comest to me with a sword and with a spear … but I come to thee in the name of the Lord
2 Chronicles 32:8	With him is an arm of flesh; but with us is the Lord to help us, and to fight our battles
Psalm 9:19–20	Lord, let not man prevail … put them in fear: that [they] may know themselves to be but men
Isaiah 31:3	The Egyptians are men and not God … when the Lord shall stretch out his hand … they all shall fail

(See also Hosea 1:7.)

D. They may seem strong, but their strength has departed:

Numbers 14:9	Neither fear the people … for they are bread for us: their defense is departed from them
Jeremiah 46:17	Pharaoh king of Egypt is but a noise; he hath passed the time appointed [his time is up]

E. God decides the outcome, not physical might:

1 Samuel 2:4	The bows of the mighty men are broken, [whereas] they that stumbled are girded with strength
2 Chronicles 25:8	God hath power to help, and to cast down
Psalm 33:16–17	There is no king saved by the multitude of an host: a mighty man is not delivered by much strength. An horse is a vain thing for safety: neither shall he deliver any by his great strength
Psalm 35:10	The Lord deliverest the poor from him that is too strong for him
Psalm 44:3–7	They got not the land … by their own sword, neither did their own arm save them: but thy arm

F. You are not to trust in physical might to fight your foes:

2 Kings 18:21	Thou trusteth upon … this bruised reed … on which if a man lean, it will [pierce] his hand
Psalm 44:5–6	Through thee will we push down our enemies: I will not trust in … my sword [to] save me
Isaiah 31:1	Woe to them that go to Egypt for help … because they are very strong; but look not unto … the Lord

G. You are not to fear the power of man:

Deuteronomy 3:22	Ye shall not fear them: the Lord shall fight for you

Psalm 27:1–3	Of whom shall I be afraid? Though an host should encamp against me, my heart shall not fear
Psalm 118:6	The Lord is on my side; I will not fear: what can man do unto me?
Proverbs 29:25	The fear of man bringeth a snare
Isaiah 2:22	Cease [fearing] man, whose breath is in his nostrils
Isaiah 51:12–13	[Why] art thou ... afraid of a man that shall die ... as grass; and forgettest the Lord thy maker
Jeremiah 1:8	Be not afraid of their faces: for I am with thee to deliver thee, saith the Lord
Luke 12:4–5	Be not afraid of them that kill the body

H. If God is on your side, you will win:

Deuteronomy 31:8	The Lord ... doth go before thee; he will be with thee
Romans 8:31	If God be for us, who can be against us?
	(See also 2 Chronicles 14:11–12; 20:12–25; Zephaniah 3:17.)

I. The armies of heaven are on your side:

2 Kings 6:14–17	[Elisha said:] They that be with us are more than they that be with them
2 Chronicles 32:7–8,21	[Hezekiah said:] There be more with us than with him
	(See also Joshua 5:13–14; Psalm 68:17; 91:11; Isaiah 37:33–36.)

J. With God, you are more powerful than your adversaries:

Joshua 23:9–10	One shall chase a thousand, for God fighteth for you
1 John 4:4	Greater is he that is in you, than he ... in the world
	(See also Deuteronomy 11:25; 28:7.)

K. God can help you win against overwhelming odds:

1 Samuel 14:6	No restraint to the Lord to save by many or by few
2 Chronicles 14:11	Lord, it is nothing with thee to help, whether with many, or with them that have no power
2 Chronicles 16:8–9	A huge host ... because thou didst rely on the Lord, he delivered them into thine hand

PROTECTION

1. TRUSTING IN GOD IS YOUR ONLY SURE REFUGE:

A. Safety and protection are in God's hands:

Psalm 127:1	Except the Lord keep the city, the watchman waketh but in vain
Proverbs 21:31	The horse is prepared … but safety is of the Lord

B. God is able to protect you:

Exodus 6:6–7	I will redeem you with a stretched out arm, and with great judgements
Isaiah 59:1	The Lord's hand is not shortened, that it cannot save
Zephaniah 3:17	The Lord in the midst of thee is mighty; he will save
Romans 4:21	What he [has] promised, he [is] able also to perform
Ephesians 3:20	He is able to do exceeding abundantly above all … we ask

C. God is your defence and protective shield:

Deuteronomy 33:27	The eternal God is thy refuge
Psalm 3:3	Thou, O Lord, art a shield for me
Psalm 5:12	With favour wilt thou compass him as with a shield
Psalm 89:18	For the Lord is our defence
Psalm 115:11	Trust in the Lord: he is their help and their shield
Isaiah 33:16	He shall dwell on high: place of defence … the rocks

(See also Psalm 18:35; 107:41.)

D. He is your tower and fortress, your high rock:

2 Samuel 22:2–3	The Lord is my rock, and my fortress, and my deliverer
Psalm 9:9	The Lord will be a refuge … in times of trouble
Psalm 61:3	Thou hast been a shelter for me, and a strong tower from the enemy
Psalm 62:6	He only is my rock and my salvation: he is my defence
Psalm 71:2–4	Be thou my strong habitation … deliver me, O my God, out of the hand of the wicked
Psalm 91:2	He is my refuge and my fortress, in him will I trust
Proverbs 18:10	The name of the Lord is a strong tower: the righteous runneth into it, and is safe

E. He is your protection in times of great danger:

Isaiah 25:4	A refuge from the storm … when the blast of the terrible ones is as a storm against the wall
Nahum 1:6–7	The Lord is … a strong hold in the day of trouble; and he knoweth them that trust in him
Zephaniah 2:3	Seek ye the Lord, all ye meek of the earth … ye shall be hid in the day of the Lord's anger

(See also Psalm 46:1–5.)

F. He is your hiding place:

Psalm 27:5	In the time of trouble he shall hide me
Psalm 32:7	Thou art my hiding place; thou shalt preserve me from trouble; thou shalt compass me about
Psalm 119:114	Thou art my hiding place and shield: I hope in they word
Psalm 143:9	I flee unto thee to hide me

2. GOD WILL PROTECT YOU BECAUSE HE LOVES YOU:

A. God delivers His people who trust Him:

2 Samuel 8:6	The Lord preserved David withersoever he went
Psalm 37:28	The Lord forsaketh not his saints; they are preserved
Psalm 37:40	The Lord ... shall deliver them from the wicked, and save them, because they trust in him
Psalm 91:9–10	Because thou hast made the Lord ... thy habitation; there shall no evil befall thee
2 Timothy 4:18	The Lord shall deliver me from every evil work

B. God loves, favours, and will protect you:

Deuteronomy 33:12	The beloved of the Lord shall dwell in safety by him
2 Samuel 22:20	He delivered me, because he delighted in me
Job 1:10	Hast not thou made an hedge about him [Job], and about his house, and all that he hath on every side
Psalm 17:8–9	Keep me as the apple of the eye, hide me under the shadow of thy wings ... from my deadly enemies
Psalm 41:11	By this I know that thou favourest me, because mine enemy doth not triumph over me
Psalm 56:9	When I cry unto thee, then shall mine enemies turn back ... for God is with me
Psalm 91:7	A thousand shall fall at thy side, and ten thousand at thy right hand; but it shall not come nigh thee
Psalm 105:12–15	He reproved kings for their sakes; saying, touch not mine anointed, and do my prophets no harm
Matthew 10:29–31	[God even watches over sparrows, and] ye are of more value than many sparrows

(See also Psalm 4:3; 40:17; 125:2.)

C. He is always close by to protect you:

Genesis 28:15	I am with thee, and will keep thee in all places whither thou goest
Deuteronomy 33:12	The Lord shall cover him all the day long, and he shall dwell between his shoulders
Deuteronomy 33:27	The eternal God is thy refuge, and underneath are the everlasting arms

Psalm 46:1	God is our refuge … a very present help in trouble
Psalm 109:31	He shall stand at [his] right hand … to save him

D. God's guardian angels protect you:

Psalm 34:7	The angel of the Lord encampeth round about them that fear him, and delivereth them
Psalm 91:11–12	He shall give his angels charge over thee, to keep thee in all thy ways
Isaiah 63:9	In affliction … angel of his presence saved them
Daniel 3:28	God … hath sent his angle, and delivered his servants that trusted in him
Daniel 6:20,22	God hath sent his angel, and shut the lions' mouths
	(See also Exodus 14:19–20; 23:20; 2 Kings 6:15–18; 2 Chronicles 32:20–21; 2 Kings 19:35; Acts 5:19; 12:6–10.)

E. Rest in God, trusting Him to protect you:

Exodus 14:14	Lord shall fight for you, and ye shall hold your peace
Exodus 33:14	My presence shall go with thee, I will give thee rest
Psalm 112:7–8	He shall not be afraid of evil tidings: his heart is fixed [steadfast], trusting in the Lord
Psalm 118:6–7	The Lord is on my side; what can man do unto me?

F. Thank God for protecting you:

Psalm 5:11	Let them shout for joy, because thou defendest them
Psalm 28:7	I am helped … with my song will I praise him
Psalm 59:16–17	I will sing of thy power … for thou hast been my defence and refuge in the day of my trouble
Psalm 98:1	Sing unto the Lord … his right hand, and his holy arm, hath gotten him the victory

3. GOD CAN PROTECT YOU FROM …

A. Traps and snares:

Psalm 91:3	He shall deliver thee from the snare of the fowler
Psalm 124:6–7	Blessed be the Lord, who hath not given us as a prey … [we are] escaped as a bird out of the snare
Psalm 141:10	Let wicked fall into their own nets, whilst I escape

B. Disease and epidemics:

Exodus 15:26	I will put none of these diseases upon thee
Deuteronomy 7:15	The Lord will take way from thee all … evil diseases … but will lay them upon all them that hate thee
Psalm 91:3	He shall deliver thee from … the [perilous] pestilence
Psalm 91:10	There shall no evil befall thee, neither shall any plague come nigh thy dwelling

C. Injury:

Psalm 34:20	He keepeth all his bones: not one of them is broken
Psalm 91:11–12	Angels … bear thee up … lest thou dash thy foot
Mark 16:18	If they drink any deadly thing, it shall not hurt them

D. Fire and burning:

Psalm 29:7	The voice of the Lord divideth the flames of fire
Isaiah 43:2	When thou walkest through the fire, thou shalt not be burned; neither shall the flame kindle upon thee
Daniel 3:25,27	These men, upon whose bodies the fire had no power, nor was an hair of their head singed

E. Drowning:

Psalm 107:23–30	[God can save you from terrible storms at sea]
Isaiah 43:2	When thou passest through the waters, I will be with thee … they shall not overflow thee
Matthew 8:23–27	There arose a great tempest … he rebuked the winds and sea … was a great calm (See also Matthew 14:23–32.)
Acts 27:14–44	Exceedingly tossed with a tempest … all hope taken away … it came to pass, they all escaped safe to land (See also Jonah 1:4,11–17; 2:3,10; 1 Peter 3:20; Genesis 7:23.)

F. Death:

Psalm 41:2	The Lord will preserve him, and keep him alive
Daniel 6:27	He delivereth and rescueth, and he … hath delivered Daniel from the power of the lions

G. Dangers while travelling:

Genesis 28:15	I will keep thee in all places whither thou goest, and will bring thee again into this land
Exodus 23:20	I send an angel before thee, to keep thee in the way, and to bring thee into the place which I have prepared
Deuteronomy 28:6	Blessed shalt thou be when thou comest in, and blessed shalt thou be when thou goest out
Psalm 105:13–15	When they went from one nation to another … he suffered no man to do them wrong
Psalm 121:8	The Lord shall preserve thy going out and thy coming in
John 10:4	When he putteth forth his sheep, he goeth before them (See also Exodus 33:14–15; Psalm 37:23; Isaiah 55:12; 63:9.)

H. Every kind of evil:

Job 5:19–22	He shall deliver thee in six troubles: yea, in seven there shall no evil touch thee
Psalm 46:1–3	God is our refuge … therefore will not we fear, though … the mountains be carried into the … sea

Psalm 121:7	The Lord shall preserve thee from all evil
Luke 10:19	I give you power … nothing shall by any means hurt you
2 Thessalonians 3:3	The Lord is faithful, who shall … keep you from evil
2 Timothy 4:18	The Lord shall deliver me from every evil work

4. PROTECTION FROM THOSE WHO SEEK TO HARM YOU:

2 Samuel 22:49	Thou hast lifted me above them that rose up against me: thou hast delivered me from the violent man
2 Chronicles 32:8	With us is the Lord our God … to fight our battles
Job 5:12–13	He disappointeth the devices of the crafty, so that their hands cannot perform their enterprise
Psalm 3:6	I will not be afraid of ten thousands of people … against me
Psalm 21:8,11	They intended evil … which they are not able to perform
Psalm 37:32–33	The wicked … seeketh to slay [the righteous]. The Lord will not leave him in his hand
Psalm 91:7	A thousand shall fall at thy side, and ten thousand at thy right hand; but it shall not come nigh thee
Psalm 97:10	He delivereth them out of the hand of the wicked
Psalm 118:13	Thou has thrust sore at me … but the Lord helped me
Isaiah 54:17	No weapon that is formed against thee shall prosper
Jeremiah 1:19	They shall fight against thee; but they shall not prevail … for I am with thee to deliver thee
Jeremiah 39:17	I will deliver thee … thou shalt not be given into the hand of the men of whom thou art afraid

5. SPECIAL PROTECTION PROMISED IN THE LAST DAYS:

Luke 21:17–18	Ye shall be hated of all nations … but there shall not an hair of your head perish
Revelation 7:3	Hurt not the earth … till we have sealed the servants of our God in their foreheads
Revelation 9:3–4	[Locusts will] hurt … only those men which have not the seal of God in their foreheads
Revelation 11:3,5–6	If any man will [try to] hurt them [the two witnesses], fire … devoureth their enemies

6. CONDITIONS FOR HAVING GOD'S PROTECTION:

A. Faith in God is essential:

Psalm 37:40	The Lord shall … deliver them from the wicked … because they trust in him
Daniel 6:23	No manner of hurt was found upon him [Daniel], because he believed in his God

1 Peter 1:5	Who are kept by the power of God through faith (See also Psalm 33:22.)

B. Pray in time of need:

Genesis 32:1–12	[Jacob's earnest prayer for protection from Esau and his 400 men] (See also 32:24–30.)
2 Samuel 22:4	I will call on the Lord, so shall I be saved from enemies
Psalm 34:17	The righteous cry, and the Lord … delivereth them
Psalm 50:15	Call upon me in the day of trouble: I will deliver (See also Psalm 18:6; 59:1–3.)

C. Love and reverence God:

2 Chronicles 16:9	[God shows] himself strong in the behalf of them whose heart is perfect toward him
Psalm 31:23	Love the Lord … for the Lord preserveth the faithful
Psalm 33:18–19	The eye of the Lord is upon them that fear him … to deliver their soul from death
Psalm 34:7	Angel of the Lord encampeth round about them that fear him, and delivereth them
Psalm 91:14–15	Because he hath set his love upon me, I will deliver
Psalm 145:20	The Lord preserveth all them that love him (See also Proverbs 16:7.)

D. Stay close to God:

Psalm 57:1	In the shadow of thy wings will I make my refuge, until these calamities be over past
Psalm 91:1	He that dwelleth in the secret place of the most High shall abide under the shadow of the Almighty

E. Be obedient and do good:

Exodus 23:22	If thou indeed obey his voice … [God will protect]
Psalm 34:17	The righteous cry, and the Lord … delivereth them
Psalm 41:1–2	Blessed is he that considereth the poor: the Lord will deliver him in time of trouble
Psalm 81:13–14	Oh that my people had hearkened unto me … I should have … turned my hand against their adversaries
Proverbs 1:33	Whoso hearkeneth unto me shall dwell safely
Daniel 6:16	God whom thou servest continually … will deliver thee
1 Peter 3:12	The eyes of the Lord are over the righteous, and his ears are open unto their prayers (See also Psalm 7:10; 1 Peter 3:13.)

F. Do your part:

Hebrews 11:7	Noah … prepared an ark to the saving of his house (See also Genesis 6:12–14,22; 7:1,11,17–23.)

Hebrews 11:31	The harlot Rahab perished not … when she [hid the spies and hung down the red cord] (See also Joshua 2:4–21.)
Exodus 12:21–23	[The Hebrews were required to paint blood on their doorpost so that the destroyer would pass over]

G. Don't be reckless, foolhardy, or disobedient:

1 Kings 22:1–4,29–37	[King warned not to go to battle; he went, disguised as a common soldier, and was killed by a stray arrow]
2 Chronicles 35:20–24	[King Josiah rashly went out to fight the Egyptians, who didn't want to battle with him, and he was killed]
Proverbs 16:5	Though hand join in hand [join forces for strength], he [the proud in heart] shall not be unpunished
Hosea 8:3	Israel hath cast off the thing that is good: the enemy shall pursue him
Matthew 4:5–7	The devil … saith unto him, cast thyself down … Jesus saith, thou shalt not tempt the Lord thy God
Acts 19:29–31	[The disciples and Paul's friends advise him not to "adventure himself" into the bloodthirsty mob]
Acts 21:17–30	[Paul went to Jerusalem despite God's warnings] (See also Acts 20:22–23; 21:4,10–14.)

7. SOME EXAMPLES OF DIVINE PROTECTION:

Genesis 19:15–17	[Angels helped Lot and his family to escape the doomed city of Sodom]
Genesis 35:5	[God made the Canaanites afraid to pursue His people]
Genesis 45:5–7	[Jacob's brothers sold him as a slave into Egypt, but God preserved him and turned the situation to good]
Exodus 12:21–23	[The Angel of Death smote the Egyptians, but passed over the Hebrews' houses]
Exodus 14:9–10,19–20	[The pillar of fire moved between the Hebrews and the pursuing Egyptian army]
Joshua 3:10–17	[God held back the swollen, flooded Jordan River, so that the Hebrews could cross safely]
Joshua 10:11–14	[God sent hailstones to smite Joshua's enemies, as well as delaying the sun's setting for him]
1 Samuel 17:34–39	[God delivered David from a lion, a bear, and Goliath]
2 Kings 6:24; 7:5–7	[The Syrians besieged Samaria, but] the Lord made [them] to hear a noise of chariots ... and they ... fled
Daniel 6:16–22	[God protected Daniel in the lion's den]
Jonah 1:15,17; 2:10	The Lord prepared a great fish to swallow up Jonah [it kept him from drowning, and took him to his destination]

Matthew 2:13–16 [God warned Joseph in a dream to flee with Mary and baby Jesus into Egypt]

Special chapter about protection: Psalm 91—the "Protection Psalm" (See also Psalm 121; 124.)

SUPPLY

1. GOD CAN SUPPLY ALL OUR NEEDS:

A. He has promised to supply our needs:

Psalm 23:1	The Lord is my shepherd; I shall not want [lack]
Psalm 34:10	They that seek the Lord shall not [lack] any good thing
Psalm 37:25	I [have] not seen righteous forsaken ... begging bread
Matthew 6:33	Seek ye first the kingdom of God ... and all these things shall be added unto you
Matthew 7:7–11	Every one that asketh receiveth ... your Father [shall] give good things to them that ask him
Romans 8:32	He that spared not his own son ... shall he not also freely give us all things?
Philippians 4:19	God shall supply all your need according to his riches (See also Deuteronomy 2:7; Psalm 68:19; 81:10; Malachi 3:10; Matthew 6:8,25–34.)

B. God is the source of all supply:

1 Chronicles 29:14	All things come of thee, and of thine own have we given thee
Psalm 104:13–15	He causeth ... herb [to grow] for man: that he may bring forth good out of the earth
Psalm 145:15–16	Thou openest thine hand, and satisfiest the desire of every living thing
James 1:17	Every good gift ... is from above, and cometh from [God] (See also Psalm 65:9–13; Genesis 1:29; 9:3.)

C. He owns the entire world:

Exodus 19:5	All the earth is mine
Psalm 24:1	The earth is the Lord's, and the fullness thereof
Psalm 50:10–11	Every beast is mine ... and the cattle upon a thousand hills
Psalm 89:11	The earth is thine: the world and the fullness thereof

2. GOD CAN DO MIRACLES TO SUPPLY:

Numbers 11:21–23	[God promised meat for a month, Moses doubted it, so] the Lord said, "Is the Lord's hand waxed short?"
2 Kings 4:1–6	[The prophet's widow borrowed vessels and they miraculously filled with enough oil to pay her debts]

A. Food:

Exodus 16:12–15	[God miraculously supplied quail and manna in desert]
Numbers 11:18–20	[God sent a month's supply of quail] (See also 11:31–32.)
Psalm 78:23–29	He opened the doors of heaven, and rained down manna ... corn of heaven ... angel's food ... meat to the full (See also Psalm 105:40.)

Psalm 132:15	I will abundantly bless her provision: I will satisfy her poor with bread
1 Kings 17:4	I have commanded the ravens to feed thee there
1 Kings 17:16	The barrel of meal wasted not, neither did the cruse of oil fail [during the 3½-year famine]
1 Kings 19:5–8	An angel said unto [Elijah], "Arise and eat" … and behold, a cake baken on the coals, and a cruse of water
2 Kings 4:42–43	[Elisha fed 100, multiplying 20 loaves and some corn]
Mark 6:34–44	[Jesus fed 5,000 men, besides women and children, by multiplying five loaves and two fishes] (See also Matthew 14:21.)
Mark 8:1–9	[Jesus fed 4,000, multiplying seven loaves]
Revelation 12:6,14	[Church "fed, nourished" for 3½ years in the wilderness] (See also Psalm 23:5; Luke 5:4–7; John 21:5–6,11.)

B. Water:

Genesis 21:14–19	[Hagar dying of thirst, God showed her a well]
Exodus 17:1–6	[At Horeb, God brought water out of a rock]
Numbers 20:2,7–11	[At Meribah, God again brought water from a rock]
Judges 15:15–19	[God supplied water from a jawbone for Samson]
2 Kings 3:9,17,20	[God miraculously supplied water for an army] (See also Psalm 78:15–16; 105:41; Isaiah 41:17–18.)

C. God can even purify impure food and water:

Exodus 15:23–25	[Bitter waters of Marah miraculously made sweet]
2 Kings 2:19–22	[Undrinkable waters of Jericho healed]
2 Kings 4:38–41	[Poisonous gourd in the pottage rendered harmless] (See also Mark 16:18.)

D. Clothing and other necessities:

Deuteronomy 29:5	I have led you forty years … your clothes are not waxen old … thy shoe is not waxen old upon thy foot
Matthew 6:25–26,30	If God clothe the grass … shall He not … clothe you? (See also Genesis 3:21.)

3. SUPPLY DURING FAMINE:

A. Famines predicted in the last days:

Matthew 24:3,7	[In] the end of the world … there shall be famines … in diverse places
Mark 13:8	There shall be famines and troubles

B. God promises to feed us during famines:

Job 5:19–20	In famine he [God] shall redeem thee from death

Psalm 33:18–19	The eye of the Lord is upon them that fear him … to keep them alive in famine
Psalm 37:18–19	The Lord knoweth the days of the upright … in the days of famine they shall be satisfied
Proverbs 10:3	The Lord will not suffer [allow] … the righteous to famish
Ezekiel 36:29–30	I will increase [the corn], and lay no famine upon you. I will multiply the fruit of the tree, and … of the field

C. He sometimes warns His people so they can make preparations:

Genesis 41:25–36,47–49	[God showed Joseph and Pharaoh that a famine was coming and they prepared for it by storing away food]
Acts 11:27–30	[God warned that a dearth was coming, and believers sent relief money to their affected brethren]

(See also Amos 3:7.)

4. CONDITIONS TO GOD'S SUPPLY:

A. We must please God and be obedient:

Matthew 6:33	Seek first the kingdom of God … and all things shall be added unto you
2 Chronicles 1:7–12	[God gave King Solomon fabulous riches and wealth when he sought the good of the kingdom first]
Psalm 34:9–10	There is no want [lack] to them that fear him ... They that seek Lord shall not [lack] any good thing
Psalm 37:3	Do good … and verily thou shalt be fed
Psalm 37:18–19	The Lord knoweth … the upright … in the days of famine they shall be satisfied
Psalm 37:25	I have been young, and now am old; yet have I not seen the righteous forsaken … begging bread
Psalm 84:11	No good thing will he withhold from them that walk uprightly
Proverbs 13:25	Righteous eateth to satisfying … wicked shall [lack]
Isaiah 1:19	If ye be willing and obedient, ye shall eat the good of the land
1 John 3:22	Whatsoever we ask, we receive … because we keep his commandments, and do … things … pleasing in his sight

(See also Deuteronomy 11:10–15; 29:9; Psalm 111:5.)

B. Examples of obeying and doing our part first:

1 Kings 17:2–5	Get thee hence … and hide by the brook of Cherith … ravens feed thee there. So he went
1 Kings 17:9–10	Arise, get thee to Zarepath. So he arose and went
2 Kings 4:1–6	Go borrow … of all thy neighbours empty vessels, borrow not a few. So she went and [did]

Matthew 17:27	Go cast an hook, and take up the fish … thou shalt find a piece of money [in its mouth]
Luke 5:4–6	Launch out into the deep, and let down your nets
John 2:1–10	Fill the waterpots with water. And they filled them
John 11:39	Take [roll] ye away the stone
John 21:5–6	Cast the net on right side of the ship … they cast

C. Pray, believe God's Word, and depend on Him to supply:

Matthew 7:7	Ask, and it shall be given; knock, and it shall be opened
Matthew 21:22	All things, whatsoever ye shall ask in prayer, believing, ye shall receive
Hebrews 11:6	He is a rewarder of them that diligently seek him

(See also 2 Chronicles 26:5; Isaiah 45:11; Matthew 9:29.)

D. Remember to thank Him for supplying:

Psalm 68:19	Blessed be the Lord, who daily loadeth us with benefits
Psalm 116:12–14,17–18	What shall I render unto the Lord for all his benefits? I will offer to thee the sacrifice of thanksgiving

5. REASONS WHY WE SOMETIMES LACK:

A. Because of sin:

Jeremiah 5:25	Your sins have withholden good things from you

(See also Psalm 81:15–16; James 4:3.)

B. Lack of faith or failure to ask:

James 1:6–7	[Wavering and not asking in faith]
James 4:2	Ye have not, because ye ask not

C. Laziness:

2 Thessalonians 3:10	If any would not work, neither should he eat
Proverbs 13:4	The soul of the sluggard desireth, and hath nothing
Proverbs 20:4	Sluggard will not plow … therefore shall have nothing
Proverbs 21:25	The desire of the slothful killeth him; for his hands refuse to labour (See also Proverbs 23:21.)

D. To keep us dependent upon God and His supply:

Deuteronomy 31:20	When they … have eaten and filled themselves, and waxen fat; then will they turn to other gods
Proverbs 30:8–9	Give me [not] riches … lest I be full and deny Thee

(See also 1 Timothy 6:10,17; Revelation 3:17–19.)

E. To show us that it's time for change:

1 Kings 17:7–9	[When the brook dried, it was time for Elijah to move]

(See also Genesis 26:1–3; Ruth 1:1–6; 2 Kings 8:1–2.)

6. GOD LOVES YOU AND WANTS TO SUPPLY:

A. He knows what you need and is looking after you:

Matthew 6:8	Your Father knoweth what things ye have need of, before ye ask him
Matthew 6:25,31–32	Take no thought for your life, what ye shall eat, or drink … [God] knoweth that ye need all these things

B. If God provides for the unbelievers …

(See Matthew 5:45; Acts 14:15–17.)

C. ... if He even provides the needs of animals …

(See Genesis 1:30; 6:14–22; Psalm 104:21,26–28; 147:8–9.)

D. ... won't He much more care for you?

(See Matthew 6:26,30; Psalm 34:10; 145:15–16; 2 Corinthians 9:8.)

7. WE SHOULD DO OUR PART:

A. Our responsibility to provide:

1 Timothy 5:8	If any provide not for ... those of his own house, he hath denied the faith, and is worse than an infidel

B. Working for our needs:

Acts 20:35	How that labouring ye ought to support the weak
Ephesians 4:28	Let him labour, working with his hands thing which is good
1 Thessalonians 4:11–12	Work with your own hands … that ye may lack nothing
2 Thessalonians 3:10–12	Some work not at all … if any would not work, neither should he eat
Titus 3:14	Let ours learn to maintain good works [profess honest trades] for necessary uses (See also Genesis 41:39–44; Daniel 2:48–49; 6:1–3; 8:27.)

C. God blesses diligent, hard work:

Genesis 31:38–40	[Jacob's example of diligent shepherding]
Genesis 39:1–6	[God blessed Joseph's hard work] (See also 39:20–23.)
Proverbs 10:4	The hand of the diligent maketh rich (See also Proverbs 13:4; 22:29; 21:25; Ecclesiastes 5:18.)
Proverbs 28:19	He that tilleth his land shall have plenty of bread, but he that followeth vain persons … poverty
Matthew 25:14–30	[The reward of the diligent servants who increased their talents]

8. WHEN GOD USES OTHERS TO SUPPLY HIS WORKERS' NEEDS:

A. Well-off supporters often helped God's messengers:

Genesis 47:1–6 [Pharaoh gave the best land in Egypt, Goshen, to Joseph's father and brothers]

1 Kings 18:3,13 [Governor Obadiah risked his life to save and feed 100 of God's prophets]

2 Kings 4:8–11 [Rich woman of Shunem supplied food and lodging for Elisha and his servant]

Nehemiah 2:7–8 [King Artaxerxes gave Nehemiah permission to take as much timber as he needed from the king's forest]

Jeremiah 37:15–21 [King Zedekiah defied Jeremiah's enemies and commanded Jeremiah be given bread continually]

Daniel 2:48–49 [King Nebuchadnezzar gives Daniel power and "many great gifts," and gave his friends high positions]

Luke 8:1–3 [Joanna and other wealthy women helped support Jesus]
(See also Romans 16:23; Philemon 1:1–2,7,22.)

B. Don't abuse others' generosity:

1 Corinthians 7:31 They that use this world, as not abusing it

C. God's workers to be supported by those to whom they minister:

2 Kings 4:42 A man … brought [Elisha] bread of the firstfruits, twenty loaves and corn [to feed his 100 disciples]

Matthew 10:9-10 Provide neither gold, nor silver in your purses … for the workman is worthy of his meat

Luke 22:35 When I sent you without purse … lacked ye any thing? And they said, "Nothing."

1 Corinthians 9:7-14 The Lord ordained that they which preach the gospel should live of the gospel

1 Timothy 5:18 Shalt not muzzle ox that treadeth the corn. The labourer is worthy of his hire (See also Deuteronomy 25:4; Luke 10:7.)
(See also Acts 28:7–10.)

D. Staying as a guest at someone's house:

Matthew 10:11 In whatsoever city or town ye shall enter, enquire who is worthy; and there abide

Luke 10:7–8 In the same house remain, eating [what] they give
(See also 1 Kings 17:8–16,24; Acts 10:5–6; 16:14–15; 17:5,7; 18:2–4; Romans 16:23; Philemon 1:22.)

E. But don't overstay your welcome:

Proverbs 25:17 Withdraw thy foot from thy neighbour's house; lest he be weary of thee; and so hate thee

F. Accepting invitations to a meal:

Matthew 9:9–10	[Jesus and disciples ate with Matthew] (See also Luke 5:29.)
Luke 7:36	One of the Pharisees desired that he would eat with him
Luke 19:1–6	[Jesus invited himself to eat at Zacchaeus' house]
1 Corinthians 10:27	If any [unbelievers] bid you to a feast, and ye be disposed to go; whatsoever is set before you, eat

G. Refusing invitations to a meal:

1 Kings 13:7–9,15–17	[Young prophet ordered by God to refuse invitations] (See also 13:18–24.)
Proverbs 15:17	Better is a dinner of herbs where love is, than [steak] and hatred therewith (See also Daniel 1:5,8,12–16.)
Proverbs 23:6–8	Eat not the bread of him that hath an evil eye

H. Share amongst yourselves what God has already given you:

Acts 2:44–45	[They] parted them to all men, as every man had need
Acts 4:32	They had all things common
Acts 4:35	Distribution was made unto every man according as he had need
Acts 11:29	Every man according to his ability [sent] relief
2 Corinthians 8:12–15	That … your abundance may be a supply for their want [lack] that there may be equality … He that gathered much had nothing over; and he that gathered little had no lack (See also Exodus 16:18.)

9. GIVING TO GOD'S WORK:

1 Samuel 25:2–8	[David sent men to ask Nabal, a great and rich—but wicked—man, to donate food to him and his men]
1 Samuel 27:5,7	[David asked for place to stay for sixteen months]
Mark 11:1–7	[Jesus' disciples requested a donkey for Him to ride]
Mark 14:12–16	[Jesus' disciples asked for the use of an upper room, already furnished and prepared]
Luke 5:1–3	[Jesus asked for the use of a boat to preach from]
John 4:6–7	[Jesus asked for a drink of water]

10. GOD PROMISES TO PROSPER OUR WORK AND BUSINESSES:

A. Financially:

Deuteronomy 28:1–13	[Mighty promises of prosperity to the faithful]
Psalm 112:1,3	Blessed is the man … that delighteth greatly in His commandments … wealth shall be in his house
Proverbs 10:22	Blessing of the Lord maketh rich, he addeth no sorrow

B. Other ways God prospers His people:

(See Genesis 39:2; Leviticus 26:3–13; Deuteronomy 29:9; 30:9; 2 Chronicles 26:5; Psalm 107:35–38; 127:3–5; Isaiah 3:10; Ezekiel 34:26; Acts 14:17.)

11. GOD SUPPLIES OUR NEEDS, NOT ALWAYS OUR WANTS:

A. Be content and do not desire more than you need:

Psalm 37:16	A little that a righteous man hath is better than the riches of many wicked
Proverbs 15:16	Better is little with the fear of the Lord than great treasure and trouble therewith
Proverbs 30:8	Give me neither poverty nor riches; feed me with food convenient for me
Luke 12:15	Beware of covetousness, for a man's life consisteth not in abundance of things which he possesseth
2 Corinthians 6:10	As poor … having nothing, and yet possessing all things
Philippians 4:11	I have learned, in whatever state I am … to be content
1 Timothy 6:6-8	Godliness with contentment is great gain … having food and raiment let us be therewith content
Hebrews 13:5	Let your [life] be without covetousness; and be content with such things as ye have

(See also Psalm 62:10; 119:36; Proverbs 17:1; 23:5.)

B. Dangers of discontent and murmuring:

Exodus 16:3	[Longing for fleshpots of Egypt, and complaining that God will let them die of hunger]
Numbers 21:5–6	[The people complained against the manna and were attacked by fiery serpents]
1 Samuel 15:3,9,22–23	[Saul disobeyed God's orders to utterly destroy, saving the best of the goods. God rejected Saul as king]
Psalm 73:3–20	[Warning not to envy the prosperity of worldly wicked]
Psalm 78:15–21	[Israelites miraculously received water, then doubtingly murmured for meat. God judged them]

TRIALS, TEMPTATIONS, AND TRIBULATIONS

1. TRIALS AND TESTS ARE TO BE EXPECTED:

Psalm 34:19	Many are the afflictions of the righteous: but the Lord delivereth him out of them all
Acts 14:22	We must through much tribulation enter the kingdom
1 Corinthians 10:13	No temptation taken you but such as is common to man
1 Thessalonians 3:3	No man should be moved by these afflictions: for yourselves know that we are appointed thereunto
Hebrews 12:7	What son is he whom the father chasteneth not?
1 Peter 4:12	Beloved, think it not strange concerning the fiery trial which is to try [test] you
1 Peter 4:17	Judgement must begin at the house of God … at us
1 Peter 5:9	Knowing that the same afflictions are accomplished in your brethren
	(See also Psalm 26:2; 139:23–24.)

2. TRIALS OFTEN RESULT WHEN THINGS DON'T GO OUR WAY:

A. Often God will grant our heart's desire:

Psalm 37:4	Delight thyself in the Lord; and he shall give thee the desires of thine heart
Psalm 84:11	No good thing will he withhold from them [the upright]
Psalm 145:19	He will fulfill the desire of them that fear him
Proverbs 10:24	The desire of the righteous shall be granted
	(See also Psalm 21:2; 145:16.)

B. But sometimes He withholds it because it's not His time:

Ecclesiastes 3:1–8	There is … a time to every purpose under the heaven
	(See also Psalm 37:34; Ecclesiastes 8:5–6.)

C. Or because it would choke out our fruitfulness:

Mark 4:7,19	The lusts of other things entering in, choke the word, and it becometh unfruitful (See also Matthew 13:22; Luke 8:14.)

D. Or seriously stumble or offend others:

1 Thessalonians 5:22	Abstain [even] from all appearance of evil
Romans 14:14–16,21	Destroy not him with thy meat, for whom Christ died
	(See also 1 Corinthians 8:8–13.)

E. Or bring reproach on God's work or ministry:

2 Corinthians 6:3	Giving no offence … that the ministry be not blamed
	(See also 2 Peter 2:2.)

F. Or because of unrepented sin in our heart:

Jeremiah 5:25	Your iniquities have turned away these things, and your sins have withholden good things from you (See also Psalm 66:18; Isaiah 59:1–2.)

G. Or because we're asking with the wrong motives:

James 4:2–3	Ye ask and receive not, because ye ask amiss, that ye may consume it upon your lusts

H. It's not always good to get the desire of our heart:

Psalm 73:3,7,16–22	I was envious at … prosperity … they have more than heart could wish … then understood I their end
1 Timothy 6:9–10	They that will [desire to] be rich fall into temptation … and many hurtful lusts … erred from the faith

I. We may miss something better God had planned for us:

Psalm 81:10–13,16	He would have fed them the finest of wheat … honey

J. Nonetheless, we have trials when we can't have something:

1 Samuel 1:6–8,10	The Lord had shut up her womb … therefore she wept … heart grieved … bitterness of soul
Proverbs 13:12	Hope deferred maketh the heart sick (See also 2 Samuel 13:1–2.)

K. Warning against stubbornly insisting on getting our way:

Psalm 78:27–31	He gave them their own desire … their lust. But … the wrath of God came (See also Psalm 81:12.)
Psalm 106:14–15	He gave them their request; but sent leanness into their soul (See also Numbers 11:4–34.) (See also 1 Samuel 8:4–22; 12:1,13,16–19, on asking for a king.)

L. What we give up for God, He will often return:

Matthew 19:29	Every one that hath forsaken … father, or mother, or wife, or children … shall receive an hundredfold
Hebrews 6:15	After he patiently endured, he obtained the promise (See also Ecclesiastes 11:1; Hebrews 10:36.)

3. WHY GOD ALLOWS TRIALS AND TESTS:

A. To draw us closer to Him:

Psalm 107:12–13	He brought down their heart with labour … then they cried unto the Lord in their trouble

B. To see if we will remain true:

Exodus 20:20	God is come to prove [test] you

Deuteronomy 8:2	The Lord … [tested you] to know what was in thine heart, whether thou wouldest keep his commandments
Deuteronomy 13:3–4	God … proveth you, to know whether ye love the Lord
Judges 2:21–22	[God kept adversaries in the land to] prove Israel, whether they keep the way of the Lord, or not
Jeremiah 12:3	Thou knowest me … Thou hast … tried my heart
Jeremiah 17:10	I the Lord search the heart … to give every man according to his ways, and … the fruit of his doings
John 6:5–6	This He said to prove [test] him, for he himself knew

C. To draw us closer to His Word:

Psalm 94:12	Blessed is the man whom Thou chastenest, O Lord, and teachest him out of Thy law
Psalm 119:71	It is good for me that I have been afflicted; that I might learn Thy statutes

D. To prune away dead wood so we can be more fruitful:

John 15:2	Every branch that beareth fruit, he purgeth [prunes], that it may bring forth more fruit

E. To teach obedience:

Hebrews 5:8	Though he were a son, yet learned he obedience by the things which he suffered (See also Hebrews 2:10.)
1 Peter 4:1–2	He that … suffered in the flesh hath ceased from sin

F. To make you a better and more useful vessel:

Jeremiah 18:4	The vessel that he [the potter] made of clay was marred … so he made it again another vessel
1 Corinthians 5:7	Purge out the old leaven, that ye may be a new lump
2 Timothy 2:21	[If purged] … he shall be a vessel … meet for the master's use, and prepared unto every good work

G. To purify us, as precious metal is refined:

Malachi 3:3	He shall sit as a refiner and purifier of silver
Zechariah 13:9	I will bring [them] through the fire, and refine them
Psalm 66:10	Thou, O God, hast … tried us, as silver is tried
Job 23:10	When he hath tried me, I shall come forth as gold
Proverbs 17:3	The fining pot is for silver, and the furnace for gold: but the Lord trieth the hearts
Isaiah 48:10	I have refined thee … in the furnace of affliction
Daniel 11:35	[They] shall fall, to try them … and to make them white
1 Peter 1:7	The trial of your faith [is] much more precious than gold … though it be tried with fire

(See also Isaiah 1:25.)

H. To prepare us for future blessings and ministries:

Deuteronomy 8:16	That he might humble thee … and prove thee, to do thee good at thy latter end
Psalm 105:17–22	[Joseph imprisoned, abased and tested, then exalted]
Proverbs 18:12	Before honour is humility

I. To teach us patience:

Romans 5:3	Tribulation worketh [teaches us] patience
James 1:3–4	The trying of your faith worketh patience

J. To make us wiser through sorrow:

Ecclesiastes 7:3–4	Sorrow is better than laughter: for by … sadness … the heart is made better

K. To teach us compassion toward others:

Hebrews 4:15	Be touched with the feeling of [others'] infirmities
2 Corinthians 1:4	That we may be able to comfort them … in trouble

4. TRIALS OVER SUFFERING PERSONAL LOSS:

A. Be willing to suffer loss of position or possessions:

Job 1:21	The Lord gave, and the Lord hath taken away; blessed be the name of the Lord
Acts 20:23–24	Bonds and afflictions … none of these things move me, neither count I [even] my life dear
Philippians 3:8	I have suffered the loss of all things, and do count them but dung, that I may win Christ
Hebrews 10:34	Ye … took joyfully the spoiling of your goods

B. Lay aside weights to run the race:

Hebrews 12:1	Let us lay aside every weight … and let us run the race
1 Corinthians 9:24	So run, that ye may obtain [the prize]
Philippians 3:13–14	Forgetting those things which are behind … I press toward the mark of the prize of the high calling

C. The futility of trying to hang onto things:

Proverbs 23:5	Wilt thou set thine eyes upon that which is not? For riches certainly … fly away
Luke 12:15	A man's life consisteth not in … things he possesseth (See also Ecclesiastes 5:13–15; 1 Timothy 6:7.)

D. Paul's trials in missing loved ones:

(See Philippians 1:7–8; 1 Thessalonians 2:17–18; 1 Thessalonians 3:10; 2 Timothy 1:3–4.)

E. God wants you to love Him first of all:

Psalm 73:25	Whom have I in heaven but thee? And there is none upon earth that I desire beside thee
Psalm 142:4–5	Refuge failed me; no man cared … thou art my refuge and my portion in the land of the living
Isaiah 54:1,5–6	Sing … for thy maker is thine husband … the Lord hath called thee as a woman forsaken
John 16:32	Ye … shall leave me alone: and yet I am not alone, because the father is with me

5. SOME BIBLE EXAMPLES OF TRIALS AND TESTS:

Genesis 26:34–35	[Esau disobeyed and married pagans] which were a grief of mind to Isaac and Rebekah (Also Genesis 27:46; 28:8.)
Exodus 4:10–13	[Moses felt incapable to speak to the Hebrew nation]
Numbers 11:10–12,14	[Moses said:] I am not able to bear all this people alone, because it is too heavy for me
Judges 6:14–15	[Gideon felt incapable to be the deliverer of Israel]
Ruth 1:12–13	[Naomi, unable to help her daughters-in-law, said:] It grieveth me much for your sakes
1 Samuel 30:1–6	[David's men grieved at the loss of wives and families]
1 Kings 19:1–4,10	[Elijah, persecuted and feeling all alone, prayed to die]
Psalm 6:6–8	[David's tears and grief because his enemies triumphed]
Psalm 38:4–9	[David's trials about an unhealed affliction]
Psalm 102:1–8	[David's deep trial because of his enemies' reproach] (See also Psalm 69:16–20.)
Isaiah 53:3–9	[Jesus' sorrows and trials]
Jeremiah 15:10	[Jeremiah's depths of despair over being rejected, despised, and mocked] (See also Jeremiah 20:7–10,14,18.)
Jonah 3:4–5,10; 4:1–9	[When things didn't work as he'd hoped, Jonah was so angry and displeased, he wished to die]
Luke 10:40	[Martha, working alone, felt unfairly over-burdened]
John 21:17	Peter grieved [because Jesus seemed to be bringing his love and loyalty into question]
2 Corinthians 1:8	[Paul's] trouble … we were pressed above strength, so we despaired even of life (See also 2 Corinthians 4:8; 7:5.)

6. WHY IT'S WORTH IT TO ENDURE TESTS AND TEMPTATIONS:

A. For the sake of lost souls:

Isaiah 53:10–12	[God "put Jesus to grief" to save our souls]
2 Timothy 2:10	I endure all things for the elect's sakes, that they may also obtain … salvation

B. Because you'll be spiritually stronger as a result:

2 Corinthians 4:16	We faint not; [for] though our outward man perish, yet the inward man is renewed day by day
2 Corinthians 12:9–10	My [Jesus'] strength is made perfect in weakness … that the power of Christ may rest upon me [Paul]

C. Because God will reward you after testing you:

Psalm 66:12	Thou hast caused [us to go] through fire and water: but thou broughtest us out into a wealthy place
Hebrews 12:11	No chastening for the present seemeth to be joyous, but grievous: nevertheless afterward … [good] fruit
James 5:11	Endure. Ye have heard of … Job, and have seen the end … the Lord is of tender mercy (See also Job 42:10–17.)

(See also Psalm 118:5; Lamentations 3:32.)

D. Heavenly rewards:

Romans 8:18	The sufferings of this present time are not worthy to be compared with the glory which shall be … in us
2 Corinthians 4:17	Our light affliction, which is but for a moment, worketh for us [an] eternal weight of glory
James 1:12	Blessed is the man that endureth temptation … he shall receive the crown of life
1 Peter 4:13	Ye are partakers of Christ's sufferings … when his glory shall be revealed, ye may be glad also

(See also 1 John 2:17; Revelation 21:7.)

7. BE THANKFUL FOR YOUR TRIALS AND TEMPTATIONS:

A. God uses your trials and temptations for good:

Romans 8:28	All things work together for good to … the called
James 1:2–4	Count it joy when ye fall into diverse temptations
1 Peter 1:6	Rejoice, though now for a season ye are in heaviness

B. Chastenings prove God loves you and that you're His child:

Deuteronomy 8:5	As a man chasteneth his son, so the Lord chasteneth
Proverbs 3:11–12	My son, despise not the chastening of the Lord
Hebrews 12:5–12	Whom the Lord loveth he chasteneth … every son
Revelation 3:19	As many as I love, I rebuke and chasten

(See also Job 5:17; Psalm 11:5; 1 Corinthians 11:32.)

C. Remember that sorrow will give way to joy:

Psalm 30:5	Weeping may endure for a night, but joy cometh in the morning
Matthew 5:4	Blessed are they that mourn: for they shall be comforted

1 Peter 5:10	God … after that ye have suffered a while, make you perfect, stablish, strengthen, settle you

8. HELPING OTHERS WHO ARE GOING THROUGH TRIALS:

A. How to help them:

Job 6:14	To him that is afflicted pity should be showed
Job 19:21	Have pity upon me … the hand of God hath touched me
Romans 15:1–2	We … ought to bear the infirmities of the weak
1 Corinthians 12:25–26	Whether one member suffer, all … suffer with it
Galatians 6:2	Bear ye one another's burdens
Hebrews 13:3	Remember them … which suffer, as being yourselves also in the body

B. Encourage and strengthen them:

Job 16:4–5	I would strengthen you with my mouth ... assuage grief
Proverbs 12:25	Heaviness in the heart of man maketh it stoop: but a good word maketh it glad
Isaiah 50:4	Speak a word in season to him that is weary

C. Admonish them with hearty counsel:

Proverbs 27:9	Ointment and perfume rejoice the heart: so doth sweetness of a man's friend by hearty counsel
Colossians 3:16	Let the Word of Christ dwell in you … teaching and admonishing one another … singing

9. WHERE TEMPTATIONS COME FROM:

A. From our own lusts:

James 1:13–14	Every man is tempted, when he is drawn away of own lust, and enticed
1 John 2:15–16	The lust of the flesh and … eyes … is of the world

B. They are also instigated by the Devil:

Genesis 3:1–6,13	[Eve:] The serpent beguiled me, and I did eat
1 Chronicles 21:1,7–8	Satan … provoked David to [sin and do foolishly]
Matthew 4:1–7	[Jesus was tempted by the Devil, "the tempter"]
Luke 22:31	Simon, Satan hath desired to ... sift you as wheat

(See also 2 Corinthians 11:3; 1 Thessalonians 3:5.)

10. AVOIDING TEMPTATION:

Matthew 6:13	[Pray:] Lead us not into temptation

A. Avoid the pathway to temptation:

Proverbs 4:14–15	Enter not into the path of the wicked, and go not ... Avoid it, pass not by it, turn from it, and pass away

Matthew 7:13–14	Enter ye in at the strait [narrow] gate: for wide is the gate, and broad is the way … to destruction
2 Timothy 2:22	Flee also youthful lusts

B. Beware of those who would entice you:

Psalm 1:1–2	[Walk] not in the counsel of the ungodly
Proverbs 1:10	If sinners entice thee, consent thou not
Proverbs 16:29	A violent man enticeth his neighbour, and leadeth him into the way that is not good
2 Peter 3:17	Beware lest ye also being led away with the error of the wicked, fall from your steadfastness (See also Proverbs 22:24–25; 2 Peter 2:18–19.)

C. Know your weaknesses, and be on guard against them:

Romans 13:14	Make not provision [forethought, plans] for the flesh, to fulfil the lusts thereof
Galatians 6:1	Considering thyself, lest thou also be temped

D. Warning about evil, beguiling influences:

Deuteronomy 7:25–26	[Do not] bring an abomination into thine house, lest thou be a cursed thing like it: utterly detest it
Psalm 101:3	I will set no wicked thing before mine eyes
Psalm 106:35–36	They were mingled among the heathen, and learned their works. Their idols … were a snare unto them
2 Corinthians 11:3	Lest … as the serpent beguiled Eve though his subtlety, so your mind should be corrupted
2 Peter 2:7–8	Lot … in seeing and hearing [the wickedness of Sodom], vexed his righteous soul … with their unlawful deeds

11. HOW TO RESIST AND OVERCOME TEMPTATION:

A. Keep your eyes on Jesus:

Hebrews 11:27	He [Moses] endured, as seeing him who is invisible
Hebrews 12:2–3	Looking unto Jesus … consider him … lest ye … faint (See also Proverbs 4:25; Colossians 3:2–3.)

B. Pray and ask God to help you:

Psalm 17:5	Hold up my going in thy paths … that my footsteps slip not
Psalm 56:13	Thou hast delivered my soul from death: wilt not thou deliver my feet from falling
Matthew 6:13	Lead us not into temptation … deliver us from evil
Matthew 18:19–20	[Have others pray with you in special times of temptation] (See also James 5:16.)
Matthew 26:41	Watch and pray, that ye enter not into temptation (See also Luke 21:36.)

C. Resist the Devil:

Ephesians 4:27	Neither give place to the devil
James 4:7	Resist the devil, and he will flee from you

D. Cling to the Word:

Psalm 119:80	Let my heart be sound in thy statutes; that I be not ashamed
John 15:3	Now ye are clean through the word
2 Peter 1:4	Precious promises: that by these ye might [escape] the corruption that is in the world through lust
Revelation 3:10	Because thou hast kept the word … I will keep thee

E. Be willing to give up your own desires out of love for Jesus:

Galatians 5:16	Walk in the Spirit, and ye shall not fulfil the lust of the flesh
Galatians 5:24	They that are Christ's have crucified the flesh with the affections and lusts
Ephesians 4:20–23	Put off … the old man … the deceitful lusts

(See also Romans 6:16; Philippians 3:8.)

F. Exercise willpower and determine not to yield to temptation:

Romans 6:13	Neither yield ye your members … unto sin
1 Corinthians 9:27	I keep under my body, and bring it into subjection
1 Corinthians 16:13	Watch ye, stand fast in the faith, quit you [behave] like men, be strong
2 Timothy 2:3	Endure hardness, as a good soldier of Jesus Christ
2 Timothy 2:22	Flee youthful lusts: but follow righteousness
1 Peter 1:14	As obedient children, not [conforming] to former lusts
1 Peter 2:11	Abstain from fleshly lusts, which war against the soul

(See also 1 Corinthians 10:5–6.)

G. Fear God and be afraid to disobey Him:

1 Samuel 12:24	Fear the Lord, and serve him in truth with all your heart
Proverbs 14:27	The fear of the Lord is a fountain of life, to depart from the snares of death
Proverbs 16:6	By the fear of the Lord men depart from evil
Proverbs 23:17	Let not thine heart envy sinners: but be thou in the fear of the Lord all the day long

H. Be serious and sober about being a believer:

1 Thessalonians 5:8	Let us … be sober, putting on the [armour of God]
Titus 2:12	Denying … worldly lusts, we should live soberly … in this present world
1 Peter 1:13	Gird up … your mind, be sober, and hope to the end
1 Peter 4:7	The end … is at hand: be ye therefore sober

1 Peter 5:8	Be sober, be vigilant; because your adversary the devil ... walketh about, seeking whom he may devour

I. Keep your heart and mind on the final goal:

Hebrews 11:25–26	Choosing rather to suffer affliction … than to enjoy the pleasures of sin … for he had respect to the reward
Hebrews 12:2	[Jesus,] for the joy set before him, endured the cross

12. GOD WILL DELIVER YOU:

A. God's promises to help you:

1 Corinthians 10:13	God … will not suffer you to be tempted above that ye are able; but will … also make a way to escape
1 Corinthians 15:57	Thanks be to God, which giveth us the victory through our Lord Jesus Christ
Hebrews 2:18	He is able to succour them that are tempted
2 Peter 2:9	Lord knoweth how to deliver godly out of temptations

B. Jesus has compassion on us, knowing what it's like:

Hebrews 4:15	[Jesus] was in all points tempted like as we are

C. He is with us when we are tempted:

Isaiah 43:1–2	Fear not: I have called thee by name; thou art mine. When thou passest through the waters, I will be with thee
1 Peter 4:19	Let them that suffer … commit the keeping of their souls to him … as unto a faithful Creator

(See also Deuteronomy 4:30–31.)

13. HOW RIGHTEOUS MEN FELL THROUGH TEMPTATION:

A. Example of Balaam the prophet:

(See Numbers 22:1–21; 24:2,10–11,15,19; 25:1–3; 31:16; Joshua 13:22; 2 Peter 2:15; Jude 1:11; Revelation 2:14.)

B. The fall of King Solomon:

2 Samuel 12:24	The Lord loved him
1 Kings 11:1–11	King Solomon loved many strange women … his wives turned away his heart after other gods ... The Lord was angry with Solomon [and said], I will rend the kingdom from thee, and give it to thy servant
Nehemiah 13:26	Solomon … was beloved of his God … nevertheless even him did outlandish women cause to sin

C. Other examples of people falling through temptation:

Genesis 3:1–6	[Eve] saw the tree was good for food ... pleasant to the eyes, and to be desired to make one wise ... did eat
Genesis 25:29–34	[Esau sold his birthright to Jacob for some pottage]
Joshua 7:1,20–21	[Achan coveted] a godly Babylonish garment ... silver and a wedge of gold
2 Kings 5:20–27	[Gehazi coveted Namaan's goods; was struck leprous]

14. EXAMPLES OF RESISTING TEMPTATION:

Genesis 14:21–23	[Abraham refused rewards from the king of Sodom]
2 Kings 5:15–16	[Naaman urged Elisha to take gifts; Elisha refused]
Job 2:9–10	[Job refused to sin with his lips and curse God]
Jeremiah 35:5–6	[The Rechabites obediently refused to drink wine]
Daniel 1:8	[Daniel refused to defile himself eating unclean food]
Acts 8:18–20	[Peter refused Simon the sorcerer's money]

SUFFERING

1. WHO CAUSES SUFFERING?—GOD OR THE DEVIL?

A. The Devil causes much of humanity's suffering:

2 Thessalonians 2:9–12	Him, whose coming is after the working of Satan with all power and signs and lying wonders … that they all might be damned
1 Peter 5:8–9	Be sober, be vigilant; because your adversary the devil, as a roaring lion, walketh about, seeking whom he may devour: Whom resist stedfast in the faith, knowing that the same afflictions are accomplished in your brethren that are in the world.
Revelation 12:12	Woe to the inhabiters of the earth and of the sea! for the devil is come down unto you, having great wrath

(See also Matthew 15:22; Luke 8:29; Acts 10:38; 2 Timothy 2:26.)

B. But it is God who allows the Devil to bring suffering:

Job 1:8–19	[God allowed Satan to bring Job to ruin with fire, raiding bandits, and a violent storm]
Job 2:3–7	[God allowed the Devil to afflict Job with boils]

(See also 1 Corinthians 5:5; 1 Timothy 1:20.)

C. God is ultimately responsible for allowing suffering:

Exodus 4:11	Who maketh the dumb, or deaf, or blind? Have not I?
1 Samuel 2:6–7	The Lord killeth, maketh alive, maketh poor … rich
Isaiah 45:7	I make peace, and create evil; I the Lord do all these
Amos 3:6	Shall there be evil in a city, and the Lord hath not done it?

(See also Deuteronomy 32:39; 2 Chronicles 15:2,5–6; Job 12:14–25; Psalm 66:10–12; Micah 1:12.)

2. WHY DOES GOD ALLOW THE RIGHTEOUS TO SUFFER?

A. He has a loving reason for everything He does:

Genesis 45:4–8	Be not grieved … that ye sold me [as a slave]: for God did send me before you to preserve life
Genesis 50:20	Ye thought evil against me; but God meant it unto good
Psalm 119:71	It is good for me that I have been afflicted; that I might learn thy statutes
Jeremiah 37:15–16; 38:28	[Jeremiah spent a long time in prison, but was safe there when Jerusalem was destroyed] (See also Jeremiah 39:11–14.)
Jonah 2:1–7	[Jonah suffered in the fish's belly but it saved him from drowning and took him to land] (See also Jonah 1:15,17; 2:10.)
Romans 8:28	All things work together for good to … the called

B. Suffering is often God's loving chastisement:

Proverbs 3:11–12	Whom the Lord loveth he correcteth
Hebrews 12:5–12	Whom the Lord loveth he chasteneth
Revelation 3:19	As many as I love, I rebuke and chasten
	(See also Deuteronomy 8:5; Job 5:17; 1 Corinthians 11:32.)

C. God's chastisements are righteous:

Nehemiah 9:33	Thou art just in all that is brought upon us
Psalm 119:75	I know that thy judgements are right, and that thou in faithfulness hast afflicted me
Psalm 19:9	The judgements of the Lord are true and righteous
Proverbs 26:2	The curse causeless shall not come
Jeremiah 17:10	I the Lord search the heart … to give every man … according to the fruit of his doings
	(See also Ezekiel 14:22–23; Hebrews 12:11.)

D. Our suffering is less than we deserve:

Ezra 9:13	God hast punished us less than our iniquities deserve
Psalm 78:38–39	Full of compassion … many a time turned he his anger
Psalm 103:10,14	He hath not dealt with us after our sins

E. Continue to trust Him, even though you don't understand:

Proverbs 3:5	Trust in Lord … lean not unto thine own understanding
Isaiah 55:8–9	Neither are your ways my ways, saith the Lord

3. SOME SPECIFIC REASONS THAT GOD ALLOWS SUFFERING:

A. Suffering has been a fact of life since the fall of man:

Genesis 3:16–19	[Suffering brought into the world by the fall of man]
Job 5:6–7	Man is born unto trouble, as the sparks fly upward
	(See also Job 14:1; Psalm 90:10.)

B. We often bring on suffering by our sins:

Genesis 42:21	We are guilty … therefore is distress come upon us
Job 4:8	They that plow iniquity and sow wickedness reap the same
Psalm 31:9–10	I am in trouble … grief … because of mine iniquity
Psalm 38:1–8	There is no soundness in my flesh … because of my sin
Psalm 107:17	Fools … because of their iniquities, are afflicted
Isaiah 66:4	[Ignoring God and doing evil brings on mental anguish, fears and delusions]
Jeremiah 5:25	Your sins have withholden good things from you
	(See also Jeremiah 30:15; Lamentations 1:20.)

C. We sometimes suffer due to disregarding God's Word:

Deuteronomy 11:28	A curse, if ye will not obey the commandments
Psalm 78:32–33	They believed not … their years he consumed in trouble
Psalm 89:30–32	If [they] forsake my law … visit transgression with rod

(See also Psalm 107:11–12.)

4. SUFFERING BECAUSE OF OBEDIENCE AND RIGHTEOUSNESS:

A. Sufferings and privations while serving God:

Acts 20:19	Serving the Lord with many tears and temptations
1 Corinthians 4:11	We hunger, thirst, are naked, buffeted
2 Corinthians 1:8	[Paul's] trouble … pressed out of measure, above strength, despaired even of life
2 Corinthians 11:23–30	[Paul's many sufferings and troubles]
Philippians 2:27,30	Sick nigh unto death, to supply your lack of service

(See also 2 Corinthians 6:4–10.)

B. Suffering caused by persecution:

Philippians 1:29	For unto you it is given … not only to believe on him, but also to suffer for his sake
2 Timothy 3:12	All that live godly in Jesus shall suffer persecution
2 Timothy 1:8	Be not ashamed, but partaker of afflictions of gospel
Hebrews 11:25	Choosing to suffer affliction with the people of God
Hebrews 11:35–38	[Saints tortured, cruelly mocked, scourged, imprisoned, slain, destitute, afflicted, tormented]

(See also Romans 8:35–37; 1 Peter 2:19–21; 3:16–17; Revelation 2:10.)

5. THE BENEFITS AND GOOD FRUITS OF SUFFERING:

A. Suffering causes us to depend on God's Word:

Deuteronomy 8:2–3	That he might make thee know that man doth not live by bread only, but by [the] word
Psalm 94:12	Blessed is the man whom thou chastenest, O Lord, and teachest him out of thy law
Psalm 119:71	I have been afflicted; that I might learn thy statutes

B. Suffering refines and purifies:

Job 23:10	When he hath tired me, I shall come forth as gold
Psalm 66:10	Thou, O God, hast proved us … tried us, as silver
Isaiah 48:10	I have refined thee … in the furnace of affliction
Zechariah 13:9	And I will … refine them as silver is refined
Hebrews 12:9–11	Chastened … that we be partakers of his holiness

(See also Proverbs 17:3; Isaiah 1:25.)

C. It teaches us obedience:

Psalm 119:67	Before I was afflicted I went astray: but now have I kept thy word
Hebrews 5:8	Yet learned he obedience by things which he suffered
	(See also 2 Corinthians 7:10–11)

D. It causes us to bring forth more good fruit:

John 15:2	He [prunes] it, that it may bring forth more fruit

E. It humbles us:

Deuteronomy 8:2,16	The Lord led thee in the wilderness, to humble thee
2 Chronicles 33:12	When he was in affliction, he humbled himself greatly
Lamentations 3:1,17–20	Remembering mine affliction … my soul … is humbled

F. It teaches us patience:

Romans 5:3	Tribulation worketh patience

G. It makes us wiser:

Ecclesiastes 7:2–3	Sorrow is better … the living will lay it to heart

H. It gives us compassion and mercy on others:

2 Corinthians 1:4	That we may be able to comfort them which are in any trouble, by the comfort wherewith we are comforted
Hebrews 2:17–18	He himself hath suffered … he is able to succor them
Hebrews 4:15	Be touched with the feeling of [others'] infirmities

I. It draws us close to, and makes us appreciate, our loved ones:

2 Corinthians 7:4–7	We were troubled on every side … nevertheless, God … comforted us by the coming of Titus

6. REWARDS IN HEAVEN FOR EARTHLY SUFFERING:

Luke 16:19–25	[Lazarus the beggar rewarded and comforted]
Romans 8:18	Sufferings of present time not worthy to be compared
2 Corinthians 1:7	As ye are partakers of the sufferings, so shall ye be also of the consolation
2 Corinthians 4:17	Our light affliction … worketh for us a far more exceeding and eternal weight of glory
2 Timothy 2:12	If we suffer, we shall also reign with him
Revelation 21:4	Shall be no more death … sorrow … crying … pain

7. REMEMBER, JESUS ALSO SUFFERED:

Hebrews 4:15	[He] was in all points tempted [tested] like as we are
Hebrews 12:3	Consider him that endured such contradiction of sinners … lest ye be wearied and faint in your minds

A. The reasons for Jesus' suffering:

Isaiah 53:4–5	He hath borne our griefs, and carried our sorrows ... He was wounded for our transgressions … and with his stripes we are healed (See also 1 Peter 2:24.)
Hebrews 2:9–10	Captain of their salvation perfect through sufferings
1 Peter 2:21	Christ suffered for us, leaving us an example
1 Peter 4:1	As Christ hath suffered for us, arm yourselves

8. THE RIGHT ATTITUDE TOWARD SUFFERING:

Job 13:15	Though he slay me, yet will I trust in him: but I will maintain mine own ways before him
Philippians 3:8	Yea doubtless, and I count all things but loss for the excellency of the knowledge of Christ Jesus my Lord: for whom I have suffered the loss of all things, and do count them but dung, that I may win Christ

A. Endure suffering patiently:

Jeremiah 10:19	Truly this is a grief, and I must bear it
Lamentations 3:24–26	Lord is my portion … hope and quietly wait in him
Romans 12:12	Rejoicing in hope; patient in tribulation
2 Timothy 4:5	Watch thou in all things, endure afflictions
Hebrews 12:7	If ye endure … God dealeth with you as with sons
1 Peter 4:19	Let them that suffer … commit the keeping of their souls to him [God] in well doing

B. Pray for strength to endure suffering:

Luke 18:1	Men ought always to pray, and not to faint
James 5:13	Is any among you afflicted? Let him pray

C. Expect afflictions and trials:

Psalm 34:19	Many are the afflictions of the righteous
Acts 14:22	Must through much tribulation enter into the kingdom
1 Thessalonians 3:3–4	No man should be moved by these afflictions: for … we are appointed thereunto
1 Peter 4:12	Think it not strange concerning the fiery trial (See also 1 Corinthians 10:13; 1 Peter 5:9.)

D. Stand strong, endure hardness:

Acts 20:23–24	None of these things move me … that I might finish
2 Timothy 2:3	Thou therefore endure hardness, as a good soldier
Hebrews 11:25–27	Choosing rather to suffer affliction … he endured
James 5:10–11	Take the prophets, for an example of suffering affliction … we count them happy which endure

E. Be happy despite suffering:

John 16:33	Ye shall have tribulation: but be of good cheer
Romans 5:3	We glory in tribulations … worketh patience
2 Corinthians 7:4	I am exceeding joyful in all our tribulation
1 Peter 4:13,16	Rejoice … ye are partakers of Christ's sufferings

F. Don't murmur against God:

Job 1:20–22	Job sinned not, nor charged God foolishly (See also 2:9–10.)
Psalm 17:3	I am purposed that my mouth shall not transgress
1 Thessalonians 5:18	In everything give thanks: for this is the will of God

G. Remain faithful:

Psalm 119:143	Trouble and anguish … yet thy commandments my delights

9. WRONG ATTITUDES TOWARD SUFFERING:

Exodus 6:9	[Despair:] They [Israelites] hearkened not unto Moses for anguish of spirit, and for cruel bondage
Ruth 1:20–21	[Complaint:] for Almighty hath dealt very bitterly with me
Job 2:7–9	[Bitterness:] Then said [Job's wife], Curse God, and die
Proverbs 24:10	[Giving up:] If thou faint in the day of adversity
Jeremiah 15:18	[Questioning:] Wilt thou be unto me as a liar? (See also Proverbs 18:14; Lamentations 3:39.)

10. GOD COMFORTS AND STRENGTHENS US WHEN WE SUFFER:

Exodus 3:7	I have seen the affliction of my people … heard their cry … I know their sorrows
Matthew 5:4	Blessed are they that mourn … they shall be comforted
John 14:18	I will not leave you comfortless: I will come to you
Romans 8:26	The Spirit helpeth our infirmities
1 Peter 5:10	But God … after that ye have suffered a while, make you perfect, stablish, strengthen, settle you (See also Psalm 23:4; 37:24; 145:14.)

11. DELIVERANCE FROM SUFFERING:

A. God promises to deliver us from our suffering:

Psalm 30:5	Weeping may endure a night, joy cometh in the morning
Psalm 34:19	Many are the afflictions … but the Lord delivereth
Psalm 103:9–14	He will not always chide … he knoweth our frame
Isaiah 54:7–8	For a small moment have I forsaken thee; but … mercy
Lamentations 3:31–32	Lord will not cast off for ever: though he cause grief (See also Exodus 3:7,9–10; Deuteronomy 26:6–8; Psalm 66:11–12; 94:12–14; 107:11–14; 118:17–18.)

B. Pray for deliverance:

Psalm 34:6	Lord heard him, and saved him out of all his troubles
Psalm 34:17	The righteous cry, and the Lord … delivereth them out
Psalm 50:15	Call upon me in the day of trouble: I will deliver thee

(See also specific examples in Ezra 9:5–15; Isaiah 38:1–3.)

C. God's conditions:

2 Chronicles 6:27–30	[Release from suffering if men repent and seek God]
2 Chronicles 7:13–14	If my people … shall humble themselves, and pray, and turn from wicked ways; I will hear … forgive … heal
Job 33:27–29	If any say, "I have sinned" … He will deliver his soul
Job 36:8–11	If they obey and serve him, they shall [have] prosperity
Jonah 2:1–10	[Jonah praised God in his trouble, and was delivered]

12. OUR DUTY TOWARD THE SUFFERING AND AFFLICTED:

Job 6:14	To him that is afflicted pity should be showed
Job 16:5	I would strengthen you … assuage your grief
Isaiah 50:4	Speak a word in season to him that is weary
Luke 10:30–37	[The Good Samaritan] Go, and do thou likewise
Romans 12:15	Weep with them that weep
1 Corinthians 12:25–26	Whether one member suffer, all … suffer with it
Galatians 6:2	Bear ye one another's burdens
Hebrews 13:3	Remember them which suffer adversity
James 1:27	Visit the fatherless and widows in their affliction

(See also Job 19:21; Matthew 25:34–45; 1 Timothy 5:10.)

13. THE SUFFERING OF THE WICKED:

Deuteronomy 28:20	The Lord shall send upon thee cursing … because of the wickedness of thy doings
Deuteronomy 28:15–67	If thou wilt not hearken ... these curses shall come ...
Job 15:20	The wicked man travaileth with pain all his days
Psalm 32:10	Many sorrows shall be to the wicked
Isaiah 42:24–25	Neither were they obedient unto his law. Therefore he hath poured upon him the fury of his anger
Isaiah 57:20–21	Wicked are like troubled sea … no peace to the wicked
Hebrews 2:15	Who through fear of death were … subject to bondage
1 John 4:18	Fear hath torment

(See also Job 20:all; Ecclesiastes 2:22–23; Lamentations 3:42–47.)

14. MUCH SUFFERING IS ACTUALLY SELF-INFLICTED:

A. Drug abuse, alcoholism, etc.:

1 Corinthians 3:17	If any man defile [his body], him shall God destroy
Proverbs 23:29–35	[Alcoholism brings on woe, sorrow, wounds] (See also Proverbs 23:21; 31:4–5; Isaiah 5:11; 28:7.)

B. Overeating:

Numbers 11:19–20, 31–34	[Hebrews gluttonously overate quails and as a result, “the fattest of them” died] (See also Psalm 78:26–31.)
Philippians 3:19	Whose end is destruction, whose God is their belly (See also Proverbs 23:1–3,21.)

C. Overdoing physically:

Ecclesiastes 12:12	Much study is a weariness of the flesh
Philippians 2:2,30	He was [sick] nigh unto death, not regarding his life

D. Pollution by pesticides, chemicals, etc.:

Isaiah 24:5	The earth is defiled under the inhabitants thereof
Jeremiah 2:7	Ye defiled my land, and made [it] an abomination
Amos 7:17	Thou shalt die in a polluted land
Micah 2:10	Because it is polluted, it shall destroy you
Zephaniah 3:1	Woe to her that is filthy and polluted, to the oppressing city
Romans 1:30,32	Inventors of evil things … worthy of death
Revelation 11:18	[God will] destroy them which destroy the earth (See also Genesis 4:8,16–17; Isaiah 5:8; 14:21, on unnatural cities and industrialisation.)

E. Greed and oppression cause wars, suffering, and misery:

Joshua 7:1–26	[Achan’s covetousness caused many Israelites to die]
Proverbs 15:27	He that is greedy of gain troubleth his own house
Nahum 3:1	Woe to the bloody city! It is full of lies and robbery
1 Timothy 6:9–10	They that will be rich … drown in destruction … sorrows
James 4:1–2	From whence come wars? … even of your lusts … ye kill
James 5:1–6	Rich men … ye have condemned and killed the just (See also Psalm 73:3–20; Micah 6:12–15.)

15. SUFFERING CAN BRING SOME TO GOD:

Deuteronomy 31:7	Many evils and troubles shall befall them [to make them realise they’ve forsaken God]
2 Chronicles 15:4	When they in their trouble … sought him: and returned
2 Chronicles 33:9–13	[Manasseh’s suffering in prison turned him to God]
Job 34:31–32	I have borne chastisement, I will not offend any more

Psalm 78:34	When he slew them, then they sought him: and returned
Isaiah 26:16	Poured out prayer when thy chastening was upon them
Jeremiah 2:27	They have turned the back ... but in the time of trouble
Daniel 4:30–37	[King Nebuchadnezzar's abasement and salvation]
Luke 15:16–20	[Suffering caused the Prodigal Son to repent]
Revelation 11:13	Earthquake [killed] 7,000 ... remnant gave glory to God
	(See also Hosea 2:6–7.)

COMFORT

1. GOD WILL HELP AND COMFORT YOU:

A. His promises of comfort:

Psalm 71:21	Thou shalt … comfort me on every side
Psalm 86:17	Thou, Lord, hast holpen me, and comforted me
Psalm 91:15	I will be with him in trouble; I will deliver him
Psalm 116:6	I was brought low, and he helped me
Psalm 138:7	Though I walk in the midst of trouble, thou wilt revive me
Isaiah 42:6	I the Lord … will hold thine hand, and will keep thee
Isaiah 43:2	When thou passest through waters, I will be with thee
Isaiah 49:13	The Lord hath comforted his people, and will have mercy upon his afflicted
Isaiah 51:12–13	I, even I, am he that comforteth you
Isaiah 66:13	As one his mother comforteth, so will I comfort you
John 14:1–3	Let not your heart be troubled: believe … in me
John 14:18	I will not leave you comfortless: I will come to you
2 Corinthians 1:3	Blessed be God … the Father of mercies, and the God of all comfort
2 Corinthians 7:6	God … comforteth those that are cast down
2 Thessalonians 2:16–17	Our Lord Jesus Christ … which hath loved us, and given us everlasting consolation … comfort your hearts

(See also Psalm 103:6; Philippians 2:1–2.)

B. God is always with you to comfort you:

Psalm 121:4	He that keepeth [thee] shall neither slumber nor sleep
2 Corinthians 1:4	[He] comforteth us in all our tribulation

C. The Holy Spirit, the "Comforter," will comfort you:

John 14:16–17	[God] shall give you a Comforter, that he may abide with you for ever; even the Spirit … shall be in you
John 14:26	The Comforter … is the Holy Ghost
John 15:26	The Comforter … whom I will send unto you from [God]
Acts 9:31	Then had the churches rest … in the comfort of the Holy Ghost

2. HOW TO RECEIVE GOD'S COMFORT:

A. Pray and ask for His help:

2 Chronicles 15:4	When they in their trouble … sought [God]
Psalm 34:17	The righteous cry, and the Lord heareth, and delivereth them out of all their troubles
Psalm 86:7	In the day of my trouble I will call upon thee: for thou wilt answer me
Psalm 119:76	Let, I pray, thy merciful kindness be for my comfort

Psalm 145:18–19	The Lord is nigh unto them that call upon him
Philippians 4:6–7	By prayer … let your requests be made known unto God. And the peace of God … shall keep your hearts
Hebrews 4:16	Come boldly unto the throne of grace, that we may obtain mercy, and find grace to help in time of need

B. Examples of King David's prayers seeking comfort:

(See Psalm 31:9–12; 38:9; 51:all; 69:1–2; 102:1–7.)

C. Read and meditate on God's Word:

Psalm 119:50	This is my comfort in my affliction: for thy word hath quickened me
Romans 15:4	[God's Word was] written … that we through the patience and comfort of the Scriptures might have hope

D. Stay close to Him:

Psalm 103:17–18	The mercy of the Lord is from everlasting to everlasting upon them that fear him
John 8:29	The Father hath not left me alone; for I do always those things that please him

E. Continue trusting and have patience:

Genesis 28:15	[God tells Jacob:] I will not leave thee, until I have done that which I have spoken to thee of
Psalm 42:3–11	Why art thou cast down, O my soul? Hope thou in God: for I shall yet praise him
Psalm 119:81–83	I hope in thy word. When wilt thou comfort me? For I am become like a bottle in the smoke
Hebrews 10:35–36	Cast not away … your confidence … ye have need of patience, that, after … ye might receive the promise

F. Remember God's past miracles and mercies:

Psalm 77:1–12	My spirit was overwhelmed … this is my infirmity: but I will remember the works of the Lord
Psalm 119:52	I remembered thy judgements of old, O Lord; and have comforted myself

G. Encourage and remind yourself of God's faithfulness:

1 Samuel 30:6	David was greatly distressed … but David encouraged himself in the Lord his God

H. Remember, God will never forsake you:

Isaiah 49:14–16	[They] said, The Lord hath forsaken me, and forgotten me. Yet will I not forget thee
Psalm 9:9–10	They that know thy name will put their trust in thee: for thou hast not forsaken them that seek thee

Psalm 31:22	I said in my haste, I am cut off from before thine eyes: [but] thou heardest ... when I cried unto thee
Matthew 28:20	I am with you always, even unto the end of the world
2 Timothy 2:13	[Even] if we believe not, yet he abideth faithful
Hebrews 13:5	I will never leave thee, nor forsake thee

(See also Isaiah 54:10.)

I. Trust and commit yourself into His hands:

Romans 8:28	All things work ... for good to them that love God
1 Peter 4:19	Let them that suffer ... commit the keeping of their souls to him ... as unto a faithful Creator

J. He will keep you:

Psalm 23:4	Thy rod and thy staff they comfort me
Psalm 37:5	Commit thy way unto the Lord; trust also in him
Psalm 55:22	Cast thy burden upon the Lord, and he shall sustain thee
Psalm 138:8	The Lord will perfect that which concerneth me
Philippians 1:6	He which hath begun a good work in you will perform [complete] it until the day of Jesus Christ
1 Thessalonians 5:24	Faithful is he that calleth you, who ... will do it
2 Timothy 1:12	[I] am persuaded that he is able to keep that which I have committed unto him
1 Peter 5:7	Casting all your care on him; for he careth for you

3. GOD LOVES YOU AND CARES FOR YOU:

A. He knows every tear you've shed:

2 Kings 20:5	I have heard thy prayer, I have seen thy tears
Psalm 56:8	Put my tears in thy bottle: are they not in thy book?

(See also Mark 9:24.)

B. He knows exactly what you're experiencing:

Exodus 3:7	I have seen the affliction of my people ... and have heard their cry ... I know their sorrows
Psalm 103:13–14	The Lord pitieth [us] for he knoweth our frame
Isaiah 53:4	He hath borne our griefs, and carried our sorrows
Isaiah 63:9	In all their affliction he was afflicted
Hebrews 4:15	Touched with the feeling of our infirmities [He] was in all points tempted like as we are

C. Though He chastises us, He loves and comforts:

Psalm 30:5	His anger endureth but a moment ... weeping may endure for a night, but joy cometh in the morning
Psalm 71:20	Thou, which hast showed me great and sore troubles, shalt quicken me again

Psalm 103:9	He will not always chide; neither … keep his anger forever
Isaiah 12:1	Though thou wast angry with me, thine anger is turned away, and thou comfortedst me
Lamentations 3:31–33	Though he cause grief, yet will he have compassion

(See also Hosea 6:1–3.)

4. GOD'S LOVING HANDS UPHOLD YOU:

A. He is always there, supporting you ...

Deuteronomy 33:27	Underneath are the everlasting arms
Psalm 37:17	The Lord upholdeth the righteous
Psalm 37:24	Thou he fall, he shall not be utterly cast down: for the Lord upholdeth him with his hand
Psalm 145:14	The Lord upholdeth all that fall, and raiseth up all those that be bowed down
Isaiah 41:10	I am with thee: be not dismayed; I will uphold thee with [my] right hand
Isaiah 63:9	In his love and pity he … bare them, and carried them

B. … even in distant lands and lonesome situations:

Psalm 139:8–12	If I make my bed in hell, behold, thou art there. If I … dwell in the uttermost parts of the sea; even there shall thy hand … hold me
Matthew 28:20	I am with you always, even unto the end of the world

5. IF YOU FEEL YOU'RE IN THE DARK, TRUST IN GOD FOR LIGHT:

Psalm 18:28	The Lord my God will enlighten my darkness
Psalm 112:4	Unto the upright there ariseth light in the darkness: he is gracious, and full of compassion
Isaiah 42:16	I will make darkness light before them, and … not forsake them
Isaiah 50:10	Who is among you … that walketh in darkness, and hath no light? Let him trust in the Lord
Micah 7:8	When I sit in darkness, Lord shall be a light unto me

(See also Isaiah 58:10–11.)

6. LOOK ON THE BRIGHT SIDE:

A. You're blessed, so be joyful and happy:

Matthew 5:10–12	Blessed are ye, when men shall revile and persecute you. Rejoice and be exceeding glad
John 16:33	In the world ye shall have tribulation: but be of good cheer; I have overcome the world

2 Corinthians 7:4	I am filled with comfort, I am exceeding joyful in all our tribulation
Philippians 4:4	Rejoice in the Lord always: and again I say, Rejoice
1 Peter 4:12–13	Rejoice … ye are partakers of Christ's sufferings

B. Happy days will come again:

Isaiah 51:11–12	The redeemed of the Lord shall … obtain gladness and joy; and sorrow and mourning shall flee away
1 Thessalonians 4:15–18	[Jesus will soon come to take us to heaven] Comfort one another with these words (See also 5:10–11.)
	(See also Isaiah 40:2; 52:9; 57:16–18; Jeremiah 31:12–14; Zechariah 1:12–17.)

C. Sorrow will soon be gone:

Job 11:16	Thou shalt forget thy misery, and remember it as waters that pass away
Psalm 30:5	Weeping may endure a night, but joy cometh in the morning
Psalm 30:11	Thou put off my sackcloth, and girded me with gladness
Isaiah 49:13	Sing … be joyful break forth into singing: for the Lord hath comforted his people … his afflicted
Isaiah 54:11	O thou afflicted … and not comforted, behold, I will lay thy stones with fair colours

D. Think about and be thankful for His comforts:

Psalm 94:19	In the multitude of my thoughts within me thy comforts delight my soul

7. WHY AND HOW TO COMFORT ONE ANOTHER:

A. Sometimes we need the help of others:

Jeremiah 8:18	When I would comfort myself … my heart is faint
2 Corinthians 2:7	Ye ought … to comfort him, lest [he] be swallowed up with overmuch sorrow
	(See also Ecclesiastes 4:9–10,12.)

B. We should comfort one another:

Genesis 37:34–35	And all his [Jacob's] sons and daughters rose up to comfort him (See also 1 Chronicles 7:22; Job 2:11.)
Isaiah 40:1	Comfort ye, comfort ye my people, saith your God
Isaiah 61:1–3	The spirit of the Lord is upon me … he hath sent me to bind up the brokenhearted … comfort all that mourn ... give unto them the beauty of ashes, oil of joy for mourning, the garment of praise for spirit of heaviness

1 Corinthians 12:25	In the body … the members should have the same care one for another
2 Corinthians 2:8	I beseech you that ye confirm your love toward him
2 Corinthians 7:6	God … comforted us by the coming of Titus [a fellow-labourer] (See also Ephesians 6:22; Colossians 4:7–8; 1 Thessalonians 3:2.)
Galatians 6:2	Bear ye one another's burdens, and so fulfill the law of Christ
Colossians 2:2	Hearts … comforted, being knit together in love
Colossians 4:11	My fellow-workers … which have been a comfort unto me
1 Thessalonians 5:11	Comfort yourselves together, and edify one another
1 Thessalonians 5:14	Comfort the feebleminded [fainthearted, timid]

C. How to comfort others:

Genesis 50:21	[Joseph] comforted them, and spake kindly unto them
Ruth 2:13	Thou hast comforted me … thou hast spoken [kindly]
Proverbs 17:22	A merry heart doeth good like a medicine
Romans 12:15	Weep with them that weep
1 Thessalonians 2:11	We … comforted … you, as a father doth his children

D. Use your own experiences to comfort others:

Psalm 66:12,16	I will declare what he hath done for my soul
2 Corinthians 1:4	That we may be able to comfort [others] in trouble, by the comfort wherewith we are comforted of God

E. The comforting, consoling power of inspired music:

1 Samuel 16:14–16	An evil spirit … troubleth thee. [A musician] shall play … and thou shalt be well (See also 16:23.)
Psalm 32:7	Thou shalt compass me about with songs of deliverance
Psalm 42:5–8	My soul is cast down within me … yet … in the night his song shall be with me
Proverbs 25:20	[Caution: Make sure you sing fitting songs]

F. Encouraging words of prophecy are a comfort:

1 Corinthians 14:3	He that prophesieth speaketh unto men to … comfort

G. When you don't know what to say, just being there is a help:

Job 2:13	They sat down with him … and none spake a word unto him: for they saw that his grief was very great
Colossians 2:2	Hearts … comforted, being knit together in love

H. Make sure you are comforting, not condemning:

Job 16:2–5	Miserable comforters are ye all. [Job said if they were in his place, he would have comforted them]

8. WHEN FEELING ABANDONED, OR SUFFERING HEARTBREAK OR LOSS:

A. Even when all others leave you, God will always remain:

Psalm 27:10	When father and mother forsake me, Lord will take me up
Psalm 34:22	None of them that trust in him shall be desolate
Psalm 142:4–5	Refuge failed me; No man cared for my soul. Thou art my refuge and my portion in the land of the living
Isaiah 54:1,5–6	The Lord hath called thee as a woman forsaken and grieved in spirit … when thou wast refused
Isaiah 54:10	The mountains shall depart … but my kindness shall not depart from thee
2 Timothy 4:16–17	All men forsook me … notwithstanding the Lord stood with me, and strengthened me
Hebrews 13:5	He hath said, I will never leave thee nor forsake thee

B. God's special care for the brokenhearted:

Psalm 34:18	The Lord is nigh unto them that are of a broken heart
Psalm 51:17	A broken and a contrite heart … thou wilt not despise
Psalm 61:2	When my heart is overwhelmed: lead me to the rock that is higher than I
Psalm 147:3	He healeth the broken heart, and bindeth up their wounds
Isaiah 61:1	He hath sent me [Jesus] to bind up the brokenhearted (See also Luke 4:18.)
Ezekiel 34:16	I … will bind up that which was broken (See also Isaiah 57:15.)

C. When suffering bereavement:

2 Samuel 12:15–23	[When David's sick child died, he stopped fasting and weeping, saying:] I shall go to him [in heaven]
1 Corinthians 15:17–21	[Jesus is raised from the dead, therefore our loved ones also live, and we are not to be miserable]
1 Thessalonians 4:13	Concerning them which are asleep [departed] ... sorrow not, as others which have no hope
1 Thessalonians 4:16–18	The dead in Christ shall rise … we shall be … with them … comfort one another with these words

D. It is sometimes better for them to be with God:

2 Corinthians 5:8	We are … willing rather to be absent from the body, and to be present with the Lord
Philippians 1:23	Desire to depart … to be with Christ … is far better
Revelation 7:16–17	[The happiness of our departed loved ones in heaven]

E. When suffering remorse over mistakes or sin:

(See Psalm 31:9–24; 38:1–22; 51:all; Lamentations 1:20; Luke 18:13–14; 2 Corinthians 2:6–8. Also compare Matthew 26:69–75 and Mark 16:6–7.)

9. HEAVENLY CONSOLATION FOR PRESENT SUFFERING AND SORROW:

A. Comforted by heavenly rewards:

Psalm 37:9	Those that wait on the Lord ... shall inherit the earth
Matthew 5:4	Blessed are they that mourn … they shall be comforted
Luke 6:21	Blessed are ye that weep now: for ye shall laugh
Luke 12:32	Fear not, little flock; for it is your Father's good pleasure to give you the kingdom (See also Matthew 25:34.)
Luke 16:19–22	[The suffering beggar Lazarus] carried by the angels into Abraham's bosom
John 16:20	Ye shall weep and lament … and ye shall be sorrowful, but your sorrow shall be turned into joy
Romans 8:18	The sufferings of this present time are not worthy to be compared with the glory [heavenly reward]
2 Corinthians 1:7	As ye are partakers of the sufferings, so shall ye be also of the consolation
2 Corinthians 4:17	Our light affliction, which is but for a moment, worketh for us [an] eternal weight of glory
2 Timothy 2:12	If we suffer, we shall also reign with him

B. There will be no more sorrow or tears in heaven:

Isaiah 25:8	He will swallow up death in victory; and the Lord God will wipe away tears from off all faces
Revelation 21:4	God shall wipe away all tears from their eyes; and there shall be no more … sorrow, nor crying (See also 7:17.)

HEALING

1. HEALING WAS PART OF JESUS' MINISTRY:

Matthew 4:23–24	Jesus went … healing all manner of sickness and disease
Matthew 9:35	Healing every sickness and disease among the people
Matthew 12:15	Great multitudes followed him and he healed them all
	(See also Matthew 15:30; 21:14; Acts 10:38.)

2. GOD'S HEALING PROMISES ARE STILL VALID TODAY:

Malachi 3:6	I am the Lord, I change not
Mark 16:17–18	These signs shall follow them that believe; lay hands on the sick and they shall recover
John 14:12–14	He that believeth on me, the works I do shall he do
1 Corinthians 12:7,9	To another the gifts of healing by the same Spirit
Hebrews 13:8	Jesus Christ the same yesterday, and to day, and for ever
James 5:14–15	Is any sick among you? Call elders … let them pray

3. IT IS WITHIN GOD'S WILL TO HEAL:

A. Scriptural authority for asking for healing:

Exodus 15:26	I am the Lord that healeth thee
Deuteronomy 7:15	The Lord will take away from thee all sickness
Psalm 84:11	No good thing will he withhold from them
Psalm 103:3	[He] forgiveth all iniquities, healeth all thy diseases
Psalm 107:20	He sent his word, and healed them
Jeremiah 30:17	For I will restore health unto thee, and will heal
Malachi 4:2	Sun of righteousness arise with healing in his wings
Matthew 10:1	He gave them power … to heal all manner of sickness and … disease
Mark 1:40–41	Lord, if thou wilt … Jesus saith, I will; be thou clean
Acts 9:34	Jesus Christ maketh thee whole
James 5:15	The prayer of faith shall save the sick … and the Lord shall raise him up
	(See also Ezekiel 34:16; 3 John 1:2.)

B. God prefers not to afflict; He'd rather heal:

Psalm 22:24	He hath not despised … affliction of the afflicted; neither hath he hid his face from him
Lamentations 3:33	He doth not afflict willingly
Hebrews 12:13	Let it rather be healed

C. Jesus' physical suffering paid for our healing:

Isaiah 53:5	He was wounded … with his stripes we are healed
Matthew 8:16–17	Himself took our infirmities and bare our sicknesses
1 Corinthians 11:23–24	This is my body, which is broken for you

1 Corinthians 11:29–30	Not discerning Lord's body … many are weak and sickly
1 Peter 2:24	By whose stripes ye were healed

4. NOTHING IS TOO SERIOUS FOR GOD TO HEAL:

Jeremiah 32:17	Ah Lord God! There is nothing too hard for thee
Jeremiah 32:27	I am the Lord … is there anything too hard for me?
Psalm 34:19	The Lord delivereth him out of them [afflictions] all
Psalm 103:3	Who healeth all thy diseases
Matthew 10:1	Power to … heal all manner of sickness, and all disease
Matthew 19:26	With God all things are possible
Mark 9:23	All things are possible to him that believeth
Luke 1:37	With God, nothing shall be impossible
Luke 5:17	The power of the Lord was present to heal them

5. CONDITIONS FOR HEALING:

2 Kings 20:5	I have … seen thy tears, behold, I will heal thee
2 Chronicles 7:14	If my people humble themselves, and pray and turn from their wicked ways; then will I hear and heal
Isaiah 19:22	They shall return to the Lord … and he shall heal them
Isaiah 58:6–8	[Help others:] Then thine health … spring forth speedily
Hosea 6:1	Come, let us return … and he will heal us
James 5:16	Confess your faults … and pray one for another, that ye may be healed

6. PRACTICAL STEPS FOR OBTAINING HEALING:

A. Begin with a clean heart; unconfessed sin will hinder faith:

Psalm 66:18–19	If I regard iniquity in my heart, Lord will not hear
Proverbs 28:13	He that covereth his sins shall not prosper
James 5:16	Confess your faults one to another, and pray one for another
1 John 3:21	If our heart condemn us not, then have we [faith]

(See also 2 Chronicles 7:14; Psalm 51:10; 139:23; 1 John 1:8–9.)

B. Prepare by memorising promises; find authority in God's Word, and faith will come:

Joshua 23:14	Not one thing hath failed of all that … God spake
1 Kings 8:56	Hath not failed one word of all his good promise
Proverbs 7:2–3	Write [My commandments] upon table of thine heart
Matthew 24:35	Heaven and earth shall pass away, but [not] my words
Romans 10:17	Faith cometh by hearing the word of God
2 Corinthians 1:20	All the promises of God in him are yea and … amen
2 Peter 1:4	Great and precious promises: by these ye might partake

C. Be definite:

Isaiah 45:11	Concerning the work of my hands, command ye me
James 1:6–8	Ask in faith, nothing wavering

D. Expect results from God:

Mark 11:23–24	Whoever … shall believe … shall have whatsoever he saith ... When ye pray, believe that ye receive and ye shall have
Hebrews 4:16	Come boldly … and find grace to help in time of need
Hebrews 11:6	He that cometh to God must believe … he is a rewarder

E. Accept God's decision:

Joshua 7:10	Get thee up; wherefore liest thou thus upon thy face?
Luke 1:38	Mary said, "Be it unto me according to thy word"

F. Stand your ground in faith and trust:

Numbers 23:19	God is not a man, that he should lie. Hath he said, and shall he not do it?
Psalm 112:7	Not be afraid of evil tidings … trusting in the Lord
Acts 27:25	I believe God, that it shall be even as was told me
Romans 3:4	Let God be true, but every man a liar
Romans 4:19–21	Being fully persuaded that what he had promised
Galatians 6:9	In due season we shall reap, if we faint not
Ephesians 4:27	Neither give place to the devil [his doubts and lies]
Ephesians 6:13	Withstand … and having done all, stand
Ephesians 6:16	Taking the shield of faith … to quench fiery darts
Hebrews 10:23	Hold fast [your] faith without wavering; he is faithful that promised
Hebrews 10:35–36	Ye have need of patience, that, after ye have done the will of God, ye might receive the promise
1 Peter 1:7	The trial of your faith … more precious than gold

(See also Proverbs 24:10; John 2:8.)

G. Real faith puts into action what it believes:

2 Kings 5:1,9–14	[Naaman obeyed Elisha, dipped in the Jordan, and was healed]
2 Chronicles 20:21–22	[When they went forth singing and praising God for the victory, He performed the miracle]
Matthew 14:28–29	[Peter believed Jesus and stepped out on the water]
Mark 2:11–12	Take up thy bed, and go … and immediately he arose
Mark 3:1,5	[A man stretches out his withered hand and is healed]
Luke 17:14	As they went, they were cleansed [healed]
John 4:47–53	Believed the word Jesus had spoken … and went his way
2 Corinthians 5:7	For we walk by faith, not by sight
James 2:17–26	As body without spirit … faith without works is dead

H. Thank Him for hearing and answering your prayer:

Luke 17:15–16	When he saw that he was healed … fell down on his face at his feet, giving him thanks
Romans 4:20	He was strong in faith, giving glory to God

7. PRAY FOR THE SICK:

A. Pray for healing in Jesus' name:

(See John 14:13–14; Acts 3:6; 4:10; 9:34.)

B. Laying hands on and touching the sick:

Mark 16:18	They shall lay hands on the sick and they shall recover
Luke 4:40	He laid his hands on every one of them, and healed them

(See also Matthew 9:29; Mark 3:10; 5:28; 6:56; 7:33–35; Luke 5:13; 6:19; 22:51.)

C. Anointing with oil for healing:

(See Mark 6:13; James 5:14.)

D. The power of united, group prayer:

Deuteronomy 32:30	One [shall] chase a thousand, and two put ten thousand to flight
Matthew 18:19–20	If two of you shall agree [in prayer] … it shall be done

E. Who should pray for the sick:

Luke 8:50–51	[Have the unbelieving leave the room before you pray]
James 5:14–16	Call for the elders … and let them pray over him. The fervent … prayer of a righteous man availeth much

8. FIGHT IN THE SPIRIT FOR HEALING:

Matthew 17:19–21	[Unusual, stubborn sicknesses require extra faith and prayer and fasting]
1 Timothy 6:12	Fight the good fight of faith, lay hold on eternal life

A. Sing and praise:

(See also Psalm 34:1; 51:15; 66:17; 77:2,10–11; 109:30.)

B. Quote Scripture:

Matthew 4:3–10	He answered and said, "It is written…"
Ephesians 6:17	Take … the sword of the Spirit, which is the word of God

9. REASONS WHY GOD ALLOWS AFFLICTIONS AND ILLNESSES:

A. To keep us righteous and close to Him:

Psalm 34:19	Many are the afflictions of the righteous
Psalm 119:71	It is good for me that I have been afflicted

2 Corinthians 12:7	Lest I should be exalted ... given a thorn in the flesh
Hebrews 12:6,11	Whom the Lord loveth he chasteneth, and scourgeth
Revelation 3:19	As many as I love, I rebuke and chasten

B. To glorify God when He heals:

Matthew 15:31	The multitude wondered … and they glorified God
John 9:1–3	[The blind man's healing was to glorify God]
Acts 9:36–42	It was known throughout all Joppa; and many believed

C. Sickness is often caused by sin:

Psalm 38:2–5	My wounds stink and are corrupt ... because of my sin … because of my foolishness
Psalm 107:17	Fools, because of their … iniquities, are afflicted
Psalm 119:67	Before I was afflicted, I went astray: but now
Proverbs 26:2	The curse causeless shall not come
	(See also Numbers 12:1–15; 1 Samuel 5:1–12; 25:2–11,37–38; 2 Chronicles 21:9–19; 26:16–21; Acts 12:21–23.)

D. Some sickness is an attack of the Devil:

Matthew 9:32–33	When the devil was cast out, the dumb spake
Mark 9:17–20,25	[Jesus rebuked an unclean spirit, healing a child]
Luke 13:11,13,16	This woman … whom Satan hath bound 18 years
Acts 10:38	Healing all that were oppressed of the devil

E. To teach and to test us:

Job 2:3–7	[The Devil was allowed to afflict Job to test him]
Job 5:17–18	Behold, happy is man whom God correcteth
Psalm 94:12	Blessed is the man whom thou chasteneth and teachest
2 Corinthians 4:17	[Our temporary afflictions teach us eternal lessons]

F. Emotional or physiological causes:

Psalm 147:3	He healeth the broken in heart, bindeth their wounds
Proverbs 11:17	He that is cruel troubleth his own flesh
Proverbs 14:30	Envy [is] the rottenness of the bones
Proverbs 15:13	By sorrow of the heart the spirit is broken
Proverbs 17:22	A broken spirit drieth the bones
Proverbs 18:14	A wounded spirit who can bear?

G. God will show you the reason if you ask Him:

1 Samuel 6:3	Then ye shall be healed, and it shall be known to you why his hand is not removed from you
Job 36:9–11	Then he sheweth them their … transgressions
Philippians 3:15	God shall reveal even this unto you

H. How to help from getting sick:

Exodus 15:26	If thou wilt diligently hearken … I will put none of these diseases upon thee
Psalm 91:9–10	Because thou hast made the Lord thy … habitation
Proverbs 4:20,22	Attend to my words … they are health to [your] flesh

I. Physical reasons for sickness:

Exodus 8:24	The land was corrupted by the swarm of flies
Proverbs 23:3	Be not desirous of dainties: they are deceitful meat
Proverbs 23:29–35	[Eating unclean meats, seafood, etc.]
Proverbs 25:16,27	[Overindulgence in sweets:] Not good to eat much honey
Mark 7:3–4	[Lack of cleanliness: Jews washed often, lived long]
Romans 1:24–27	[Unclean or perverted sex]
Philippians 2:27,30	[Overdoing physically:] Sick … not regarding his life

10. POINTS TO REMEMBER AFTER PRAYER:

A. Reasons why we're sometimes not healed:

Isaiah 59:1–2	The Lord's hand is not shortened, but your sins have separated you
Hosea 5:15	I will return to my place, till they acknowledge their offence
2 Corinthians 12:7–9	[Paul prayed 3 times to be healed, but the Lord left him with a thorn in the flesh to keep him humble]
Hebrews 10:36	After ye have done the will of God ye [shall] receive the promise
James 1:3	The trying of your faith worketh patience
1 Peter 1:7	Trial of your faith [is] much more precious than gold

B. Testify publicly about your healing:

Job 36:24	Remember that thou magnify his work, which men behold
Psalm 107:2	Let the redeemed of the Lord say so
Mark 5:19	Go home to thy friends and tell them how great things the Lord hath done for thee
Acts 4:10	Be it known unto you all, that by the name of Jesus … doth this man stand here before you whole

(See also Psalm 22:22,25; 35:18; 107:31–32.)

C. Obey God once healed, or your sickness may return:

John 5:14	Thou art made whole, sin no more, lest a worse thing
Psalm 85:8	But let them not turn again to folly

11. MIRACULOUS OR NATURAL HEALING?

A. Doctors don't always have the answers:

2 Chronicles 16:12–13	Asa was diseased in his feet … he sought not to the Lord, but to the physicians. And Asa died
Psalm 118:8	Better to trust in the Lord than to put confidence in man
Jeremiah 46:11	In vain shalt thou use many medicines ... not be cured
Mark 5:25–26	Suffered many things of many physicians … grew worse (See also Hosea 5:13.)

B. Doctors and medicines can help:

Proverbs 17:22	A merry heart doeth good like a medicine
Luke 10:34	He bound up his wounds … pouring in oil and wine

C. God ordained natural remedies:

2 Kings 20:1–7	Take a lump of figs ... lay it on the boil (See also Isaiah 38:21.)
Jeremiah 51:8	Take balm for her pain, if so be she may be healed
Ezekiel 47:12	And the leaf thereof [shall be] for medicine
1 Timothy 5:23	Use a little wine for thy stomach's sake and ... infirmities

D. Eat wholesome, nourishing food:

Psalm 103:5	[God] saftisfieth thy mouth with good things; so that thy youth is renewed like the eagle's

12. NO SICKNESS IN HEAVEN:

1 Corinthians 15:42–43	So is the resurrection … It is sown in corruption, raised in incorruption: sown in weakness … raised in power (See also Isaiah 33:24; Revelation 21:4.)

OVERCOMING THE DEVIL

"We are not ignorant of his devices." (2 Corinthians 2:11)

1. WHERE DID THE DEVIL COME FROM?

A. God created the Devil:

Proverbs 16:4	The Lord hath made all things ... even the wicked
Isaiah 45:7	I form the light, and darkness ... and create evil: I the Lord do all these things
Ezekiel 28:14–15	Anointed cherub ... from the day thou wast created
John 1:3	All things were made by him [Jesus]
Colossians 1:16	By him [Jesus] were all things created

B. The Devil's fall through pride:

Isaiah 14:12–15	Thou hast said ... I will be like the most High
1 Timothy 3:6	Lest being lifted up with pride he fall into the [same] condemnation [as] the devil

2. THE DEVIL IS UNDER GOD'S RESTRICTIONS:

A. Satan could only afflict Job as God permitted:

Job 1:6–12	All he hath is in thy power; only on him put not ... hand
Job 2:1–7	He is in thine hand; but save his life

B. God rules over the entire world:

Daniel 4:17	The most High ruleth in the kingdom of men, and giveth it to whomsoever he will
Daniel 4:34–35	He doeth according to his will ... and none can stay his hand, or say unto him, What doest thou?
Psalm 24:1	The earth is the Lord's (See also Acts 17:24.)
Psalm 89:11	The heavens are thine, the earth also is thine
Job 41:11	Whatsoever is under the whole heaven is mine

C. But, within limitations, He allows the Devil to rule it:

Jeremiah 27:5	I [God] have made the earth ... and have given it to whom it seemed meet [appropriate] unto me
Luke 4:5–6	All the kingdoms of the world ... all this power and the glory of them ... is delivered unto [Satan]
John 12:31	The prince of this world (See also John 14:30; 16:11.)
2 Corinthians 4:4	The god of this world
Ephesians 2:2	Prince of the power of the air

D. The Devil rules over the fallen angels:

(See Matthew 12:24; Luke 11:15; Revelation 12:3–4,7–9.)

3. VICTORY OVER THE DEVIL:

A. God's power is much greater than the Devil's:

Luke 10:17	The devils are subject unto us through thy name
Luke 10:19	I give unto you power … over all the power of the enemy: and nothing shall … hurt you
Philippians 2:9–11	At the name of Jesus every knee should bow
James 2:19	Thou believest that there is one God; the devils also believe, and tremble
1 John 4:4	Greater is he [Jesus] that is in you than he [the Devil] that is in the world

(See also Zechariah 3:2; Jude 1:9.)

B. Jesus defeated the Devil:

Luke 10:18	I saw Satan fall as lightning from heaven
Colossians 2:15	Spoiling principalities and powers … triumphing over them
Hebrews 2:14	Through death he [destroyed] him that had the power of death, that is, the devil
1 John 3:8	The Son of God was manifested, that he might destroy the works of the devil

C. Jesus' power to exorcise (cast out) demons:

Matthew 8:16	He cast out the [devils] with his word
Matthew 9:32–33	When the devil was cast out, the dumb spake
Matthew 12:22	One possessed with a devil … and [Jesus] healed him
Matthew 12:28	I cast out devils by the Spirit of God
Mark 1:34,39	He cast out many devils; and suffered not [did not allow] the devils to speak
Luke 4:33–36	With authority and power he commandeth unclean spirits
Luke 8:27–33	[Jesus rebuked Legion; the devils went into the herd of swine] (See also Mark 5:1–15.)
Luke 9:42	Jesus rebuked the unclean spirit, and healed the child
Acts 10:38	Jesus [healed] all that were oppressed of the devil

(See also Mark 1:17–23; 7:25–30; 9:17–27.)

D. Jesus gave His disciples power over the Devil:

Matthew 10:1	He gave them [his disciples] power against unclean spirits, to cast them out
Luke 9:1	He … gave them power and authority over all devils
Acts 5:16	There came [to the disciples] them which were vexed with unclean spirits: and they were healed every one
Romans 16:20	The God of peace shall bruise Satan under your feet

(See also Acts 8:6–7; 19:11–12; 26:17–18.)

E. Jesus gives all believers power over the Devil—including you:

Mark 16:17	These signs shall follow them that believe; In my name shall they cast out devils
Luke 9:49–50	We saw one casting out devils in thy name [It wasn't only the apostles who had this power]
John 14:12	He that believeth on me, the works I do shall he do also
1 John 2:14	The word of God abideth in you and ye have overcome the wicked one

4. THE SPIRITUAL WARFARE:

A. Our war against the Devil:

2 Corinthians 10:3–5	The weapons of our warfare are not carnal, but mighty through God
Ephesians 6:10–13	Be strong … put on armour … stand against the devil ... wrestle ... against the rulers of darkness of this world, against spiritual wickedness
	(See also 1 Samuel 16:23; Revelation 12:7,17.)

B. Be on guard against and resist and defy the Devil:

Matthew 4:10	Get thee hence, Satan: for it is written, Thou shalt worship the Lord thy God, and him only
Mark 8:33	Get thee behind [away from] me, Satan
Ephesians 4:27	Neither give place to the devil
1 Peter 5:8–9	Be sober, be vigilant; because your adversary the devil walketh about, seeking whom he may devour: whom resist stedfast in the faith

C. Promises to claim when fighting and overcoming the Devil:

Isaiah 59:19	When the enemy shall come in like a flood, the Spirit of the Lord shall lift up a standard against him
Matthew 16:19	Whatsoever thou shalt bind on earth shall be bound
Luke 10:19	I give unto you power … over all the power of the enemy
Romans 16:20	The God of peace shall bruise Satan under your feet
James 4:7	Resist the devil, and he will flee from you
1 John 2:14	Ye are strong, and the word of God abideth in you, and ye have overcome the wicked one
1 John 4:4	Greater is he [Jesus] that is in you, than he [the Devil] that is in the world

D. Be prepared for battle when confronting the Devil:

Matthew 12:29	How can one enter into a strong man's house … except he first bind the strong man?
Mark 9:29	This kind can come forth [only] by prayer and fasting

Acts 19:13–17	[Seven sons of Sceva attempted exorcism without being full of Jesus themselves, and met disastrous results]

E. United prayer for deliverance of the oppressed:

Ecclesiastes 4:9–12	Two are better than one
Matthew 18:19–20	If two of you shall agree … ask, it shall be done

F. They must get filled up with Jesus and His Word once they're delivered, or they may end up worse than they were at first:

Luke 11:24–26	Unclean spirit, gone out of a man [returns to him, finds him empty, and re-enters with 7 other spirits] (See also Matthew 12:43–45.)

5. THE DEVIL'S DEVICES:

A. Don't be ignorant of the Devil's devices:

Genesis 3:1	The serpent was more subtil than any beast
2 Corinthians 2:11	Lest Satan should get an advantage of us: for we are not ignorant of his devices
Ephesians 6:11	Stand against the wiles of the devil

B. The Devil is a liar and deceiver:

Genesis 3:1	[Creates doubt of God's Word:] Yea, hath God said?
John 8:44	For he is a liar, and the father of it
Acts 5:1–4	Satan filled … heart to lie to the Holy Ghost
2 Corinthians 11:3	As serpent beguiled Eve … so your minds be corrupted
2 Corinthians 11:13–14	Satan … transformed into an angel of light (See also 2 Thessalonians 2:9–11.)
1 John 4:1,3	Beloved, believe not every spirit (See also 1 Timothy 4:1.)
Revelation 12:9	The devil, Satan, which deceiveth the whole world

C. The Devil tries to turn men from salvation:

Mark 4:15	When they have heard, Satan cometh immediately, and taketh away the word (See also Matthew 13:19; Luke 8:12.)
Acts 13:8,10	Elymas … child of the devil [sought] to turn away the deputy from the faith
2 Corinthians 4:4	The [Devil] hath blinded the minds of [unbelievers] lest light of the gospel … should shine unto them

D. The Devil is the hinderer:

Zechariah 3:1	Satan standing at his right hand to resist him
1 Thessalonians 2:18	We would have come … but Satan hindered us

E. Specific "devices" to be on guard against:

Matthew 16:21–23	[Leads people to contradict and doubt truth]

John 13:2	Devil, having put into the heart of Judas … to betray
Acts 13:10	Child of devil … not [ceasing] to pervert right ways
1 Corinthians 14:33	For God is not the author of confusion
Colossians 1:13	Who hath delivered us from the power of the darkness
2 Timothy 1:7	For God hath not given us the spirit of fear
1 John 3:10	[Hatred:] Children of devil … loveth not his brother

6. THE DEVIL IS THE ACCUSER AND TEMPTER:

A. Satan tempts men to sin:

(See Genesis 3:1–6; 1 Chronicles 21:1–3,7–8; Matthew 4:3–9; 1 Corinthians 7:5; Luke 4:1–13.)

B. The Devil is the accuser, like a prosecuting attorney:

Job 1:6	The sons of God came … before the Lord, and Satan came also [Note: "Satan" means "accuser."]
Revelation 12:10	The accuser of our brethren … which accused them before our God day and night

C. Jesus is our advocate, like a defense attorney:

Romans 8:34	Who is he that condemneth? Christ … at the right hand of God, maketh intercession for us
Hebrews 9:24	Christ is … entered … into heaven, to appear in the presence of God for us (See also 1 Timothy 2:5.)
1 John 2:1	If any man sin, we have an advocate with the Father, Jesus Christ the righteous

7. THE DEVIL IS A DESTROYER:

A. He causes bondage, snares, and oppression:

(See Luke 8:29; Acts 10:38; Romans 8:15; 1 Timothy 3:7; 2 Timothy 2:26.)

B. Disease:

(See Job 2:7; Luke 13:11–12,16; 2 Corinthians 12:7.)

C. And destruction:

(See John 8:44; Hebrews 2:14; 1 Peter 5:8–9.)

D. God sometimes uses the Devil to punish the disobedient:

(See 1 Samuel 16:14; 1 Corinthians 5:5; 1 Timothy 1:20.)

E. Satan seeks to subvert the saints:

Job 1:8–11	Doth Job fear God for nought? Put forth thine hand
Job 2:3–5	Put forth thine hand … and he will curse thee
Luke 22:31	Satan hath desired to ... sift thee as wheat

8. JUDGEMENT OF THE DEVIL AND HIS DEMONS, AND HIS FINAL END:

A. Some are bound, awaiting judgement:

2 Peter 2:4	Angels that sinned … into chains of darkness
Jude 1:6	Reserved in everlasting chains unto judgement

B. Apparently most are still loose, as their time is not yet come:

Matthew 8:28–29	Art thou come hither to torment us before the time

C. The Devil is not yet cast out of heaven; He has access to God's throne:

Job 1:6; 2:1	Sons of God … before God, and Satan among them
Revelation 12:10	Which accused them before God day and night
Revelation 12:7–9, 13–14	[The Devil will be cast out of heaven at the beginning of the last 3½ years, in the time of the end]

D. The Devil will be bound for 1,000 years in God's prison:

Revelation 20:1–3,7,10	[Satan bound 1,000 years, afterward released for a short time before being thrown into lake of fire]

E. The Devil and his demons will finally be thrown into the lake of fire:

Matthew 25:41	Everlasting fire prepared for devil and his angels
Revelation 20:10	The devil was cast into the lake of fire and brimstone

9. YOUR ARMOUR AND WEAPONRY TO DEFEAT THE DEVIL:

A. Your spiritual armour:

Romans 13:12	Let us cast off the works of darkness, and let us put on the armour of light
2 Corinthians 6:7	The armour of righteousness on the right hand and on the left
Ephesians 6:11,13	Put on the whole armour of God, that ye may be able to stand against the wiles of the devil

B. Your mighty shield:

Psalm 3:3	Thou, O Lord, art a shield for me (See also Psalm 28:7; 33:20; 115:9; 144:2; Proverbs 30:5.)
Psalm 91:4	His truth shall be thy shield and buckler
Ephesians 6:16	Take the shield of faith, wherewith ye shall be able to quench all the fiery darts of the wicked

C. Your invincible sword of the Spirit:

Ephesians 6:17	Take … the sword of the Spirit … the word of God
Hebrews 4:12	The word of God is … quick [alive] and powerful, and sharper than any twoedged sword

D. Your breastplate:

Ephesians 6:14	Stand ... having on the breastplate of righteousness (See also Isaiah 59:17.)

E. Your impenetrable helmet:

Ephesians 6:17	Take the helmet of salvation
1 Thessalonians 5:8	Let us ... put on for an helmet, the hope of salvation

10. POWER, FREEDOM, AND DELIVERANCE FROM THE DEVIL'S DARKNESS:

A. God gives us overcoming power:

Luke 10:19	I give you power over all the power of the enemy
Ephesians 3:16	That he would grant you ... to be strengthened with might by his Spirit in the inner man
2 Timothy 1:7	God hath not given us the spirit of fear; but of power, and of love, and of a sound mind

B. Freedom from the Devil's snares and bondage:

Psalm 91:3	He shall deliver thee from the snare of the fowler
Psalm 124:7	Our soul is escaped as a bird out of the snare of the fowlers: the snare is broken, and we are escaped
Proverbs 14:27	Fear of the Lord [helps] depart from the snares of death
2 Corinthians 3:17	Where the Spirit of the Lord is, there is liberty
2 Timothy 2:25–26	Acknowledging of the truth ... that they may recover themselves out of the snare of the devil

C. Delivered into God's glorious kingdom of light:

Acts 26:18	Open their eyes ... turn them from darkness to light, from the power of Satan unto God
Colossians 1:12–13	Who hath delivered us from the power of darkness ... partakers of the inheritance of the saints in light

D. The Devil cannot separate us from God:

Romans 8:38–39	Neither angels, nor powers ... nor any other creature, shall be able to separate us from ... Christ Jesus
1 Peter 1:5	Who are kept by the power of God ... unto salvation

11. OUR ASTONISHING ANGELIC ALLIES, THE HOSTS OF HEAVEN:

A. They outnumber the Devil's forces two to one:

2 Kings 6:16–17	They that be with us are more than they that be with them ... mountain was full of ... chariots of fire
Revelation 12:3–4	[Satan's] tail drew the third part of the stars [angels] (See also Revelation 5:11.)

B. Their fantastic flaming weapons:

Genesis 3:24	Cherubims, and a flaming sword, which turned every way
2 Kings 6:17	The mountain was full of horses and chariots of fire round about Elisha (See also Numbers 22:23; 1 Chronicles 21:16.)

C. They battle against and defeat the Devil:

Revelation 12:7–9	Michael and his angels fought against … the [Devil] and his angels [and the Devil's forces were defeated]

FEAR NOT

Includes courage, trusting, peace, and fearing God

1. GOD TELLS US NOT TO FEAR:

Isaiah 7:4	Be quiet, fear not, neither be fainthearted

A. God is with us; therefore we should not fear:

Joshua 1:9	Have not I commanded thee? Be strong and of a good courage; be not afraid … for the Lord is with thee
Psalm 118:6	The Lord is on my side; I will not fear: what can man do
Isaiah 12:2	God is my salvation; I will trust, and not be afraid
Isaiah 41:10	Fear thou not; for I am with thee … I will help thee
Luke 12:32	Fear not, little flock
	(See also Numbers 14:9; Psalm 78:53; Matthew 17:6–7.)

B. God is greater than any adversary, and He will keep us:

Psalm 27:1	The Lord is my light … whom shall I fear?
Proverbs 3:25–26	Be not afraid of sudden fear … Lord shall keep [thee]
Luke 10:19	I give you power … over all the power of the enemy
1 John 4:4	Greater is he that is in you, than he … in the world

C. Don't fear people:

Jeremiah 1:8	Be not afraid of their faces: for I am with thee
Ezekiel 3:9	Fear them not, neither be dismayed at their looks

D. God promises peace:

Job 22:21	Acquaint now thyself with him, and be at peace
Psalm 29:11	The Lord will bless his people with peace
Proverbs 3:24	When thou liest down, thou shalt not be afraid
Isaiah 26:3	Thou wilt keep him in perfect peace, whose mind is stayed on thee
John 14:27	My peace I give unto you … let not your heart be troubled, neither let it be afraid
John 16:33	In me ye [can] have peace … I have overcome the world
Galatians 5:22	The fruit of the Spirit is … peace
Philippians 4:7	The peace of God … shall keep your hearts and minds

2. TRUSTING IN GOD OVERCOMES FEAR:

A. When we trust God, we don't need to fear anything:

2 Kings 6:14–17	Fear not: for they [God's angelic army] that be with us are more than they that be with them
2 Kings 19:6–7	Be not ye afraid of the words which thou hast heard
Nehemiah 4:14	Be not afraid of them: remember the Lord, which is great and terrible, and fight
Psalm 3:6	I will not be afraid of ten thousands of people, that have set themselves against me round about

Psalm 27:1,3	Though an host should encamp against me, my heart shall not fear: though war should rise against me
Psalm 46:1–2	God is our refuge … Therefore will not we fear, though the mountains be carried into the … sea
Isaiah 43:1–3	Fear not … when thou passest through the waters, I will be with thee
Hebrews 13:6	We may boldly say, "The Lord is my helper, and I will not fear what man shall do unto me"
Revelation 2:10	Fear none of those things which thou shalt suffer … be faithful unto death, and I will give thee crown of life

B. Examples of courage and fearlessness in danger:

Joshua 14:12–14	[Caleb fearlessly conquered the giant Anakim] (See also Numbers 13:28,33; Deuteronomy 9:1–2; Joshua 15:13–15.)
Nehemiah 6:5–11	[Nehemiah refused to be bluffed into fearing, or fleeing into the temple in fright]
Daniel 3:14–17	[Three Hebrews fearlessly refused to worship the idol]
Daniel 6:4–10	[Knowing it could cost him his life, Daniel refused to compromise his faith in God]
John 19:9–11	[Jesus refused to fear Pilate's power]
Philippians 1:14	Many brethren, waxing confident [because of] my bonds, are much more bold to speak the word without fear
Hebrews 11:27	[Moses] forsook Egypt, not fearing wrath of the king (See also Ezra 8:21–23,31; Acts 4:17–18,29,33; 7:54–60.)

C. Examples of men who refused to fear, though all others did:

1 Samuel 14:1–14	[Jonathan and armourbearer attacked Philistine garrison, while everyone else was terrified] (See also 1 Samuel 13:5–7.)
1 Samuel 17:4–11, 23–37,48	[All the armies of Israel were "sore afraid" of Goliath, but David boldly attacked him]
2 Samuel 23:8–22	[David's mighty men stood their ground and defeated their enemies despite overwhelming odds]

3. SOME CAUSES OF FEAR:

A. A lack of faith and trust in God and His Word:

Isaiah 51:12–13	Who art thou, that thou [art] afraid of a man … and forgettest the Lord thy maker?
Matthew 8:26	Why are ye fearful, O ye of little faith?
Mark 4:40	Why are ye so fearful? How is it ye have no faith?

B. Looking at circumstances and conditions:

Joshua 17:14–18	[Israelites fearful to attack the Canaanites because the Canaanites had powerful chariots of iron]

Psalm 107:23–27	[Storm at sea] Their soul is melted … at wit's end
Matthew 14:30	[Peter, walking on the sea] saw the wind boisterous … was afraid; and [began] to sink
Mark 4:37–40	[Storm on Sea of Galilee throws disciples into fear]
2 Corinthians 7:5	We were troubled on every side … within were fears (See also Isaiah 7:1–2.)

C. Disregarding God's Word:

Leviticus 26:15,17	If ye despise my statutes … ye shall flee when none pursueth
Deuteronomy 28:58, 65–67	If thou wilt not observe … the Lord shall give thee a trembling heart … and thou shalt fear day and night
Jeremiah 6:19,22–25	I will bring evil … because they have not hearkened unto my words … fear is on every side

D. Unrepented sin:

2 Chronicles 29:6,8	Our fathers have trespassed … wherefore he hath delivered them to trouble
Job 18:5,11	Terrors shall make [the wicked] afraid on every side
Isaiah 48:22	There is no peace, saith the Lord, unto the wicked

E. Evil spirits:

1 Samuel 15:23; 16:14–15	Thou [Saul] hast rejected the word of the Lord … an evil spirit from the Lord troubled [terrified] him

4. WHAT FEAR CAN RESULT IN:

A. It can bind:

Proverbs 29:25	The fear of man bringeth a snare
Hebrews 2:15	Who through fear of death were … subject to bondage

B. It can cause weakness:

Job 4:14	Fear came upon me, and trembling … all my bones shake
Isaiah 13:8	They shall be afraid: pangs … shall take hold of them
Jeremiah 6:24–25	Our hands wax feeble … fear is on every side

C. It can sap your will to fight:

Leviticus 26:36–37	Ye shall have no power to stand before your enemies
Joshua 2:11	As soon as we heard these things, our hearts did melt, neither did there remain any more courage
Joshua 5:1	Their heart melted, neither was there spirit in them any more (See also 1 Samuel 13:6–7.)

D. It hinders us from witnessing or standing up for our convictions:

Matthew 26:56	Then all the disciples forsook [Jesus], and fled
Matthew 26:69–74	[Peter, fearful, denied that he knew Jesus] (See also Mark 14:66–72; Luke 22:54–60; John 18:16–17,25–27.)
John 7:13	No man spake openly of him for fear of the Jews
John 9:22	These [evasive] words spake his parents, because they feared the Jews
John 12:42–43	Many believed on him; but did not confess him … for they loved the praise of men more than praise of God
John 19:12–16	[Pilate, fearing the Jews, gave in to their demands to have Jesus crucified]
John 19:38	Joseph … a disciple, but secretly for fear of the Jews

E. It can cause us to disobey God:

Numbers 13:28,31–33	[Israelites refused to invade Canaan for fear of the giants] (See also Numbers 14:1–5; Deuteronomy 1:26–28.)
1 Samuel 15:24	I have sinned … transgressed the commandment of the Lord … because I feared the people

F. It can cause mental torment and anguish:

1 John 4:18	Fear hath torment

G. Fear can even cause sickness and death:

Luke 21:26	Men's hearts failing them for fear (See also 1 Samuel 14:15–16; 28:5.)

H. If not checked, fear can get a grip on you:

Psalm 48:6	Fear took hold of them, and pain, as a woman in travail
Psalm 55:5	Fearfulness and trembling are come upon me, horror hath overwhelmed me
Jeremiah 6:22–25	Anguish hath taken hold of us … fear is on every side

I. Unchecked fear can become extreme:

Leviticus 26:17,36	Ye shall flee when none pursueth … sound of a shaken leaf shall chase them
Deuteronomy 28:66–67	Thou shalt fear day and night, and shalt have none assurance of thy life
Job 18:11,14	Terrors shall make him afraid on every side … shall bring him to the king of terrors
Psalm 53:5	There were they in great fear, where no fear was
Proverbs 28:1	The wicked flee when no man pursueth

J. Fears can materialise and become real things:

Job 3:25	The thing which I greatly feared is come upon me
Proverbs 10:24	The fear of the wicked, it shall come upon him

Isaiah 66:4	I will choose their delusions ... bring their fears upon them

K. Fear is contagious and can affect others:

Deuteronomy 20:8	What man is fearful? Let him go … lest his brethren's heart faint as well as his heart
Judges 7:3	Whosoever is fearful and afraid, let him … depart

(See also Judges 7:19–22; 1 Samuel 14:12–16.)

5. HOW TO HAVE PEACE AND FREEDOM FROM FEAR:

A. Trust in God:

Psalm 23:4	Though I walk through the valley of the shadow of death, I will fear no evil: for thou art with me
Psalm 31:13–14	Fear was on every side … but I trusted in thee
Psalm 56:3–4	What time I am afraid, I will trust in thee. I will not fear what flesh can do unto me
Psalm 91:2,5	The Lord is my refuge … [I shall] not be afraid for the terror by night
Psalm 112:7–8	He shall not be afraid … heart [trusts] in the Lord
Isaiah 26:3	Thou wilt keep him in perfect peace, whose mind is stayed on thee: because he trusteth in thee
Matthew 10:28	Fear not them which kill the body … but fear [God]
John 14:1	Let not your heart be troubled … believe in me
Philippians 4:7	The peace of God … shall keep your hearts and minds
1 John 4:18	There is no fear in love; love casteth out fear

B. Trust in God's Word:

Psalm 119:165	Great peace have they which love thy law: and nothing shall offend them
Proverbs 1:33	Whoso hearkeneth unto me … shall be quiet from fear
Proverbs 3:1–2	Let thine heart keep my commandments … peace shall they add to thee
Isaiah 48:18	O that thou hadst hearkened to my commandments! Then had thy peace been as a river

C. Remember that God is with you and will not fail you:

Deuteronomy 1:29–30	Dread not, neither be afraid of them … God goeth before you, he shall fight for you
Deuteronomy 20:3–4	Let not your hearts faint, fear not, and do not tremble, neither be ye terrified … for God goeth with you
Deuteronomy 31:6	Fear not, nor be afraid … God … will not fail thee
Zechariah 8:13	Fear not, but let your hands be strong
Mark 5:36	Be not afraid, only believe

D. When others with you are afraid:

Isaiah 8:12	Neither fear ye their fear, nor be afraid
Isaiah 35:4	Say to them that are of a fearful heart, "Be strong, fear not: behold, God … will come and save you"

E. Seek God for deliverance from fear:

Psalm 34:4	I sought the Lord, and he heard me, and delivered me from all my fears
Psalm 64:1	O God … preserve my life from fear of the enemy

F. Forsake your sins:

Job 11:13–15	[Pray to God and] put [iniquity] far away … Then shalt thou … be steadfast, and shalt not fear

G. Rebuke the Devil and the spirit of fear:

James 4:7	Resist the devil, and he will flee from you
1 John 4:18	There is no fear in love; perfect love casteth out fear

H. The solution—the Holy Spirit and faith:

Acts 4:29,31	Behold their threatenings … grant unto thy servants, that with all boldness they may speak thy word
Hebrews 11:33–34	Who through faith … waxed valiant in fight

6. THE FEAR OF GOD:

(The "Fear of God" is a feeling of reverence, awe, and respect, not the unpleasant emotion of terror or dread.)

A. The Bible tells us to fear God:

Joshua 24:14	Fear the Lord, and serve him in sincerity and in truth
Psalm 19:9	The fear of the Lord is clean (Compare with Proverbs 29:25.)
Proverbs 3:7	Fear the Lord, and depart from evil
Ecclesiastes 12:13	Fear God, and keep his commandments: for this is the whole duty of man
Isaiah 8:12–13	Neither fear ye their fear, nor be afraid … Let him [God] be your fear
Luke 12:4–5	Be not afraid of [men] … I will warn you whom ye shall fear: Fear him [God] … yea, I say, Fear him
Hebrews 10:31	It is a fearful thing to fall into the hands of … God (See also Matthew 10:28.)

B. God blesses those who fear Him:

Psalm 25:12	He that feareth the Lord … shall he teach in the way
Psalm 31:19	How great is thy goodness … for them that fear thee
Psalm 34:9	There is no want [lack] to them that fear him
Psalm 103:13	The Lord [has compassion on] them that fear him

Psalm 147:11	The Lord taketh pleasure in them that fear him
Proverbs 1:7	The fear of the Lord is the beginning of knowledge
Proverbs 9:10	The fear of the Lord is the beginning of wisdom
Proverbs 14:26	In the fear of the Lord is strong confidence
Malachi 4:2	Unto you that fear my name shall the Sun of righteousness arise with healing in his wings
Acts 10:35	He that feareth him … is accepted with him
Revelation 11:18	Reward thy servants, and them that fear thy name

THANKFULNESS

Praise and thankfulness vs. murmuring and complaining

1. HAVING A THANKFUL, GRATEFUL ATTITUDE:

A. God wants and expects us to be thankful:

Psalm 50:14	Offer unto God thanksgiving
Psalm 95:2	Come before his presence with thanksgiving
Psalm 100:4	Be thankful unto him
Psalm 140:13	Surely the righteous shall give thanks unto thy name
Ephesians 5:20	Giving thanks always for all things unto God
Colossians 3:15	Be ye thankful
1 Thessalonians 5:18	In everything give thanks: for this is the will of God
	(See also Psalm 92:1.)

B. We should be content:

Philippians 4:11	In whatsoever state I am, therewith ... be content
1 Timothy 6:6	Godliness with contentment is great gain
1 Timothy 6:8	Having food and raiment let us be therewith content
Hebrews 13:5	Be content with such things as ye have
	(See also Proverbs 15:16–17.)

C. Don't take God's blessings for granted:

Psalm 68:19	Blessed be Lord ... who daily loadeth us with benefits
Psalm 103:2	Bless the Lord ... and forget not all his benefits
Luke 17:12–18	Were not ten [lepers] cleansed? Where are the nine? [None] returned to give glory to God, save [one]

D. Remember to regularly thank Him for your blessings:

2 Samuel 22:49–50	Thou hast delivered me ... therefore I will give thanks
1 Chronicles 16:8	Give thanks ... make known his deeds among the people
Psalm 136:1–3	Give thanks unto God ... for his mercy endureth forever
1 Corinthians 15:57	Thanks be to God, which giveth us the victory
2 Corinthians 2:14	Thanks be unto God, which ... causeth us to triumph
	(See also Psalm 26:7; 107:22.)

2. PRAISING GOD:

A. We are admonished to praise God:

Psalm 18:3	The Lord ... is worthy to be praised
Psalm 22:3	[God] inhabitest the praises of Israel
Psalm 66:8	O bless our God, ye people, and make the voice of his praise to be heard
Psalm 67:3	O God, let all the people praise thee
Psalm 100:4	Enter into his gates with thanksgiving, and into his courts with praise

Psalm 103:1	Bless the Lord, O my soul: and all that is within me, bless his holy name
Psalm 107:8	Oh that men would praise the Lord for his goodness, and for his wonderful works
Psalm 113:1	Praise ye the Lord, O ye servants of the Lord
Psalm 117:1	Praise the Lord, all ye nations … all ye people
Psalm 147:1	Praise ye the Lord: for … praise is comely
Psalm 150:6	Let every thing that hath breath praise the Lord
1 Peter 2:9	Ye should show forth praises of him who called you

(See also Psalm 50:23; 148:all; 150:all.)

B. Praise God in song:

Psalm 30:4	Sing unto the Lord … and give thanks
Psalm 69:30	Praise the name of God with a song … and thanksgiving
Psalm 92:1	It is a good thing to … sing praises unto thy name
Psalm 98:1	Sing unto the Lord a new song
Psalm 147:1,7	Sing unto the Lord with thanksgiving; sing praise
Ephesians 5:19	Making melody in your heart to the Lord
Colossians 3:16	Singing with grace in your hearts to the Lord

C. Praise God happily:

Psalm 5:11	Let them that love thy name be joyful in thee
Psalm 95:2	Make a joyful noise unto him with psalms
Isaiah 51:3	Joy and gladness … thanksgiving, and the voice of melody
Jeremiah 30:19	Out of them shall proceed thanksgiving and the voice of them that make merry

(See also Psalm 100:1; Jeremiah 33:11.)

D. Have a continual attitude of praising God:

Psalm 34:1	I will bless the Lord at all times: his praise shall continually be in my mouth
Psalm 35:28	My tongue shall speak of thy … praise all day long
Psalm 71:8	Let my mouth be filled with thy praise … all the day
Hebrews 13:15	Let us offer … praise to God continually … our lips giving thanks to his name

(See also Psalm 30:12; 72:15; 79:13; 104:33; 113:3.)

3. MURMURING (COMPLAINING) FORBIDDEN BY GOD:

John 6:43	Jesus said unto them, Murmur not among yourselves
1 Corinthians 10:10	Neither murmur ye, as some of them murmured
Philippians 2:14	Do all things without murmurings and disputings

(See also Psalm 144:14.)

4. CAUSES OF MURMURING:

A. Lack of gratitude for what God has given us:

Numbers 11:4–6,18 We remember the fish, cucumbers, melons, leeks … now there is nothing at all, beside this manna

Numbers 21:4–5 There is no bread … and our soul loatheth this [manna]

B. Lack of faith for God to supply our needs:

Exodus 16:2–3 The whole congregation ... murmured against Moses ... in the wilderness [when they ran out of food]

Exodus 17:1–4 People thirsted … and murmured … thou brought us out of Egypt, to kill us with thirst

(See also Exodus 15:23–24.)

C. Loss of faith in God's Word and His power:

Psalm 106:24–25 They believed not his word … but murmured

John 6:60–66 Many disciples said, This is an hard saying … his disciples murmured … many went back

(Compare Exodus 3:4–8; 4:30–31 with Exodus 14:9–12; Deuteronomy 1:19–27; Numbers 14:1–11.)

D. Giving up and losing hope:

1 Samuel 27:1 David said, "I shall perish one day by the hand of Saul"

1 Kings 19:1–4,10 Elijah … requested that he might die

Jeremiah 20:14–18 Cursed be the day I was born … wherefore came I … out of the womb to see labour and sorrow?

Jonah 4:1–9 Jonah prayed, Take my life from me; for it is better for me to die than to live

(See also Job 7:6,11; 10:1.)

E. Lack of faith that God loves us:

Deuteronomy 1:27 Ye murmured, and said, Because the Lord hated us, he brought us [to Canaan] to destroy us

(See also Psalm 73:13–14; 77:1–9.)

F. Thinking that God is far away and doesn't hear:

Job 23:2–9 Today is my complaint bitter: Oh that I knew where I might find him. I cannot perceive him

Psalm 10:1 Why standest thou afar off, O Lord? Why hidest thou?

(See also Psalm 13:1; 22:1,12.)

G. Self-righteously judging others:

Mark 14:4–10 Why was this waste … made? For it might have been sold … they murmured. Judas … went to betray him

Luke 15:2 The Pharisees murmured, This man receiveth sinners

Luke 19:7	When [the Pharisees] saw it, they all murmured ... he [has] gone to be a guest with ... a sinner

5. WHY MURMURING IS DANGEROUS:

A. Murmuring angers God:

Numbers 11:1	When the people complained, it displeased the Lord: and his anger was kindled; and fire ... consumed them
Numbers 11:10,33	[Israelites wailed for meat] and the anger of the Lord kindled greatly ... and the Lord smote the people
Numbers 21:4–6	The people spake against God ... and the Lord sent fiery serpents among the people ... and much people died
1 Corinthians 10:10	Neither murmur ye, as some of them [Israelites] also murmured, and were destroyed of the destroyer (See also Numbers 17:10.)

B. God may take us at our word:

Numbers 14:1–2	All the children of Israel murmured ... Would God that we had died in this wilderness
Numbers 14:26–35	As ye have spoken, so will I do to you: Your carcases shall fall in this wilderness ... even forty years

6. WHAT TO DO WHEN PROBLEMS ARISE:

A. Praise and rejoice even when things go wrong:

Habakkuk 3:17–18	Although the ... fields shall yield no meat; the flock shall be cut off ... yet will I rejoice in the Lord
Matthew 5:11–12	When men revile you, and persecute you, and say ... evil against you falsely ... rejoice, and be exceeding glad
Luke 6:22–23	When men shall hate you ... separate you ... reproach you ... rejoice ye ... and leap for joy
Acts 5:40–41	They called the apostles, and beat them ... they departed rejoicing that they were worthy to suffer shame
Acts 16:22–25	Beat them ... cast them into prison ... Paul and Silas prayed, and sang praises unto God
1 Thessalonians 5:18	In everything give thanks: this is the will of God
1 Peter 4:12–13	Think it not strange ... the fiery trial ... but rejoice (See also Jeremiah 15:10–11,16; Jonah 2:all; Philippians 4:4.)

B. If you have a genuine deep grievance, tell God:

Psalm 55:2–3	Hear me: I mourn in my complaint, and make a noise ... because of the enemy ... my heart is sore pained
Psalm 55:22	Cast thy burden upon the Lord, and he shall sustain thee
Psalm 77:1–4	I was troubled: I complained, my spirit ... overwhelmed

Psalm 142:2–3	I poured out my complaint before him; I showed him my trouble ... my spirit was overwhelmed
1 Peter 5:7	Casting all your care upon him; for he careth for you
	(See also Hebrews 4:14–16.)

C. Keep on praising, and victory will come:

2 Chronicles 20:22	When they began to sing and to praise, the Lord set ambushments against the [enemy]

D. Keep a thankful attitude in prayer:

Philippians 4:6	By prayer ... with thanksgiving let your requests be made known unto God
Colossians 4:2	Continue in prayer ... with thanksgiving

PRIDE, SELF-RIGHTEOUSNESS, AND HUMILITY

1. WHAT DOES GOD THINK ABOUT PRIDE?

A. He hates it:

Proverbs 6:16–17	These … doth the Lord hate: a proud look
Proverbs 16:5	Every one that is proud … is an abomination to Lord

B. We should hate it too:

Proverbs 8:13	Pride, and arrogancy, and the evil way, and the froward mouth, do I hate.

C. Pride is a sin, not a virtue:

Proverbs 21:4	An high look, and a proud heart … is sin
Habakkuk 2:4	Behold, his soul which is lifted up is not upright
1 John 2:16	Pride … is not of the Father, but is of the world

2. WHY IS IT WRONG FOR US TO BE PROUD?

A. Because only God is great; we are not:

Psalm 66:5–7	Come and see the works of God … he ruleth … let not the rebellious exalt themselves
Psalm 97:9	Thou, Lord, art high … exalted far above all
Ezekiel 28:2	Thine heart is lifted up … yet thou art a man, and not God, though thou set thine heart as … God
Philippians 2:9–10	God hath highly exalted him [Jesus], and given him a name above every name … every knee should bow

(See also Psalm 21:13; 57:5,11; 108:5; Isaiah 2:11,17.)

B. God alone should get the glory:

Acts 12:20–23	Angel … smote him, because he gave not God the glory
1 Corinthians 10:31	Whatsoever ye do, do all the glory of God

(See also Jeremiah 9:23–24; 1 Corinthians 1:28–29.)

C. Pride makes us ignore and forget God:

Deuteronomy 8:14	[When] thine heart be lifted up … thou forget the Lord
Psalm 10:4	The wicked, through … pride … will not seek after God
Hosea 13:6	Heart was exalted; therefore have they forgotten me

D. God will distance Himself from and resist the proud:

Psalm 138:6	The proud [God] knoweth afar off
James 4:6	God resisteth the proud, but giveth grace unto humble

E. Pride makes us rebel against the Word:

Nehemiah 9:16–17,29	They dealt proudly … and hearkened not to thy [word]

F. It gives us an exaggerated sense of greatness:

Obadiah 1:3	The pride of thine heart hath deceived thee, that saith, who shall bring me down?
Romans 12:3	[Thinking] of himself more highly than he ought to
Galatians 6:3	If a man think himself to be something, when he is nothing, he deceiveth himself

G. It creates self-exaltation and a desire to be honoured:

Proverbs 25:27	For men to search their own glory is not glory
Matthew 23:5–7	[The proud Pharisees] love … greetings [in public], and to be called [Master, Master]
Mark 12:38–39	Scribes … love … chief seats … and uppermost rooms
Jude 1:16	Their mouth speaketh great swelling words, having men's persons in admiration

H. When we seek to please men, we often displease God:

1 Samuel 15:30	I have sinned: [but] honour me … before the [people]
John 5:44	Ye … receive honour one of another, and seek not the honour that cometh from God only
John 12:43	They loved praise of men more than the praise of God
Galatians 1:10	If I pleased men … not be the servant of Christ

I. Pride makes us think we are "wise":

Proverbs 3:7	Be not wise in thine own eyes: fear the Lord
1 Corinthians 3:18	Let no man deceive himself. If any … seemeth wise
1 Corinthians 8:2	If any think that he knoweth any thing, he knoweth nothing ye as he ought to know

J. Pride gives us a "know-it-all" attitude:

Psalm 131:1	[The haughty exercise themselves in great matters, in things too high for them]
Proverbs 26:12	Seest thou a man "wise" in his own conceit? There is more hope of a fool than of him

(See also 1 Timothy 1:7.)

K. Pride causes arguments:

Proverbs 13:10	Only by pride cometh contention
Proverbs 28:25	He that is of a proud heart stirreth up strife

(See also Proverbs 14:3; 21:24.)

L. Prides corrupts us:

Mark 7:22–23	Pride [comes] from within, and defiles the man

M. Pride will bring about our downfall:

Proverbs 11:2	When pride cometh, then cometh shame
Proverbs 16:18	Pride goeth before destruction, and an haughty spirit before a fall

Proverbs 18:12	Before destruction the heart of man is haughty
Proverbs 29:23	A man's pride shall bring him low
Ezekiel 28:12–17	[The fall of Satan happened because he exalted himself in pride] (See also Isaiah 14:12–15.)
Daniel 5:18,20–21	God gave Nebuchadnezzar … majesty … and honour: But when his heart was lifted up … he was deposed
1 Corinthians 10:12	Him that thinketh he standeth take heed lest he fall

3. SOME CAUSES OF PRIDE:

A. Beauty:

Ezekiel 28:17	Thine heart is lifted up because of thy beauty

B. Material abundance:

Deuteronomy 8:12–14	Lest when thou … art full … and all that thou hast is multiplied; then thine heart be lifted up
Ezekiel 28:5	Thine heart is lifted up because of thy riches
Hosea 13:6	They were filled, and their heart was exalted

C. Being overly secure:

Psalm 73:5–6	They are not in trouble as other men … therefore pride compasseth them about as a chain

D. Being overly affected by exaltation:

2 Chronicles 26:15–16	He was marvelously helped, till he was strong. But when he was strong, his heart was lifted up
Daniel 11:11–12	[Victory over enemies causes heart to be lifted up]
1 Timothy 3:6	Not a novice, lest being lifted up with pride he fall

4. WARNINGS AGAINST PRIDE:

A. We should avoid proud boasting:

1 Samuel 2:3	Talk no more so exceeding proudly; let not arrogancy come out of your mouth
Proverbs 27:2	Let another man praise thee, and not thine own mouth
2 Corinthians 10:18	Not he that commendeth himself is approved, but whom the Lord commendeth

B. We shouldn't exalt ourselves:

Proverbs 25:6–7	Put not forth thyself in the presence of the king, and stand not in the place of great men
Luke 14:10	When thou art bidden … sit down in the lowest room

C. If we're proud, we're in a dangerous position:

Psalm 18:27	Thou [God] wilt bring down high looks
Proverbs 15:25	The Lord will destroy the house of the proud

Ecclesiastes 7:16	Be not righteous over much [overly righteous] … why shouldst thou destroy thyself?
Jeremiah 48:25–26,29	[Exceeding proud, lofty, arrogant, haughty Moabites magnified selves against God and were destroyed]

5. WHY IS IT WRONG TO THINK THAT WE—IN OURSELVES—ARE GOOD AND RIGHTEOUS?

A. Because we are not:

Job 15:14–16	What is man, that he should be clean? … righteous? ... the heavens are not clean in his sight. How much more abominable and filthy is man
Psalm 130:3	If thou shouldest mark iniquities, who shall stand?
Proverbs 20:9	Who can say, I have made my heart clean, I am pure?
Ecclesiastes 7:20	There is not a just man upon earth, that doeth good and sinneth not
Isaiah 64:6	We are all as an unclean thing, and all our righteousnesses are as filthy rags
Romans 3:10,23	There is none righteous, no, not one … all have sinned
Romans 7:18	In me, that is, in my flesh, dwelleth no good thing

B. Only God is good:

Job 9:2	But how should man be just with God?
Psalm 71:16	I will make mention of thy righteousness, thine only
Matthew 19:17	There is none good but one, that is, God

C. Doing so causes us to be lifted up in pride:

Proverbs 30:12–13	[They] are pure in their own eyes … O how lofty are their eyes! And their eyelids are lifted up
Luke 18:11	God, I thank thee, that I am not as other men … unjust

D. It separates us from God:

Job 13:16	An hypocrite shall not come before him
Romans 10:3	They … going about to establish their own righteousness, have not submitted unto the righteousness of God

E. It makes us unable to see our sins:

Job 32:1	Job … was righteous in his own eyes (See also Proverbs 16:2; 21:2.)
Proverbs 30:12	A generation that are pure in their own eyes, and yet is not washed from their filthiness
Luke 6:41–42	Why perceivest not the beam that is in thine own eye?
John 9:41	Ye say, "We see"; therefore your sin remaineth

F. True righteousness means trusting God:

Galatians 3:6	Abraham believed God, it was accounted … righteousness

Philippians 3:9	Not having mine own righteousness ... but ... of God
Titus 3:5	Not by works of righteousness which we have done, but according to his mercy he saved us

6. WHY IS IT WRONG TO THINK THAT WE—IN OURSELVES—ARE BETTER THAN OTHERS?

A. Because we're not:

John 8:7	He that is without sin ... let him first cast a stone
Romans 3:23	All have sinned, and come short of the glory of God

B. A proud attitude displeases and angers God:

Isaiah 65:5	[They] say, "I am holier than thou." These are a smoke in my [God's] nose
Luke 16:15	Ye are they which justify yourselves ... but ... that which is highly esteemed among men is abomination [to] God

C. It makes us despise and be unmerciful to others:

Matthew 23:29	Ye have omitted the weightier matters ... mercy
Luke 18:9	[They] trusted in themselves that they were righteous, and despised others
Luke 18:11	God, I thank thee, that I am not as other men are ... unjust ... or even as this publican [tax collector] (See also Matthew 9:13.)

D. We only are what we are by God's grace:

1 Corinthians 4:7	Who maketh thee to differ from another? And what hast thou that thou didst not receive?
1 Corinthians 15:10	By the grace of God I am what I am
2 Corinthians 3:5	Not that we are sufficient of ourselves to think any thing as of ourselves

7. THE HUMBLING OF THE PROUD:

A. God can—and does—humble the proud:

Genesis 11:1–8	[Men were building the tower of Babel in pride, so God confused and scattered them]
1 Samuel 13:8–14	[Saul presumed to offer the sacrifice without waiting for Samuel, and lost the kingdom as a result]
2 Chronicles 32:24–25	Heart was lifted up: therefore ... wrath [was] upon him
Job 33:15–17	[God works on our hearts at night to remove pride]
Psalm 101:5	Him that hath an high look and a proud heart will not I suffer [allow to continue]
Isaiah 2:11–12	The lofty looks of man shall be humbled, and the haughtiness of men shall be bowed down ... every one that is proud and lofty ... shall be brought low

Isaiah 13:11	I will cause the arrogancy of the proud to cease
Daniel 4:30–35	[King Nebuchadnezzar, lifted up in pride, was deposed by God, abased as a beast, and learned humility]
Daniel 4:37	Those that walk in pride he is able to abase
Daniel 5:20–21	When his … mind [was] hardened in pride … was deposed
2 Corinthians 12:7	Lest I [Paul] should be exalted above measure … there was given to me a thorn in the flesh

(See also Jeremiah 50:31–32; Obadiah 1:4.)

B. It is a spiritual law: If we're proud, we will be humbled:

Matthew 23:12	Whosoever shall exalt himself shall be abased
Luke 14:11	Whosever exalteth himself shall be abased
Luke 18:14	Every one that exalteth himself shall be abased

C. Being humbled teaches us that God is in charge:

Job 42:1–6	[After being humbled, Job said:] I know that thou canst do every thing … I … repent
Daniel 4:32–35	Eat grass … until thou know that the most High ruleth

8. WHY WE SHOULD WANT TO BE HUMBLE:

A. Because God loves and delights in the humble:

Psalm 51:17	The sacrifices of God are a broken spirit: a broken and a contrite heart, O God, thou wilt not despise
Psalm 138:6	The Lord be high, yet hath he respect unto the lowly
1 Peter 3:4	A meek and quiet spirit … is in the sight of God of great price
1 Peter 5:5	God … giveth grace to the humble

B. He is close to the humble:

Psalm 34:18	The Lord is nigh unto them that are of a broken heart
Isaiah 57:15	The high and lofty one that inhabiteth eternity [dwells] with him that is of a contrite and humble spirit

C. He requires us to be humble:

Micah 6:8	What doth the Lord require … walk humbly with thy God
Colossians 3:12	Put on, as the elect of God … humbleness of mind

D. Humility brings honour and blessing:

Proverbs 22:4	By humility … are riches, and honour, and life
Proverbs 29:23	Honour shall uphold the humble spirit

E. If we are humble, God will exalt us:

Matthew 23:12	He that shall humble himself shall be exalted
Luke 1:52	He put down the mighty … and exalted them of low degree

F. God helps the humble:

Psalm 9:12	He forgetteth not the cry of the humble
Psalm 25:9	The meek will he guide … and meek will he teach his way
Psalm 34:18	The Lord … saveth such as be of a contrite spirit
Psalm 147:6	The Lord lifteth up the meek: He casteth wicked down
Isaiah 57:15	[I] revive spirit of the humble, and heart of contrite ones
Luke 1:48	He hath regarded the low estate of his handmaiden
1 Peter 5:5	God resisteth the proud, and giveth grace to the humble

G. Humility can spare us from trouble:

1 Kings 21:17,25–29	[Wicked king Ahab humbled himself before God, so God didn't bring judgement during his lifetime]
2 Chronicles 32:26	Hezekiah humbled himself for the pride of his heart … so that the wrath of the Lord came not

H. God gives the humble true wisdom:

Proverbs 11:2	[Pride causes shame] but with the lowly is wisdom
1 Corinthians 3:18	Let him become a fool, that he may be wise
	(See also Luke 10:21.)

I. Humility is true greatness in God's eyes:

Ecclesiastes 7:8	The patient in spirit is better than proud in spirit
Matthew 18:4	Whosoever shall humble himself is greatest in the kingdom of heaven
Matthew 19:30	The last shall be first
Mark 10:43	Whosoever will be great … shall be your minister
Luke 22:26	He that is greatest … let him be as the younger

J. God uses and exalts the humble:

1 Samuel 15:17	When thou wast little in thine own sight … the Lord
Proverbs 15:33	Before honour is humility
James 4:10	Humble yourselves … and he shall lift you up
1 Peter 5:6	Humble yourselves … that he may exalt you in due time

K. Other blessings upon the meek:

Psalm 37:11	The meek shall inherit the earth; and shall delight
Psalm 149:4	The Lord … will beautify the meek with salvation
Matthew 5:5	Blessed are the meek: for they shall inherit the earth

9. KEEPING A HUMBLE ATTITUDE:

A. Remind yourself that anything good is only Jesus, not you:

Genesis 41:15–16	Joseph answered Pharaoh, saying, It is not in me: God shall give Pharaoh an answer
Daniel 2:26–30	God … revealeth secrets. But as for me, this secret is not revealed to me for any wisdom that I have

1 Corinthians 4:7	What hast thou that thou didst not receive [from God]? Why dost thou glory?
1 Corinthians 15:9–10	I am not meet [worthy] to be called an apostle … but by the grace of God I am what I am
2 Corinthians 10:17	He that glorieth, let him glory in the Lord (See also Jeremiah 9:23–24.)
Galatians 6:14	God forbid I should glory, save in the cross of Jesus (See also Romans 2:11; Galatians 6:3.)

B. Read and obey the Word:

Deuteronomy 17:19–20	[Read and obey the Word, so that your] heart be not lifted up

C. Realistically admit your limitations:

Romans 12:3	[Don't] think of [yourself] more highly than [you] ought to think; but think soberly
Romans 12:16	Be not wise in your own conceits

10. HUMILITY WITH ONE ANOTHER:

A. Follow Jesus' example of humility:

Matthew 21:5	Thy King [Jesus] cometh unto thee, meek … upon an ass
Luke 22:27	He that sitteth at meat [is greater] … but I am among you as he that serveth
John 13:5,12–15	He began to wash the disciples' feet, and wipe them … I have given you an example, that ye should do as I
Philippians 2:5–8	Let this mind be in you … Jesus made himself of no reputation … [became] a servant … humbled himself

B. Other examples of true humility:

1 Samuel 25:40–41	[Abigail, when asked to marry David, said:] Let [me] be a servant to wash the feet of [his] servants
Mark 7:25–30	[Syrophenician woman said:] Yet the dogs under the table eat of the children's crumbs
Luke 7:2–7	[Pharisees said:] he was worthy for whom he should do this. The centurion [said], I am not worthy
John 1:27	[Jesus'] shoe's latchet I am not worthy to unloose

C. Submit humbly to one another:

Luke 22:25–26	Kings … exercise lordship. But ye shall not be so. He that is greatest … let him be as the younger
Ephesians 5:21	Submitting yourselves one to another in fear of God
1 Peter 5:5	All of you be subject one to another, and be clothed with humility: for God resisteth the proud

D. Love and honour others:

Romans 12:10	With brotherly love; in honour preferring one another
Romans 12:16	Mind not high things, condescend to men of low estate
Romans 14:2–3	Let not him that eateth despise him that eateth not
1 Corinthians 13:4	Charity [love] vaunteth not itself, is not puffed up
Philippians 2:3	Let nothing be done through strife or vainglory but in lowliness of mind let each esteem other better than themselves

E. Be humble when pointing out other's errors:

Luke 6:42	Cast out first the beam out of thine own eye
Galatians 6:1	Restore such an one in the spirit of meekness
2 Timothy 2:25	In meekness instructing those that oppose themselves

11. THE SOLUTION:

A. Confess your faults and inabilities and humble yourself before God:

James 4:10	Humble yourselves in the sight of the Lord
1 Peter 5:6	Humble yourselves ... under the mighty hand of God

B. Ask others to pray for you to overcome pride:

Matthew 18:19–20	If two of you shall agree [in prayer] it shall be done
James 5:16	Confess your faults one to another, and pray one for another

C. Examples of humbling oneself before God:

2 Samuel 24:2–4,8–10	[In pride, David took a census of his kingdom to see how great he was, then repented and sought mercy]
Job 40:1–5; 42:1–6	[Self-righteous Job—see 32:1; 35:2—humbled himself, confessed he was vile, and repented]
Psalm 51:1–4	I acknowledge my ... sin ... that thou mightiest be justified when thou speakest
Daniel 4:33–35,37	[King Nebuchadnezzar humbled himself and confessed that only God was great]

(See also 1 Samuel 9:21, about Saul; 2 Samuel 7:18, about David; 1 Kings 3:7, about Solomon; Matthew 3:14, about John the Baptist.)

12. SPECIAL PASSAGES:

1 Kings 12:1–16	[Rehoboam "answered the people roughly"]
2 Chronicles 26:14–23	[King Uzziah, "lifted up," presumed to offer incense]
Daniel 4:all	[Nebuchadnezzar's pride, humiliation, and restoration]
Luke 18:9–14	[The parable of the Pharisee and the tax collector]

THE POWER OF THE TONGUE

"Death and life are in the power of the tongue." (Proverbs 18:21)

1. THE POWER OF POSITIVE SPEECH:

A. Loving, wholesome speech has a great effect:

2 Chronicles 10:7	If thou be kind unto this people … and speak good words to them, they will be thy servants forever
Proverbs 15:1	A soft answer turneth away wrath
Proverbs 15:23	A word spoken in due season, how good is it
Proverbs 25:15	By long forbearing is a prince persuaded, and a soft tongue breaketh the bone.

B. Wise speech is health and life:

Proverbs 10:11	The mouth of a righteous man is a well of life
Proverbs 12:18	The tongue of the wise is health
Proverbs 15:4	A wholesome tongue is a tree of life
Proverbs 16:24	Pleasant words are … sweet to the soul, and health

C. Other points on wholesome speech:

Proverbs 8:6	The opening of my lips shall be right things
Proverbs 14:3	The lips of the wise shall preserve them
Proverbs 31:26	In her tongue is the law of kindness
Ecclesiastes 10:12	If any man offend not in word, the same is a perfect [complete, mature] man

(See also Psalm 37:30; Proverbs 10:31; 15:7; 24:26; Malachi 2:6–7.)

D. Speaking of the right things at the right time:

Proverbs 10:32	The lips of the righteous know what is acceptable
Proverbs 25:11	A word fitly spoken is like apples of gold in pictures of silver
Ecclesiastes 8:5	A wise man's heart discerneth both time and judgement

E. Speaking encouraging words to strengthen others:

Genesis 50:21	And he comforted them, and spake kindly unto them
Deuteronomy 3:28	Encourage him, and strengthen him
Job 4:4	Thy words have upholden him that was falling, and thou hast strengthened the feeble knees
Job 16:5	I would strengthen you with my mouth
Isaiah 35:3–4	Strengthen the weak hands … say to them, be strong
Isaiah 50:4	Speak a word in season to him that is weary

F. Talking about God's Word:

Deuteronomy 6:6–7	Thou shalt talk of [the word] when thou sittest … when thou walkest … when thou liest down … and risest up
Psalm 119:172	My tongue shall talk of thy word
John 6:63	The words that I speak unto you, they are spirit, and … life

Ephesians 5:19	Speaking to yourselves in psalms and hymns and … songs
1 Peter 4:11	If any man speak, let him speak as the oracles of God

G. Sharing testimonies about the great things God has done:

Psalm 9:11	Sing praises … declare among the people his doings
Psalm 35:28	My tongue shall talk of thy righteousness and of thy praise all the day long
Psalm 66:16	I will declare what he hath done for my soul
Psalm 145:1–7,10,12,21	I will speak of … thy majesty, and of thy wondrous works … make known to men his mighty acts
Acts 12:17	He … declared unto them how the Lord had brought him out of the prison
	(See also Psalm 37:30; 40:9–10; 71:17; Isaiah 12:4.)

H. Have a sense of humour and be able to laugh:

Psalm 126:2	Then was our mouth filled with laughter (See also Job 8:21.)
Proverbs 17:22	A merry heart doeth good like a medicine (See also Proverbs 15:13,15.)
	(See also Genesis 21:6; Ecclesiastes 3:4; 10:19.)

2. Silence and restrained speech:

Ecclesiastes 3:7	[There is] a time to keep silence, and a time to speak

A. The dangers of speaking too much:

Proverbs 10:19	In the multitude of words there wanteth [lacks] not sin
Proverbs 14:23	In all labour there is profit: but the talk of the lips tendeth only to penury

B. The wisdom of being slow to speak:

Proverbs 18:13	He that answereth a matter before he heareth it, it is folly and shame unto him
Ecclesiastes 5:2,6	Be not rash [hasty] with thy mouth … wherefore should God be angry … and destroy the work of thine hands?
John 8:1–9	[Example of Jesus avoiding being rushed into answering]
James 1:19	Let every man be swift to hear, slow to speak

C. It can be wise to speak little:

Proverbs 17:27	He that hath knowledge spareth his words
Ecclesiastes 5:3	A fool's voice is known by multitude of words (See also Matthew 5:37.)

D. It is often wise not to speak at all:

Job 13:5	O that ye would altogether hold your peace. And it should be your wisdom
Proverbs 10:19	He that refraineth his lips is wise

Proverbs 11:12	A man of understanding holdeth his peace
Proverbs 17:28	Even a fool, when he holdeth his peace, is counted wise: and he that shutteth lips is … a man of understanding
Proverbs 21:23	Who keepeth … his tongue keepeth his soul from troubles

E. Watch your words:

Psalm 39:1	To … sin not with my tongue: I will keep my mouth with a bridle, while the wicked is before me
Psalm 141:3	Set a watch, O Lord, before my mouth; keep … my lips.
Proverbs 13:3	He that keepeth his mouth keepeth his life
Matthew 12:36	Every idle word that men shall speak, they shall give account thereof in the day of judgement

F. Keeping secrets:

Proverbs 11:13	A talebearer [gossip] revealeth secrets: but he that is of a faithful spirit concealeth the matter
Proverbs 25:9	Debate thy cause with thy neighbour himself; and discover [disclose] not a secret to another
Micah 7:5	Keep the doors of thy mouth from her that lieth in thy bosom (See also Judges 14:15–17; 16:4–6,15–21.)
Matthew 9:30	Jesus straitly charged them … see that no man know it
Matthew 12:14–16	[Jesus] charged them they should not make him known
Mark 1:43–45	See thou say nothing to any man (See also Matthew 8:4.)
Mark 9:9–10	[Jesus] charged them that they should tell no man what things they had seen (See also Matthew 17:9; Luke 9:36.)
Luke 8:56	He charged them that they should tell no man what was done (See also Mark 5:43.)
Luke 9:20–21	He … commanded them to tell no man that thing (See also Matthew 16:20.)
Acts 23:22	Tell no man that thou hast shewed these things to me (See also Joshua 2:14,20.)

G. Learning how to be quiet:

Job 6:24	Teach me, and I will hold my tongue
1 Thessalonians 4:11	Study to be quiet, and to do [mind] your own business

H. The foolish simply cannot keep their mouth shut:

Proverbs 15:2	The mouth of fools poureth forth foolishness
Proverbs 20:3	Honour … to cease … but every fool will be meddling
Proverbs 29:11	A fool uttereth all his mind

3. THE DAMAGE AN UNCONTROLLED TONGUE WILL DO:

A. An uncontrolled tongue will defile you and others:

Matthew 15:11	That which cometh out of the mouth … defileth a man
Matthew 15:18	Those things which proceed out of the mouth come forth from the heart; and they defile a man
James 3:6	The tongue is … a world of iniquity … it defileth the whole body

B. A gossiping tongue is a fire:

Proverbs 16:27	Ungodly man … in his lips there is as a burning fire
James 3:5–6	The tongue is a fire … it setteth on fire … and is set on fire of hell

C. A slanderous, wicked tongue is a deadly poison:

Psalm 140:3	Adders' poison is under their lips
Ecclesiastes 10:11	The serpent will bite without enchantment; and a babbler is no better
Romans 3:13	The poison of asps is under their lips
James 3:8	The tongue … is … full of deadly poison

D. A sharp tongue can inflict deep wounds:

Proverbs 12:18	There is that speaketh like the piercings of a sword
Proverbs 25:18	Man that beareth false witness … is a maul, and a sword
Proverbs 26:22	The words of a talebearer are as wounds, and they go down into the innermost parts

E. A malicious tongue destroys and kills:

Proverbs 11:9	An hypocrite with his mouth destroyeth his neighbour
Proverbs 18:21	Death and life are in the power of the tongue
Proverbs 26:28	A flattering mouth worketh ruin

F. It destroys love and friendship:

Proverbs 16:28	A whisperer [gossiper] separateth chief friends
Acts 14:2	Made their minds evil affected against the brethren

4. FOOLISH AND EVIL SPEECH:

A. Evil speech comes from an evil heart:

Proverbs 15:2	The mouth of fools poureth out foolishness
Proverbs 15:28	The mouth of the wicked poureth out evil things
Matthew 12:35	An evil man out of [his heart] bringeth forth evil things

B. Evil, foolish speech corrupts:

Ecclesiastes 10:1	Dead flies … send forth a stinking … so doth a little folly in him that is in reputation for wisdom

1 Corinthians 15:33	Evil communications corrupt good manners

C. The perverse and contrary tongue:

Proverbs 8:13	The froward [contrary] mouth do I hate
Proverbs 15:4	Perverseness [in a tongue] is a breach in the spirit
Proverbs 26:18–19	As a madman who casteth firebrands and death, so is the man that deceiveth … and saith, am not I [joking]?

D. Foolishness and vain talk leads to mischief and ungodliness:

Proverbs 14:7	Go from the presence of a foolish man, when thou perceivest not in him the lips of knowledge
Proverbs 15:14	The mouth of fools feedeth on foolishness
Ecclesiastes 10:13	The beginning of [his] words … is foolishness
2 Timothy 2:16	Shun profane and vain babblings: for they will increase unto more ungodliness

E. An uncontrolled tongue brings disaster:

Psalm 109:17–20	As he loved cursing, so let it come unto him
Proverbs 10:10	A prating [idly chattering] fool shall fall
Proverbs 10:14	The mouth of the foolish is near destruction
Proverbs 12:13	The wicked is snared by the transgression of his lips
Proverbs 13:3	He that openeth wide his lips shall have destruction
Proverbs 17:20	He that hath a perverse tongue falleth into mischief
Proverbs 18:7	A fool's mouth … and his lips are the snare of his soul
Ecclesiastes 10:12	The lips of a fool will swallow up himself

5. CONTROLLING YOUR TONGUE:

A. Refrain from corrupt communication:

Proverbs 4:24	Put away from thee a froward mouth, and perverse lips
Ephesians 4:29	Let no corrupt communication proceed out of your mouth
Ephesians 5:4	Neither filthiness [obscenity], nor foolish talking, nor jesting, but rather giving of thanks
Colossians 3:8	Put … filthy communication out of your mouth
1 Timothy 6:20	Avoiding profane and vain babblings

B. Speak edifying things, not corrupt:

Proverbs 8:8–9	All the words of my mouth are in righteousness; there is nothing froward or perverse in them
Ephesians 4:29	No corrupt communication … but that which is … edifying, that it may minister grace unto the hearers
Colossians 4:6	Let your speech be always with grace, seasoned with salt
Titus 2:8	Sound speech, that cannot be condemned (See also Romans 15:2.)

C. You can't control your own tongue by yourself:

James 3:8	The tongue can no man tame

D. Only God can, so yield to Him:

Psalm 45:1	My tongue is the pen of a ready writer [God]
Proverbs 16:1	The preparations of the heart of man, and the answer of the tongue, is from the Lord
Isaiah 50:4	The Lord God hath given me the tongue of the learned, that I … know how to speak [an encouraging] word
Luke 12:12	The Holy Ghost shall teach you … what ye ought to say
1 Peter 4:11	If any man speak, let him speak as the oracles of God

E. Read and obey God's Word, and let it change you:

Psalm 119:9	[How] shall a young man cleanse his way? By taking heed … to thy word
John 15:3	Now ye are clean through the word
Ephesians 5:26	That he might sanctify and cleanse it with the washing of water by the word
1 Peter 1:22	Ye have purified your souls in obeying the truth

(See also Proverbs 6:20–23; Hebrews 10:22.)

6. GOSSIPING, BACKBITING, AND SLANDERING:

A. God forbids you to gossip:

Exodus 23:1	Thou shalt not raise a false report
Leviticus 19:16	Thou shalt not go up and down as a talebearer among thy people: I am the Lord
Ephesians 4:31	Let all … evil speaking, be put away … with all malice
Titus 3:2	Speak evil of no man
James 4:11	Speak not evil one of another, brethren
1 Peter 2:1	[Lay] aside all malice, and guile … and all evil speakings

B. Warning against backbiting:

Proverbs 25:9	Debate thy cause with thy neighbour himself; and [tell] not a secret to another
2 Corinthians 12:20	I fear … I shall not find you such as I would … lest there be … backbitings, whisperings

C. Gossiping shows a lack of true faith and love:

Proverbs 10:18	He that uttereth a slander, is a fool
1 Timothy 5:11–13	When they have begun to wax wanton against Christ … they learn to be … tattlers and busybodies
James 1:26	If any man seem to be religious, and bridleth not his tongue … this man's religion is vain

D. Gossiping is born of hatred:

Psalm 38:12	They that seek my hurt speak mischievous things, and imagine deceits
Psalm 41:7	All that hate me whisper together against me

E. Gossiping is of the Devil:

1 Timothy 3:11	So must their wives be grave, not slanderers [literally: "diabolos," meaning false accuser, devil]
Revelation 12:10	The accuser of our brethren [the Devil]

7. THE PUNISHMENT FOR GOSSIPING:

A. Scriptural response to backbiters and talebearers:

Psalm 32:9	[They] have no understanding: whose mouth must be held in with bit and bridle
Proverbs 25:23	Angry countenance [driveth away] a backbiting tongue
Titus 1:10–11	There are many unruly and vain talkers … whose mouths must be stopped

B. Part company with them if they don't change:

Psalm 101:5	[King David said:] Whoso [privately] slandereth his neighbour, him will I cut off
Psalm 101:7	He that telleth lies shall not tarry in my sight
Proverbs 20:19	He that goeth about as a talebearer revealeth secrets: therefore [have nothing to do] with him
Proverbs 22:10	Cast out a scorner, and contention shall go out
Proverbs 26:20	Where there is no talebearer, the strife ceaseth

C. God will judge them:

Matthew 12:36–37	Every idle word that men shall speak, they shall give account thereof in the day of judgement

8. HOW TO AVOID CRITICIZING AND GOSSIPING:

A. Think about others' virtues:

Philippians 4:8	Whatsoever things are … pure … lovely … if there be any virtue … think on these things (See also Philippians 1:3.)

B. Remember the blessings for not backbiting:

Psalm 15:1,3	Who shall abide [before God]? He that backbiteth not … nor taketh up a reproach against his neighbour
1 Peter 3:10	He that will … see good days, let him refrain his tongue from evil, and his lips [from] guile
Revelation 14:5	In their mouth was … no guile: they are before the throne

C. Make an effort to not speak evil:

Psalm 17:3	I am purposed that my mouth shall not transgress
Psalm 39:1	I will take heed … that I sin not with my tongue
Proverbs 30:32	If thou hast thought evil, lay thine hand upon thy mouth [before you speak what you were thinking]

D. Don't even think evil:

Psalm 19:14	Let the words of my mouth, and the meditation of my heart, be acceptable in thy sight
Ecclesiastes 10:20	Curse not the king, no not in thy thought
Mark 7:21	For out of the heart of men, proceed evil thoughts
2 Corinthians 10:5	Bringing … every thought to the obedience of Christ

E. You can't speak good if your heart is full of evil:

Matthew 12:34	How can ye, being evil, speak good things? For out of the abundance of the heart the mouth speaketh

F. Beware of hypocritical flattery:

Psalm 12:2	They speak vanity … with flattering lips and double heart
Psalm 28:3	Wicked … speak peace, but mischief is in their hearts
Psalm 55:21	The words of his mouth were smoother than … oil, yet were they drawn swords
Psalm 62:4	They bless with their mouth, but curse inwardly
Proverbs 26:23	Burning [fervently agreeing] lips [with] a wicked heart are like [earthenware] covered with silver
Proverbs 26:25–26	When he speaketh fair, believe him not: for there are … abominations in his heart
Ezekiel 33:31	With their mouth they shew much love, but their heart goeth after their covetousness

9. WARNING AGAINST JUDGING OTHERS:

Matthew 7:1–5	Judge not, that ye be not judged. For with what judgement ye judge, ye shall be judged ... Why beholdest thou the mote … in thy brother's eye, but considerest not the beam … in thine own eye?
John 7:24	Judge not according to appearance … but righteous
Romans 2:1	Thou art inexcusable … wherein thou judgest another … for thou that judgest doest the same things
Romans 2:3	Thinkest thou … that judgest … and doest the same, that thou shalt escape the judgement of God?
Romans 14:13	Let us not therefore judge one another any more

10. WHAT TO DO WHEN OTHERS SPEAK EVIL OF YOU:

A. Ignore it if you can; don't be offended:

Psalm 119:165	Great peace have they which love Thy [word]: and nothing shall offend them
Ecclesiastes 7:21–22	Take no heed unto all words spoken … thine own heart knoweth thou thyself likewise hast cursed others

B. Don't speak evil of them in return:

1 Peter 2:21–23	Follow [Christ's] steps … who, when he was reviled, reviled not again (See also Isaiah 53:7,9.)
1 Peter 3:9	Not rendering evil for evil, or railing for railing: but contrariwise blessing

C. Let your good works disprove their lies:

Titus 2:7–8	Sound speech, that cannot be condemned; that he that is … contrary [have] no evil thing to say of you
1 Peter 2:12	Whereas they speak against you as evildoers, they may by your good works, glorify God
1 Peter 2:15	With well doing … put to silence … foolish men
1 Peter 3:16	Having a good [way of life]; that, whereas they speak evil of you … they may be ashamed

D. Jesus remained silent before His accusers:

Isaiah 53:7	He was oppressed … yet he opened not his mouth
Matthew 27:14	[Jesus] answered him [Pilate] to never a word
Luke 22:67–68	[Jesus knew that to answer His enemies was pointless]
Luke 23:9	He [Herod] questioned him [Jesus] in many words; but he answered him nothing

E. But there are times to speak out and answer:

Acts 21:40	[Paul gave his defense to the mob in Jerusalem]
Acts 24:10	[Paul defended himself before Felix]
Acts 26:1	[Paul's self-defense before Festus and Agrippa]
1 Peter 3:15	Be ready always to give an answer to every man that asketh you a reason (See also Matthew 10:18–20.)

11. ARGUMENTS AND CONTENTIONS:

A. Avoid getting drawn into arguments:

Proverbs 17:14	Leave off contention, before it be meddled with
Proverbs 26:4	Answer not a fool according to his folly, lest thou also be like unto him
Proverbs 29:11	A wise man keepeth [his comments] in till afterwards

Philippians 2:3	Let nothing be done through strife
2 Timothy 2:24	The servant of the Lord must not strive; but be patient
1 Peter 3:9	Not rendering evil [insult] for [insult], or railing [reviling] for [reviling]: but contrariwise blessing
	(See also 2 Kings 18:36.)

B. Listen carefully, and think about what you say:

Proverbs 15:28	The heart of the righteous studieth to answer
Proverbs 18:13	He that answereth a matter before he heareth it, it is folly and shame unto him
James 1:19	Be swift to hear, slow to speak, slow to wrath

C. Don't get provoked and answer rashly:

Proverbs 15:18	He that is slow to anger appeaseth strife
Proverbs 16:32	He that is slow to anger is better than the mighty
Proverbs 25:8	Go not forth hastily to strive
Proverbs 29:20	Seest thou a man that is hasty in his words? There is more hope of a fool than of him
Ecclesiastes 5:2	Be not rash with thy mouth [nor] hasty to utter any thing … let thy words be few

D. Speak calmly:

Proverbs 15:1	A soft answer turneth away wrath
Proverbs 22:11	For the grace of his lips the king shall be his friend

E. What causes arguments and contention:

Proverbs 10:12	Hatred stirreth up strifes
Proverbs 13:10	Only by pride cometh contention
Proverbs 15:1	Grievous words stir up anger
Proverbs 15:18	A wrathful man stirreth up strife
Proverbs 18:6	A fool's lips enter into contention
Proverbs 26:21	As wood to fire; so a contentious man [kindles] strife
Proverbs 28:25	He that is of a proud heart stirreth up strife
Proverbs 29:22	An angry man stirreth up strife
Acts 13:45	They were filled with envy, and spake against those things … contradicting and blaspheming
1 Timothy 6:4	He is proud, knowing nothing, but doting about questions and … words, whereof cometh … strife
James 4:1	Wars and fightings … come … of your lusts
	(See also Proverbs 26:17.)

F. The futility of arguing:

Job 6:25	How forcible are right words! but what doth your arguing reprove?
Proverbs 9:7–8	He that reproveth a scorner getteth to himself … shame

	… reprove not a scorner, lest he hate thee
Proverbs 23:9	Speak not in the ears of a fool: he will despise wisdom
Proverbs 29:9	If a wise man contendeth with a foolish man, whether he [the foolish man] rage or laugh, there is no rest

G. Ending an argument:

Proverbs 17:9	He that covereth [lets pass] a transgression seeketh love
Proverbs 20:3	It is an honour for a man to cease from strife
Proverbs 22:10	Cast out the scorner, and contention shall … cease
Colossians 3:13	Forbearing [putting up with] one another, and forgiving one another, if any man have a quarrel against any

(See also Genesis 50:20–21.)

H. Warning to those who "love a good argument":

Proverbs 17:9	He loveth transgression that loveth strife
1 Corinthians 3:3	Whereas there is among you … strife … are you ye not carnal, and walk as [carnal, worldly] men?
James 3:14–15	If ye have bitter … strife in your hearts, glory not … this wisdom is devilish

I. The bad fruit of arguments:

Psalm 106:33	They provoked his [Moses'] spirit, so that he spake unadvisedly with his lips
Proverbs 18:19	A brother offended is harder to be won than a strong city … contentions are like bars of a castle
Acts 15:39	The contention was so sharp between them, that they departed asunder one from the other
Galatians 5:15	If ye bite and devour one another, take heed that ye be not consumed one of another
James 3:16	Where … strife is, there is confusion and every evil work

J. When it is right to contend:

Proverbs 26:5	Answer a fool according to his folly, lest he be wise in his own conceit
Proverbs 28:4	Such as keep the law contend with [the wicked]
Proverbs 28:23	He that rebuketh a man afterwards shall find more favour than he that flattereth
Acts 15:1–2	Paul … had no small dissension and disputation with them
Jude 1:3	Ye should earnestly contend for the faith

K. Humbly explain, correct, and instruct:

Galatians 6:1	Restore such an one in the spirit of meekness
2 Timothy 2:25	In meekness instructing those that oppose themselves

	(See also James 5:20.)
1 Peter 3:15	Be ready always to give an answer to every man that asketh you a reason ... with meekness

12. LYING, DECEIVING, AND BEARING FALSE WITNESS:

A. God's Word warns us not to lie:

Leviticus 19:11	Neither deal falsely, neither lie one to another
Proverbs 24:28	Be not a witness against thy neighbour without cause; and deceive not with thy lips
Ephesians 4:25	Putting away lying, speak every man truth with his neighbour
Colossians 3:9	Lie not to one another, seeing ye have put off the old man with his deeds

B. What God thinks about lying:

Proverbs 12:22	Lying lips are an abomination to the Lord

C. God's judgement on wicked liars:

Psalm 63:11	The mouth of the them that speak lies shall be stopped
Proverbs 19:5	A false witness shall not be unpunished, and he that speaketh lies shall not escape
Proverbs 19:9	He that speaketh lies shall perish
Acts 5:1–10	[Ananias and Sapphira lied to the Holy Ghost and died]
	(See also Psalm 31:18; 35:11–20; Proverbs 12:19.)

Special chapter about the tongue: James 3

UNITY

1. UNITY OR DISUNITY?

A. God wants us to have unity:

Psalm 133:1	How good and how pleasant it is for brethren to dwell together in unity
1 Corinthians 1:10	I beseech you … that there be no divisions among you, but … be perfectly joined together in the same mind
2 Corinthians 13:11	Be ye of one mind, live in peace; and the God of love and peace shall be with you
Philippians 1:27	Stand fast in one spirit, with one mind striving together

B. What He thinks of disunity:

Proverbs 6:16,19	These … doth the Lord hate: [they] are an abomination unto him: he that soweth discord among brethren
James 3:14–15	But if ye have … strife in your hearts, glory not … this descendeth not from above, but is devilish

2. HOW TO WORK AT KEEPING UNITED:

Ephesians 4:3	Endeavouring to keep the unity of the Spirit

A. Have the Word as a unifying standard:

1 Corinthians 14:37	Let him acknowledge that the things I write are the commandments of the Lord
Philippians 3:16	Let us walk by the same rule … mind the same thing
1 Thessalonians 2:13–14	Ye received the word of God which ye heard of us, ye … became followers

B. Be agreeable and likeminded:

Romans 12:16	Be of the same mind one toward another … condescend to men of low estate
Romans 15:5–6	God … grant you to be likeminded one toward another … that ye may with one mind and one mouth glorify God
1 Corinthians 1:10	I beseech you … that ye all speak the same thing
Philippians 2:2	Be likeminded, having the same love, being of one accord, of one mind

(See also Acts 2:46; Philippians 4:2.)

C. Be at peace with fellow-workers:

Romans 14:19	Let us follow after the things which make for peace, and things wherewith one may edify another
Colossians 3:15	Let the peace of God rule in your hearts, to the which ye are called in one body
1 Thessalonians 5:13	Be at peace among yourselves

D. Have love and concern for one another:

Proverbs 10:12	Hatred stirreth up strifes: but love covereth all sins
Romans 12:10	Be kindly affectioned with brotherly love; in honour preferring one another (See also 1 Thessalonians 2:7–8.)
1 Corinthians 12:25–26	There should be no schism in the body; but the members should have the same care one for another
Ephesians 4:16	The whole body fitly joined together … maketh increase of the body unto the edifying of itself in love

E. Be kind, gentle, and courteous to one another:

1 Corinthians 11:33	When ye come together to eat, tarry one for another
Ephesians 4:32	Be ye kind … tenderhearted, forgiving one another
2 Timothy 2:24	Not strive … be gentle unto all men, patient
1 Peter 3:8	Be ye all of one mind, having compassion … love as brethren, be pitiful [sympathetic], be courteous (See also Proverbs 18:24.)

F. Take people where they're at:

Romans 14:1	Him that is weak in the faith receive ye, but not to doubtful disputations (See also Romans 14:2–21.)

G. Avoid offending people:

Proverbs 18:19	Brother offended is harder to be won than a strong city
1 Corinthians 10:32–33	Give none offence, neither … to the church of God … I please all men in all things

H. Be careful what you say:

Proverbs 17:9	He that repeateth a matter separateth very friends
2 Timothy 2:23	Foolish questions avoid … they do gender strifes
Titus 3:2	Speak evil of no man … gentle … meekness unto all men (See also James 3:16–17; Ecclesiastes 5:2.)

I. Control your temper; be slow to speak:

Proverbs 14:29	He that is slow to wrath is of great understanding
Proverbs 15:1	A soft answer turneth away wrath
Proverbs 15:18	He that is slow to anger appeaseth strife
Proverbs 25:8	Go not forth hastily to strive [with thy neighbour]
Philippians 2:3	Let nothing be done through strife or vainglory
James 1:19	Let every man be … slow to speak, slow to wrath (See also Proverbs 3:30; 26:17.)

J. Humbly discuss disagreements with elders:

1 Timothy 5:1	Rebuke not an elder, but entreat him as a father

K. Sort out frictions before doing anything else:

Matthew 5:23–24	First be reconciled to thy brother, then … offer gift
Mark 11:25	When … praying, forgive, if ye have ought against any
James 5:9	Grudge not one against another, lest ye be condemned

L. Avoid being partial or playing favourites:

1 Timothy 5:21	[Not] preferring one before another, doing nothing by partiality (See also James 3:7.)
James 2:1	Have not the faith of Jesus … with respect of persons

M. Value peace above selfish interests:

Romans 12:18	As much as lieth in you, live peaceably with all men
Romans 14:19–21	Let us follow after the things which make for peace (See also 1 Corinthians 6:7; Philippians 2:4.)

N. Share unselfishly with others:

Acts 4:32	And the multitude of them that believed were of one heart and of one soul … they had all things common (See also 1 Corinthians 10:33; 2 Corinthians 8:9.)

O. Return good for evil:

Matthew 5:44	Love your enemies, bless them that curse you
Romans 12:21	Overcome evil with good
1 Thessalonians 5:15	See that none render evil for evil … among yourselves

P. Retaliation forbidden:

(See Leviticus 19:18; Proverbs 20:22; 24:29; Romans 12:17,19; 1 Peter 3:9.)

3. THE FRUITS OF UNITY:

A. Working together for a common goal:

2 Kings 10:15	Is thine heart right, as my heart is with thine heart? If it be, give me thine hand
Amos 3:3	Can two walk [or work] together, except they be agreed?
Matthew 18:19–20	Where two or three are gathered in my [Jesus'] name, there am I in the midst of them
Acts 2:14	Peter, standing up with the eleven, lifted up his voice
Philippians 1:27	With one mind, striving together for … the gospel

B. There is strength in unity:

Judges 20:11	The men [army] were gathered against the city, knit together as one man
1 Samuel 14:6–7	Jonathan said, Let us go over. His armourbearer said, Behold I am with thee according to thy heart
Ecclesiastes 4:9–10	Two are better than one … for if they fall, the one will lift up his fellow

Ecclesiastes 4:12	If one [a foe] prevail against him, two shall withstand [the foe], and a three-fold cord is not ... broken (See also Nehemiah 4:16–17.)

C. Good fruit of united outreach:

Acts 2:1–2,41	[Believers] all with one accord in one place [were filled with the spirit, witnessed, and 3,000 souls were saved]

4. UNITY OF BELIEVERS IN JESUS:

A. Jesus' prayer that we be united as one:

John 17:11,21–23	That they all may be one; as Thou, Father, art in me, and I in thee, that they also may be one in us ... that they may be one, even as we are one: I in them, and thou in me, that they may be made perfect in one

B. We should be one body, working together unitedly:

Romans 12:5	We, being many, are one body in Christ, and every one members one of another
1 Corinthians 12:12–13	All the members of one body, being many, are one body (See also 1 Corinthians 10:17.)
1 Corinthians 12:27	Ye are the body of Christ, and members in particular
Ephesians 2:22	Ye are builded together ... through the Spirit (See also Ephesians 1:10; 2:19–21; 4:11–12; 1 Corinthians 12:4–16.)
Colossians 1:17–18	[Jesus] is head of our body (See also Ephesians 4:15–16.) (See also 1 Corinthians 3:9; 2 Corinthians 6:1.)

C. Jesus' Spirit gives us peace with one another:

1 Corinthians 14:33	God is the author ... of peace, as in all the churches
2 Corinthians 13:11	Brethren ... live in peace; God of peace shall be with you
Galatians 5:22	The fruit of the Spirit is ... peace
Ephesians 2:14	He is our peace ... hath broken down the wall between
Colossians 2:2	Your hearts comforted, being knit together in love

D. There should be no divisions because of race or sex:

1 Corinthians 12:13	Whether Jews or Gentiles, [we] have been all made ... one
Galatians 3:26,28	Neither Jew nor Greek ... male or female: for ye are all one in Jesus

E. Or social or financial statuses:

1 Corinthians 12:13	Whether ... bond or free, [we] have been all made ... one
Galatians 3:28	Neither bond nor free ... for ye are all one in Jesus

5. CAUSES OF DISUNITY:

A. Pride and lust:

Proverbs 13:10	Only by pride cometh contention
Proverbs 28:25	He that is of a proud heart stirreth up strife
James 4:1–3	Whence come fightings among you? From your lusts

B. Not walking in the Spirit:

1 Corinthians 3:3	Ye are carnal: there is among you strife and divisions
Galatians 5:19–21	Works of the flesh: hatred, wrath, strifes

C. Ill feelings and hatred:

Proverbs 10:12	Hatred stirreth up strifes: but love covereth all sins
Proverbs 16:28	A froward man soweth strife, and a whisperer separateth
Proverbs 26:24	He that hateth dissembleth with his lips

D. Envy and jealousy:

Romans 13:13	Let us walk honestly … not in … strife and envying
1 Corinthians 13:4	Love … envieth not; love vaunteth not itself
Galatians 5:26	Let us not be desirous of vain glory, provoking one another, envying one another
James 3:14–16	If ye have bitter envying … in your hearts, glory not. For where envying … is, there is … every evil work

(See also Proverbs 14:30; 27:4; Galatians 5:19–21; Titus 3:3.)

E. Favouritism and partiality:

Acts 6:1	There arose a murmuring of the Grecians against the Hebrews, because their widows were neglected

F. Self-exaltation and desire for leadership:

Numbers 12:1–15	[Miriam and Aaron rebel against Moses, desiring power]
Numbers 16:1–35	[Korah rebels against Moses, desiring leadership]
Luke 22:24	There was a strife among them, [who] should be greatest
Acts 20:30	Of your own selves shall men arise … to draw away disciples after them
Galatians 5:26	Let us not desire vain glory, provoking … one another
3 John 1:9–11	Diotrephes, who loveth to have the preeminence among them receiveth us not

G. Arguing over minor doctrines and theorizing:

1 Timothy 6:3–5	Knowing nothing, doting about questions and strifes of words, whereof cometh … strife

H. Bitterness:

Hebrews 12:15	Lest any root of bitterness springing up trouble you, and thereby many be defiled

I. Anger and a quick temper:

Proverbs 15:18	A wrathful man stirreth up strife
Proverbs 29:22	An angry man stirreth up strife, and a furious man

J. Repeating things we know we shouldn't:

Proverbs 17:9	He that repeateth a matter separateth very friends
Proverbs 26:20	Where there is no talebearer, the strife ceaseth

(See also James 1:26.)

K. Inability to stop arguing:

Proverbs 17:14	The beginning of strife is as when one letteth out water … leave off contention
Proverbs 20:3	It is an honour to cease from strife: but every fool will be meddling

6. RESULTS OF DISUNITY:

A. Not being able to work together:

Amos 3:3	Can two walk together, except they be agreed?
Acts 15:36–40	Contention so sharp [between Paul and Barnabus] that they departed asunder [and went separate ways]

B. It destroys God's work:

Matthew 12:25	Every house divided against itself … shall not stand
Mark 3:24	If kingdom be divided against itself … cannot stand

(See also Numbers 32:1–7.)

C. Longstanding divisions:

Proverbs 18:19	A brother offended is harder to be won than a strong city

D. Creates sectarian divisions and man-worship:

1 Corinthians 3:3–4	There [are] divisions … For one saith, I am of Paul; and another, I am of Apollos

(See also 1 Corinthians 3:21–23; 11:18.)

E. Backbiting and rumours:

Proverbs 16:28	A whisperer separateth chief friends
2 Corinthians 12:20	I fear … lest there be backbitings, whisperings

F. Opens the door to every kind of evil:

James 3:16	For where … strife [is], there is confusion and every evil work

7. HOW TO DEAL WITH DISUNITY:

1 Thessalonians 5:14 Warn them that are unruly

A. When it's just between us and a fellow worker:

Proverbs 25:9	Debate thy cause with thy neighbour himself; and discover not a secret to another
Matthew 18:15	Tell him his fault between thee and him alone
Luke 17:4	If he trespass seven times in a day, and seven times a day turn again, saying, I repent … forgive
1 Peter 4:8	Charity [love] shall cover the multitude of sins

(See also Matthew 18:21–22.)

B. When there is a division in the work, let the pastors and elders settle the disputes:

Acts 15:2	When [they] had no small dissension, they determined [to] go to the elders about this question
Acts 15:7,12	When there had been much disputing, Peter rose up, and [spoke]. Then all the multitude kept silence
Galatians 6:1	If a man be overtaken in a fault, ye which are spiritual, restore such an one

C. Let it pass if it's not an important disagreement:

Romans 14:2	One believeth that he may eat all things: another … eateth [only] herbs
Romans 14:5–6	One man esteemeth one day above another: another esteemeth every day alike

8. DISASSOCIATING FROM THOSE WHO CAUSE DIVISION:

Proverbs 22:10	Cast out the scorner, and … strife shall cease
Matthew 18:15–17	If he neglected to hear the church, let him be unto thee as an heathen
Romans 16:17	Mark them which cause divisions and offences … and avoid
1 Corinthians 5:11–13	With such an one no, not to eat … put away wicked
2 Thessalonians 3:6	We command you … that ye withdraw yourselves from every brother that walketh disorderly
2 Thessalonians 3:14–15	If any obey not … have no company with him … yet count him not as an enemy, but admonish as a brother
1 Timothy 6:3,5	If any man teach otherwise, and consent not to … the doctrine … from such withdraw thyself
Titus 3:10	An heretick after first and second admonition, reject
2 John 1:10–11	If any … bring not this doctrine, receive him not

(See also 1 Timothy 6:3–5; Jude 1:12.)

9. RESTORATION TO FELLOWSHIP:

Galatians 6:1	If a man be overtaken in a fault … restore [him]
2 Timothy 2:25–26	In meekness instructing those … that they may recover
James 5:19–20	If any of you err from the truth ... convert him
	(See also Luke 15:11–24, on the return of the Prodigal Son.)

10. WHEN CONTENTIONS AND DISPUTES ARE NECESSARY:

To refute false doctrine or serious wrong behaviour:

John 7:43	There was a division among people because of [Jesus]
Acts 15:1–2	"Except ye be circumcised, ye cannot be saved." Paul … had no small dissension and disputation with them
Galatians 2:11–14	When Peter was come to Antioch, I withstood him to the face … I [rebuked] Peter before them all
1 Timothy 5:20	Them that sin, rebuke before all that others may fear
Jude 1:3	Ye should earnestly contend for the faith

Special chapters about unity: Psalm 133; John 17; 1 Corinthians 12; Ephesians 4; Romans 12

DISCIPLESHIP

1. WHAT IS A DISCIPLE?

A. A "follower of the teaching" and the Master Teacher:

Matthew 10:24–25	The disciple [should] be as his master (See also Luke 6:40.)
John 8:31	If ye continue in my word, then are ye my disciples
John 12:26	If any man serve me, let him follow me
John 13:15	I have given you an example, that ye should do as I have done
1 Peter 2:21	Christ [left] us an example ... follow his steps

B. A disciple abides [lives, dwells] in Jesus:

John 15:4	Abide in me, and I in you
John 15:9–10	If ye keep my commandments, ye shall abide in my love
1 John 2:6	He that ... abideth in him ought ... to walk as he walked
1 John 3:24	He that keepeth his commandments dwelleth in him (See also 2 Corinthians 5:17; 1 John 2:5,10,24,28.)

C. A disciple serves Jesus out of love and gratitude:

John 14:21,23	If a man love me, he will keep my words
1 Corinthians 6:19–20	Ye are not your own ... for ye are bought with a price
2 Corinthians 5:14	The love of Christ constraineth [motivates] us
Ephesians 5:1–2	Be followers of God ... walk in love, as Christ loved us
Philippians 1:21	For me to live is Christ, and to die is gain (See also Exodus 21:5–6.)

2. A DISCIPLE'S JOB:

A. To win souls ("bear fruit"):

Matthew 4:19	Follow me, and I will make you fishers of men
Mark 16:15	Go ye into all the world and preach the gospel to every creature
Luke 9:59–60	Let the dead bury their dead: but go thou and preach
John 15:8	Bear much fruit, so shall ye be my disciples (See also Matthew 7:20; Romans 7:4.)

B. To train more disciples:

Matthew 28:19	Go therefore and teach [make disciples of] all nations
John 21:15–17	Lovest thou me? Feed [teach and instruct] my sheep
2 Timothy 2:2	Things which thou hast heard ... [teach] faithful men (See also Acts 20:20.)

3. DEDICATING ONESELF TO GOD:

A. Subordinating other pursuits to follow Jesus:

Matthew 13:44–46	Kingdom of heaven is like ... treasure hid in a field … selleth all that he hath, and buyeth that field ... pearl of great price … sold all that he had and bought it
Luke 14:33	He … that forsaketh not all … cannot be my disciple

B. Having the right priorities—spiritual over material:

Matthew 6:19–20	Lay not up for yourselves treasures upon earth
Mark 10:21	Sell whatsoever thou hast … and take up cross and follow
Luke 12:15	A man's life consisteth not in the abundance of the things which he possesseth
Acts 4:34–35	Possessors of lands or houses sold them, and brought the prices … and laid them down at apostles' feet
Philippians 3:8	Jesus … for whom I have suffered the loss of all things, and do count them but dung

(See also Matthew 19:22; Luke 12:33.)

C. Forsaking materialistic ambitions:

Matthew 6:24	Ye cannot serve God and mammon
Mark 4:19	The cares of this world, and deceitfulness of riches … choke the word … it becometh unfruitful
Mark 10:17–25	[Jesus challenged the rich young ruler to forsake all]
John 6:27	Labour not for the meat which perisheth, but for
2 Timothy 2:4	No man that warreth entangleth himself with … this life
Hebrews 12:1	Lay aside every weight … let us run the race

(See also 2 Corinthians 6:17.)

D. Start by counting the cost:

Proverbs 24:6	By wise counsel thou shalt make thy war
Luke 14:27–32	Intending to build … sitteth down and counteth the cost

E. Commit and don't look back:

Luke 9:61–62	No man … looking back, is fit for the kingdom of God
Philippians 3:13–14	Forgetting things which are behind, and reaching forth … I press toward the … high calling of God
Hebrews 11:27	[Moses] forsook Egypt … endured, as seeing him [God]

F. Some made a sudden decision to follow:

1 Kings 18:21	How long halt ye … ? If the Lord be God, follow him
Matthew 9:9	As Jesus passed … he saw Matthew sitting at receipt of custom: Follow me. And he arose, and followed him
John 4:35	Say not ye, There are yet four months, and then cometh harvest? Look on the fields, they are white already

Hebrews 4:7	Today if ye … hear his voice, harden not your hearts

G. Delay and excuses can result in never serving God:

Luke 9:57–62	Let me first go bid them farewell, which are at home

H. Some took more time to count the cost:

Luke 14:28–30	Sit … down first, and count the cost

- Peter and Andrew first met Jesus at the Jordan River (John 1:37–42)
- They followed Him back to Galilee (John 1:43; 2:1–2)
- He called them some time later, and they then forsook all to follow Him (Matthew 4:18; Mark 1:16–20)

4. DIFFERENT MINISTRIES OF DISCIPLES:

A. Being a disciple does not always mean abandoning all other pursuits:

Matthew 27:57	Rich man … named Joseph, who also was Jesus' disciple
John 19:38–40	Joseph of Arimathaea, a disciple of Jesus, secretly
Acts 9:36,39	A disciple named Tabitha [made coats and garments] (See also Mark 14:8.)

B. Some disciples had prominent positions in society:

Mark 15:43	Joseph of Arimathaea, an honourable counselor (See also Luke 23:50–51.)
Acts 10:24; 44–48	[Cornelius the centurion, his relatives and friends]
Acts 19:31	Certain of the chief of Asia … were [Paul's] friends
Romans 16:23	Erastus the chamberlain of the city saluteth you

C. Sacrificial giving—a requirement for all disciples:

Luke 8:3	Joanna the wife of Chuza … and Susana, and many others, which ministered unto him of their substance
2 Corinthians 8:14–15	That … your abundance may be a supply for their want
Acts 11:29	The disciples, every man according to his ability
1 Timothy 6:17–18	[Command] them that are rich ... to distribute

D. The disciple's attitude toward those who can't devote their time to serving God:

Mark 10:21	[Jesus loved the rich young ruler, even though he didn't forsake all]
Luke 9:49–50	We forbad him, because he followeth not with us. But Jesus said, Forbid him not

E. Not all are called to be disciples:

Matthew 22:14	For many are called, but few are chosen
Luke 8:38–39	The man … besought him that he might be with him: but Jesus sent him away, saying, Return to thine house (See also Mark 5:18–20.)
John 6:53–61,66	[Jesus weeded out weak followers who were there for the wrong motives] (See also Jeremiah 12:5; Matthew 13:47–48.)

F. Different degrees of discipleship:

- The 3 innermost disciples (Mark 9:2; 14:32–33)
- The 12 apostles (Mark 3:13–19)
- The "other 70" (Luke 10:1)
- The "multitude of the disciples" (Luke 19:37)

5. DISCIPLESHIP AND "LOSING YOUR OWN LIFE":

A. Disciples must subordinate their own life, plans, ambitions:

Matthew 6:21	Where your treasure is, there will your heart be also
Matthew 16:25	Whosoever will lose his life for my sake shall find it
Luke 9:59,61	[Wrong attitude:] I will follow thee, but … me first
Luke 14:26	If any … hate not his own life, he cannot be my disciple

B. Discipleship—A life of death to self-centeredness:

Matthew 6:33	Seek first the kingdom of God
Matthew 10:38	He that taketh not his cross, and followeth after me
Matthew 16:24	If any man come after me, let him deny himself
Mark 10:21	Come, take up the cross, and follow me
John 12:24–25	[If] a corn of wheat fall into the ground and die ... it bringeth forth much fruit. He that loveth his life shall lose it
2 Corinthians 5:15	They should not live unto themselves, but unto him which died for them

6. THE PATH THE DISCIPLE FOLLOWS:

A. A disciple heeds God's will and follows:

Numbers 22:18	I cannot go beyond the word of the Lord, to do less or more
Luke 6:46	Why call me, Lord, Lord, and do not the things I say?
Luke 14:27	Whosoever doth not … come after me, cannot be my disciple
John 2:5	Whatsoever he saith unto you, do it
John 8:31	If ye continue in my word, then are ye my disciples indeed
Revelation 14:4	They follow the Lamb whithersoever he goeth

B. A disciple follows godly leaders and examples:

1 Corinthians 11:1	Be ye followers of me, even as I also am of Christ
Philippians 3:17	Be followers of me and … them which walk as ye have us for an [example]
1 Thessalonians 1:6	Ye became followers of us, and of the Lord, having received the word
Hebrews 13:7	Them which have rule over you … whose faith follow

C. Disciples follow God, even without understanding all the details:

John 21:21–22	What will [he] do? What is that to thee? Follow thou me
2 Corinthians 5:7	We walk by faith, not by sight
Hebrews 11:8	Abraham went out, not knowing whither he went

D. Disciples adapt and change:

Luke 9:3	Take nothing for your journey, neither … money
Luke 22:35–36	I sent you without purse … but now … take it

E. Disciples love other disciples and work in unity with them:

John 13:35	Ye are my disciples, if ye have love one to another
Philippians 1:27	With one mind striving together for the … gospel

7. THE LIFE OF A DISCIPLE:

A. Give sacrificially and be willing to call nothing your own:

Matthew 5:42	Give to him that asketh thee … turn not thou away
Luke 3:11	He that hath two coats, [give] to him that hath none
Luke 6:30	Him that taketh thy goods, ask them not again
Acts 2:44–45	And all that believed … had all things common
Acts 4:32–35	Neither said any that ought of the things which he possessed was his own; they had all things common
1 Timothy 6:7–8	Having food and raiment let us be therewith content

(See also Luke 9:23–26.)

B. Disciples must be willing to endure hardships:

Luke 9:57–58	I will follow thee … foxes have holes, but the son of man hath not where to lay his head
2 Timothy 2:3	Endure hardness as a good soldier of Jesus Christ

(See also 2 Corinthians 11:23–28.)

C. Be willing to endure persecution:

Acts 15:26	Men that have hazarded their lives for Jesus Christ
Philippians 1:29	Not only to believe on him, but also to suffer
2 Timothy 3:12	All that live godly in Jesus shall suffer persecution

(See also John 16:33.)

D. Be zealous and enthusiastic:

Ecclesiastes 9:10	Whatsoever thy hand findeth to do, do it with thy might
Galatians 4:18	It is good to be zealous … always in a good thing
Revelation 3:15	I would thou wert cold or hot

8. THE BENEFITS OF DISCIPLESHIP:

A. Discipleship is a privilege:

Psalm 4:3	Lord hath set apart him that is godly for himself
Matthew 22:14	For many are called, but few are chosen
Philippians 3:14	The prize for the high calling of God in Christ Jesus
2 Timothy 1:9	Who hath saved us, and called us with an holy calling
	(See also Matthew 11:25; 13:16–17; Luke 8:10.)

B. Rewards for serving Jesus:

Matthew 10:39	He that loseth his life for my sake shall find it
Matthew 19:27–29	We have forsaken all, and followed; what shall we have? … Ye shall sit upon thrones … receive an hundredfold
Mark 10:28–30	Shall receive an hundredfold now in this time
Luke 12:33	Sell that ye have … provide yourselves a treasure in the heavens that faileth not
John 12:26	If any man serve me, him will my Father honour
1 Corinthians 2:9	Eye hath not seen … the things which God hath prepared for them that love him
	(See also Matthew 5:10–12; 16:25,27; John 12:25; 2 Timothy 2:12.)

C. Faithful overcomers rewarded:

Matthew 25:14–29	[The parable of the talents] (See also Luke 19:12–26.)
Luke 12:42–44	Faithful steward ... Lord will make him ruler (See also Luke 12:35–38.)
Revelation 2:26–28	He that overcometh … will I give power over nations
Revelation 3:21	Him that overcometh will I grant to sit with me

9. JESUS' LAST WORDS AND PRAYER FOR HIS DISCIPLES:

(See John 14–17; Acts 1:8.)

THE CHRISTIAN'S RELATIONSHIP TO SOCIETY

1. CHRISTIANS DO NOT BELONG TO THIS WORLD:

John 15:19	Ye are not of the world, but I have chosen you out of the world

A. We are citizens of heaven:

John 14:2–3	I go to prepare a place for you … that where I am, there ye may be also
Hebrews 11:14	They … declare plainly that they seek a country
Hebrews 11:16	Now they desire a better country … an heavenly
Hebrews 13:14	Here have we no continuing city … we seek one to come

(See also John 18:36.)

B. We are sojourners in this world, pilgrims passing through:

Psalm 39:12	I am a stranger with thee, and a sojourner
Psalm 119:19	I am a stranger in the earth
Hebrews 11:13	Confessed they were strangers and pilgrims on the earth

C. Earthly lands and homes are only temporary:

Leviticus 25:23	The land is mine [God's]; for ye are strangers and sojourners with me

D. Our life on earth is brief:

1 Chronicles 29:15	We are strangers before thee, and sojourners … our days on the earth are as a shadow
1 Peter 1:17	Pass time of your sojourning here in fear [of God]

(See also Psalm 39:4–5.)

E. Guard against thinking this world is your permanent home:

Psalm 49:11–12	Their inward thought is, that their houses shall continue for ever, and their dwelling places

2. THOUGH IN THIS WORLD, WE ARE NOT PART OF IT:

A. Christians are not of this world:

John 17:14–16	They are not of the world, even as I [Jesus] am not
Romans 12:2	Be not conformed to this world
Galatians 6:14	The cross of … Christ, by whom the world is crucified [dead] unto me, and I unto the world
Ephesians 2:2–3	In time past ye walked according to the course of this world
Philippians 2:15	The sons of God … in the midst of a crooked and perverse nation, among whom ye shine as lights in the world
1 John 4:4–6	They are of the world … we are of God

1 John 5:19	We are of God, and the whole world lieth in wickedness

B. We are not to have close friendship with those who reject Christ:

Proverbs 1:15	My son, walk not thou … with them; refrain thy foot
Proverbs 24:1	Be not envious against [of] evil men, neither desire to be with them
Isaiah 52:11	Go ye out from thence, touch no unclean thing; go ye out of the midst of [them]; be ye clean
1 Corinthians 10:20–21	I would not that ye should fellowship with devils. Ye cannot drink the cup of the Lord, and … of devils
2 Corinthians 6:14–15	Be not unequally yoked together with unbelievers: what fellowship hath righteousness with unrighteousness? What part hath he that believeth with an infidel?
2 Corinthians 6:17	Come out from among them, and be separate … touch not
Ephesians 5:11	Have no fellowship with the … works of darkness
Revelation 18:4	Come out of her, my people, that ye be not partakers

(See also Proverbs 4:14–17; 13:20.)

C. Do not become entirely separate; we must witness:

Mark 16:15	Go ye into all the world, and preach the gospel
John 17:15	Not that thou shouldest take them out of the world, but … keep them from the evil
John 17:18	As thou has sent me into the world, even so have I sent them into the world [to witness]

D. Marriage with the unbelieving and worldly is discouraged:

Deuteronomy 7:3–4	Neither shalt thou make marriages with them … for they will turn away thy son from following me
Joshua 23:12–13	If ye do in any wise … make marriages with them … they shall be snares and traps unto you
1 Kings 11:1–8	King Solomon loved many strange women … his wives turned away his heart after other gods
Nehemiah 13:26–27	Solomon … was beloved of his God … nevertheless even him did outlandish women cause to sin
1 Corinthians 7:12–16	[If already married to an unbeliever, have faith, you may yet win them by your Christian example]
1 Corinthians 7:39	She is at liberty to be married to whom she will; only [let her marry] in the Lord

(See also Genesis 26:34–35; 27:46; Judges 14:1–3; Ezra 9:1–2; Malachi 2:11–12.)

3. OUR ATTITUDE TOWARD WORLDLY VALUES:

A. Caution not to love this present world:

James 4:4	The friendship of the world is enmity with God
1 John 2:15–16	Love not the world, neither the things that are in the world

B. The pilgrim's attitude:

Titus 2:12–13	Denying ungodliness and worldly lusts … live soberly … in this present world; looking for that blessed hope
Hebrews 11:24–27	Moses … choosing rather to suffer affliction with the people of God … forsook Egypt
James 1:27	Pure religion ... to keep unspotted from the world
1 Peter 1:17	[God] judgeth … every man's work, [so] pass the time of your sojourning here in fear
1 Peter 2:11	As strangers and pilgrims, abstain from fleshly [worldly] lusts, which war against the soul
2 Peter 3:11,14	Seeing then that all these things shall be dissolved, what manner of persons ought ye to be
1 John 2:16–17	The lust of the flesh, and the lust of the eyes … is of the world. And the world passeth away

C. We should resist being influenced by trends, fads, and media:

Exodus 23:2	Thou shalt not follow a multitude to do evil
Romans 12:2	Be not conformed to this world: but be ye transformed
1 Corinthians 7:31	The fashion of this world passeth away
Colossians 2:8	Beware lest any man spoil you through … vain deceit

D. Warning against indiscriminate worldly entertainment:

2 Kings 17:15	They followed vanity, and became vain, and went after the heathen that were round about them
Psalm 101:3	I will set no wicked thing before mine eyes
Psalm 119:37	Turn away mine eyes from beholding vanity
Isaiah 33:15	He that walketh righteously … shutteth his eyes from seeing evil

E. The detrimental effect of this wicked world on believers:

2 Peter 2:7–8	[The inhabitants of Sodom] vexed his [Lot's] righteous soul … with their unlawful deeds
2 Peter 3:17	Beware lest ye also, being led away with the error of the wicked, fall from your steadfastness

F. Peer pressure and influence:

2 Kings 12:3–16	[King Rehoboam foolishly followed the counsel of] the young men that were grown up with him

G. Don't compromise or tolerate ungodly ways:

Exodus 23:32–33	Make no covenant with them, nor with their gods. They shall not dwell in thy land … for if thou serve their gods, it will surely be a snare unto thee
1 Timothy 5:22	Neither be partaker of other men's sins: keep … pure

H. Avoid wanton parties and activities:

Romans 13:13–14	Not in rioting and drunkenness, not in chambering [licentiousness] … fulfil [not] lusts
1 Peter 4:3–4	[We are not to indulge in drunken parties and reveling] (See also Ephesians 2:2–3; Titus 2:12.)

I. But don't go to the opposite extreme:

Matthew 9:9–13	[The self-righteous demanded:] Why eateth your master with publicans and sinners?
1 Corinthians 10:27	[We can accept invitations to banquets and feasts]

4. IF POSSIBLE, LIVE PEACEABLY WITH OTHERS IN ORDER TO WIN THEM TO GOD:

A. Peaceable relations with others are preferable:

Proverbs 16:7	Lord … maketh even his enemies to be at peace with him
Jeremiah 29:7	Seek the peace of the city … and pray unto the Lord for it: for in the peace thereof shall ye have peace
Matthew 5:25	Agree with thine adversary quickly … lest at any time
Romans 12:18	As much as lieth in [depends upon] you, live peaceably with all men
Colossians 4:5	Walk in wisdom toward them that are without
1 Timothy 2:1–2	[Pray] that we may lead a quiet and peaceable life

B. Try to relate to their way of thinking, in order to win them:

1 Corinthians 9:19–22	Unto the Jews I became as Jew, that I might gain Jews. I am made all things to all men
1 Corinthians 10:32–33	Give none offence, neither to Jews nor to Gentiles ... I please all men in all things … that they may be saved

C. Identify with them by giving your background and credentials:

Acts 21:39	I am … of Tarsus, a citizen of no mean city
Acts 22:3	I am a man … brought up in this city … taught according to the law of the fathers … as ye all are (See also Acts 16:36–38; 22:25–28.)

5. CAUTIONS AGAINST COMPROMISING WITH THE WORLD:

Galatians 1:10	Do I seek to please men? If I yet pleased men, I should not be the servant of Christ

A. Caution against pleasing to the point of compromising:

2 Kings 5:17–18	In this thing the Lord pardon thy servant, that … I bow myself in the house of Rimmon [a heathen god]
Luke 6:26	Woe unto you, when all men speak well of you

B. WE SHOULD STAND UP FOR, AND NOT BE ASHAMED OF, OUR FAITH:

Mark 8:38	Whosoever shall be ashamed of me and of my words in this … sinful generation; of him shall [I] be ashamed
Romans 1:16	I am not ashamed of the gospel of Christ
2 Timothy 1:8	Be not thou ashamed of the testimony of our Lord
1 Peter 4:16	If any suffer as a Christian, let him not be ashamed

C. We are not of this world, and it hates us for that:

Luke 6:22	Men … shall separate you from their company, and reproach
John 15:18–19	Because ye are not of the world … world hateth you
1 Peter 4:4	They think it strange that ye run not with them to the same excess of riot, speaking evil of you

6. THE IMPORTANCE OF AN HONEST, SINCERE EXAMPLE:

A. Be a good example:

Matthew 5:16	Let your light so shine … that they may see your good works, and glorify your Father in heaven
Luke 6:27	Love your enemies, do good to them which hate you
Romans 13:3	Do … good, and thou shalt have praise of the [rulers]
1 Thessalonians 5:22	Abstain from all appearance of evil
1 Timothy 4:12	Be thou an example of the believers, in word, in conversation, in charity [love]
1 Peter 2:13	Submit yourselves to every ordinance of man for the Lord's sake
1 Peter 2:15	With well doing … put to silence ignorance of foolish

B. We are commanded to be honest in our dealings:

Romans 12:17	Provide things honest in the sight of all men
2 Corinthians 8:21	Providing for honest things … in the sight of men
1 Thessalonians 4:12	Walk honestly toward them that are without
Titus 2:10	Not purloining [stealing, pilfering], but showing all good fidelity
1 Peter 2:12	Having your [way of life] honest among the Gentiles (See also Romans 13:13; Hebrews 13:18.)

C. Do not bring reproach upon the cause of Christ:

Romans 14:16	Let not then your good be evil spoken of

2 Corinthians 6:3	Giving none offence in any thing, that the ministry be not blamed
1 Timothy 5:14	Give none occasion to adversary to speak reproachfully

(See also Romans 2:23–24; 1 Timothy 6:1; Titus 2:5.)

D. Be blameless and innocent:

Matthew 10:16	Sheep in the midst of wolves: be ye therefore wise as serpents, and harmless as doves
Philippians 2:15	Blameless and harmless, the sons of God, without rebuke
Titus 1:6	Blameless ... having children not accused of riot

E. Don't let your liberties become a "stumbling block" to others:

Romans 14:13–21	No man put a stumblingblock ... in his brother's way [that we may be] ... approved of men
1 Corinthians 6:12	All things are lawful ... but all things not expedient
1 Corinthians 8:8–13	Take heed lest by any means this liberty of yours become a stumbling block to them that are weak
1 Peter 2:16	Not using your liberty for a cloak of maliciousness

7. WORK AND EMPLOYMENT:

A. Christians are instructed to do honest work:

Ephesians 4:28	Let him labour, working with his hands the thing [profession] which is good
1 Thessalonians 4:11–12	Work with your own hands, as we commanded you; that ye may have lack of nothing
2 Thessalonians 3:10–12	If any would not work, neither should he eat
Titus 3:14	Let ours learn to maintain good works [honest trades] for necessary uses

B. We must keep our priorities straight:

Luke 12:15	Beware of covetousness ... a man's life consisteth not in the abundance of the things which he possesseth
Acts 20:35	Labouring ye ought to support weak ... blessed to give
Ephesians 4:28	Let him labour, working ... that he may have to give
1 Corinthians 7:31	They that use this world, as not abusing it
1 Timothy 6:8	Having food and raiment let us therewith be content

C. Consider the fate of those who covet riches:

Psalm 49:16–20	[The fate of those who seek riches in this world]
Mark 10:24–25	How hard is it for them that trust in riches to enter
1 Timothy 6:9–10	They that will [desire to] be rich fall into ... snare ... erred from the faith ... pierced with sorrows
James 1:10–11	The rich ... is made low ... withereth ... perisheth

(See also James 5:1–4.)

D. Warning regarding wrong attitudes:

Job 31:24–25,28	If I have … said to gold, Thou art my confidence … I should have denied God that is above
Haggai 1:9	It came to little … because ... ye run every man unto his own house [and neglected God's work]
Luke 12:19–21	Soul, thou hast much goods laid up … take thine ease
1 Timothy 6:10	The love of money is the root of all evil
Revelation 3:15–18	Thou sayest, "I am rich, and increased with goods, and have need of nothing." Thou art wretched, poor, naked

8. THE WORK OF PASTORS, FULL-TIME CHRISTIAN WORKERS, AND MISSIONARIES:

A. The compensation of pastors and teachers:

1 Corinthians 9:7	Who feedeth a flock, and eateth not of the milk of the flock?
1 Corinthians 9:13	They which minister about holy things live of the things of the temple
1 Timothy 5:17–18	They who labour in the word and doctrine … the labourer is worthy of his reward [wages]

B. The work of missionaries is preaching the gospel; they are reapers in God's harvest and deserve wages:

Matthew 9:37–38	The harvest [of souls] is plenteous, but the labourers are few … send labourers into his harvest
John 4:35–36	Look on the [mission] fields; for they are white already to harvest. And he that reapeth receiveth wages, and gathereth fruit unto life eternal
1 Corinthians 9:10	He that ploweth … and thresheth … should be partaker
1 Corinthians 9:13–14	The Lord ordained that they which preach the gospel should live of the gospel

C. Christians with secular jobs should help to support God's workers:

Luke 8:3	Joanna, the wife of Chuza, Herod's steward … ministered unto him [Jesus] of their substance
Luke 10:7	Eating such things as they give: for the labourer is worthy of his hire
Romans 15:27	If [they] have been made partakers of their spiritual things, their duty is to minister … carnal things
1 Corinthians 9:11	If we have sown unto you spiritual things … we shall reap your carnal things
Galatians 6:6	Let him that is taught in the word communicate [give materially] unto him that teacheth

D. God's workers can hold secular jobs also:

Acts 18:1–3	He [Paul] was of the same craft, he … wrought: for by

	their occupation they were tentmakers (See also Acts 20:34–35.)

9. A CHRISTIAN'S RELATIONSHIP TO GOVERNMENTS:

A. Try to be good citizens and obey the government:

Romans 13:1	Let every soul be subject unto the higher powers. The powers that be [the authorities] are ordained of God
Titus 3:1	Put them in mind to be subject … to obey magistrates
1 Peter 2:17	Honour all men ... Fear God. Honour the king

B. Most governments and laws are for our good and protection:

Acts 21:30–35	[Roman soldiers rescued Paul from a hostile mob]
Acts 23:10	[Romans prevented Jews from pulling Paul in pieces]
Acts 25:15–16	It is not the manner of the Romans to deliver any man to die [without defence]

C. Pray for the government and officials:

Ecclesiastes 10:20	Curse not the king, no not in thy thought
1 Timothy 2:1	I exhort that … prayers … be made for kings, and for all that are in authority

D. Perform required national and community duties:

Matthew 22:21	Render unto Caesar the things which are Caesar's
Romans 13:7	Render to all their dues: tribute to whom tribute

E. However, we must obey God above all:

Acts 4:19–20	[We are not bound to obey secular laws which cause us to disobey God, or which forbid witnessing]
Acts 5:29	We ought to obey God rather than men

10. THE GOVERNMENTS OF MAN:

A. God rules the governments of men:

Proverbs 8:15–16	By me kings reign, and … princes rule … even all the judges of the earth
Daniel 4:32,35	The most High ruleth in the kingdom of men, and giveth it to whomsoever he will
John 19:10–11	Thou [Pilate] couldst have no power at all against me except it were given thee from above

B. God has allowed the Devil a certain amount of control:

Luke 4:5–6	All the kingdoms of the world [are] delivered unto me [Satan]; and to whomsoever I will give it
2 Corinthians 4:4	[Satan is called] the god of this world

PERSECUTION

1. PERSECUTION PROMISED TO ALL FOLLOWERS OF JESUS:

Matthew 10:17	Beware of men: they will deliver you up … scourge
Matthew 24:9	Deliver you up … ye shall be hated of all nations
Mark 10:30	Shall receive an hundredfold now … with persecutions
Luke 21:12	They shall lay their hands on you and persecute you
John 15:20	If they have persecuted me, they will also persecute you
John 16:33	In the world ye shall have tribulation
Philippians 1:29	Given not only to believe on him, but also to suffer
2 Timothy 3:12	Yea, and all that will live godly in Christ Jesus shall suffer persecution

(See also Matthew 23:24; 1 John 3:13.)

2. BENEFITS OF PERSECUTION:

A. Heavenly rewards for enduring persecution:

Matthew 5:10	Blessed are … persecuted … for theirs is the kingdom
Romans 8:17–18	Sufferings … not worthy to be compared with the glory
2 Corinthians 2:12	If we suffer, we shall also reign with him
2 Corinthians 4:17	Affliction … worketh for us … eternal weight of glory
Hebrews 11:25–26	Choosing to suffer affliction … respect unto reward
Hebrews 11:35	Tortured, not accepting deliverance; that they might obtain a better resurrection
1 Peter 4:12–13	Fiery trial … when his glory revealed, ye may be glad

B. God is with and helps those being persecuted:

Psalm 37:32–33	The Lord will not leave him [the righteous] in his [the wicked's] hand
Psalm 46:1	God is … a very present help in trouble
Isaiah 50:7–9	The Lord God will help me … who is mine adversary?
Matthew 10:18–20	Brought before governors … it shall be given you what ye shall speak … [God's] Spirit speaketh in you
Acts 7:55	[Stephen] saw the glory of God, and Jesus standing
Romans 8:35–39	Persecution [can't] separate us from the love of God
2 Corinthians 4:8–11	Persecuted, but not forsaken
Hebrews 13:5–6	The Lord is my helper, and I will not fear what man shall do unto me
1 Peter 4:14	If ye be reproached for Christ … spirit of glory and God resteth upon you

C. God allows persecution to spread His message and messengers:

Matthew 10:23	When they persecute you in this city, flee ye into another
Acts 8:1,4	Scattered … went everywhere preaching the word
Acts 11:19	Scattered … travelled as far as Cyprus, preaching

D. When condemning God's messengers, enemies often broadcast God's message—thus arousing interest in it:

John 19:4–8	The Jews answered, "[Jesus] ought to die, because he made himself the Son of God"
Acts 17:5–7	These [say] there is another king, one Jesus
Acts 19:23–26	This Paul persuaded … saying that [idols] be no gods
Acts 24:14	This I confess … the way which they call heresy, so worship I God
Acts 25:18–19	[Paul's] accusers … had questions against him of Jesus, which was dead, whom Paul affirmed to be alive
Acts 28:22	Everywhere [this sect] is spoken against … but we desire to hear of thee, what thou thinkest
Philippians 1:15–18	Notwithstanding … Christ is preached

E. The Word can be preached even from prison:

Jeremiah 38:13–18	[King Zedekiah consulted with imprisoned Jeremiah]
Matthew 10:18–20	Brought before governors and kings for a testimony
Acts 16:23–31	[Philippian jailor converted after earthquake]
Acts 28:16	[In bonds, Paul preached in Rome] (See also 28:30–31.)
Philippians 1:12–14	[In bonds, Paul converts Caesar's household] (See also Philippians 4:22.)

F. God gets good out of seeming bad:

Genesis 50:20	Ye thought evil … but God meant it to good
Exodus 14:1–28	[God hardened Pharaoh's heart to pursue the Hebrews, so that his entire army drowned and empire collapsed]
Psalm 76:10	Surely the wrath of man shall praise thee

3. ATTITUDE TO HAVE DURING PERSECUTION:

A. Be fearless and unmovable:

Jeremiah 1:17–19	Be not dismayed … they shall fight … but I am with thee
Ezekiel 3:8–9	Fear them not, neither be dismayed at their looks
Matthew 10:28	Fear not them which kill the body
Acts 20:24	None of these … move me, neither count I my life dear
1 Thessalonians 3:3	That no man should be moved by these afflictions … we are appointed thereunto
1 Peter 2:20	When ye do well, and suffer for it … take it patiently
Revelation 12:11	And they loved not their lives unto the death (See also Philippians 1:14.)

B. Have joy in persecution:

Matthew 5:12	Rejoice and be exceeding glad … for so persecuted
Luke 6:22–23	When men hate you … rejoice … leap for joy

Acts 5:40–41	Rejoicing they were counted worthy to suffer shame
Romans 5:3	We glory in tribulations
2 Thessalonians 1:4	We glory in you for your patience and faith in all your persecutions and tribulations that ye endure
1 Peter 3:14	If ye suffer for righteousness' sake, happy are ye
1 Peter 4:12–14	If ye be reproached for … Christ, happy are ye

C. Do not be ashamed:

Isaiah 50:7	I set my face like a flint … I shall not be ashamed
1 Peter 4:16	If any suffer as a Christian, let him not be ashamed

D. Suffer willingly for a righteous cause:

Jeremiah 15:15	For thy sake I have suffered rebuke
Matthew 5:10	Blessed are they … persecuted for righteousness' sake
2 Corinthians 12:10	I take pleasure in persecutions … for Christ's sake
2 Thessalonians 1:5	Counted worthy of kingdom of God, for which ye suffer
1 Peter 2:19	For conscience toward God … suffering wrongfully

E. Examples of enduring persecution courageously:

- Jeremiah (Jeremiah 26:11–15)
- Paul and his companions (1 Corinthians 4:12)
- Paul (2 Corinthians 6:4–5,8–10; 2 Corinthians 11:23–27)
- Timothy (2 Timothy 1:8)
- Early Christians (Hebrews 10:32–33)
- Moses (Hebrews 11:25)
- Old and New Testament saints (Hebrews 11:35–40)

F. Remain faithful to the truth despite persecution:

Psalm 119:51	Proud have me … in derision, yet have I not declined
Psalm 119:86–87	They persecuted me wrongfully; they almost consumed me … but I forsook not thy precepts
Psalm 119:157	Many are my persecutors … yet I do not decline
Revelation 2:13	Thou holdest fast … and hast not denied my faith, even in those days wherein … my martyr was slain

G. Endure persecution because of love for the lost:

2 Timothy 2:10	I endure all things for the elect's sake, that they may obtain salvation (See also John 10:11.)
Hebrews 5:7–9	He suffered … became the author of eternal salvation
1 Peter 2:21	Christ suffered for us … ye should follow his steps

H. Examples of men of God imprisoned for their faith:

- Old Testament saints (Hebrews 11:36)
- Samson (Judges 16:21)
- Micaiah (1 Kings 22:26–27)

- Hanani (2 Chronicles 16:10)
- Jeremiah (Jeremiah 37:11–16)
- Daniel (Daniel 6:16–17)
- John the Baptist (Matthew 14:3–4)
- Peter and John (Acts 4:1–3)
- Apostles (Acts 5:16–18)
- Men and women Christians in Jerusalem (Acts 8:3; 9:1–2,14; 22:4–5,19; 26:10)
- Peter (Acts 12:1–4)
- Paul and Silas (Acts 16:22–24)
- Paul's imprisonments (2 Corinthians 11:23)
- Paul's final imprisonment (Acts 24:27; 26:29; 28:16)

4. REASONS WHY PERSECUTORS ATTACK CHRISTIANS:

A. Their goal is to stop the witness:

Jeremiah 11:21	Prophesy not … that thou die not by our hand
John 11:47–48,53	If we let him alone, all men will believe on him. Then they took counsel to put him to death
Acts 4:17	That it spread no further … Let us threaten them (See also Revelation 6:9; 11:7.)

B. Wicked men hate the righteous:

Psalm 38:20	They are adversaries; because I follow … good
Proverbs 29:27	He that is upright is abomination to the wicked
Isaiah 59:15	He that departeth from evil maketh himself a prey
Acts 7:52	Which of the prophets have not your fathers persecuted?
Galatians 4:29	He that was born after the flesh persecuted him
1 Peter 4:3–4	[Righteous despised for not joining drunken parties]
1 John 3:12	Cain slew [Abel] because his own works were evil

C. Because truth is a witness against evil:

1 Kings 22:17–27	[Micaiah imprisoned for prophesying the truth]
2 Chronicles 16:7–10	[Asa imprisons Hanani for prophesying against him]
2 Chronicles 24:20–21	[King has Zechariah stoned for rebuking the people]
Jeremiah 32:2–3	[Jeremiah imprisoned for prophesying the truth]
Amos 5:10	They abhor him that speaketh uprightly
John 7:7	It [the world] hateth me [Jesus], because I testify of it
Acts 6:10–15	[Stephen stoned for rebuking Jews] (See also Acts 7:51–60.)
Revelation 1:9	[John exiled to Patmos for preaching the word] (See also Revelation 12:17; 20:4.)

D. Ignorance of the truth:

Acts 3:13–14	I wot that through ignorance ye did it (See also 3:17.)
1 Timothy 1:13	[I] was a persecutor … I did it ignorantly in unbelief

E. Not truly knowing God:

John 5:18,38,42	Ye have not his word … ye have not the love of God
John 8:37	Ye seek to kill me, because my word hath no place
John 15:21	They [persecutors] know not him [God] that sent me
John 15:24	Now have they ... hated both me and my Father
John 16:3	Because they have not known the Father, nor me
Acts 13:27–28	They knew him not … nor yet the voices of prophets

F. Self-righteous, misguided religious zeal:

John 16:2	Whosoever killeth you will think that he doeth God service (See also Isaiah 66:5.)
Acts 13:50	Jews stirred up the devout and honourable women
Acts 21:27–32	Men of Israel, help: This is the man that teacheth
Acts 22:3–4	Zealous … I persecuted this way unto the death
Acts 23:12–14	[40 men vowed and conspired to kill Paul]
Acts 26:9–11	I thought I ought to do many things contrary to Jesus
Galatians 1:13–14	Persecuted … being exceedingly zealous of traditions
Philippians 3:6	Concerning zeal, persecuting the church

G. For breaking religious traditions and doctrines:

Matthew 12:10–14	Is it lawful to heal on the Sabbath days?
John 5:16	[Angry Jews seek to kill Jesus for healing on Sabbath]
John 10:31–33	For a good work we stone thee not; but for blasphemy

H. Religious jealousy and fear of competition:

Matthew 27:18	For he knew that for envy they had delivered him
Mark 11:18	Feared him, because people astonished at his doctrine
Acts 13:44–45	When the Jews saw the multitudes … filled with envy
Acts 17:5	Jews which believed not, moved with envy … assaulted

I. Because we do not belong to this world:

John 15:19	Because ye are not of world … the world hateth you
John 17:14	World hated them, because they are not of the world
1 John 4:5–6	They are of the world … we are of God

J. Persecution by corrupt rich:

Acts 19:23–27	By this craft we have our wealth … but Paul persuaded
James 2:6–7	Rich men oppress, draw you before judgement seat
Revelation 17:1–6,18	That great city … drunken with the blood of saints

K. Wickedness, pride:

Psalm 10:2	The wicked in his pride doth persecute the poor
Psalm 74:22	The foolish man reproacheth thee daily
Psalm 119:69	The proud have forged a lie against me

L. For refusing to compromise faith:

Daniel 3:14–20	We will not serve thy god, nor worship the … image
Daniel 6:4–5	[Jealous princes accuse Daniel regarding his faith]

M. For refusing to worship the Antichrist and his image:

Revelation 13:14–17	As many as would not worship the image … be killed
Revelation 20:4	Beheaded … had not worshipped the beast

N. For no valid reason at all:

Psalm 119:86	They persecute me wrongfully
Psalm 119:161	Princes have persecuted me without a cause
John 15:25	They hated me without a cause (See also Psalm 69:4.)

5. PERSECUTION USUALLY BEGINS WITH VERBAL ATTACKS:

A. Slander, infamy, lies:

Psalm 69:9–12	I became a proverb to them … they speak against me
Psalm 119:51	The proud have had me greatly in derision
Matthew 5:11	Men shall revile you … and say all manner of evil
Luke 6:22	Men shall reproach you, and cast out your name as evil
Luke 22:63–65	Men that held Jesus mocked him … blasphemously spake
Acts 14:2	Made their minds evil affected against the brethren
Acts 28:22	This sect … everywhere it is spoken against
1 Corinthians 4:13	Defamed … we are made as the filth of the world (See also Psalm 35:16,21.)

B. Persecutors twist words to defame:

Isaiah 29:21	Make a man an offender for a word … lay a snare
Isaiah 56:5	Every day they wrest my words … their thoughts evil
Matthew 22:15	Took counsel how they might entangle him in his talk
Mark 12:13	They send Pharisees … to catch him in his words
Luke 11:54	Seeking to catch something out of his mouth, that they might accuse him
Luke 20:20	Take hold of his words … deliver him to the governor

C. Lying accusations and false charges:

Psalm 35:11	False witnesses … laid to my charge things I knew not
Jeremiah 38:4	[Treason:] seeketh not the welfare … but the hurt
Matthew 26:59–61	Chief priests … sought false witness against Jesus
Luke 23:2	We found this fellow perverting the nation, and forbidding to give tribute [pay taxes]
Luke 23:5	[Sedition:] He stirreth up the people
Acts 6:11–13	We have heard him speak blasphemous words
Acts 16:19–21	These men exceedingly trouble city … teach customs
Acts 17:5–7	These … do contrary to the decrees of Caesar

Acts 18:12–13	Persuadeth men to worship God contrary to the law
Acts 24:5	Pestilent, mover of sedition, ringleader of sect
2 Timothy 2:8–9	I suffer trouble as an evil doer, even unto bonds

(See also Psalm 94:20.)

D. Character assassination:

Luke 7:34	Behold a gluttonous man and a wine-bibber
Luke 7:12	Nay; but he deceiveth the people
John 9:24	We know that this man [Jesus] is a sinner

E. Accusations of being "of the Devil":

Matthew 10:24–25	They called [Jesus] Beelzebub, how much more [us]
Matthew 9:34	He casteth out devils through the prince of devils
Mark 3:22	He hath Beelzebub, and by the prince of the devils
John 10:20	Many said, he hath a devil … why hear ye him?

F. Charges of religious insanity:

Mark 3:21	Went to lay hold on him: said, He is beside himself
Acts 26:24	Much learning [of the scriptures] doth make thee mad

G. Persecution through fear of society's disapproval:

John 9:22	Parents feared Jews: for Jews had agreed that if any
John 12:42	[Some believing] chief rulers … did not confess him, lest they be put out of the synagogue

6. PERSECUTION FROM FAMILY AND FRIENDS:

Jeremiah 12:6	Thy brethren … have called a multitude after thee
Matthew 10:21	Brother shall deliver up the brother to death
Matthew 10:35–36	A man's foes shall be they of his own household
Mark 3:21	Friends … went out to lay hold on him
Mark 6:4	Prophet is … without honour among kin, and in own house
Luke 12:51–53	There shall be five in one house divided
Luke 21:16	Ye shall be betrayed by parents, brethren, friends
John 7:1–5	[Jesus' brethren taunt Him]
1 Thessalonians 2:14–16	Ye also have suffered … of your own countrymen

(See also Micah 7:2; John 1:11.)

7. THE WORLD PERSECUTED AND REJECTED JESUS:

A. Evil plots and persecution against Jesus:

Matthew 12:14	Held council against him, how they might destroy him
Matthew 26:3–4	Consulted that they might take him by subtilty and kill
Luke 4:28–29	Led him unto the hill … that they might cast him down
Luke 6:11	Filled with madness; and communed what they might do

Luke 19:47	Chief priests and scribes ... sought to destroy him
John 5:16	Therefore did Jews persecute Jesus, and sought to slay
John 11:57	Given commandment, if any man knew where he were
	(See also Luke 20:20.)

B. Look to Jesus' example of suffering persecution:

Isaiah 53:3,7–8	Despised and rejected of men ... afflicted ... cut off
John 15:18	The world ... hated me before it hated you
John 15:20	If they have persecuted me, they will persecute you
Hebrews 12:2–4	Consider him who endured such contradiction
Hebrews 13:13	Let us go forth unto him ... bearing his reproach
1 Peter 2:21–23	Christ suffered for us, leaving us an example
1 Peter 4:1	Christ suffered ... arm yourselves with the same mind

C. When persecuting Christians, they persecute Jesus:

Zechariah 2:8	He that toucheth you toucheth the apple of his eye
Matthew 25:40	Inasmuch as ye have done it unto one of the least of these ... ye have done it unto me
Acts 9:1–5	Saul, Saul, why persecutest thou me?
Acts 5:38–39	Refrain from these men ... lest ye fight against God

8. COMPROMISING, FLEEING, AND AVOIDING PERSECUTION:

A. Bad examples of compromising to avoid persecution:

2 Kings 5:15,17–18	[Naaman believed in God, but bowed down to the pagan idol of Rimmon]
Luke 6:26	Woe unto you, when all men speak well of you
John 12:42	Rulers ... did not confess him, lest they be put out
Galatians 6:12	Lest they suffer persecution for cross of Christ

B. Fleeing from persecution (discretion, not cowardice):

1 Kings 19:2–3	[Elijah fled from the wicked queen Jezebel]
Jeremiah 26:20–21	[Urijah fled from king Jehoiakim to Egypt]
Jeremiah 36:19,26	Go, hide thee ... and let no man know where ye be
Matthew 2:13–14	Arise, and take the young child ... and flee into Egypt
Matthew 10:23	When they persecute you in this city, flee ye to another
Matthew 12:14–15	When Jesus knew it, he withdrew himself from thence
John 7:1	He would not walk in Jewry, because the Jews
John 10:39–40	They sought again to take him: but he escaped
John 11:53–54	He walked no more openly among the Jews; but went
Acts 9:23–25	Took [Paul] by night, and let him down in a basket
Acts 14:5–6	An assault made ... they were ware of it, and fled
Acts 17:5,10	Assaulted ... brethren sent away Paul and Silas by night
Acts 17:13–14	Jews ... stirred up to people ... brethren sent away Paul
Acts 23:12–35	[470 Roman soldiers helped Paul flee a conspiracy]

C. Pray to avoid persecution, if possible:

2 Thessalonians 3:1–2	Pray … that we may be delivered from wicked men
1 Timothy 2:1–2	Prayers … that we may lead a quiet and peaceable life

D. Use wisdom to avoid stirring up unnecessary persecution:

Proverbs 15:1	A soft answer turneth away wrath
Proverbs 16:7	When a man's ways please the Lord, he maketh even his enemies to be at peace with him
Matthew 5:25	Agree with thine adversary quickly … lest he deliver
Romans 12:18–21	If it be possible, as much as lieth in you, live peaceably with all men … overcome evil with good

9. GOD WILL JUDGE YOUR PERSECUTORS:

A. The Psalmist's prayers for God to protect His people and judge their enemies:

(See Psalm 3:all; 5:8–12; 6:10; 7:all; 9:3–5,9–10,13–20; 10:all; 12:all; 13:all; 17:4–15; 18:37–50; 21:7–13; 23:5; 27:1–6,11–14; 28:all; 31:all; 34:1–7; 35:all; 37:all; 38:12–22; 40:13–17; 41:5–11; 43:all; 52:all; 53:1–5; 54:all; 55:1–9,18,23; 56:all; 57:1–6; 58:all; 62:1–8; 63:8–11; 64:all; 68:1–3; 69:4,22–30; 70:all; 71:4,10–13; 82:3–4; 83:1–4,12–18; 94:1–7,16,21–23; 105:12–15; 109:all; 118:5–14; 119:84,126; 120:2; 124:all; 125:3–5; 129:1–6; 139:19–22; 140:all; 143:3–4,9–12; 144:6–11; 149:5–9.)

B. Other prayers:

(See Jeremiah 15:15; 17:18; 18:18–23; Lamentations 3:59–66; Revelation 6:9–10.)

C. God's judgement on persecutors:

Deuteronomy 30:7	Lord put curses on enemies which persecuted thee
2 Chronicles 36:16	Wrath of the Lord arose … till there was no remedy
Psalm 7:11–16	He ordaineth his arrows against the persecutors
Psalm 11:2,5–6	Upon the wicked he shall rain fire and brimstone
Psalm 37:12–15,17	The Lord shall laugh at him, for he seeth that his day is coming
Psalm 105:14–15	Touch not mine anointed, and do my prophets no harm
Isaiah 54:15	Whosoever shall gather against thee shall fall
Jeremiah 20:2–6	[Pashur persecuted Jeremiah, then Jeremiah prophesied God's judgements against him]
Luke 11:49–51	Blood of prophets … be required of this generation
1 Thessalonians 2:15–16	Forbidding us to speak … wrath is come upon them
2 Thessalonians 1:6–9	Recompense tribulation to them that trouble you
	(See also Revelation 16:1–6; 18:2,4–8.)

10. ENDTIME PERSECUTION:

A. Suffering persecution in the last days:

Matthew 24:9–10	Then shall they deliver you up to be afflicted
Mark 13:12–13	Brother shall betray brother to death
Luke 21:12,16–17	They shall lay their hands on you, and persecute
2 Timothy 3:1–3	In the last days … despisers of them that are good

B. Persecution during the great tribulation:

Deuteronomy 4:30–31	When thou art in tribulation … in the latter days
Daniel 11:33–35	They shall fall by sword, flame, captivity, spoil … they shall be helped
Matthew 24:21–22	Then shall be great tribulation
Mark 13:19	In those days shall be affliction, such as was not
Revelation 12:12–13,17	Dragon persecuted the woman [church] … war with remnant
Revelation 13:7	It was given unto him to make war with the saints
Revelation 13:15	As many as would not worship the image … killed
Revelation 20:4	Beheaded for witness … had not worshipped the beast

C. The tribulation saints will be greatly rewarded:

Revelation 7:13–17	Came out of great tribulation … before throne of God
Revelation 20:4	Beheaded … reigned with Christ a thousand years

BACKSLIDING
(Falling away from God)

1. DANGER SIGNS THAT LEAD TO LOSING FAITH:

A. Cooling off and losing "first love" for Jesus:

Revelation 2:4–5	Thou hast left thy first love … remember from whence thou art fallen, and repent … or else I will remove
Revelation 3:15–16	Thou art lukewarm, and neither cold nor hot

B. Being filled with own ways and desires:

Proverbs 14:14	Backslider in heart shall be filled with his own ways
Ezekiel 14:3,5	These men have set up their idols in their heart … they are estranged from me through their idols
Ezekiel 14:7–8	Every one which … setteth up his idols in his heart … I will cut him off from the midst of my people
1 Timothy 6:9	Hurtful lusts … drown men in perdition

C. Losing sight of the heavenly goal in favour of temporal gain:

Proverbs 29:18	Where there is no vision, the people perish
Malachi 3:14	Ye said, It is vain to serve God … what profit is it?
Luke 15:12–13	[The Prodigal Son] wasted his substance with riotous living
Hebrews 12:16–17	Esau, for one morsel of meat sold his birthright
2 Peter 1:9	He … cannot see afar off, and hath forgotten that he was purged from his old sins

D. Quitting when the going gets tough:

Matthew 13:20–21	When persecution ariseth … by and by he is offended
John 10:12–13	An hireling … seeth the wolf coming, and leaveth the sheep, and fleeth. He careth not for the sheep

E. Desiring worldly pleasures and riches:

Genesis 19:26	[Lot's] wife looked back … and became a pillar of salt
Numbers 11:5–6	[Lusting for things of Egypt] (See also Exodus 16:3.)
Psalm 73:2–3	My steps had well night slipped. For I was envious at … the prosperity of the wicked
Matthew 13:22	The care of this world, and the deceitfulness of riches, choke the word
2 Timothy 4:10	Demas hath forsaken me, having loved present world
Hebrews 11:14–15	If they had been mindful of that country from whence they came out, they might have … returned
1 John 2:15–17	If any man love the world, love of the Father not in him
Revelation 3:17	I am rich and increased with goods and have need of nothing

(See also 1 Corinthians 10:5–6.)

F. Not being grounded in the Word:

Matthew 7:26–27	[He] that heareth these sayings … and doeth them not … house upon the sand … great was the fall of it
Luke 8:13	These have no root … in time of temptation fall away
1 Timothy 1:19	Faith … which some having put away made shipwreck
2 Timothy 4:3–4	They shall turn away their ears from the truth

G. Having an unbelieving attitude:

John 6:60,66	Many disciples said, this is an hard saying; who can hear it? Many went back, and walked no more with him
Romans 11:20	Because of unbelief they were broken off
Colossians 2:8	Beware lest any man spoil you through philosophy
Hebrews 3:12	Take heed, lest there be in you an evil heart of unbelief, in departing from the living God
Jude 1:5	The Lord, having saved the people out of Egypt, afterward destroyed them that believed not

H. Hardening heart to the truth:

Matthew 13:15	Ears dull of hearing … their eyes they have closed
Ephesians 4:18–19	Having understanding darkened, being alienated from the life of God through blindness … past feeling

I. Double-mindedness and wavering:

2 Chronicles 25:2,14	He did that which was right, but not with a perfect heart [and soon worshipped other gods] (See also Psalm 78:36–37.)
Psalm 78:8–9	[They] set not their heart aright … spirit was not steadfast
Hosea 10:2	Their heart is divided; now [are] they found faulty
James 1:6–8	A double-minded man is unstable in all his ways (See also Ephesians 4:14.)

J. Refusing to receive correction:

Job 33:9–10	I am clean … I am innocent; neither is there iniquity in me
Proverbs 14:9	Fools make a mock at sin [as if it's not serious]
Proverbs 15:10	Correction is grievous unto him that forsaketh the way

K. Not confessing problems and sins:

Proverbs 28:13	He that covereth his sins shall not prosper
John 3:19–20	Neither cometh to light, lest his deeds be reproved (See also Isaiah 29:15 and Saul's problem in 1 Samuel 15.)

L. Not responding to God's reproofs:

Proverbs 29:1	He that being often reproved, and hardeneth his neck
Isaiah 1:5	Why should ye be striken any more? Ye revolt more
Isaiah 57:17	I was wroth, and smote him [but] he went on forwardly in the way of his heart

Jeremiah 2:30	In vain have I smitten your children; they received no correction
	(See also Isaiah 42:25; Jeremiah 5:3; Daniel 9:13.)

M. Allowing bitterness to grow:

Hebrews 12:15	Lest any man fail of the grace of God, lest any root of bitterness springing up, trouble you
	(See also James 3:14–15; Ephesians 4:31.)

N. Being led astray with vain imaginations:

Jeremiah 7:24	They walked in the imagination of their evil heart, and went backward
	(See also Jeremiah 13:10; 16:12.)

O. Idleness and gossiping:

1 Timothy 5:12–13	They have cast off their faith. They learn to be idle, wandering … tattlers and busybodies
2 Timothy 2:16	Vain babblings … will increase unto more ungodliness
	(See also Ephesians 1:14; 1 Timothy 6:20–21.)

P. Murmuring and ingratitude:

Numbers 14:27–30	[Murmurers not allowed to enter the promised land]
	(See also Numbers 11:1; 21:5–6; 1 Corinthians 10:10; Jude 1:15–16.)

Q. Fellowshipping with the wrong crowd:

Proverbs 6:12–16,19	Frowardness is in his heart … he soweth discord
Proverbs 13:20	A companion of fools shall be destroyed
1 Corinthians 15:33	Evil communications corrupt good manners
Galatians 5:7	Who did hinder you that ye should not obey the truth?
James 4:4	Whoever will be a friend of the world is enemy of God
	(See also Luke 6:45; 1 Kings 11:4.)

R. A lack of the fear of God:

Jeremiah 2:19	Thou hast forsaken the Lord … my fear is not in thee

2. GOD'S PROMISES OF MERCY TO THOSE WHO RETURN TO HIM:

2 Chronicles 30:9	God is gracious and merciful, and will not turn away his face from you, if ye return unto him
Isaiah 54:7–8	For a small moment have I forsaken thee; but with great mercies will I gather thee
Isaiah 55:7	Let the wicked forsake his way and return, and he will have mercy upon him
Jeremiah 3:12	Return, backsliding Israel … for I am merciful
Jeremiah 3:14	Turn, O backsliding children, for I am married to you
Jeremiah 3:22	Return … and I will heal your backslidings
Hosea 14:4	I will heal their backsliding … mine anger turned away

Joel 2:12–13	Turn ye to me with all your heart, and with weeping … God is gracious and merciful, and of great kindness
Zechariah 10:6	I will have mercy upon them: and they shall be as though I had not cast them off

(See also Job 14:7; Isaiah 1:18; Ezekiel 36:26–27; Daniel 9:9.)

3. ATTITUDE FOR REPENTANT PRODIGALS TO HAVE:

2 Chronicles 7:14	If my people … humble themselves and seek my face, and turn from their wicked ways … I will forgive
Psalm 41:4	Lord … heal my soul; for I have sinned against thee
Psalm 51:3	I acknowledge my transgressions: and my sin is before me
Psalm 84:10	I had rather be a doorkeeper in the house of my God, than to dwell in the tents of wickedness
Psalm 119:176	I have gone astray like a lost sheep; seek [me]
Jeremiah 14:7	Our backslidings are many … have sinned against thee
Jeremiah 24:7	I will be their God: for they shall return unto me with their whole heart
Ezekiel 36:31	Then shall ye remember … and shall loathe yourselves … for your iniquities
Hosea 6:1	Come, let us return unto the Lord … he will heal us
Luke 15:19,21	I am no more worthy to be called thy son: make me as one of thy hired servants

(See also Job 40:1–5; 42:1–6; Psalm 51:all; Daniel 9:3–20; James 4:6–10.)

4. HOW TO AVOID LOSING THE FAITH:

A. Love God and keep the heavenly vision:

Matthew 6:21	Where your treasure is, there will your heart be also
Matthew 6:24	Hate the [world], and love the [Lord] … hold on to the [Lord], and despise the [world]
Colossians 2:6–7	Rooted and built up in him, and stablished in the faith
Colossians 3:1–2	Set your affection on things above, not on … earth
Hebrews 12:2–3	Looking unto Jesus … lest ye faint in your minds

B. Remember that Jesus is worth it all:

1 Corinthians 15:58	Be steadfast, unmoveable … in the work of the Lord, your labour is not in vain in the Lord
Galatians 6:9	Let us not be weary in well doing: for in due season we shall reap, if we faint not
Hebrews 10:35	Cast not away your confidence … hath great recompense
Hebrews 11:26–27	Esteeming … Christ greater riches than the treasures of Egypt … endured, as seeing him who is invisible

James 1:12	Blessed is the man that endureth temptation … he shall receive the crown of life (See also 2 Timothy 4:7–8.)
Revelation 3:11	Hold fast which thou hast, that no man take thy crown (See also John 15:2–7, about "abiding in the vine"; 2 Corinthians 4:16–18; Revelation 2:26–28.)

C. Trust God to keep you faithful:

Psalm 17:5	Hold up my goings in thy paths that my [feet] slip not
Psalm 26:1	I have trusted in the Lord; I shall not slide
Jude 1:24	He [God] is able to keep you from falling

D. Hide the Word in your heart:

Psalm 37:31	Law of God is in his heart; none of his steps slide
Psalm 119:9	Cleanse his way by taking heed … to thy word
Psalm 119:11	Word hid in mine heart, that I might not sin
Psalm 119:165	Great peace have they which love thy law: and nothing shall offend them (See also 2 Thessalonians 2:15; 2 Peter 1:4.)

E. Have conviction; you know what you believe:

1 Kings 18:21	How long halt ye between two opinions? If the Lord be God, follow him
John 6:67–68	Jesus [said] unto the twelve, Will ye also go away? To whom shall we go? Thou hast the words of life
Acts 20:24	None of these things move me … that I might finish [my] ministry … to testify the gospel
Romans 14:5	Let every man be fully persuaded in his own mind
2 Peter 1:10	Make your calling and election sure … shall never fall

F. Be open to correction and reproof:

Psalm 141:5	Let righteous reprove me … shall be an excellent oil
Proverbs 6:23	Reproofs of instruction are the way of life (See also Proverbs 10:17.)
Proverbs 27:5–6	Faithful are the wounds of a friend
Hebrews 3:13	Exhort one another daily, lest any of you be hardened
Hebrews 12:5–13	Endure chastening … lest [ye] be turned out of the way

G. Confess your problems and sins:

Proverbs 28:13	Whoso confesseth and forsaketh [sins] shall have mercy
Hebrews 12:1	Lay aside every weight, and the sin … and run the race
James 5:16	Confess your faults one to another, and pray one for (See also Job 11:14; 1 John 1:8–10.)

H. Withdraw yourself from those who turn away from the truth:

Psalm 1:1–2	[Walk] not in the counsel of the ungodly, nor [stand] in the way of sinners, nor [sit] in the seat of the scornful

Psalm 119:63	I am a companion of them that fear thee, and of them that keep thy precepts (See also Proverbs 13:20.)
Romans 16:17–18	Avoid them … by fair speeches deceive the simple
Ephesians 5:11	Have no fellowship with … but rather reprove them
2 Thessalonians 3:6	Withdraw selves from brother that walketh disorderly
1 Timothy 6:3–5	Perverse disputing … from such withdraw thyself
2 Peter 3:17	Beware lest ye being led away with the wicked, fall

(See also Exodus 23:2; Proverbs 1:10,15.)

I. Love not the world:

Romans 12:2	Be not conformed to his world, but be ye transformed
Galatians 6:14	Cross of Christ, [whereby] world is crucified unto me
2 Timothy 2:4	No man that warreth entangleth self with … this world
1 John 2:15	Love not the world, neither the things in the world

(See also Colossians 3:2; 1 Corinthians 7:31.)

J. Endure hardships:

Psalm 44:14–18	All this is come upon us: yet … our heart is not turned back, neither have our steps declined
2 Timothy 2:3	Endure hardness, as a good soldier of Jesus Christ
Hebrews 11:24–25	Choosing rather to suffer affliction … than to enjoy the pleasures of sin for a season

(See also Hebrews 12:1–3.)

K. Remember how much you've already endured:

Galatians 3:4	Have ye suffered so many things in vain?
Hebrews 10:32	Call to remembrance the former days, in which … ye endured a great fight

(See also Hebrews 6:11.)

L. Be thankful and content:

Philippians 4:11	Have learned, in whatever state I am … to be content
1 Thessalonians 5:18	In everything give thanks
1 Timothy 6:6–8	Having food and raiment let us be therewith content

(See also Proverbs 15:16; Ecclesiastes 6:9; Hebrews 13:5.)

M. Be thankful for what He's delivered you from:

Psalm 40:2	He brought me out of an horrible pit … and set my feet upon a rock

N. Consider what backsliding leads to:

Proverbs 13:15	The way of the transgressor is hard
1 Corinthians 3:11–15	If any build … wood, hay, stubble … he shall suffer loss
2 Peter 2:20	If after they have escaped the … world … they are again

	entangled therein, the latter end is worse
	(See also Psalm 106:15; Galatians 6:7–8; Revelation 3:11.)

5. THE ATTITUDE TO HAVE TOWARD FORMER BRETHREN:

A. Try to win them back, if possible:

Jeremiah 31:20	Since I spake against him, I remember him still
Luke 15:4–6	What man ... having an hundred sheep, if he lose one, doth not seek
Luke 15:20–24	[Father rejoiced and welcomed the Prodigal Son back home]
	(See also Galatians 6:1,2; 2 Timothy 2:24–26.)

B. Don't give up on them:

Jeremiah 31:17	There is hope in thine end ... that thy children shall come again to their own border
	(See also the story of Simon Peter in Luke 22:54–62; Mark 16:7; Acts 2:14,38,40.)
	(See also the story of John Mark in Acts 13:5,13; 14:36–40; 2 Timothy 4:11.)

C. Some people were never really part of your fellowship:

Galatians 2:4	False brethren unawares ... came in privily to spy out
1 John 2:19	They went out from us, but they were not of us; for if they had been of us, they would have continued
Jude 1:4	Men crept in ... who were ordained to condemnation

D. Some become antagonistic:

Matthew 12:30	He that gathereth not with me, scattereth abroad
Philippians 3:18	For many walk ... they are enemies of the cross
	(Judas' backsliding: Matthew 26:14–15,47–50; 27:5.)
	(Alexander's backsliding: 1 Timothy 1:19–20; 2 Timothy 4:14–15.)

Special passages about falling away from the faith: Nehemiah 9:15–37; Psalm 78; 106; Luke 15:11–32

CHRISTIANITY IN CRISIS

"I would that thou wert cold or hot." (Revelation 3:15)

(This section is a detailed study on the pitfalls of complacency and even apostasy that individual Christians, as well as entire churches and denominations, can fall into.

It is the editors' prayer that the reader will not merely reflect on the failings of other Christians when studying this section, but will, in Christian maturity, use it as a spiritual thermometer to measure his or her own depth of devotion to Jesus Christ, and know whether they are "cold or hot.")

1. PREDICTIONS OF A GREAT APOSTASY IN THE LAST DAYS:

Matthew 24:12	Iniquity shall abound, the love of many shall wax cold
2 Thessalonians 2:1–3	The day of Christ … shall not come, except there come a falling away [apostasy] first
1 Timothy 4:1	The Spirit speaketh expressly, that in the latter times some shall depart from the faith
2 Timothy 4:3–4	The time will come when they will not endure sound doctrine … turn away their ears from the truth

2. IGNORANCE OF THE WORD OF GOD:

A. Many don't study the Word or know what it really says:

Hosea 4:6	My people are destroyed for lack of knowledge
Matthew 12:3–5	Have ye not read what David did … or have ye not read in the law (See also Matthew 19:4.)
Matthew 22:29	Ye do err, not knowing the scriptures
Acts 13:27	They knew [understood] not … the prophets which are read every Sabbath day (See also 2 Corinthians 3:14–15.)
1 Timothy 1:7	Understanding neither what they say, nor whereof they affirm (See also Jeremiah 5:4; Acts 13:27.)

B. The dangers of being unlearned in the Word:

2 Peter 3:16	In all [Paul's] epistles … things hard to be understood, which they that are unlearned … wrest [distort]

C. The ignorant can be easily led astray by false teachers:

Galatians 1:6–7	Ye are so soon removed from him that called you … unto another gospel
2 Thessalonians 2:2–3,5	Let no man deceive you … Remember ye not … I told you these things?

D. Even many who know the Word don't obey it:

Jeremiah 5:5	The great men … have known the way of the Lord … but these have altogether broken the yoke [disobeyed]

Jeremiah 8:8–9	How do ye say, We are wise, and the law of the Lord is with us? Lo … the pen of the scribes is in vain
Matthew 23:3	Do not ye after their works: for they say, and do not
Romans 2:17–24	Thou … knowest his will … hast … the truth … makest thy boast of the law, through breaking the law dishonourest thou God

E. Some, though familiar with the Word, are not even saved:

Jeremiah 2:8	They that handle the law knew me not
John 3:1–10	Art thou a master of Israel, and knowest not these things [about being born again]

3. DOCTRINES AND TRADITIONS OF MAN VS. GOD'S WORD:

A. Beware of exalting doctrines of man above the Word:

Isaiah 29:13	Their fear toward me is taught by the precept of men
Matthew 15:3	Ye also transgress the commandment of God by your tradition
Matthew 15:9	Teaching for doctrines the commandments of men
Mark 7:9	Ye reject the commandment of God, that ye may keep your own tradition
Mark 7:13	Making the word … of none effect through your traditions
2 Timothy 4:3–4	After their own lusts shall they heap to themselves teachers, having itching ears

B. "Denominationalism" and needless doctrinal divisions:

Romans 14:1–6	[Avoid arguing over minor personal doctrines]
1 Corinthians 1:10–13	One … saith, I am of Paul; and I of Apollos; and I of Cephas … Is Christ divided? (See also 1 Corinthians 3:21–23.)
1 Timothy 6:3–4	Proud … doting about questions and strifes of words (See also John 4:20–21; Acts 15:5,24.)

C. Prestige-seeking leaders create their own factions:

Acts 20:30	Of your own selves shall men arise, speaking perverse [erroneous] things, to draw away disciples after them
2 Timothy 1:15	All they which are in Asia be turned away from [Paul]; of whom [the leaders] are Phygellus and Hermogenes
3 John 1:9–10	Diotrephes, loveth to have the preeminence among them [and rejected the apostle John's authority]

D. Splitting theological hairs, while disobeying the Word:

Matthew 23:24	Ye … strain at a gnat, and swallow a camel
Luke 11:42	Ye tithe [but] pass over judgement and the love of God

E. Twisting the Word to suit personal doctrines:

1 Timothy 1:5–6	The commandment is charity … from which some … have turned aside unto vain jangling
2 Peter 1:20	No prophecy of the scripture [should be] of any private interpretation
2 Peter 3:16	They that are unlearned and unstable wrest … the scriptures, unto their own destruction

F. Stick to solid Scriptural doctrines:

1 Timothy 4:6–7	Nourished up in the words of faith and of good doctrine
1 Timothy 6:3–4	If any … consent not to … the words of our Lord Jesus Christ … he is proud, knowing nothing
Titus 1:14	Not giving heed to … commandments of men, that turn from the truth
	(See also Colossians 2:8–9; 2 Timothy 1:13; 2:14–16,23; Titus 1:9; 2:1,8; 3:9.)

G. Beware of those who deny biblical beliefs:

Jeremiah 8:9	The wise men … have rejected the word of the Lord; and what wisdom is in them?
Acts 23:8	[They] say that there is no resurrection, neither angel, nor spirit
1 Corinthians 15:12–17	How say some among you that there is no resurrection
Galatians 1:9	If any man preach any other gospel … let him be accursed
2 Timothy 3:5	Having a form of godliness, but denying the power thereof
2 Peter 2:1	Damnable heresies, even denying the Lord

4. THE DWELLING PLACE OF GOD:

A. Your body is the true temple of the Holy Spirit:

John 4:20–24	Neither in this mountain, nor yet at Jerusalem, worship … true worshippers shall worship the Father in spirit
1 Corinthians 3:16	Ye are the temple of God … the Spirit of God dwelleth in you
1 Corinthians 6:19	Your body is the temple of the Holy Ghost which is in you
2 Corinthians 6:16	Ye are the temple of the living God … I will dwell in them

B. The true church is the body of believers:

Acts 2:41–47	[Scriptural definition of what the church is]
Romans 12:4–5	We, being many, are one body in Christ
1 Corinthians 12:13–28	Ye are the body of Christ, and members in particular
Colossians 1:18,24	[Jesus] is the head of the body, the church

1 Peter 2:5	Ye also, as lively stones, are built up a spiritual house [church] (See 1 Corinthians 10:17; Ephesians 4:4,12,15–16.)

C. The early church only had homes to meet in:

(See Romans 16:3,5; 1 Corinthians 16:19; Colossians 4:15; Philemon 1:2.)

D. Does God dwell in church buildings?

1 Kings 8:27	The heaven and heaven of heavens cannot contain thee; how much less this house that I [Solomon] have builded?
Isaiah 66:1	Earth is my footstool: where is the house that ye build unto me?
Hosea 8:14	Israel hath forgotten his Maker, and buildeth temples
Acts 7:48	The most High dwelleth not in temples made with hands
Hebrews 9:24	Christ is not entered into the holy places made with hands

5. THE DANGER OF COMPLACENCY:

A. Lukewarmness and satisfaction with material things:

Jeremiah 5:31	The prophets prophesy falsely, and the priests bear rule by their means; and my people love to have it so
1 Timothy 6:5	Supposing that gain is godliness [the "abundant life"]
Revelation 3:15–17	I know thy works, that thou art … lukewarm ... thou sayest, I am rich, and increased with goods, and have need of nothing; and knowest not that thou art wretched

B. Closing our minds to the truth is spiritual blindness:

Isaiah 30:9	Rebellious people … that will not hear the law of the Lord
Zechariah 7:11–12	They refused to hearken … and stopped their ears … lest they should hear the … words [given by] the prophets
Matthew 13:14–15	Their eyes they have closed; lest … they should see
Matthew 15:14	They be blind leaders of the blind (See also Matthew 23:16–17,24,26; Romans 10:3; 2 Corinthians 4:4; Ephesians 4:18.)

C. Even many who boast that they "see" are blind:

John 9:40–41	Are we blind also? Jesus said … ye say, We see; therefore your sin remaineth
Revelation 3:17	Thou … knowest not that thou art … blind

D. Compromise due to fear of man:

Mark 8:38	Whosoever shall be ashamed of me … of him shall the Son of man be ashamed
John 12:42–43	Many believed … but … did not confess him, lest they should be put out of the synagogue

6. DISOBEDIENCE TO THE GREAT COMMISSION:

A. What we as Christians are supposed to do:

Mark 16:15	Go ye into all the world, and preach the gospel to every creature

B. Beware of anyone who is not concerned with winning the lost:

Isaiah 56:10–11	His watchmen are blind … dumb dogs, they cannot bark … shepherds that … look to their own way … for his gain
Jeremiah 50:6	Lost sheep: their shepherds have caused them to go astray
Ezekiel 34:4–6	Neither have ye sought that which was lost
Ezekiel 34:8	Neither did my shepherds search for my flock, but the shepherds fed themselves, and fed not my flock
John 10:12–13	The hireling fleeth … and careth not for the sheep (See also Ezekiel 33:6.)

C. Hypocrisy among believers turns men from salvation:

Romans 2:17–24	For the name of God is blasphemed among the Gentiles through you (See also Matthew 23:13; Luke 11:52.)

7. FAILURE TO SHEPHERD THE FLOCK:

A. Jesus' commands to pastors:

Proverbs 27:23	Be thou diligent to know the state of thy flocks
John 21:16	Lovest thou me? … Feed my sheep
Acts 20:28	Feed the church of God, which he hath purchased with his own blood
1 Peter 5:2	Feed the flock of God which is among you

B. Many neglect to spiritually feed their flocks:

Ezekiel 34:2–3	Should not the shepherds feed the flocks? Ye feed not
Ezekiel 34:18–19	My flock … drink that which ye have fouled with your feet

C. They don't minister to and care for them:

Jeremiah 6:14	They have healed also the hurt … of my people slightly
Ezekiel 34:4	The diseased have ye not strengthened, neither … healed … neither … bound up … neither … brought again

D. Unshepherded members are a scattered flock:

Jeremiah 13:17,20	Weep … because the Lord's flock is carried away captive … Where is … thy beautiful flock?
Jeremiah 23:2	The pastors that feed my people; Ye have scattered my flock … and have not visited them
Ezekiel 34:5–8	They were scattered, because there is no shepherd
Matthew 9:36	[Jesus] was moved with compassion on them, because they … were scattered abroad, as sheep having no shepherd

8. WARNINGS AGAINST COVETING FINANCIAL GAIN:

A. Preaching for money, not to win souls or feed the flock:

Jeremiah 6:13	Given to covetousness; and from the prophet even unto the priest every one dealeth falsely
Micah 3:11	Priests thereof teach for hire, and the prophets thereof divine for money
Matthew 6:24	No man can serve … God and mammon [materialism]
Titus 1:10–11	Vain talkers … teaching … for filthy lucre's sake
1 Peter 5:2	Feed the flock of God … not for filthy lucre
2 Peter 2:1,3	False teachers … through covetousness shall they with feigned words make merchandise of you

(See also Zechariah 11:4–5.)

B. Unjustly robbing the poor:

Isaiah 56:11	They all look to their own way, every one for his gain
Ezekiel 33:31	With their mouth they show much love, but their heart goeth after their covetousness
Ezekiel 34:2–3	Woe be to the shepherds … that do feed themselves … Ye eat the fat, and ye clothe you with the wool
Matthew 23:14	Ye devour widows' houses, and for a pretence make long prayer

C. Selfishness toward the needy shows a lack of love:

Matthew 25:42–43	I was an hungered, and ye gave me no meat
1 John 3:17	Whoso hath this world's good, and seeth his brother have need [and doesn't help] how dwelleth the love of God in him?

(See also James 2:15–16.)

9. WARNINGS AGAINST HYPOCRISY:

A. To those who pretend to be Christians, but are not:

Jeremiah 7:4	Lying words, saying, The temple of the Lord, are these

Matthew 7:21	Not every one that saith unto me, Lord, Lord, shall enter into … heaven; but he that doeth the will of my Father
Matthew 15:9	In vain they do worship me
Matthew 23:2–3	Do not ye after their works: for they say, and do not
Matthew 23:14	For a pretence make long prayer
Luke 6:46	Why call ye me Lord, Lord, and do not the things I say?
Titus 1:16	They profess that they know God; but in works they deny him
	(See also Matthew 7:22–23.)

B. Some appear outwardly good, but are inwardly wicked:

Matthew 7:15	In sheep's clothing, but inwardly they are ravening wolves
Matthew 23:5	All their works they do for to be seen of men
Matthew 23:27–28	Like unto whited sepulchres, which indeed appear beautiful outward … full of hypocrisy and iniquity
Luke 18:11–12	I thank thee, that I am not as … this publican. I fast
	(See also Jeremiah 7:9–10.)

C. False holiness and religious standards:

Matthew 23:4	They bind heavy burdens … on men's shoulders
Acts 15:10	Why … put a yoke upon the neck of the disciples
	(See also Matthew 6:2,5,16.)

D. False professions of love for God:

Isaiah 29:13	This people draw near me with their mouth, and with their lips do honour me, but have removed their heart far from me
Jeremiah 2:32	My people have forgotten me days without number
Jeremiah 5:1–2	Though they say, The Lord liveth; surely they swear falsely
Ezekiel 33:31–32	They come … as my people, and they hear thy words, but they will not do them
Matthew 15:8	Draweth nigh unto me with their mouth, and honoureth me with their lips; but their heart is far from me (See also Mark 7:6.)
1 John 4:20	If a man say, I love God, and hateth his brother, he is a liar
	(See also Isaiah 58:1–2; Malachi 1:6.)

10. RELIGIOUS PERSECUTION:

A. Misled religious zeal frequently results in persecution:

Isaiah 66:5	Your brethren … cast you out for my name's sake
Matthew 23:31–35	Children of them which killed the prophets … from the blood of righteous Abel … Zacharias

John 16:2	Whosoever killeth you will think that he doeth God service
Galatians 4:29	He that was born after the flesh persecuted him that was born after the Spirit, even so it is now (See also Lamentations 4:13–14; Matthew 27:40–43; John 19:6–7.)

B. Religious jealousy motivates persecution:

Mark 15:10	The chief priests had delivered [Jesus] for envy (See also John 11:47–50,53.)
Acts 13:44–45	When the Jews saw the multitudes, they were filled with envy

Special chapters about Christianity in crisis: Ezekiel 13; 34; Jeremiah 23; Matthew 23; Revelation 2–3

THE LAW OF CHRIST

"The perfect law of liberty" vs. religious legalism

1. SALVATION IS PURELY BY GRACE, NOT WORKS:

Romans 3:28	A man is justified by faith without the deeds of the law
Ephesians 2:8–9	By grace [undeserved mercy] are ye saved through faith ... it is the gift of God: Not of works
Titus 3:5	Not by works of righteousness which we have done, but according to his mercy he saved us

A. Salvation is not partly by grace and partly by good works:

Romans 11:6	If by grace, then is it no more of works: otherwise grace is no more grace

B. Salvation was always by grace, even in the Old Testament:

Genesis 6:8	But Noah found grace in the eyes of the Lord
Genesis 15:6	[Abraham] believed in the Lord; and he counted it to him for righteousness (See also Romans 4:3,5–8,21–22.)
Habakkuk 2:4	The just shall live by his faith

C. Scrupulously keeping the Mosaic law never justified anyone:

John 1:17	Law was given by Moses, but grace and truth came by Jesus Christ
Romans 3:20	By the deeds of the law there shall no flesh be justified
Romans 9:31	Israel, which followed after the law ... hath not attained to the law of righteousness
Galatians 2:16	A man is not justified by the works of the law, but by the faith of Jesus Christ (See also Galatians 3:11.)
Hebrews 7:19	The law made nothing perfect, but ... a better hope did

2. WHAT WAS THE MOSAIC LAW?

A. It was a legal code that God gave Moses:

Exodus 24:12	And the Lord said unto Moses, Come up to me into the mount ... and I will give thee ... a law

B. It was a strict system of justice and retribution:

Exodus 21:23–25	Thou shalt give life for life, eye for eye, tooth for tooth, hand for hand ... Burning for burning
Hebrews 10:28	He that despised [broke] Moses' law died without mercy

C. The Ten Commandments were not merely "helpful moral guidelines," but strict laws, most carrying the death penalty:

Exodus 20:2–3	(#1) Thou shalt have no other gods before me [Death penalty: Exodus 22:20; Deuteronomy 13:1–18]

Exodus 20:4–5	(#2) Thou shalt not make unto thee any graven image [Death penalty same as (#1)] (See also Leviticus 26:1,30; Deuteronomy 4:23–26.]
Exodus 20:7	(#3) Thou shalt not take the name of the Lord thy God in vain [Death penalty: Leviticus 24:10–16]
Exodus 20:8–10	(#4) Remember the sabbath day, to keep it holy. [Death penalty: Exodus 31:14–15; 35:2]
Exodus 20:12	(#5) Honour thy father and thy mother [Death penalty: Exodus 21:15,17; Leviticus 20:9; Deuteronomy 21:18–21]
Exodus 20:13	(#6) Thou shalt not kill [Death penalty: Exodus 21:12; Leviticus 21:17,21; Numbers 35:16–31]
Exodus 20:14	(#7) Thou shalt not commit adultery [Death penalty: Leviticus 20:10; Deuteronomy 22:22]
Exodus 20:15	(#8) Thou shalt not steal [Punishment: Exodus 22:7; Proverbs 6:20; death penalty: Exodus 21:16]
Exodus 20:16	(#9) Thou shalt not bear false witness [Punishment and/or death penalty: Deuteronomy 19:16–21]
Exodus 20:17	(#10) Thou shalt not covet … any thing that is thy neighbour's
Galatians 4:21	Tell me, ye that desire to be under the law, do ye not hear the law?

D. The Ten Commandments were only the beginning; Moses' law contained hundreds of other commandments:

Deuteronomy 27:26	Cursed be he that confirmeth not all the words of this law to do them (See also Galatians 3:10.) (See also Deuteronomy 4:13–14.)

E. If guilty of breaking one law, guilty of breaking it all:

James 2:10	Whosoever shall keep the whole law, and yet offend in one point, he is guilty of all

3. THE LAW SERVED A PURPOSE ONLY FOR A TIME:

Galatians 3:19	Wherefore then serveth the law? It was added because of transgressions, till the seed [Jesus] should come
Galatians 3:23	Before faith came, we were kept under the law
Hebrews 9:10	Carnal ordinances, imposed on them until the time of reformation

A. It was merely a copy, a shadow, of the real thing:

Colossians 2:16–17	Sabbath days … are a shadow of things to come; but the body [the reality that casts the shadow] is of Christ
Hebrews 8:5	The example and shadow of heavenly things
Hebrews 9:8–9	First tabernacle … a figure for the time then present

Hebrews 10:1	The law having a shadow of good things to come, and not the very image of the things
1 John 2:8	A new commandment … because the darkness is past, and the true light now shineth.

B. The Law was hard to keep:

John 7:19	Did not Moses give you the law, and yet none of you keepeth the law (See also Acts 7:53.)
Acts 15:10	A yoke upon the neck … which neither our fathers nor we were able to bear
Romans 7:14–19	The law is spiritual: but I am carnal, sold under sin … how to perform that which is good I find not

C. This showed that humans were sinners in need of grace:

Romans 3:19–20	That … all the world may become guilty before God ... by the law is the knowledge of sin
Romans 7:7	I had not known sin, but by the law
Galatians 3:24	The law was our schoolmaster to bring us unto Christ (See also Romans 4:15.)

D. The old Law was unprofitable and eventually replaced:

Romans 8:3	What the law could not do, in that it was weak
Hebrews 7:18	For there is verily a disannulling of the [Mosaic law] … for the weakness and unprofitableness thereof

4. ATONEMENT (PAYMENT) FOR BREAKING THE LAW:

A. Because the Law was constantly being broken, forgiveness was needed, and a blood sacrifice was required:

Leviticus 4:1–4	If a soul shall sin … against any of the commandments of the Lord … kill the bullock before the Lord
Leviticus 17:11	It is the blood that maketh an atonement for the soul
Hebrews 9:22	Without shedding of blood is no remission (See also Leviticus 6:2–3,6–7; 16:3,5–11,15–22.)

B. But this never permanently erased sin:

Hebrews 10:1–4,11	It is not possible that the blood of bulls and of goats should take away sins … can never take away sins

C. But Jesus made a perfect and permanent sacrifice:

Matthew 26:28	This is my blood … which is shed for many for the remission of sins
Hebrews 9:7–14	By his own blood … obtained eternal redemption for us
Hebrews 9:25–28	Christ was once offered to bear the sins of many
Hebrews 10:10–12	We are sanctified through the offering of the body of Jesus Christ once for all

1 Peter 1:18–19	Ye were not redeemed … with the precious blood of Christ
1 John 1:7	The blood of Jesus Christ … cleanseth us from all sin (See also John 1:29; Romans 5:9.)

5. THE NEW LAW, THE LAW OF CHRIST:

A. God promised a new law to replace the old Mosaic law:

Jeremiah 31:31–33	The days come … that I will make a new covenant … I will … write [my law] in their hearts
Hebrews 8:7–10	Finding fault with [the old covenant], he saith … I will make a new covenant

B. Names of the new law:

- A new covenant (Jeremiah 31:31)
- The law of faith (Romans 3:27)
- The law of the Spirit of life (Romans 8:2)
- The law of righteousness (Romans 9:31)
- The law of Christ (Galatians 6:2)
- The new testament (Hebrews 9:15)
- The perfect law of liberty (James 1:25)
- The royal law (James 2:8)
- The holy commandment (2 Peter 2:21)

C. Jesus' death on the cross fulfilled and ended the Law:

Matthew 5:17	I am not come to destroy [the Law], but to fulfil
John 19:30	[Jesus] said, It is finished [When He died for our sins, the Mosaic law ended for believers]
Romans 10:4	For Christ is the end of the law for righteousness to every one that believeth
Colossians 2:14	Blotting out [wiping the slate completely clean of] the … ordinances [Law] … nailing it to his cross

D. The old Mosaic law is now discarded (for believers in Jesus):

Hebrews 8:6	A better covenant … established upon better promises
Hebrews 8:13	He hath made the first [covenant] old. Now that which decayeth and waxeth old is ready to vanish away
Hebrews 10:9	He taketh away the first [Law], that he may establish the second

E. Believers are no longer bound by the rigid Mosaic law:

Romans 6:14	Ye are not under the law, but under grace
Galatians 3:24–25	The law was our schoolmaster … But after that faith is come, we are no longer under a schoolmaster
1 Timothy 1:9	The law is not made for a righteous man, but for the lawless … ungodly … profane … murderers

F. Jesus has liberated us from the Mosaic law:

Romans 7:4	Ye also are become dead to the law by the body of Christ
Romans 7:6	Now we are delivered from the law
Romans 8:1–2	The law of the Spirit of life in Christ Jesus hath made me free from the law of sin and death
Galatians 3:13	Christ hath redeemed us from the curse of the law

G. Jesus' Spirit and truth gives us freedom:

John 8:36	If the Son therefore shall make you free, ye shall be free indeed
2 Corinthians 3:17	Where the Spirit of the Lord is, there is liberty
Galatians 5:1	The liberty wherewith Christ hath made us free
Galatians 5:5	Through the Spirit wait for the hope of righteousness by faith
Galatians 5:18	If ye be led of the Spirit, ye are not under the law

H. Read Jesus' liberating words to be set free:

John 8:31–32	Ye shall know the truth, and the truth shall make you free
Romans 10:17	Faith cometh by hearing … the word of God
James 1:25	Whoso looketh into the perfect law of liberty, and continueth therein … shall be blessed in his deed

6. NOW THE COMMANDMENT IS TO LOVE GOD AND OUR NEIGHBOUR:

A. This fulfils the Law:

Matthew 7:12	All things … ye would that men should do to you, do … to them: for this is the law (See also Luke 6:31.)
Matthew 22:36–40	Thou shalt love … God … Thou shalt love thy neighbour … On these two commandments [depend] all the law
Romans 13:8	He that loveth another hath fulfilled the law
Romans 13:10	Love worketh no ill to his neighbour: therefore love is the fulfilling of the law
Galatians 5:14	All the law is fulfilled in one word, even in this; Thou shalt love thy neighbour as thyself
James 2:8	If ye fulfil the royal law … Thou shalt love thy neighbour as thyself, ye do well (See also Mark 12:29–31.)

B. Deeds done in pure, unselfish love are lawful:

Luke 11:41	All things are clean unto you
1 Corinthians 6:12	All things are lawful unto me (See also 1 Corinthians 10:23.)
Galatians 5:22–23	Fruit of the Spirit is love … against such there is no law
Titus 1:15	Unto the pure all things are pure

C. But you have to have faith for your actions:

Romans 14:14	To him that esteemeth [thinks] any thing to be unclean, to him it is unclean
Romans 14:22–23	Happy is he that condemneth not himself in that thing which he alloweth … for whatsoever is not of faith is sin
Titus 1:15	Unto the … defiled and unbelieving is nothing pure

7. LIVING THE NEW LAW:

A. In some ways, the law of Christ is stricter than Moses' law:

Matthew 5:38–42	[The Law] said, An eye for an eye, and a tooth for a tooth: But I say unto you, That ye resist not evil
Matthew 5:43–45	[The Law] said, Thou shalt love thy neighbour, and hate thine enemy. But I say unto you, Love your enemies
Luke 10:25–37	Thou shalt love … thy neighbour as thyself [even those you'd normally dislike]
James 4:17	Him that knoweth to do good, and doeth it not … it is sin

B. Only Jesus can give you the power to live His law:

Philippians 2:13	For it is God which worketh in you both to will and to do of his good pleasure
Philippians 4:13	I can do all things through Christ which strengtheneth me
2 Corinthians 5:14	For the love of Christ constraineth [compels] us
2 Corinthians 12:9	My [God's] grace is sufficient for thee

8. WARNINGS AGAINST MISUSING THE NEW LAW:

A. Selfish, unloving liberties:

Romans 14:15	If thy brother be grieved … now walkest thou not charitably. Destroy not him with thy [liberty]
Romans 14:20	All things indeed are pure; but it is evil for that man who eateth with offence
1 Corinthians 6:12	All things are lawful unto me, but all things are not expedient
1 Corinthians 8:9,12	Take heed lest … this liberty of yours become a stumblingblock to them that are weak (See also 1 Corinthians 8.)
1 Corinthians 10:23	All things are lawful for me, but all things edify not

B. Walk in love, not in lust and sin:

Romans 6:1–2	Shall we … sin, that grace may abound? God forbid
Galatians 5:13	Use not liberty for an occasion to the flesh, but by love serve one another
1 Peter 2:16	As free, and not using your liberty for a cloak of maliciousness, but as the servants of God (See also Romans 3:8; 14:all; 15:1–2.)

9. BEWARE OF FALLING INTO RELIGIOUS LEGALISM:

A. The concision: Believers still bound by the Law:

Acts 21:20	Many thousands of Jews … which believe; and they are all zealous of the law
Philippians 3:2–3	Beware of evil workers, beware of the concision (See also Acts 15:1,24; Romans 2:28–29; Galatians 6:12–13.)

B. Don't be entangled again by the Law:

Galatians 3:1,3	Are ye so foolish? having begun in the Spirit, are ye now made perfect by the flesh?
Galatians 5:1	Stand fast therefore in the liberty … and be not entangled again with the yoke of bondage [to the Law]
Colossians 2:20–22	If ye be dead with Christ … are ye subject to … the commandments and doctrines of men?

C. Legalism is self-righteousness and denies Jesus' sacrifice:

Romans 10:3	Going about to establish their own righteousness, have not submitted themselves unto the righteousness of God
Galatians 2:21	If righteousness come by the law, then Christ is dead in vain [no reason] (See also Galatians 5:4.)

D. The Law can't save you or make you righteous:

Acts 13:39	By him all that believe are justified from all things, from which ye could not be justified by the Law
Romans 9:31–32	Israel, which followed after the law of righteousness, hath not attained to the law of righteousness
Philippians 3:3–9	Not having mine own righteousness, which is of the law, but that which is through the faith of Christ

E. Those who attempt to obey the Law are under bondage:

Galatians 3:10	Cursed is every one that continueth not in all things
Galatians 4:21–31	[The allegory of the two covenants, one of freedom, and the other of bondage]
Galatians 5:2–4	[Anyone who tries to keep the Law] is a debtor to do the whole law
James 2:10	For whosoever shall keep the whole law, and yet offend in one point, he is guilty of all

10. TRYING TO LEGALISTICALLY KEEP THE LAW IS NOT GOD'S WILL:

A. Legalists completely miss the main issue:

Matthew 15:2–6	Why do thy disciples transgress the tradition of the elders? ... Ye transgress the commandment of God by your tradition
Matthew 23:23–24	For ye pay tithe of [spices] and have omitted the weightier [more important] matters of ... mercy, and faith ... Ye ... strain at a gnat, and swallow a camel
Mark 7:6–8	Their heart is far from me ... ye hold the tradition of men, [such] as the washing of pots and cups
John 5:8–11	[Jesus told a lame man, "Take up thy bed and walk." The legalists ignored the miraculous healing and told him it was not lawful to carry his bed on the Sabbath]

B. Legalism is a crushing weight to those it is imposed upon:

Matthew 23:4	They bind heavy burdens and grievous to be borne, and lay them on men's shoulders
2 Corinthians 3:6	The letter killeth, but the spirit giveth life

C. The solution: Walk in God's love and Spirit:

Micah 6:8	What doth the Lord require of thee, but to do justly, and to love mercy, and to walk humbly with thy God?
John 6:63	It is the spirit that quickeneth [brings life]; the flesh profiteth nothing
Romans 7:6	We should serve in newness of spirit, and not in the oldness of the letter [of the Law]
2 Corinthians 3:6	Not of the letter, but of the spirit
Galatians 6:2	Bear ye one another's burdens, and so fulfil the law of Christ

11. EVEN UNDER THE MOSAIC LAW, GOD'S LOVE AND MERCY PREVAILED:

A. God always wanted love and mercy more than legalism:

Hosea 6:6	I desired mercy, and not sacrifice; and the knowledge of God more than burnt offerings. (See also Matthew 12:7.)
Micah 6:6–8	Shall I come before him with burnt offerings? ... what doth the Lord require of thee, but to ... love mercy
Mark 12:33	To love him with the heart ... and to love his neighbour ... is more than all ... offerings and sacrifices

(See also Deuteronomy 10:12; 1 Samuel 15:22; Psalm 40:6; 51:16–17; 69:30–31; Isaiah 1:11–16; Jeremiah 7:22–23.)

B. He allowed exceptions and the Mosaic law to be broken:

2 Chronicles 30:1–3	[King Hezekiah celebrated the Passover Feast in the second month instead of the first, as was commanded in Exodus 12] (See also Numbers 9:1–11.)
2 Chronicles 30:16–20	Many in the congregation that were not sanctified … yet did they eat the passover otherwise than it was written. But Hezekiah prayed for them, saying, The good Lord pardon every one … though he be not cleansed … the Lord hearkened to Hezekiah
Matthew 12:3–5	[David] did eat the shewbread, which was not lawful for him to eat ... on the sabbath days the priests … profane the sabbath, and are blameless (See also 1 Samuel 21:6; John 7:22–23.)

Special chapters about Christ's law: Romans 3–5; 7; 9–10; 14; Galatians 2–5; Hebrews 3–11

CREATION vs. EVOLUTION

1. GOD CREATED THE WORLD, NOT CHANCE EVOLUTION:

Genesis 1:1 — In the beginning God created the heaven and the earth
Nehemiah 9:6 — Thou hast made … the earth, and all things that are therein
Isaiah 45:12 — I have made the earth, and created man upon it
John 1:1–3 — All things were made by [Jesus]; and without him was not any thing made that was made
Colossians 1:16 — For by [Jesus] were all things created
Hebrews 1:2 — His Son … by whom also he made the worlds
(See also Psalm 105:25; Isaiah 48:13; Acts 4:24; 14:15; 17:24; Ephesians 3:9.)

2. GOD'S WORD CREATED (AND MAINTAINS) THE UNIVERSE:

Psalm 33:6 — By the word of the Lord were the heavens made
Psalm 33:9 — For he spake, and it was done; he commanded, and it stood fast
Colossians 1:17 — [Jesus] is before all things, and by him all things consist [hold together]
Hebrews 1:3 — Upholding all things by the word of his power
Hebrews 11:3 — The worlds were framed by the word of God, so that things which are seen were not made of things which do appear

3. GOD'S CREATION IS PROOF OF HIS EXISTENCE:

Job 12:7–9 — The earth … shall teach thee … Who knoweth not … that the hand of the Lord hath wrought this?
Psalm 19:1 — The heavens declare the glory of God; and the firmament [sky] showeth his handiwork
Romans 1:20 — The invisible things of him [are] understood by the things that are made … so that they are without excuse

4. JESUS BELIEVED IN AND QUOTED FROM GENESIS:

Matthew 19:4–5 — Have ye not read … he … made them at the beginning
(See also Genesis 1:27; 2:24.)
John 5:46–47 — If ye believe not [Moses'] writings, how shall ye believe my words?

5. THE BIBLE AND SCIENCE:

A. Prophetic descriptions of "discoveries" about creation:

Job 26:7 — He … hangeth the earth upon nothing
Job 36:27–28 — [Hydrological cycle:] Rain according to the vapour thereof: Which the clouds do drop and distil

Job 38:22	Hast thou entered into the treasures of the snow? [No two snowflakes are alike]
Ecclesiastes 1:7	All the rivers run into the sea … from whence the rivers come, thither they return again
Isaiah 40:22	It is he that sitteth upon the circle of the earth

B. "Prehistoric" beasts are mentioned in the Bible coexisting with man:

Genesis 1:21	God created great whales [Hebrew: great sea monsters]
Job 40:15–24	Behold now behemoth … moveth his tail like a cedar
Job 41:1–34	Leviathan … shall not one be cast down even at the sight of him?

C. Each species created distinct and separate; the unbridgeable gap of sterility separates species:

Genesis 1:11–12 21,24–25	Every [plant and] living creature … brought forth after their kind

6. GOD, AS THE CREATOR, HAS OWNERSHIP RIGHTS OVER EVERYTHING:

Job 41:11	Whatsoever is under the whole heaven is mine
Psalm 24:1–2	Earth is the Lord's … and they that dwell therein
Psalm 50:10–12	Every beast of the forest is mine … the world is mine
Psalm 89:11	The heavens are thine, the earth also is thine
Psalm 95:3–5	The sea is his, and he made it: and his hands formed the dry land.

(See also Psalm 102:25; Isaiah 45:18.)

7. HE EXPECTS REVERENCE AND WORSHIP FROM HIS CREATIONS:

Psalm 33:6–9	By the word of the Lord were the heavens made … Let all the earth fear the Lord [and] stand in awe of him
Psalm 148:5	Praise the name of the Lord: for he … created
Ecclesiastes 12:1	Remember now thy Creator in the days of thy youth
Isaiah 45:9	Woe unto him that striveth with his Maker
Isaiah 48:12–13	Hearken unto me … Mine hand also hath laid the foundation of the earth, and … spanned the heavens
Jeremiah 32:17	Thou hast made the heaven and the earth by thy great power and … there is nothing too hard for thee
Jeremiah 33:2–3	Thus saith the Lord the maker … call unto me
Acts 14:15	Turn from these vanities unto … God, which made heaven, and earth, and the sea, and all things that are therein

(See also Jeremiah 5:22; Isaiah 42:5; Amos 4:13.)

8. GOD HAS POWER TO CONTROL HIS CREATIONS:

Job 38:8–11	Here shall thy proud waves be stayed [stopped]
Psalm 104:5–35	[A description of God's control of creation]
Psalm 135:5–7	Whatsoever the Lord pleased, that did he … in earth
	(See also Job 26; 28; 38–41; Psalm 148:6–14; Matthew 8:26; Mark 4:39; Luke 8:24.)

THE ENDTIME

1. THE LAST DAYS; SIGNS OF THE TIMES:

A. We should discern the signs of the times:

Matthew 16:3	Can ye not discern the signs of the times?
Matthew 24:3	What should be the sign of thy coming, and of the end of the world?
Matthew 24:39	[Unbelievers] knew not until the flood came
1 Thessalonians 5:2,4	Ye, brethren, are not [to be] in darkness
2 Peter 3:3–4	Scoffers saying, "Where is His coming?" All things continue as they were"

B. Greatly increased learning:

Daniel 12:4	Time of the end: Many shall run to and fro, and knowledge shall be increased
Matthew 24:14	Gospel preached in all the world [now possible by radio, TV, etc.] ... then the end
2 Timothy 3:1,7	[Modern education:] Ever learning, and never able to come to the knowledge of the truth

C. Natural disasters:

Matthew 24:7	There shall be famines, and pestilences, and earthquakes
Luke 21:26	Men's hearts failing them for fear [unprecedented rate of heart attacks today]

D. Wickedness and wars:

Matthew 24:6–7	Wars and rumours of wars ... nation against nation
Matthew 24:37–38	As the days of Noah were [corrupt and violent] so shall also [it] be
Luke 21:25	Upon earth distress of nations [civil unrest]
2 Timothy 3:1,13	In the last days ... evil men shall wax worse and worse

E. Great falling away from true faith:

Matthew 24:12	Iniquity shall abound ... the love of many shall wax cold
Matthew 24:5,11,24	There shall arise false Christs, and false prophets ... deceive many
2 Thessalonians 2:2–3	The day of Christ shall not come, except there come a falling away [apostasy] first
1 Timothy 4:1	In latter times some shall depart from the faith, giving heed to ... doctrines of devils

F. Increased persecution of Christians:

Matthew 24:9–10	Ye shall be hated of all nations ... many be offended
Luke 21:16–17	Ye shall be betrayed ... and some of you ... put to death

G. What all these fulfilled signs mean:

Matthew 24:33	When ye see all these things, [Jesus' coming is] near
Luke 21:28	When these things begin to come to pass ... your redemption draweth nigh
Luke 21:31–32	This generation shall not pass away, till all be fulfilled

2. HOW TO RECOGNISE THE ANTICHRIST WORLD GOVERNMENT:

Daniel 8:25	By peace [he] shall destroy many
Daniel 11:21,23–24	Come in peaceably, and obtain the kingdom by flatteries [intrigue] ... work deceitfully ... become strong with a small people ... enter peaceably even upon the fattest [richest] places
Daniel 11:39	He shall divide the land for gain
Daniel 11:36–37	Exalt himself ... speak things against the God of gods

3. THE RISE OF THE ANTICHRIST:

Daniel 8:23	In the latter time ... a king of fierce countenance ... shall stand up. Daniel 11:37
Daniel 11:37	Neither shall he regard the God of his fathers, nor the desire of women, nor regard any god
2 Thessalonians 2:1–4	That day [of Jesus' coming] shall not come, except ... that man of sin be revealed
2 Thessalonians 2:9–12	[His] coming is after the working of Satan ... God shall send them strong delusion [the Antichrist] who believed not the truth
1 John 2:18	It is the last time: [the] antichrist shall come
Revelation 13:4	The dragon [Satan] which gave power unto the beast
Revelation 13:7	Power was given him over all ... nations

4. THE SIGNING OF THE COVENANT:

Daniel 9:27	He shall confirm the covenant for one week [7 years]
Daniel 11:30	The holy covenant [Involves religious issues]

5. THE BREAKING OF THE COVENANT AND STOPPING OF THE DAILY SACRIFICE (JEWISH TEMPLE WORSHIP):

Daniel 8:11–12	By him [the Antichrist] daily sacrifice was taken away
Daniel 9:27	In the midst of the week [3½ years into the 7-year covenant] he shall cause the sacrifice to cease
Daniel 11:31	Take away the daily sacrifice, place the abomination that maketh desolate
2 Thessalonians 2:4	He [the Antichrist] as God sitteth in the temple of God

6. THE GREAT TRIBULATION:

A. A time of intense trouble and persecution:

Daniel 12:1	There shall be a time of trouble, such as never was
Matthew 24:15,21–22	When ye see the abomination of desolation … then shall be great tribulation ... except those days should be shortened, there should no flesh be saved

B. The Antichrist blasphemes by saying that he is God:

Daniel 7:25	[The Antichrist] speaks great words against the most High
2 Thessalonians 2:3–4	[The Antichrist] exalteth himself above all that is called God
Revelation 13:6	[The Antichrist] opened mouth in blasphemy against God

C. Much of the world worships him:

Revelation 13:8	All that dwell upon the earth worship him, whose names are not written in the book of life
Revelation 13:13–14	[The Antichrist] doeth great wonders … and deceiveth them that dwell on the earth

D. The mark, the image, and the enforced worship of the beast:

Revelation 13:15–18	Image of the beast … speak, and cause that as many as would not worship [it] be killed ... no man might buy or sell, save he that had the mark … or the number of his name ... the number … is [666]
Revelation 14:9–11	If any man worship the beast … and receive his mark … shall be tormented

E. The false prophet:

Revelation 13:11–16	He causeth the earth … to worship the [Antichrist] and deceiveth them
Revelation 19:20	The false prophet wrought miracles … he deceived them

F. The Antichrist's persecution of Christians:

Daniel 7:21	Made war with the saints, and prevailed against them
Daniel 7:25	He shall wear out the saints of the most High [God]
Daniel 11:35	Some of them of understanding shall fall
Revelation 13:7	To make war with the saints, and to overcome them: and power was given him over all … nations

G. Why God allows us to suffer tribulation:

Isaiah 48:10	I have refined thee … in the furnace of affliction
Daniel 11:35	To try them, and to purge, and to make them white
Daniel 12:10	Many shall be purified, and made white, and tried

(See also Proverbs 17:3; Ephesians 5:27.)

H. Future heavenly reward for enduring tribulation:

Revelation 7:9,13–17	These came out of great tribulation … therefore are they before the throne of God day and night
Revelation 20:4	Them … which had not worshipped the beast … lived and reigned with Christ

I. Christians overcome and survive despite persecution:

Daniel 11:32	People that know their God shall be strong, and do exploits
Romans 8:35–37	In all these things we are more than conquerors
1 Corinthians 15:51–52	We shall not all sleep [die], but we shall all be changed
1 Thessalonians 4:16–17	We which are alive and remain [Many Christians still alive at Jesus' second coming]
Revelation 12:11	They overcame him [the Antichrist] by the blood of the Lamb, and by the word of their testimony

J. Protection and provision during tribulation:

Revelation 9:3–4	[The wicked will be tormented, but Christians will be spared]
Revelation 11:3,5–7	Two witnesses … have power … to smite the earth with all plagues
Revelation 12:6	Fled into the wilderness, where she hath a place prepared of God, that they should feed her there
Revelation 12:14	Fly into the wilderness … where she is nourished

K. Witnessing during the tribulation:

Daniel 11:33	They that understand … shall instruct many

L. Length of the great tribulation:

Daniel 7:25	A time, times, and an half
Revelation 11:2	Forty and two months
Revelation 12:6	[1,260] days
Revelation 12:14	A time, and times, and half a time

7. THE SECOND COMING OF JESUS CHRIST:

A. After the great tribulation:

Matthew 24:29–30	Immediately after the tribulation … they shall see the Son of man coming in the clouds
2 Thessalonians 2:1–3	That day [of Jesus' coming] shall not come, except … first that man of sin [the Antichrist] be revealed

B. Jesus' coming will not be a secret event:

Matthew 24:23–26	If any man say unto you, Here is Christ, or there … in the secret chambers; believe it not
Matthew 24:30	The tribes of the earth [shall] mourn, and see the Son of man coming … with power and great glory
Acts 1:9–11	Jesus … shall so come in like manner [in the clouds]
1 Thessalonians 5:1–4	Ye are not in darkness [We will be expecting Jesus, but the world will be surprised]
Revelation 1:7	He cometh with clouds; and every eye shall see him

C. The tremendous signs of His coming:

Matthew 24:27	For as the lightning … shineth … so shall also the coming … be [Jesus lights up the sky]
Matthew 24:29	Sun be darkened … moon not give light
1 Thessalonians 4:16	Lord shall … shout … voice of the archangel … trump of God [Lots of noise and commotion]

8. THE RESURRECTION AND RAPTURE:

A. The living raptured, the dead resurrected:

Isaiah 26:19	Thy dead men shall live, together with my dead body shall they arise
Matthew 24:31	Sound of a trumpet … gather together [rapture] his elect
1 Corinthians 15:51–52	We shall not all sleep [die], but we shall all be changed ... at the last trump … the dead shall be raised incorruptible, and we shall be changed [transformed]
1 Thessalonians 4:14–17	Them which sleep in Jesus [the departed who were saved] will God bring with him ... the dead in Christ [their bodies] shall rise first ... then we which are alive shall be caught up [raptured]
Revelation 20:6	Blessed and holy … hath part in the first resurrection

(See also 1 Corinthians 15:53–54; 2 Corinthians 5:1–4.)

B. Our powerful, immortal resurrection bodies:

Luke 20:19,26	The doors were shut … Jesus stood in the midst
Luke 20:36	Neither can they die any more … equal unto the angels … being the children of the resurrection
Luke 24:30–31	As he sat at meat … he vanished out of their sight.
Luke 24:36–40	A spirit hath not flesh and bones, as ye see me have
Luke 24:42–43	He took it [fish and an honeycomb], and did eat
Acts 10:40–41	We did eat and drink with him after he rose from the dead
1 Corinthians 6:14	God hath raised up [Jesus], and will also raise up us
Philippians 3:20–21	Jesus … change our body … like his glorious body
1 John 3:2	When he shall appear, we shall be like him

(See also 1 Corinthians 15:19–55—"The Resurrection Chapter.")

9. THE MARRIAGE SUPPER OF THE LAMB:

Hosea 2:19–20	I [God] will betroth thee unto me for ever (See also Isaiah 62:5; 2 Corinthians 11:2.)
Romans 7:4	[Christians are married to Jesus]
Revelation 7:9,13–17	Great multitude [of Christians] which came out of great tribulation … are before the throne of God
Revelation 19:1,6–9	Much people in heaven … the marriage of the Lamb

is come

10. THE JUDGEMENT SEAT OF CHRIST:

A. Christians rewarded or punished for their work:

Romans 14:10–12	Judgment seat … every one shall give account of himself
2 Corinthians 5:10	We [Christians] must appear before the judgment seat of Christ … receive [rewards for] things done
Revelation 22:12	My reward is with me, to give every man according as his work shall be.

B. Jesus praises and rewards some, is ashamed of others:

Daniel 12:2–3	Many shall awake … some to shame and ... contempt ... they that turn many to righteousness [shall shine] as the stars for ever and ever
Matthew 25:21	Well done, thou good and faithful … enter into the joy of thy lord
Mark 8:38	Of him [some Christians] shall the Son … be ashamed
1 Corinthians 3:14–15	If any man's work abide … he shall receive a reward. If any man's work … burned, he shall suffer loss: but he himself shall be saved

C. The crown of life—A reward for faithful service:

2 Timothy 4:7–8	I have kept the faith … a crown of righteousness
James 1:12	Crown of life … Lord hath promised to them that love him
Revelation 2:10	Be thou faithful … I will give thee a crown of life

11. THE WRATH OF GOD UPON THE EARTH:

A. God's wrath upon the remaining unsaved:

Isaiah 13:9–11	The day of the Lord cometh with wrath and anger … he shall destroy the sinners ... punish the world
Isaiah 26:19–21	Dead men shall live … then the Lord cometh … to punish the inhabitants of the earth
Revelation 14:9–10	If any man worship the beast … the same shall drink of the wine of the wrath of God
Revelation 16:1–21	[Description of the plagues of God's wrath]

B. The utter destruction of Babylon by fire:

Revelation 17:1,5,18	The great whore … Babylon the Great … that great city, which reigneth over the kings of the earth
Revelation 17:16	Ten horns [leaders of nations] shall make her desolate … and burn her with fire
Revelation 18:2–3,11	[Babylon is the world merchant/commercial system]
Revelation 18:8	In one day … she shall be utterly burned with fire

Revelation 18:17	In one hour so great riches is come to nought

12. THE BATTLE OF ARMAGEDDON:

A. The Antichrist, his allies, and eastern kings gather to fight:

Ezekiel 38:1–9	Gog … in the latter years thou shalt come into … Israel … many people with thee
Revelation 16:12	Water thereof [the Euphrates River] was dried up, that the way of the kings of the east might be prepared
Revelation 16:14	Demons … go out unto [the Antichrist's] kings … to gather them to the battle
Revelation 16:16	He gathered them together into a place called … Armageddon
Revelation 19:19	Kings of the earth … gathered together to make war against him
Revelation 17:12–14	Ten kings … these shall make war with the Lamb

B. God and His armies destroy the Antichrist's forces:

Deuteronomy 32:41–43	Rejoice … for he will avenge the blood of his servants
Isaiah 11:4	With the breath of his lips shall he slay the wicked
2 Thessalonians 1:7–9	Jesus shall be revealed from heaven … taking vengeance on [the wicked]
Jude 1:14–15	The Lord cometh with ten thousands of his saints, to execute judgment upon all
Revelation 19:11	[Jesus comes riding on a white horse to make war]
Revelation 19:14–15	Armies in heaven [saints] followed him upon white horses
Revelation 19:20–21	The beast was taken, and the false prophet … these both were cast alive into a lake of fire burning with brimstone. And the remnant were slain

C. The cleanup after the battle:

Isaiah 66:15–16	The slain of the Lord shall be many
Ezekiel 39:17–20	[Carrion eaters] filled … with all men of war
Ezekiel 39:11–12	Seven months shall the house of Israel be burying them
Revelation 19:17–18	Saying to all the fowls … Come … that ye may eat [corpses]

13. THE MILLENNIUM:

A. One thousand years of peace:

Revelation 20:1–3	Satan bound a thousand years, and cast into the bottomless pit

B. The saints rule with Jesus over all the earth:

Daniel 2:44	In the days of these kings shall God set up a kingdom
Daniel 7:13–14	There was given [Jesus] a kingdom, that all people, nations, and languages, should serve him
Daniel 7:18,22,27	The kingdom … given to the people of the saints
Revelation 2:26–27	He that overcometh will I give power over the nations ... He shall rule them with a rod of iron [authority]
Revelation 5:10	Made us kings and priests: and we shall reign on earth
Revelation 20:4,6	They lived and reigned with Christ a thousand years (See also 2 Timothy 2:12; 1 Corinthians 6:2; 15:24–25; Psalm 22:27–28; 47:2–3,7–8; 72:6–8,11,19.)

C. His rule will be just and righteous:

Psalm 67:4	Let the nations be glad … thou shalt judge the people righteously
Psalm 72:3–4	He shall judge the poor … he shall save the children of the needy
Psalm 98:8–9	With righteousness shall he judge the world (See Psalm 45:6; Isaiah 14:5,7.)

D. Heavenly conditions of the millennium:

Isaiah 11:6–9	[Peace with animals and nature during the millennium] The wolf shall dwell with the lamb … calf and the young lion ... They shall not hurt nor destroy in all my holy mountain
Isaiah 65:25	The wolf and the lamb shall feed together, and the lion shall eat straw
Hosea 2:18	In that day will I make a covenant with the beasts … and I will break … the sword

E. Men will live for centuries, like before the flood:

Isaiah 65:20	The child shall die an hundred years old

F. Peace on earth:

Psalm 46:9	He maketh wars to cease [and weapons are destroyed]
Isaiah 2:4	Neither shall they learn war any more (See also Micah 4:3.)
Isaiah 14:5–7	The whole earth is at rest, and is quiet

G. Everyone on earth will know about God:

Psalm 22:27	All the kindreds of the nations shall worship thee
Isaiah 2:2–3	All nations shall flow unto … the mountain of the Lord [to learn God's Word]
Jeremiah 31:34	They shall teach no more … "Know the Lord": for they shall all know me
Habakkuk 2:14	The earth shall be filled with the knowledge of … the Lord

H. Some will disobey and be punished:

Psalm 2:8–10	Shalt break them with a rod of iron
Isaiah 26:10	The wicked will not learn righteousness: in the land of uprightness will he deal unjustly
Zechariah 14:16–17	Whoso will not … worship the King … upon them shall be no rain

14. THE BATTLE OF GOG AND MAGOG:

Psalm 2:1–5	The kings of the earth set themselves ... against the Lord
Psalm 78:69	The earth which he hath established for ever [Only earth's crust melts; globe is permanent]
Isaiah 40:4	Every valley shall be exalted, and every mountain and hill shall be made low [earth's surface melted down evenly]
2 Peter 3:10–13	Elements shall melt with fervent heat, the earth also … shall be burned up … [the atmosphere] being on fire shall be dissolved
Revelation 20:7–9	When the thousand years are expired, Satan shall be loosed ... shall … deceive the nations … gather them ... to battle ... fire came down from God out of heaven, and devoured them [the rebels]

15. THE GREAT WHITE THRONE JUDGEMENT:

Job 34:10–11	For the work of a man shall he render unto him
Luke 12:47–48	He that knew not … shall be beaten with few stripes [Differences of punishment] (See also Romans 2:12,14.)
John 5:29	And they shall come forth unto the resurrection
Revelation 20:5	Rest of the dead lived not again until the thousand years were finished
Revelation 20:10–13	The devil ... was cast into the lake of fire ... And I saw a great white throne ... The dead ... judged according to their works
Revelation 20:15; 21:8	[Those] not written in the book of life cast into the lake of fire … the second death

16. THE NEW HEAVEN AND NEW EARTH:

A. The heavenly city comes down to earth:

Revelation 21:1–3	I saw a new heaven and a new earth … and there was no more sea [3–4 times more land area] ... I ... saw ... new Jerusalem, coming down ... [The city] of God is with men, and he will dwell with them
Revelation 21:10	Holy Jerusalem, descending out of heaven

B. Description of the heavenly city:

John 14:2–3	In my Father's house are many mansions
Hebrews 11:10	A city … whose builder and maker is God.
Revelation 21:16–21	He measured the city … twelve thousand furlongs [2,200 kilometres]. The length and the breadth and the height ... are equal. And he measured the wall thereof, an hundred and forty and four cubits [65 metres] … the city was pure gold … the foundations of the wall of the city were garnished with all manner of precious stones … the twelve gates were twelve pearls … and the street of the city was pure gold
Revelation 21:23,25	The city had no need of the sun … for the glory of God did lighten it … no night there
Revelation 22:1–2	A pure river of water of life [flows through the city] ... On either side of the river, was ... the tree of life

C. Only the saved live in the city; the unsaved nations are outside:

Hebrews 11:13–16	Strangers and pilgrims … [God] prepared for them a city
Revelation 21:24,27	[Only] they which are written in the Lamb's book of life
Revelation 22:2	Leaves of the tree were for the healing of the [sick] nations

D. Eternal life and happiness in heaven forever:

Psalm 36:7–9	Make them drink of the river of thy pleasures
Hebrews 13:14	Here have we no city, but we seek one to come
Revelation 7:17	God shall wipe away all tears from their eyes
Revelation 21:4–5	There shall be no more death, neither sorrow, nor crying, neither shall there be any more pain: for the former things are passed away ... Behold, I make all things new
Revelation 21:7	He that overcometh shall inherit all things
Revelation 22:3	And there shall be no more curse

MARRIAGE AND THE HOME

Includes marital relations and parental duties

1. MARRIAGE:

A. God has ordained and blessed marriage:

Genesis 2:18	The Lord God said, it is not good that man should be alone; I will make him an help meet for him
Proverbs 5:18	Be blessed: and rejoice with the wife of thy youth
Proverbs 18:22	Whoso findeth a wife findeth a good thing, and obtaineth favour of the Lord
Ecclesiastes 9:9	Live joyfully with the wife whom thou loveset all the days of thy life ... which he [God] hath given thee
Matthew 19:4–5	[God] made them male and female ... for this cause shall a man leave father and mother, and cleave to his wife

B. Marriage gives strength and companionship:

Genesis 2:18	God said, it is not good that man should be alone
Ecclesiastes 4:9–11	Two are better than one ... They have a good reward
1 Peter 3:7	Heirs together of the grace of life

C. Marriage is a commitment:

Matthew 19:4–6	[God] made them male and female ... for this cause shall a man leave father and mother, and cleave to his wife ... What therefore God hath joined together, let not man put asunder.
1 Corinthians 7:10	Unto the married I command ... let not the wife depart from her husband (See also 7:1–17.)

2. A HUSBAND'S RESPONSIBILITY TOWARD HIS WIFE:

A. The husband is to tenderly love his wife:

Ephesians 5:25	Husbands, love your wives, even as Christ also loved the church, and gave himself for it
Ephesians 5:28	So ought men to love their wives as their own bodies
Ephesians 5:33	Let every one of you ... to love his wife even as himself
Colossians 3:19	Husbands, love your wives, and be not bitter against them

B. The husband is to honour, praise, and please his wife:

Proverbs 31:28	Her husband also [arises up], and he praiseth her
1 Corinthians 7:33	He that is married careth ... how he may please his wife
1 Peter 3:7	Husbands, dwell with them according to knowledge, giving honour unto the wife ... the weaker vessel

C. He is to listen to and heed his wife's wise counsel:

Judges 13:19–23	[Manoah's wife wisely explained that there was no need to fear]
1 Samuel 25:9–33	[Abigail, the wife of Nabal, wisely pacified David]
2 Samuel 20:1–2,7, 13–22	[Wise woman of Abel "went unto all the people in her wisdom" and spared her city from destruction]
2 Kings 4:8–10	[Woman of Shunem] said to her husband … [Elisha] is an holy man of God. Let us make [him] a chamber (See also 2 Samuel 14:1–15; Daniel 5:10–12; Matthew 27:19.)

3. A WIFE'S ATTRIBUTES AND RESPONSIBILITIES:

A. The Bible's description of a virtuous wife:

Proverbs 11:16	A gracious woman retaineth honour
Proverbs 12:4	A virtuous woman is a crown to her husband
Proverbs 19:14	A prudent [wise] wife is from the Lord
Proverbs 31:10–12	Who can find a virtuous woman? Her price is far above rubies (See also all of Proverbs 31:10–31.)
Proverbs 31:26	She openeth her mouth with wisdom: and in her tongue is the law of kindness
1 Timothy 3:11	Their wives [should] be grave [reverent], not slanderers
Titus 2:4	Teach the young women to be sober [serious]
Titus 2:5	To be discreet [wise], chaste … good, obedient

B. She should guide the home and children:

Psalm 128:3	Thy wife shall be as a fruitful vine
Proverbs 14:1	Every wise woman buildeth her house
Proverbs 31:27	She looketh well to the ways of her household, and eateth not the bread of idleness
1 Timothy 3:11	Even so must their wives be … faithful in all things
1 Timothy 5:14	Marry, bear children, guide the house
Titus 2:4	Teach the young women … to love their children
Titus 2:5	To be … keepers at home [homemakers]

C. Examples of how wives should not be:

Proverbs 7:11	She is loud and stubborn, her feet abide not in her house
1 Timothy 5:13	They learn to be idle, wandering about from house to house … tattlers and busybodies

D. Virtue is more important than physical beauty:

Proverbs 11:22	As a jewel of gold in a swine's snout, so is a fair woman which is without discretion [good judgement]
Proverbs 31:30	Beauty is vain, but a woman that feareth the Lord, she shall be praised

1 Peter 3:3–5	Whose adorning let it not be outward [rather] the ornament of a meek and quiet spirit which is [very precious]

4. A WIFE'S RESPONSIBILITY TOWARD HER HUSBAND:

A. To be a companion:

Proverbs 31:11	The heart of her husband doth safely trust in her
Malachi 2:14	She [is] thy companion, and the wife of thy covenant

B. To love and please her husband:

Proverbs 31:12	She will do him good and not evil all days of her life
1 Corinthians 7:34	She that is married careth for the things of the world, how she may please her husband
Titus 2:4	Teach the young women to … love their husbands

C. To respect her husband:

Ephesians 5:33	[Let] the wife see that she reverence her husband
Colossians 3:18	Wives, submit yourselves unto your own husbands, as it is fit in the Lord
1 Peter 3:1–6	Wives, be in subjection to your own husbands [with] … a meek and quiet spirit … in the sight of God (See also 1 Corinthians 11:3,8–9; Ephesians 5:22; Titus 2:5.)

5. SPIRITUAL MINISTRIES ARE NOT RESTRICTED TO MEN:

A. Women's place in spiritual ministries may equal or surpass men's:

Romans 2:11	For there is no respect of persons with God
Galatians 3:28	There is neither Jew nor Greek, there is neither bond nor free, there is neither male nor female: for ye are all one in Christ Jesus

B. Women disciples and leading workers of the early church:

Mark 16:9	[Mary Magdalene was honoured by being the first person to see Jesus after his resurrection] (See also Luke 8:1–3; John 20:1–18.)
John 19:25	[When all his male followers—except John—fled and hid, faithful women stayed with Jesus at his crucifixion] (See also Matthew 27:55–56.)
Romans 16:1–4	I commend to you Phebe … receive her in the Lord … assist her in whatsoever business she hath need of you ... Priscilla and Aquila my helpers [Priscilla, was often respectfully listed before her husband] (See also Acts 18:2,18.)
1 Corinthians 16:16	Submit yourselves unto … every one [women included] that helpeth with us, and laboureth (See also 1 Thessalonians 5:12–13.)

Philippians 4:3	Help those women which laboured with me in the gospel (See also Romans 16:6,12–13; 1 Timothy 5:1–2; 2 Timothy 4:21.)

C. Wives who were honoured and exalted:

Judges 13:1–10	[Angel appeared to Manoah's wife twice, later to him]
1 Samuel 25:38–39	[God slew wicked Nabal, but honoured his wife, Abigail, by having her marry David, the future king of Israel]
2 Kings 4:8–37	[The "great woman of Shunem," not her husband, was the honoured one in this story] (See also 2 Kings 8:1–6.)
Luke 1:26–35	[The Archangel Gabriel appeared to Mary first; and only three months later to Joseph] (See also Matthew 1:18–21; Luke 1:56.)
Luke 1:46–48	[Mary prophesied:] All generations shall call me blessed (See also Judges 4:17–23; 5:24; 2 Samuel 20:1–2,7,13–22.)

D. Women prophetesses, anointed of the Spirit:

Exodus 15:20–21	Miriam the prophetess [sang a victory song]
Judges 5:1–31	[The victory song of the prophetess Deborah, and Barak]
Luke 1:39–55	[Elizabeth and Mary, filled with the Spirit, prophesied]
Luke 2:36–38	Anna, a prophetess … served God night and day
Acts 2:17	I will pour out of My Spirit upon all flesh: your sons and your daughters shall prophesy (See also Joel 2:28.)
Acts 21:8–9	Philip … had four daughters … which did prophesy

E. A woman who judged God's people:

Judges 4:4	Deborah, a prophetess … judged Israel at that time
Judges 5:6–7	The inhabitants of the villages ceased … until Deborah arose … a mother in Israel (See also Judges 4:1–10, 23–24.)

6. HARMONY AND MARITAL PEACE:

A. Harmony is important to a Christian marriage:

Colossians 2:2	Hearts … be comforted, being knit together in love
1 Timothy 3:4–5	If a man know not how to rule his own house, how shall he take care of the church of God?
1 Peter 3:7	Heirs together of the grace of life; that your prayers be not hindered
1 Peter 4:8	Have fervent charity [love] among yourselves: for charity shall cover the multitude of sins (See also Titus 2:5.)

B. Arguments should be avoided:

Proverbs 14:1	Every wise woman buildeth her house: but the foolish plucketh [pulls] it down (See also Proverbs 24:3.)

Proverbs 17:9	He that covereth [over] transgression seeketh love
Proverbs 17:14	Leave off contention, before it be meddled with
Proverbs 21:19	It is better to dwell in the wilderness, than with a contentious and an angry woman (See also Proverbs 25:24.)
Proverbs 27:15	A continual dropping [dripping] in a very rainy day and a contentious woman are alike (See also Proverbs 19:13.)
Philippians 2:3	Let nothing be done through strife
Colossians 3:13	Forbearing one another, and forgiving one another, if any have a quarrel against any (See also 1 Peter 3:9.)

7. MARRIAGE AND LOVEMAKING:

A. Sex in marriage is pure, holy, and ordained of God:

1 Corinthians 7:28	If thou marry, thou hast not sinned (See also 7:36.)
Hebrews 13:4	Marriage is honourable in all, and the bed undeflied

B. It was ordained for the procreation of the race:

Genesis 1:27–28	Male and female created he them. And God blessed them, and God said unto them, "Be fruitful, and multiply"
Malachi 2:15	Did not he make [them] one? Wherefore one? That he might seek a godly seed (See also Jeremiah 29:6.)

C. In marriage, man and woman are joined as "one flesh":

Genesis 2:23	[She] is now bone of my bones, and flesh of my flesh
Mark 10:6–8	God made them male and female … a man [shall] cleave to his wife; and they shall be one flesh (See also Genesis 2:24.)
1 Corinthians 6:16	Two, saith he, shall be one flesh
Ephesians 5:31	A man … shall be joined unto his wife, and they two shall be one flesh

D. Conjugal pleasures are gifts from God:

Proverbs 5:18–19	Let thy fountain be blessed: and rejoice with the wife of thy youth ... let her breasts satisfy thee at all times; and be thou ravished always with her love
Song of Solomon 7:6–12	How pleasant art thou, O love, for delights (See also Psalm 19:5; Song of Solomon 1:1,4,13; 2:3,6,16–17; 4:6,10–16; 5:4–5; 8:3,14.)

E. Sex is a marital right, not to be used to punish or reward:

1 Corinthians 7:3–5	Let the husband render unto the wife due benevolence: and likewise also the wife unto the husband. The wife hath not [exclusive] power over her body, but the husband [and vice versa]. Defraud [deprive] ye not one the other, except it be with [mutual] consent for a time

F. Husbands should treat their wife with honour and love, not merely as sexual objects:

1 Thessalonians 4:4–5	Possess his vessel [wife] in … honour; not in the lust of concupiscence [excessive desire]

8. MARRIAGE VS. CELIBACY:

A. Those who forbid marriage are in error:

1 Timothy 4:1–3	Some shall depart from the faith … forbidding to marry

B. Even priests, bishops, and church officials are advised to marry:

Leviticus 21:10,13	[The high priest was allowed to marry]
Ezekiel 44:21–22	[Jewish priests were given specific instructions concerning whom they could marry]
Matthew 8:14	[The apostle Peter was married] (See also 1 Corinthians 9:5.)
1 Timothy 3:2	A bishop then must be … the husband of one wife (See also 1 Timothy 3:11–12.)

C. Celibacy pros and cons:

Genesis 2:18	God said, It is not good that the man should be alone
Isaiah 56:4–5	Unto the eunuchs that … choose the things that please me … I will give an everlasting name
Matthew 19:10–12	There be eunuchs, which have made themselves eunuchs for the kingdom of heaven's sake
1 Corinthians 7:9	Let them marry: for it is better to marry than to burn

9. DIVORCE, REMARRIAGE, MARITAL INFIDELITY, AND FORGIVENESS:

Regarding the Scriptures on divorce, remarriage, infidelity, and forgiveness, there are such wide differences of opinion, interpretation, and application between leading Christian theologians and denominations today, the editors felt it best to refrain from outlining them here in order to avoid appearing dogmatic about such a sensitive and personal issue.

Some churches believe that the New Testament forbids divorce and remarriage in any form. Others read the passages in question as guidelines, to be tempered with love, mercy, understanding, and judicial allowances.

There are many sincere Christians on both sides of the fence, so the editors felt that the task of doctrinally defining this point was best left to the reader's personal faith and conviction. "Let every man be fully persuaded in his own mind" (Romans 14:5).

10. PARENTAL DUTIES TOWARD THEIR CHILDREN:

A. Parents should teach their children in love:

Ephesians 6:4	Fathers, provoke not your children to wrath: but bring them up in the nurture and admonition of the Lord
Colossians 3:21	Fathers, provoke not your children to anger, lest they be discouraged

B. They should teach them God's Word:

Deuteronomy 6:7	Thou shalt teach them [God's words] diligently unto thy children (See also Deuteronomy 4:9; 11:18–19.)
Deuteronomy 31:12–13	That their children … may learn to fear the Lord
Psalm 78:5	He commanded our fathers that they should make them known to their children
Proverbs 22:6	Train up a child in the way he should go
John 21:15	Feed my lambs

C. Parents should provide for their children's needs:

2 Corinthians 12:14	The children ought not to lay up [provide] for the parents, but the parents for the children
1 Timothy 5:8	If any provide not for his … own house, he hath denied the faith, and is worse than an infidel (See also Acts 20:35; Ephesians 4:28.)

D. Parents should oversee their children:

1 Timothy 3:4	One that ruleth well his own house, having his children in subjection with all gravity [reverence]
1 Timothy 3:12	Ruling their children and their own houses well

E. Parents should chastise children when necessary:

Proverbs 13:24	He that spareth his rod hateth his son: but he that loveth him chasteneth him betimes [promptly]
Proverbs 19:18	Chasten thy son while there is hope, and let not thy soul spare for his crying (See also Proverbs 22:15; Proverbs 23:13.)

F. The bad fruit of being an indulgent parent:

1 Samuel 3:13	His sons made themselves vile, and he restrained them not
1 Kings 1:1,5–6	His father had not displeased him at any time … saying, "Why hast thou done so?" (See also 1:16–21.)
Proverbs 29:15	A child left to himself bringeth his mother to shame
Luke 15:12–13	[Father of the Prodigal Son gave him his share, and the son then went off and wasted it with riotous living]

G. Beware of partiality:

Genesis 25:28	Isaac loved Esau, because he did eat of his venison: but Rebekah loved Jacob (See also Genesis 27:6–17.)
Genesis 37:3–4	Israel loved Joseph more than all his children … his brethren saw [it and] hated him (See also Genesis 42:4; 48:21–22.)
1 Timothy 5:21	Without preferring one before another, doing nothing by partiality

H. Examples of parental concern for children:

(See Genesis 37:14; 2 Samuel 18:29; Esther 2:11.)

I. Examples of motherly love:

(See Genesis 21:15–16; Exodus 1:22; 2:1–2; 1 Samuel 1:22–28; 2:18–19; 1 Kings 3:23–27; 2 Kings 4:17–20,27; Isaiah 49:15; Matthew 15:22–28; John 19:17–18,25; Hebrews 11:23.)

J. Examples of fatherly love:

(See Genesis 27:33–35; 2 Samuel 12:15–18; Mark 5:22–23; Luke 15:20–24.)

11. THE IMPORTANCE OF TRAINING YOUR CHILDREN RIGHT:

A. Children will often be no better than their parents:

Ezekiel 16:44	As is the mother, so is her daughter

B. Good influence of parents:

1 Kings 9:4	Walk before me, as David thy father walked, in integrity of heart, and in uprightness (See also 2 Chronicles 17:3.)
2 Chronicles 26:4	He did that which was right in the sight of the Lord [as] his father … did (See also 2 Chronicles 20:32.)
2 Timothy 1:5	The unfeigned faith that is in thee, which dwelt first in thy grandmother … and thy mother

C. Evil influence of parents:

1 Kings 22:52	He did evil … walked in way of his father … and mother
2 Chronicles 22:3	His mother was his counselor to do wickedly
Jeremiah 9:14	[They] have walked … after Baalim, which their fathers taught them
	(See also Ezekiel 20:18; Amos 2:4; Matthew 14:8.)

12. PARENTS AS "GOOD SHEPHERDS":

A. Parents' responsibility to protect their children:

Exodus 2:1–2	[Moses' mother defied Pharaoh and hid her baby] (See also Hebrews 11:23.)
2 Kings 11:1–3	[Baby Joash's aunt hid him from the wicked queen]
Matthew 2:13–22	[Joseph was warned of God to flee into Egypt with Mary and baby Jesus, and only to return when it was safe]

B. Parents' responsibility to defend their children:

Nehemiah 4:14	Remember the Lord … and fight … for your sons and daughters
John 10:11–13	The good shepherd giveth his life for the sheep

C. God will help you:

Isaiah 49:24–25	I will contend with him that contendeth with thee, and I will save thy children

CHILDREN

Includes pregnancy, the "right to life," childbirth, and raising and training children

1. PREGNANCY:

A. Children are a blessing from God:

Genesis 49:25	God … shall bless thee with blessings of … the womb
Psalm 113:9	He maketh the barren woman to keep house, and to be a joyful mother of children
Psalm 127:3–5	Children are an heritage of the Lord: and the fruit of the womb is his reward. As arrows … so are children … Happy is the man that hath his quiver full of them
Psalm 128:1,3	Blessed is every one that feareth the Lord. Thy wife shall be as a fruitful vine
Proverbs 17:6	Children's children are the crown of old men
1 Timothy 5:14	I will therefore that … women marry, bear children

(See also Genesis 30:1; Deuteronomy 33:24; 1 Samuel 1:1–18; Luke 1:42.)

B. God is the one who blesses women with pregnancy:

Genesis 4:1	Adam knew Eve … and she conceived, and bare Cain, and said, I have gotten a man from the Lord
Genesis 4:25	Adam knew his wife again; and she bare a son … God, said she, hath appointed me another seed
Genesis 25:21	Isaac entreated the Lord for his wife, because she was barren … and Rebekah his wife conceived
Genesis 30:22–23	God remembered Rachel … and opened her womb. And she conceived, and bare a son
1 Samuel 1:27	For this child I prayed; and the Lord hath given me
Hebrews 2:13	Behold I and the children which God hath given me
Luke 1:7,13	Thy prayer is heard; and thy wife … shall bear thee a son

(See also Genesis 33:5; Judges 13:3; 1 Samuel 1:19–20; Psalm 115:14.)

C. God promises to take care of believers' children:

Psalm 37:25	I have been young and now am old, yet have I not seen the righteous forsaken, nor his seed begging bread
Proverbs 11:21	The seed of the righteous shall be delivered
Isaiah 65:23	They are the seed of the blessed … and their offspring

(See also Psalm 25:12–13; 102:28; 112:1–2; Proverbs 14:26; Philippians 4:19.)

2. GOD'S HAND ON CHILDREN BEFORE BIRTH:

A. God forms children in the womb:

Job 31:15	Did not he that made me in the womb make him? And did not one fashion us in the womb?
Job 33:4	The Spirit of God hath made me, and … given me life
Psalm 71:5–6	By thee I have been holden up from the womb
Psalm 139:14–16	I am wonderfully made … in thy book all my members were written, which in continuance were fashioned (See also Isaiah 44:24.)

B. God gives life and a soul to unborn children:

Genesis 2:7	God … breathed into his nostrils the breath of life; and man became a living soul
Job 33:4	The breath of the almighty hath given me life
Acts 17:25	He giveth to all life, and breath

C. God cares for children in the womb:

Psalm 139:13	Thou hast covered me in my mother's womb
Isaiah 40:11	He … shall gently lead those that are with young

D. God loves and knows children, even before birth:

Psalm 22:10	I was cast upon thee from the womb: thou art my God from my mother's belly
Isaiah 49:1	The Lord hath called me from the womb; from the [womb] hath he made mention of my name
Jeremiah 1:5	Before I formed thee in the belly I knew thee; before thou camest out of the womb I sanctified thee
Luke 1:13	[Angel said:] Thy wife … shall bear thee a son, and thou shalt call his name John

3. THE BIBLE ON "THE RIGHT TO LIFE":

Leviticus 18:21	Thou shalt not let any of thy seed pass through the fire
Deuteronomy 27:25	Cursed be he that taketh reward to slay an innocent
Psalm 106:38	Shed innocent blood … of their sons and daughters
Jeremiah 2:34–35	In thy skirts is found the blood … of poor innocents
2 Timothy 3:1–3	In the last days … men [and women] shall be lovers of their selves … without natural affection [love]

4. CHILDBIRTH:

A. God can help in the delivery:

Psalm 22:9	Thou art he that took me out of the womb
Psalm 71:6	Thou art he that took me out of my mother's bowels
Isaiah 46:3	[They] are borne by me from the belly … from the womb

B. Promises to claim during long labour:

Isaiah 65:23	They shall not labour in vain, nor bring forth for trouble; for they are the seed of the blessed
Isaiah 66:9	Shall I bring to the birth, and not cause to bring forth? Shall I cause to bring forth, and shut the womb?
John 16:21	As soon as she is delivered of the child, she remembereth no more the anguish, for the joy that a man is born
Hebrews 11:11	Through faith Sara … was delivered of a child … because she judged him faithful who had promised

C. Promises for strength:

Isaiah 40:29–31	He giveth power to the faint; and to them that have no might he increaseth strength … renew their strength
Isaiah 41:10	Be not dismayed … I will strengthen thee

D. Conditions for claiming God's promises:

Daniel 6:16	God whom thou servest continually, will deliver thee
1 Timothy 2:15	She shall be saved in childbearing, if they continue in faith and charity [love]

5. TEACHING AND TRAINING YOUR CHILDREN:

Judges 13:8	Teach us what we shall do unto the child that shall be born

A. God's care for young children:

Matthew 18:10	In heaven their angels always behold the face of [God]
1 Corinthians 7:14	[Even if only one parent is a believer, the children are sanctified by God]

B. Their early training will guide them all through life:

Proverbs 22:6	Train up a child in the way he should go: and when he is old, he will not depart from it

C. Make a priority of the care and training of your children:

Mark 7:27	Let the children first be filled
3 John 1:4	I have no greater joy than to hear that my children walk in truth

D. If you neglect them, you'll both suffer:

Proverbs 29:15	A child left to himself bringeth his mother to shame (See also Matthew 23:23.)

E. Teach your children the Word:

Deuteronomy 6:6–7	These words … teach them diligently unto thy children

Deuteronomy 11:18–20	Lay up these my words in your heart and in your soul … and teach them [to] your children
Isaiah 38:19	The father to the children shall make known thy truth
Joel 1:3	Tell ye your children … and let your children tell their children, and their children another generation
John 21:15	Lovest thou me more than these? Feed my lambs
2 Timothy 3:15	From a child [infancy] thou hast known the scriptures (See also Deuteronomy 31:12–13; Psalm 78:1–6; 1 John 2:13.)

F. Teach your children to trust in God:

Psalm 22:9	Thou didst make me hope when I was upon my mother's breasts
Psalm 34:11	Come, ye children, hearken unto me: I will teach you the fear [reverence] of the Lord
Psalm 78:6–7	Declare them to [your] children: that they might set their hope in God
Acts 2:39	For the promise is unto you, and to your children
Hebrews 2:13	I will put my trust in him … I and the children

G. Lead them to receive Jesus:

Mark 10:14	Suffer [allow] the little children to come unto me
Galatians 4:19	My little children, of whom I travail in birth … unto Christ be formed in you
1 John 2:12	I write unto you, little children, because your sins are forgiven you for his name's sake

H. Only God and His Word can teach life's most important lessons:

Psalm 25:5	Lead me in thy truth, and teach me: for thou art … God
Proverbs 8:32–33	Hearken unto me, O ye children … keep my ways. Hear instruction, and be wise, and refuse it not
Isaiah 54:13	All thy children shall be taught of the Lord; and great shall be peace of thy children (See also John 6:45.)
1 Corinthians 2:13	We speak … words … which the Holy Ghost teacheth

I. Children worshipping with their parents:

Joshua 8:35	["Little ones" listen to Bible reading with parents]
2 Chronicles 20:13	[Children included in serious prayer meeting] (See also Joel 2:12,15–16.)

6. TEACHING CHILDREN OBEDIENCE AND RESPECT:

A. Children are to obey their parents:

Proverbs 1:8–9	My son, hear the instruction of thy father, and … mother
Ephesians 6:1	Children, obey your parents in the Lord: this is right

Colossians 3:20	Children, obey your parents in all things: for this is well pleasing unto the Lord

B. Children are to honour their parents:

Exodus 20:12	Honour thy father and mother: that thy days may be long
Leviticus 19:3	Ye shall fear every man his mother, and his father
Ephesians 6:2	Honour thy father and mother; [this] is the first commandment with promise (See also Proverbs 20:20; 23:22.)

C. The blessing of having obedient, wise children:

Proverbs 10:1	A wise son maketh a glad father
Proverbs 13:1	A wise son heareth his father's instruction
Proverbs 23:15–16	Son, if thine heart be wise, my heart shall rejoice
Proverbs 23:24–25	He that begetteth a wise child shall have joy
Proverbs 28:7	Whoso keepeth the law is a wise son
2 John 1:4	I rejoiced greatly that I found of thy children walking in truth (See also 3 John 1:4.)

D. The grief of having disobedient, foolish children:

Proverbs 10:1	A foolish son is the heaviness of his mother
Proverbs 17:21	The father of a fool hath no joy
Proverbs 17:25	A foolish son is a grief to his father, and bitterness to her that bare him [his mother]
Proverbs 19:13	A foolish son is the calamity of his father

7. LOVING INSTRUCTION BALANCED WITH DISCIPLINE:

A. Treat your children gently and with love:

Luke 1:17	He shall … turn hearts of the fathers to the children
Ephesians 6:4	Fathers, provoke not your children to wrath
Colossians 3:21	Fathers, provoke not your children to anger, lest they be discouraged
1 Thessalonians 2:7	We were gentle … as a nurse cherisheth her children
Titus 2:4	Teach the young women … to love their children

B. Patience, mercy, and truth are the most effective:

Proverbs 16:6	By mercy and truth iniquity is purged
Romans 2:4	The goodness of God leadeth thee to repentance
Ephesians 6:4	Bring them up in the nurture and admiration of the Lord
1 Thessalonians 2:11	We exhorted and comforted and charged [testified to] every one of you, as a father doth his children

C. Each child is different; seek God how to train and discipline:

Judges 13:12	How shall we order the child, and how shall we do? (See also Luke 12:47–48.)

D. The Scriptural admonition to correct and discipline when necessary:

Proverbs 13:24	He that spareth his rod hateth his son: but he that loveth him chasteneth him betimes [promptly]
Proverbs 23:13	Withhold not correction from the child
Proverbs 29:17	Correct thy son, and he shall give thee rest ... delight

E. Christians required to train their children:

1 Timothy 3:4	That ruleth well his own house, having his children in subjection with all gravity
1 Timothy 3:12	Ruling their children and their own houses well
Titus 1:6	Blameless ... having faithful children not ... unruly
	(See also Galatians 4:1–2.)

F. Even with the right training, some children will go wrong:

1 Samuel 8:1–3,5	[Righteous Samuel's sons became corrupt and covetous]
Mark 13:12–13	[In the last days, some backslidden children will betray their Christian parents] (See also Matthew 24:10.)
	(See also Proverbs 2:16–18.)

G. Partiality and favouritism cause problems:

Genesis 25:27–28	Isaac loved Esau ... but Rebekah loved Jacob [and helped Jacob deceive old father Isaac—Genesis 27:1–18]
Genesis 37:3–4	Israel loved Joseph more than all his children ... when his brethren saw [it], they hated him

8. THE GROWING YEARS:

A. Be considerate of children's limitations:

Genesis 33:12–14	The children are tender [young] ... I will lead on softly according as the ... children be able to endure

B. Growing up and maturing:

Isaiah 28:9	Whom shall he teach knowledge? And ... make to understand doctrine? Them that are weaned
Hebrews 5:14	Strong meat [doctrine] belongeth to them ... of full age

C. Becoming a teen, a young adult:

Ecclesiastes 12:1	Remember now thy creator in the days of thy youth
1 Corinthians 13:11	When I became a man, I put away childish things
1 Corinthians 14:20	Be not children in understanding: in malice be ye children, but in understanding be men [mature]
Ephesians 4:14	That we henceforth be no more children
1 Timothy 4:12	Let no man despise thy youth; but be thou an example of the believers, in conversation, charity, faith

D. Examples of teens and young men serving God:

1 Samuel 16:1,10–13	[David was anointed to be king when he was just a teen] (See also 16:14–23; 17:32–37,49.)
Jeremiah 1:4–9	[Teenage Jeremiah was called to proclaim God's words]
Acts 23:12–24	[The apostle Paul's teenage nephew saves his life]
Acts 16:1–3	[Paul chose young Timothy to be his helper and travelling companion] (See also 1 Timothy 4:12.)

9. BECOMING LIKE CHILDREN:

A. You must have the faith of a child to be saved:

Matthew 18:3–4	Except ye be converted, and become as little children, ye shall not enter into the kingdom of heaven. Whosoever therefore shall humble himself as this little child ... is greatest in the kingdom of heaven
Mark 10:15	Whosoever shall not receive the kingdom of God as a little child, he shall not enter therein

B. In relation to God, we are children:

Deuteronomy 8:5	As a man chasteneth his son, so the Lord thy God chasteneth thee
1 Kings 3:7	[King Solomon told God:] I am but a little child
Psalm 103:13	Like as a father pitieth his children, so the Lord pitieth them that fear him
Ephesians 5:1	Be ye therefore followers of God, as dear children (See also Isaiah 63:15–16; Malachi 3:17; Galatians 4:3–7.)

SLEEP

1. SLEEP CONSIDERED A BLESSING:

A. Trust in God to bless you with sleep:

Psalm 3:5	I laid me down and slept; for the Lord sustained me
Psalm 4:8	I will both lay me down in peace, and sleep
Psalm 127:2	He giveth his beloved sleep
Ecclesiastes 5:12	The sleep of a labouring man is sweet
Jeremiah 31:26	I awaked, and beheld; and my sleep was sweet unto me

B. God gives freedom from fear and sweet sleep:

Psalm 91:5	Thou shalt not be afraid for the terror by night
Proverbs 3:24	Not be afraid … shalt lie down, and thy sleep be sweet
Acts 12:6	[Peter able to sleep in prison] bound with two chains

C. Rest in God and sleep through anything:

Ezekiel 34:25	Dwell safely in the wilderness, and sleep in the woods
Matthew 8:24	Tempest … ship covered with waves: but he was asleep

2. IF YOU CAN'T SLEEP, PRAY:

Psalm 42:8	In the night his song shall be with me, and my prayer
Psalm 63:5–6	When I … meditate on thee in the night watches
Isaiah 26:9	With my soul have I desired thee in the night
Lamentations 2:19	Arise, cry out in the night … pour out thine heart

(See also Psalm 4:4; 119:55.)

3. SOME REASONS FOR NOT BEING ABLE TO SLEEP:

A. When God wants to speak to you:

1 Samuel 3:3–10	Samuel was laid down to sleep … the Lord called
Job 4:12–17	In the night, when deep sleep falleth on men, a spirit passed before my face … I heard a voice

B. Sometimes God allows it to work out His will:

Esther 6:1–3	On that night could not the king [Ahasuerus] sleep

C. When worried or troubled:

Psalm 77:3–4	Thou holdest mine eyes waking: I am so troubled
Ecclesiastes 2:23	His days are sorrows … taketh not rest in the night
Ecclesiastes 5:12	Abundance of the rich will not suffer him to sleep
Daniel 6:14–18	[King Darius passed the night fasting, unable to sleep]

(See also Psalm 6:6.)

D. Because of unusual dreams:

Job 7:13–14	Then thou scarest me with dreams, and visions
Daniel 2:1	His spirit was troubled, and his sleep brake from him

E. When God is testing you, as He did Job:

Job 7:3–4	Wearisome nights are appointed unto me … I am full of tossings to and fro unto the dawning of the day

F. Punishment for disobeying God:

Deuteronomy 28:58, 66–67	If thou wilt not observe … thou shalt fear day and night … shalt say, "Would God it were morning"

G. Be considerate of those who are sleeping:

Proverbs 27:14	He that blesseth his friend with a loud voice, rising early … it shall be counted a curse to him
Song of Solomon 2:7	Stir not up, nor awake my love, till he please

4. GOOD REASONS FOR MISSING SLEEP:

A. To pray fervently:

1 Samuel 15:11	It grieved Samuel; and he cried unto the Lord all night
Luke 6:12	[Jesus] continued all night in prayer to God
1 Thessalonians 3:10	Night and day praying exceedingly [to] see your face

B. To rise early and pray:

1 Samuel 1:19	They rose up in the morning early, and worshipped
Psalm 57:8–9	Awake, psaltery and harp: I myself will awake early. I will praise thee, O Lord
Psalm 119:147	I prevented [was up before] the dawning of the morning, and cried: I hoped in thy word
Mark 1:35	Rising up a great while before day … Jesus prayed

C. To do your job:

Genesis 31:38–40	[Jacob frequently sacrificed sleep for 20 years because of diligent shepherding]

D. Caution about getting overtired:

Psalm 127:2	It is vain for you to rise up early, to sit up late … for so he giveth his beloved sleep
Acts 20:7–9	Eutychus, being fallen into a deep sleep … fell down

5. WHEN IT IS NOT GOOD TO SLEEP:

A. Don't oversleep when you should be working:

Proverbs 6:9–11	How long wilt thou sleep, O sluggard? ... a little sleep, a little slumber … so shall thy poverty come (See also Proverbs 24:33–34.)
Proverbs 10:5	He that sleepeth in harvest … son that causeth shame
Proverbs 20:13	Love not sleep, lest thou come to poverty

Proverbs 26:14	As the door turneth upon hinges, so doth the slothful

B. Times to rise and pray:

Jonah 1:4–6	O sleeper ... arise, call upon thy God
Mark 14:37–41	Sleepest thou? Couldst thou not watch one hour? Watch ye and pray, lest ye enter into temptation
Luke 22:46	Why sleep ye? Rise and pray, lest ye enter temptation

C. When something important needs to be done first:

Psalm 132:3–5	I will not give sleep to mine eyes, until I find
Proverbs 6:1–4	Do this now ... give not sleep to thine eyes, nor slumber

D. Oversleeping can be caused by laziness or unconcern for others:

Proverbs 19:15	Slothfulness casteth into a deep sleep
Isaiah 56:10–11	Watchmen are blind ... sleeping, loving to slumber

E. Sleep can symbolise spiritual insensitivity:

Romans 13:11–12	Knowing the time ... now it is high time to awake
Ephesians 5:14	Awake thou that sleepest ... Christ shall give thee light
1 Thessalonians 5:4–8	Let us not sleep ... let us watch and be sober

6. TRUSTING GOD TO AWAKEN YOU:

A. When you've slept enough and need to rise:

Isaiah 50:4	[God] wakeneth [me] morning by morning ... to hear
Zechariah 4:1	And the angel that talked with me ... walked me

B. To flee danger:

Matthew 2:13–14	Angel ... appeareth to Joseph in a dream, saying, Arise ... flee. He arose ... by night, and [left with Jesus and Mary]
Acts 12:4–7	Peter [slept] ... angel of the Lord ... smote Peter on the side, and raised him up, saying, Arise up quickly

C. To give you something you need:

1 Kings 19:5–7	[Angel woke Elijah up twice to give him food and water]

D. God can awaken you after giving you an important message:

Matthew 1:24	Joseph being raised from sleep did as the angel ... had bidden

OLD AGE

1. THE BLESSINGS OF OLD AGE:

A. Old age has its own beauty and glory:

Proverbs 16:31 — The hoary [grey] head is a crown of glory, if it be found in the way of righteousness

Proverbs 20:29 — The beauty of old men is the grey head

B. God's Word says that the elderly should be honoured and respected:

Leviticus 19:32 — Thou shalt rise up [in respect] before the hoary head, and honour the face of the old man

Job 32:4,6 — Elihu had waited till Job [and the others] had spoken, because they were elder than he

Proverbs 23:22 — Hearken unto thy father … and despise not [respect] thy mother when she is old

C. The passing of years usually brings wisdom:

Job 12:12 — With the ancient is wisdom; and in length of days understanding

Job 32:7 — Days should speak, and multitude of years … teach wisdom

1 Kings 12:1–16 — [King Rehoboam's folly in not following the wise advice of the old men]

D. Long years of trusting God brings assurance:

Psalm 37:25 — I have been young, and now am old; yet have I not seen the righteous forsaken

E. We shouldn't be sad about old age:

Ecclesiastes 11:10 — Remove sorrow from thy heart … for childhood and youth are vanity

2. GOD'S HELP IN OUR OLD AGE:

Isaiah 46:4 — Even to your old age I am he; and even to hoar hairs will I carry you … and will deliver you

(See also Psalm 71:8–9,17–18.)

3. DESIRING LONG LIFE:

A. Before the flood, people lived to very great ages:

(See Genesis 5:1–32; 7:11; 9:28–29.)

B. After the flood, lifespans became shorter:

(See Genesis 11:10–32; 25:7–8,17; 35:28; 47:8–9; Deuteronomy 34:7; Joshua 24:29.)

C. Today's average lifespan:

Psalm 90:10	The days of our years are [seventy]; and if by reason of strength they be [eighty] years

D. Old age can be a reward for a righteous life:

Genesis 15:15	Thou shalt go to thy fathers in peace … in good old age
Genesis 25:8	Abraham … died in a good old age … full of years
Deuteronomy 34:7	Moses was [120] years old when he died: his eye was not dim, nor his natural force abated
1 Chronicles 29:28	He died in a good old age, full of days, riches, and honour
2 Chronicles 24:15	[Godly Jehoidah lived to 130 years of age, at a time when most men only lived to be 70]
Job 5:26	Thou shalt come to thy grave in a full age, like as a [sheaf of grain] in his season
Psalm 91:14,16	He hath set his love on me … with long life will I satisfy him
Isaiah 65:22	As the days of a tree are the days of my people, and mine elect shall long enjoy the work of their hands
Zechariah 8:3–4	There shall yet [be] old men and old women … every man with his staff in his hand for very age

E. How to obtain the blessing of longevity:

Deuteronomy 5:33	Walk in all the ways which the Lord … commanded you, that ye may live … prolong your days
Deuteronomy 30:20	Love the Lord thy God … obey his voice … for he is thy life, and the length of thy days
Psalm 34:12–14	What man … desireth life, and loveth many days? Keep thy tongue from evil and guile … do good; seek peace
Proverbs 3:1–2	Let thine heart keep my commandments: for length of days, and long life … shall they add to thee
Proverbs 9:10–11	For by me [wisdom] thy days shall be multiplied, and the years of thy life shall be increased
Proverbs 10:27	The fear of the Lord prolongeth days
	(See also Proverbs 3:13,16; 4:7,10; 9:10–11; 1 Peter 3:10–11; Exodus 20:12.)

F. Praying for more time to live and serve God:

2 Kings 20:1–7	[God revived ailing King Hezekiah and gave him 15 more years to live]
Psalm 71:18	Forsake me not; until I have shewed thy strength unto this generation, and … to everyone that is to come

G. Wanting to continue living in order to help others:

Philippians 1:23–25	Having a desire to depart, and to be with Christ … [but] to abide in the flesh is more needful for you

H. God sometimes revealed to men their time of departing:

Psalm 39:4	Lord, make me to know … the measure of my days, what it is; that I may know how frail I am
Psalm 90:12	Teach us to number our days, that we may apply our hearts unto wisdom
Luke 2:26	It was revealed unto him by the Holy Ghost, that he should not see death, before he had seen … Christ
2 Timothy 4:6–7	I am now ready … the time of my departure is at hand
2 Peter 1:14	Shortly I must put off this my tabernacle, even as our Lord Jesus Christ hath shewed me
2 Kings 2:3	Knowest thou that the Lord will take [Elijah] away today?

I. These were then able to give parting instructions to their family:

Genesis 49:1,33	[Dying Jacob called his sons and gave them instructions, and when finished, "gave up the ghost"] (See also Genesis 50:22–26; 1 Kings 2:1–3,10.)

J. The futility of worrying that our time has come:

Genesis 27:1–4	[Aged Isaac thought he was about to die, but lived many more years and died when 180—Genesis 35:28–29]
1 Samuel 27:1	[David despaired:] I shall perish one day by the hand of Saul [but lived over 40 years more] (See also Hebrews 2:15.)

K. Trust God to keep you until His appointed time:

Job 7:1	Is there not an appointed time to man upon earth?
Psalm 31:15	My times are in thy hand
Psalm 48:14	God … is our guide even unto death

L. Sometimes, not living to old age is the greater blessing:

Genesis 5:23–24	[Enoch lived only 1/3rd the lifespan of his day; God took him because he pleased Him] (See also Hebrews 11:5.)
Isaiah 57:1	Merciful men are taken away … the righteous is taken away from the evil to come (See also 1 Kings 14:12–13.)

4. GOD CAN MIGHTILY USE AGED BELIEVERS:

A. Promises of fruitfulness:

Psalm 92:13–14	They shall still bring forth fruit in old age; they shall be [fresh] and flourishing

B. Material ministering and good deeds:

2 Samuel 19:32–35	[Barzillai, 80 years old, helped support King David in his time of great need] (See also 2 Samuel 17:27–29.)

C. Spiritual ministries:

Exodus 7:7	[Moses was 80 years old when he led the exodus]
Daniel 9:1; 10:1	[Daniel received two of his greatest revelations between the ages of 85 and 90]
Joel 2:28	I will pour out my spirit upon all flesh; and ... your old men shall dream dreams (See also Acts 2:16–17.)
Revelation 1:1,9	[The apostle John received the Book of Revelation in exile on Patmos, in his 80s or 90s]

D. Some conditions to being used of God:

Titus 2:2–3	Aged men be sober, [reverent], temperate, sound in faith, in love, in patience [that they may teach]

E. The ministry of prayer:

1 Samuel 12:1–2,16,19	[Samuel, aged and grey-headed, prayed, and God performed a miracle to punish the errant Israelites]
Luke 2:36–37	Anna, a prophetess ... of about [84 years old], served God with fastings and prayers night and day
1 Timothy 5:5,9	[Prayer, a special ministry for women over 60]

F. Witnessing:

Luke 2:36–38	[Anna, 84 years old, witnessed to others about Jesus]
Philemon 1:9–11,16	Paul the aged [led Onesimus to receive Jesus]
Acts 28:30–31	[Paul witnessed to all those who came to visit him] (See also 2 Timothy 1:5; 3:15.)

G. God can use those who think they are too old:

Genesis 18:10–14; 21:1–2	[Sarah, at 90, laughs and doubts she can have a child] (See also Genesis 17:15–17; Luke 1:36.)

H. God sometimes doesn't really use us until we're older and wiser:

Acts 7:23–34	[Moses tried to start his life's work at 40, but was not really ready for it until he was 80]

I. Keep faithfully serving Jesus till He calls you:

2 Peter 1:12–15	I think it meet, as long as I am in this [body], to stir you up [and establish you in the truth]

J. Enduring adversity in old age:

Philemon 1:9–10	Paul the aged, and now also a prisoner ... in bonds
Revelation 1:9	[John, in his 80s or 90s, exiled to the isle of Patmos]

5. STRENGTH IN OLD AGE:

A. God can give us strength and health:

Deuteronomy 33:25	As thy days, so shall thy strength be
Deuteronomy 34:7	[Moses at 120 years old] … his eye was not dim, nor his natural force abated
Isaiah 40:29	To them that have no might he increaseth strength
Psalm 103:5	[He] satisfieth thy mouth with good things; so that thy youth is renewed like the eagle's
Joshua 14:7,10–11	I [Caleb] am this day [85] years old. As yet I am as strong this day as I was [when I was 40]

B. Courage and determination give strength and victory in old age:

Joshua 14:10–14	[Caleb, 85 years old:] Give me this mountain [inhabited by giants in strongly-fortified cities] ... the Lord will be with me … I shall ... drive them out

C. Give God the credit for keeping us during a difficult life:

Joshua 14:10	Behold, the Lord hath kept me alive

6. CAUTIONS REGARDING OLD AGE:

A. We must not assume that age alone always makes us wiser:

Job 32:9	Great men are not always wise: neither do the aged [always] understand judgement (See also Psalm 119:100.)

B. Without God, the wisdom of the aged comes to naught:

Job 12:13,20	With him [God] is wisdom … he … taketh away the understanding of the aged

C. Caution against becoming too set in our ways:

Ecclesiastes 4:13	Better is a … wise child than an old and foolish king, who will no more be admonished

D. Caution against tossing conviction aside in old age:

1 Kings 11:4	When Solomon was old, his wives turned away his heart after other gods: and his heart was not perfect with God

E. Unwisely comparing former glories to the present:

Ezra 3:11–12	[People rejoiced to see the new temple, but the old men, remembering old temple, wept] (See also Haggai 2:3.)
Ecclesiastes 7:10	Say not thou, What is the cause that the former days were better than these? Thou dost not enquire wisely

7. JOY IN CHILDREN AND GRANDCHILDREN:

Genesis 37:3	Israel loved Joseph more than all his children, because he was the son of his old age
Ruth 4:13–16	[Naomi's grandchild] a nourisher of thine old age
Proverbs 17:6	Children's children are the crown of old men; and the glory of children are their fathers

(See also Luke 1:5–7,13,18–20.)

SALVATION

- **John 1:12** As many as received him, to them gave he power to become the sons of God, even to them that believe on his name.
- **John 3:3** Except a man be born again, he cannot see the kingdom of God.
- **John 3:16** For God so loved the world, that he gave his only begotten Son, that whosoever believeth in him should not perish, but have everlasting life.
- **John 3:36** He that believeth on the Son hath everlasting life: and he that believeth not the Son shall not see life; but the wrath of God abideth on him.
- **John 6:37** All that the Father giveth me shall come to me; and him that cometh to me I will in no wise cast out.
- **John 10:28** I give unto them eternal life; and they shall never perish, neither shall any man pluck them out of my hand.
- **John 14:6** Jesus saith unto him, I am the way, the truth, and the life: no man cometh unto the Father, but by me.
- **Acts 16:31** Believe on the Lord Jesus Christ, and thou shalt be saved.
- **Romans 3:23** For all have sinned, and come short of the glory of God.
- **Romans 6:23** For the wages of sin is death; but the gift of God is eternal life through Jesus Christ our Lord.
- **Romans 10:9–10** That if thou shalt confess with thy mouth the Lord Jesus, and shalt believe in thine heart that God hath raised him from the dead, thou shalt be saved. For with the heart man believeth unto righteousness; and with the mouth confession is made unto salvation.
- **2 Corinthians 5:17** Therefore if any man be in Christ, he is a new creature: old things are passed away; behold, all things are become new.
- **Ephesians 2:8–9** For by grace are ye saved through faith; and that not of yourselves: it is the gift of God: Not of works, lest any man should boast.
- **Titus 3:5** Not by works of righteousness which we have done, but according to his mercy he saved us.
- **1 John 5:12–13** He that hath the Son hath life; and he that hath not the Son of God hath not life. These things have I written unto you that believe on the name of the Son of God; that ye may know that ye have eternal life, and that ye may believe on the name of the Son of God.
- **Revelation 3:20** Behold, I stand at the door, and knock: if any man hear my voice, and open the door, I will come in to him, and will sup with him, and he with me.

JESUS CHRIST, THE SON OF GOD

- **Isaiah 9:6** For unto us a child is born, unto us a son is given: and the government shall be upon his shoulder: and his name shall be called Wonderful, Counsellor, The mighty God, The everlasting Father, The Prince of Peace.
- **John 1:1,14** In the beginning was the word, and the word was with God, and the word was God. And the word was made flesh, and dwelt among us, and we beheld his glory, the glory as of the only begotten of the Father, full of grace and truth.
- **John 3:17** God sent not his Son into the world to condemn the world; but that the world through him might be saved.
- **John 10:11** I am the good shepherd: the good shepherd giveth his life for the sheep.
- **John 15:13** Greater love hath no man than this, that a man lay down his life for his friends.
- **Acts 10:38** God anointed Jesus of Nazareth with the Holy Ghost and with power: who went about doing good, and healing all that were oppressed of the devil.
- **Romans 5:8** God commendeth his love toward us, in that, while we were yet sinners, Christ died for us.

(See also Isaiah 53—the prophetic "Portrait of Jesus Chapter.")

THE HOLY SPIRIT

- **Luke 11:13** If ye then, being evil, know how to give good gifts unto your children: how much more shall your heavenly Father give the Holy Spirit to them that ask him?
- **John 7:38–39** He that believeth on me, as the Scripture hath said, out of his belly shall flow rivers of living water. But this spake he of the Spirit, which they that believe on him should receive.
- **John 14:26** The Comforter, which is the Holy Ghost, whom the Father will send in my name, he shall teach you all things, and bring all things to your remembrance, whatsoever I have said unto you.
- **John 16:13** When he, the Spirit of truth, is come, he will guide you into all truth: for he shall not speak of himself; but whatsoever he shall hear, that shall he speak: and he will show you things to come.
- **Acts 1:8** Ye shall receive power, after that the Holy Ghost is come upon you: and ye shall be witnesses unto me both in Jerusalem, and in all Judaea, and in Samaria, and unto the uttermost part of the earth.
- **Acts 2:17–18** And it shall come to pass in the last days, saith God, I will pour out of my Spirit upon all flesh: and your sons and your daughters shall prophesy, and your young men shall see visions, and your old men shall dream dreams: and on my servants and on my handmaidens I will pour out in those days of my Spirit; and they shall prophesy.

- **Acts 4:31** And they were all filled with the Holy Ghost, and they spake the word of God with boldness.
- **Acts 5:32** And we are his witnesses of these things; and so is also the Holy Ghost, whom God hath given to them that obey him.
- **Acts 19:2,6** He said unto them, Have ye received the Holy Ghost since ye believed? And they said unto him, We have not so much as heard whether there be any Holy Ghost. And when Paul had laid his hands upon them, the Holy Ghost came on them; and they spake with tongues, and prophesied.
- **2 Corinthians 3:17** Now the Lord is that Spirit: and where the Spirit of the Lord is, there is liberty.

THE WORD OF GOD

- **Joshua 1:8** This book of the law shall not depart out of thy mouth; but thou shalt meditate therein day and night, that thou mayest observe to do according to all that is written therein: for then thou shalt make thy way prosperous, and then thou shalt have good success.
- **Job 23:12** I have esteemed the words of his mouth more than my necessary food.
- **Psalm 119:11** Thy word have I hid in mine heart, that I might not sin against thee.
- **Psalm 119:89** For ever, O Lord, thy word is settled in heaven.
- **Psalm 119:105** Thy word is a lamp unto my feet, and a light unto my path.
- **Jeremiah 15:16** Thy words were found, and I did eat them.
- **Matthew 4:4** Man shall not live by bread alone, but by every word that proceedeth out of the mouth of God.
- **Matthew 24:35** Heaven and earth shall pass away, but my words shall not pass away.
- **John 6:63** It is the Spirit that quickeneth; the flesh profiteth nothing: the words that I speak unto you, they are spirit, and they are life.
- **John 8:31–32** If ye continue in my word, then are ye my disciples indeed. And ye shall know the truth, and the truth shall make you free.
- **Romans 10:17** So then faith cometh by hearing, and hearing by the word of God.
- **1 Corinthians 10:11** Now all these things happened unto them for ensamples: and they are written for our admonition, upon whom the ends of the world are come.
- **2 Timothy 2:15** Study to show thyself approved unto God, a workman that needeth not to be ashamed, rightly dividing the word of truth.
- **2 Timothy 3:16** All Scripture is given by inspiration of God, and is profitable for doctrine, for reproof, for correction, for instruction in righteousness.
- **1 Peter 2:2** As newborn babes, desire the sincere milk of the word, that ye may grow thereby.

- **2 Peter 1:21** For the prophecy came not in old time by the will of man: but holy men of God spake as they were moved by the Holy Ghost.

PRAYER

- **Psalm 66:18–19** If I regard iniquity in my heart, the Lord will not hear me: But verily God hath heard me; he hath attended to the voice of my prayer.
- **Jeremiah 29:13** Ye shall seek me, and find me, when ye shall search for me with all your heart.
- **Jeremiah 33:3** Call unto me, and I will answer thee, and show thee great and mighty things, which thou knowest not.
- **Matthew 7:7–8** Ask, and it shall be given you; seek, and ye shall find; knock, and it shall be opened unto you: For every one that asketh receiveth; and he that seeketh findeth; and to him that knocketh it shall be opened.
- **Matthew 18:19** If two of you shall agree on earth as touching any thing that they shall ask, it shall be done for them of my Father which is in heaven.
- **Mark 11:24** What things soever ye desire, when ye pray, believe that ye receive them, and ye shall have them.
- **John 16:23** Whatsoever ye shall ask the Father in my name, he will give it you.
- **James 1:6–7** But let him ask in faith, nothing wavering. For he that wavereth is like a wave of the sea driven with the wind and tossed. For let not that man think that he shall receive any thing of the Lord.
- **James 4:2** Ye have not, because ye ask not.
- **1 John 3:22** And whatsoever we ask, we receive of him, because we keep his commandments, and do those things that are pleasing in his sight.
- **1 John 5:14** If we ask any thing according to his will, he heareth us.

FAITH

- **Job 13:15** Though he slay me, yet will I trust in him.
- **Proverbs 3:5** Trust in the Lord with all thine heart; and lean not unto thine own understanding.
- **Matthew 9:29** According to your faith be it unto you.
- **Mark 9:23** If thou canst believe, all things are possible to him that believeth.
- **Romans 4:20–21** He staggered not at the promise of God through unbelief; but was strong in faith, giving glory to God; and being fully persuaded that, what he had promised, he was able also to perform.
- **Romans 10:17** Faith cometh by hearing, and hearing by the word of God.
- **2 Corinthians 5:7** For we walk by faith, not by sight.
- **Hebrews 10:35** Cast not away therefore your confidence, which hath great recompense of reward.

- **Hebrews 10:38** Now the just shall live by faith.
- **Hebrews 11:1,6** Faith is the substance of things hoped for, the evidence of things not seen. But without faith it is impossible to please him: for he that cometh to God must believe that he is, and that he is a rewarder of them that diligently seek him.
- **1 John 5:4** This is the victory that overcometh the world, even our faith.

LOVE

- **Matthew 7:12** Therefore all things whatsoever ye would that men should do to you, do ye even so to them.
- **Matthew 22:37–39** Jesus said unto him, Thou shalt love the Lord thy God with all thy heart, and with all thy soul, and with all thy mind. This is the first and great commandment. And the second is like unto it, Thou shalt love thy neighbour as thyself.
- **John 13:35** By this shall all men know that ye are my disciples, if ye have love one to another.
- **John 15:12** This is my commandment, That ye love one another, as I have loved you.
- **1 Corinthians 13:8** Charity [love] never faileth.
- **1 Corinthians 16:14** Let all your things be done with love.
- **1 Peter 4:8** Above all things have fervent love among yourselves: for love shall cover the multitude of sins.
- **1 John 3:16** Hereby perceive we the love of God, because he laid down his life for us: and we ought to lay down our lives for the brethren.
- **1 John 3:18** My little children, let us not love in word, neither in tongue; but in deed and in truth.
- **1 John 4:8** He that loveth not knoweth not God; for God is love.

(See also 1 Corinthians 13—"The Love Chapter.")

FORGIVENESS

- **Matthew 6:14–15** For if ye forgive men their trespasses, your heavenly Father will also forgive you: But if ye forgive not men their trespasses, neither will your Father forgive your trespasses.
- **Ephesians 4:32** Be ye kind one to another, tenderhearted, forgiving one another, even as God for Christ's sake hath forgiven you.
- **1 John 1:9** If we confess our sins, he is faithful and just to forgive us our sins, and to cleanse us from all unrighteousness.

OUR RELATIONSHIP WITH GOD

- **Psalm 111:10** The fear of the Lord is the beginning of wisdom.
- **Proverbs 8:17** I love them that love me; and those that seek me early shall find me.
- **Matthew 11:28–30** Come unto me, all ye that labour and are heavy laden, and I will give you rest. Take my yoke upon you, and learn of me; for I am meek and lowly in heart: and ye shall find rest unto your souls. For my yoke is easy, and my burden is light.
- **Matthew 22:37–38** Thou shalt love the Lord thy God with all thy heart, and with all thy soul, and with all thy mind.
- **John 14:23** If a man love me, he will keep my words: and my Father will love him, and we will come unto him, and make our abode with him.
- **Romans 7:4** Ye also are become dead to the law by the body of Christ; that ye should be married to another, even to him who is raised from the dead, that we should bring forth fruit unto God.
- **2 Corinthians 6:16** Ye are the temple of the living God; as God hath said, I will dwell in them, and walk in them; and I will be their God, and they shall be my people.
- **Ephesians 5:30** We are members of his body, of his flesh, and of his bones.
- **James 4:8** Draw nigh to God, and he will draw nigh to you.

FELLOWSHIP

- **Hebrews 10:25** Not forsaking the assembling of ourselves together, as the manner of some is; but exhorting one another: and so much the more, as ye see the day approaching.
- **Psalm 133:1** Behold, how good and how pleasant it is for brethren to dwell together in unity!
- **Matthew 18:20** Where two or three are gathered together in my name, there am I in the midst of them.
- **Acts 2:42** And they continued stedfastly in the apostles' doctrine and fellowship, and in breaking of bread, and in prayers.
- **1 John 1:7** If we walk in the light, as he is in the light, we have fellowship one with another.

WITNESSING

- **Psalm 126:6** He that goeth forth and weepeth, bearing precious seed, shall doubtless come again with rejoicing, bringing his sheaves with him.
- **Proverbs 11:30** The fruit of the righteous is a tree of life; and he that winneth souls is wise.

- **Daniel 12:3** They that be wise shall shine as the brightness of the firmament; and they that turn many to righteousness as the stars for ever and ever.
- **Matthew 4:19** Follow me, and I will make you fishers of men.
- **Matthew 5:14–16** Ye are the light of the world. A city that is set on an hill cannot be hid. Neither do men light a candle, and put it under a bushel, but on a candlestick; and it giveth light unto all that are in the house. Let your light so shine before men, that they may see your good works, and glorify your Father which is in heaven.
- **Matthew 9:37–38** Then saith he unto his disciples, The harvest truly is plenteous, but the labourers are few; Pray ye therefore the Lord of the harvest, that he will send forth labourers into his harvest.
- **Mark 16:15** And he said unto them, Go ye into all the world, and preach the gospel to every creature.
- **John 15:16** Ye have not chosen me, but I have chosen you, and ordained you, that ye should go and bring forth fruit, and that your fruit should remain.
- **1 Corinthians 9:16** For though I preach the gospel, I have nothing to glory of: for necessity is laid upon me; yea, woe is unto me, if I preach not the gospel!
- **2 Timothy 4:2** Preach the word; be instant in season, out of season; reprove, rebuke, exhort with all longsuffering and doctrine.
- **1 Peter 3:15** Be ready always to give an answer to every man that asketh you a reason of the hope that is in you with meekness and fear.

GIVING

- **Proverbs 3:27–28** Withhold not good from them to whom it is due, when it is in the power of thine hand to do it. Say not unto thy neighbour, Go, and come again, and to morrow I will give; when thou hast it by thee.
- **Proverbs 11:24–25** There is that scattereth, and yet increaseth; and there is that withholdeth more than is meet, but it tendeth to poverty. The liberal soul shall be made fat: And he that watereth shall be watered also himself.
- **Proverbs 19:17** He that hath pity upon the poor lendeth unto the Lord; and that which he hath given will he pay him again.
- **Malachi 3:10** Bring ye all the tithes into the storehouse, that there may be meat in mine house, and prove me now herewith, saith the Lord of hosts, if I will not open you the windows of heaven, and pour you out a blessing, that there shall not be room enough to receive it.
- **Luke 6:38** Give, and it shall be given unto you; good measure, pressed down, and shaken together, and running over, shall men give into your bosom. For with the same measure that ye mete withal it shall be measured to you again.
- **Acts 20:35** It is more blessed to give than to receive.

- **2 Corinthians 9:6–7** He which soweth sparingly shall reap also sparingly; and he which soweth bountifully shall reap also bountifully. Every man according as he purposeth in his heart, so let him give; not grudgingly, or of necessity: for God loveth a cheerful giver.
- **1 John 3:17–18** Whoso hath this world's good, and seeth his brother have need, and shutteth up his bowels of compassion from him, how dwelleth the love of God in him? My little children, let us not love in word, neither in tongue; but in deed and in truth.

HOW TO FIND THE WILL OF GOD

- **Judges 6:37** Behold, I will put a fleece of wool in the floor; and if the dew be on the fleece only, and it be dry upon all the earth beside, then shall I know that thou wilt save Israel by mine hand.
- **Psalm 32:8** I will instruct thee and teach thee in the way which thou shalt go: I will guide thee with mine eye.
- **Psalm 119:130** The entrance of thy words giveth light; it giveth understanding unto the simple.
- **Psalm 143:8** Cause me to know the way wherein I should walk; for I lift up my soul unto thee.
- **Proverbs 3:6** In all thy ways acknowledge him, and he shall direct thy paths.
- **Proverbs 15:22** Without counsel purposes are disappointed: but in the multitude of counsellors they are established.
- **Isaiah 30:21** Thine ears shall hear a word behind thee, saying, This is the way, walk ye in it, when ye turn to the right hand, and when ye turn to the left.
- **Romans 12:1–2** I beseech you therefore, brethren, by the mercies of God, that ye present your bodies a living sacrifice, holy, acceptable unto God, which is your reasonable service. And be not conformed to this world: but be ye transformed by the renewing of your mind, that ye may prove what is that good, and acceptable, and perfect, will of God.

OBEDIENCE TO GOD

- **1 Samuel 15:22** Hath the Lord as great delight in burnt offerings and sacrifices, as in obeying the voice of the Lord? Behold, to obey is better than sacrifice, and to hearken than the fat of rams.
- **Job 36:11** If they obey and serve him, they shall spend their days in prosperity, and their years in pleasures.
- **Isaiah 1:19–20** If ye be willing and obedient, ye shall eat the good of the land: But if ye refuse and rebel, ye shall be devoured with the sword: for the mouth of the Lord hath spoken it.
- **Luke 6:46** Why call ye me, Lord, Lord, and do not the things which I say?

- **John 13:17** If ye know these things, happy are ye if ye do them.
- **John 14:15** If ye love me, keep my commandments.
- **John 15:14** Ye are my friends, if ye do whatsoever I command you.
- **Ephesians 6:6** Not with eyeservice, as menpleasers; but as the servants of Christ, doing the will of God from the heart.
- **Hebrews 5:8** Though he were a Son, yet learned he obedience by the things which he suffered.

STRENGTH AND POWER

- **Nehemiah 8:10** The joy of the Lord is your strength.
- **Psalm 37:39** The salvation of the righteous is of the Lord: he is their strength in the time of trouble.
- **Psalm 68:35** The God of Israel is he that giveth strength and power unto his people.
- **Isaiah 30:7** Their strength is to sit still.
- **Isaiah 30:15** In quietness and in confidence shall be your strength.
- **Isaiah 40:29** He giveth power to the faint; and to them that have no might he increaseth strength.
- **Isaiah 40:31** They that wait upon the Lord shall renew their strength; they shall mount up with wings as eagles; they shall run, and not be weary; and they shall walk, and not faint.
- **Jeremiah 17:5** Cursed be the man that trusteth in man, and maketh flesh his arm, and whose heart departeth from the Lord.
- **Zechariah 4:6** Not by might, nor by power, but by my Spirit, saith the Lord of hosts.
- **2 Corinthians 4:7** But we have this treasure in earthen vessels, that the excellency of the power may be of God, and not of us.
- **2 Corinthians 12:9–10** And he said unto me, my grace is sufficient for thee: for my strength is made perfect in weakness. Most gladly therefore will I rather glory in my infirmities, that the power of Christ may rest upon me. For when I am weak, then am I strong.
- **Ephesians 6:10** Finally, my brethren, be strong in the Lord, and in the power of his might.
- **Philippians 4:13** I can do all things through Christ which strengtheneth me.

PROTECTION

- **Exodus 14:14** The Lord shall fight for you, and ye shall hold your peace.
- **Psalm 34:7** The angel of the Lord encampeth round about them that fear him, and delivereth them.
- **Psalm 34:17** The righteous cry, and the Lord heareth, and delivereth them out of all their troubles.
- **Psalm 46:1–2** God is our refuge and strength, a very present help in trouble. Therefore will not we fear, though the earth be removed, and though the mountains be carried into the midst of the sea.
- **Proverbs 1:33** Whoso hearkeneth unto me shall dwell safely, and shall be quiet from fear of evil.
- **Proverbs 18:10** The name of the Lord is a strong tower: The righteous runneth into it, and is safe.
- **Isaiah 43:2** When thou passest through the waters, I will be with thee; and through the rivers, they shall not overflow thee: when thou walkest through the fire, thou shalt not be burned; neither shall the flame kindle upon thee.

(See also Psalm 91—"The Protection Psalm.")

SUPPLY

- **Psalm 23:1** The Lord is my shepherd; I shall not want [lack].
- **Psalm 34:10** They that seek the Lord shall not want any good thing.
- **Psalm 37:3** Trust in the Lord, and do good; so shalt thou dwell in the land, and verily thou shalt be fed.
- **Psalm 37:25** I have been young, and now am old; yet have I not seen the righteous forsaken, nor his seed begging bread.
- **Psalm 68:19** Blessed be the Lord, who daily loadeth us with benefits.
- **Psalm 84:11** No good thing will he withhold from them that walk uprightly.
- **Matthew 6:25–26** Take no thought for your life, what ye shall eat, or what ye shall drink; nor yet for your body, what ye shall put on. Is not the life more than meat, and the body than raiment? Behold the fowls of the air: for they sow not, neither do they reap, nor gather into barns; yet your heavenly Father feedeth them. Are ye not much better than they?
- **Matthew 6:33** Seek ye first the kingdom of God, and his righteousness; and all these things shall be added unto you.
- **Matthew 7:9–11** What man is there of you, whom if his son ask bread, will he give him a stone? Or if he ask a fish, will he give him a serpent? If ye then, being evil, know how to give good gifts unto your children, how much more shall your Father which is in heaven give good things to them that ask him?
- **Romans 8:32** He that spared not his own Son, but delivered him up for us all, how shall he not with him also freely give us all things?

- **Philippians 4:19** my God shall supply all your need according to his riches in glory by Christ Jesus.

TRIALS, TEMPTATIONS, AND TRIBULATIONS

- **Job 23:10** He knoweth the way that I take: when he hath tried me, I shall come forth as gold.
- **Proverbs 1:10** My son, if sinners entice thee, consent thou not.
- **Matthew 26:41** Watch and pray, that ye enter not into temptation: the spirit indeed is willing, but the flesh is weak.
- **1 Corinthians 10:13** There hath no temptation taken you but such as is common to man: but God is faithful, who will not suffer you to be tempted above that ye are able; but will with the temptation also make a way to escape, that ye may be able to bear it.
- **2 Timothy 2:3** Endure hardness, as a good soldier of Jesus Christ.
- **Hebrews 12:2–3** Looking unto Jesus the author and finisher of our faith; who for the joy that was set before him endured the cross, despising the shame, and is set down at the right hand of the throne of God. For consider him that endured such contradiction of sinners against himself, lest ye be wearied and faint in your minds.
- **James 1:3** The trying of your faith worketh patience.
- **James 1:12** Blessed is the man that endureth temptation: for when he is tried, he shall receive the crown of life, which the Lord hath promised to them that love him.
- **1 Peter 1:7** That the trial of your faith, being much more precious than of gold that perisheth, though it be tried with fire, might be found unto praise and honour and glory at the appearing of Jesus Christ.
- **2 Peter 2:9** The Lord knoweth how to deliver the godly out of temptations.

SUFFERING

- **Psalm 34:19** Many are the afflictions of the righteous: but the Lord delivereth him out of them all.
- **Romans 8:18** For I reckon that the sufferings of this present time are not worthy to be compared with the glory which shall be revealed in us.
- **Romans 8:28** And we know that all things work together for good to them that love God, to them who are the called according to his purpose.
- **2 Corinthians 4:17** For our light affliction, which is but for a moment, worketh for us a far more exceeding and eternal weight of glory.
- **2 Timothy 2:12** If we suffer, we shall also reign with him: if we deny him, he also will deny us.

- **1 Peter 4:19** Wherefore let them that suffer according to the will of God commit the keeping of their souls to him in well doing, as unto a faithful Creator.

COMFORT

- **Psalm 23:4** Yea, though I walk through the valley of the shadow of death, I will fear no evil: for thou art with me; thy rod and thy staff they comfort me.
- **Psalm 30:5** For his anger endureth but a moment; in his favour is life: weeping may endure for a night, but joy cometh in the morning.
- **Psalm 119:50** This is my comfort in my affliction: for thy word hath quickened me.
- **Psalm 145:14** The Lord upholdeth all that fall, and raiseth up all those that be bowed down.
- **Psalm 147:3** He healeth up the broken in heart, and bindeth up their wounds.
- **Isaiah 54:7** For a small moment have I forsaken thee; but with great mercies will I gather thee.
- **Lamentations 3:32–33** Though he cause grief, yet will he have compassion according to the multitude of his mercies. For he doth not afflict willingly nor grieve the children of men.
- **Matthew 5:4** Blessed are they that mourn: for they shall be comforted.
- **John 14:1** Let not your heart be troubled: Ye believe in God, believe also in me.
- **John 14:18** I will not leave you comfortless: I will come to you.
- **2 Corinthians 1:4** Who comforteth us in all our tribulation, that we may be able to comfort them which are in any trouble, by the comfort wherewith we ourselves are comforted of God.
- **Hebrews 4:16** Let us therefore come boldly unto the throne of grace, that we may obtain mercy, and find grace to help in time of need.
- **Hebrews 13:5** He hath said, I will never leave thee, nor forsake thee.
- **1 Peter 5:7** Casting all your care upon him; for he careth for you.
- **Revelation 21:4** God shall wipe away all tears from their eyes; and there shall be no more death, neither sorrow, nor crying, neither shall there be any more pain: for the former things are passed away.

HEALING

- **Exodus 15:26** I am the Lord that healeth thee.
- **Psalm 34:19** Many are the afflictions of the righteous: but the Lord delivereth him out of them all.
- **Psalm 103:3** Who forgiveth all thine iniquities; who healeth all thy diseases.
- **Psalm 107:20** He sent his word, and healed them, and delivered them from their destructions.

- **Isaiah 53:5** With his stripes we are healed.
- **Jeremiah 30:17** I will restore health unto thee, and I will heal thee of thy wounds, saith the Lord.
- **Jeremiah 32:27** Behold, I am the Lord, the God of all flesh: is there any thing too hard for me?
- **Malachi 4:2** Unto you that fear my name shall the Sun of righteousness arise with healing in his wings.
- **Luke 17:14** As they went, they were cleansed.
- **James 5:14–15** Is any sick among you? Let him call for the elders of the church; and let them pray over him, anointing him with oil in the name of the Lord: and the prayer of faith shall save the sick, and the Lord shall raise him up; and if he have committed sins, they shall be forgiven him.

OVERCOMING THE DEVIL

- **Isaiah 59:19** When the enemy shall come in like a flood, the Spirit of the Lord shall lift up a standard against him.
- **2 Corinthians 2:11** Lest Satan should get an advantage of us: for we are not ignorant of his devices.
- **2 Corinthians 10:3–5** For though we walk in the flesh, we do not war after the flesh: For the weapons of our warfare are not carnal, but mighty through God to the pulling down of strong holds. Casting down imaginations, and every high thing that exalteth itself against the knowledge of God, and bringing into captivity every thought to the obedience of Christ.
- **Ephesians 4:27** Neither give place to the devil.
- **Ephesians 6:11–12** Put on the whole armour of God, that ye may be able to stand against the wiles of the devil. For we wrestle not against flesh and blood, but against principalities, against powers, against the rulers of the darkness of this world, against spiritual wickedness in high places.
- **Ephesians 6:16** Above all, taking the shield of faith, wherewith ye shall be able to quench all the fiery darts of the wicked.
- **James 4:7** Resist the devil, and he will flee from you.
- **1 Peter 5:8–9** Be sober, be vigilant; because your adversary the devil, as a roaring lion, walketh about, seeking whom he may devour: whom resist stedfast in the faith.
- **1 John 2:14** The word of God abideth in you, and ye have overcome the wicked one.
- **1 John 3:8** For this purpose the Son of God was manifested, that he might destroy the works of the devil.
- **1 John 4:4** Greater is he that is in you, than he that is in the world.

FEAR NOT

- **Psalm 27:1** The Lord is my light and my salvation; whom shall I fear? The Lord is the strength of my life; of whom shall I be afraid?
- **Psalm 34:4** I sought the Lord, and he heard me, and delivered me from all my fears.
- **Psalm 56:3** What time I am afraid, I will trust in thee.
- **Psalm 56:11** In God have I put my trust: I will not be afraid what man can do unto me.
- **Psalm 118:6** The Lord is on my side; I will not fear: what can man do unto me?
- **Proverbs 29:25** The fear of man bringeth a snare: but whoso putteth his trust in the Lord shall be safe.
- **Isaiah 12:2** Behold, God is my salvation; I will trust, and not be afraid.
- **Isaiah 26:3** Thou wilt keep him in perfect peace, whose mind is stayed on thee: because he trusteth in thee.
- **Isaiah 41:10** Fear thou not; for I am with thee: Be not dismayed; for I am thy God: I will strengthen thee; yea, I will help thee; yea, I will uphold thee with the right hand of my righteousness.
- **John 14:27** Peace I leave with you, my peace I give unto you: not as the world giveth, give I unto you. Let not your heart be troubled, neither let it be afraid.
- **2 Timothy 1:7** God hath not given us the spirit of fear; but of power, and of love, and of a sound mind.
- **1 John 4:18** There is no fear in love; but perfect love casteth out fear: because fear hath torment. He that feareth is not made perfect in love.

THANKFULNESS

- **Psalm 34:1** I will bless the Lord at all times: his praise shall continually be in my mouth.
- **Psalm 107:8** Oh that men would praise the Lord for his goodness, and for his wonderful works to the children of men!
- **Ephesians 5:20** Giving thanks always for all things unto God and the Father in the name of our Lord Jesus Christ;
- **Philippians 4:11** I have learned, in whatsoever state I am, therewith to be content.
- **1 Thessalonians 5:18** In every thing give thanks.
- **Hebrews 13:15** By him therefore let us offer the sacrifice of praise to God continually, that is, the fruit of our lips giving thanks to his name.

PRIDE, SELF-RIGHTEOUSNESS, AND HUMILITY

- **Psalm 34:2** My soul shall make her boast in the Lord: the humble shall hear thereof, and be glad.
- **Proverbs 11:2** When pride cometh, then cometh shame: but with the lowly is wisdom.
- **Proverbs 16:18** Pride goeth before destruction, and an haughty spirit before a fall.
- **Isaiah 57:15** For thus saith the high and lofty one that inhabiteth eternity, whose name is Holy; I dwell in the high and holy place, with him also that is of a contrite and humble spirit, to revive the spirit of the humble, and to revive the heart of the contrite ones.
- **Daniel 4:37** Those that walk in pride he is able to abase.
- **Matthew 23:12** Whosoever shall exalt himself shall be abased; and he that shall humble himself shall be exalted.
- **Luke 6:41–42** Why beholdest thou the mote that is in thy brother's eye, but perceivest not the beam that is in thine own eye? Thou hypocrite, cast out first the beam out of thine own eye, and then shalt thou see clearly to pull out the mote that is in thy brother's eye.
- **2 Corinthians 10:17** He that glorieth, let him glory in the Lord.
- **Philippians 2:3** Let nothing be done through strife or vainglory; but in lowliness of mind let each esteem other better than themselves.
- **1 Peter 5:5–6** All of you be subject one to another, and be clothed with humility: for God resisteth the proud, and giveth grace to the humble. Humble yourselves therefore under the mighty hand of God, that he may exalt you in due time.

THE POWER OF THE TONGUE

- **Psalm 19:14** Let the words of my mouth, and the meditation of my heart, be acceptable in thy sight, O Lord, my strength, and my redeemer.
- **Psalm 35:28** My tongue shall speak of thy righteousness and of thy praise all the day long.
- **Proverbs 16:24** Pleasant words are as an honeycomb, sweet to the soul, and health to the bones.
- **Proverbs 17:27** He that hath knowledge spareth his words: and a man of understanding is of an excellent spirit.
- **Proverbs 18:21** Death and life are in the power of the tongue.
- **Proverbs 29:11** A fool uttereth all his mind: but a wise man keepeth it in till afterwards.
- **Matthew 12:34** Out of the abundance of the heart the mouth speaketh.

- **Matthew 12:36–37** Every idle word that men shall speak, they shall give account thereof in the day of judgement. For by thy words thou shalt be justified, and by thy words thou shalt be condemned.
- **Ephesians 4:29** Let no corrupt communication proceed out of your mouth, but that which is good to the use of edifying, that it may minister grace unto the hearers.
- **James 1:19** Wherefore, my beloved brethren, let every man be swift to hear, slow to speak, slow to wrath.

(See also James 3—"The Tongue Chapter.")

UNITY

- **Psalm 133:1** Behold, how good and how pleasant it is for brethren to dwell together in unity!
- **Ecclesiastes 4:9–10,12** Two are better than one; because they have a good reward for their labour. For if they fall, the one will lift up his fellow: but woe to him that is alone when he falleth; for he hath not another to help him up. And if one prevail against him, two shall withstand him; and a threefold cord is not quickly broken.
- **Romans 12:5** We, being many, are one body in Christ, and every one members one of another.
- **Romans 14:19** Let us therefore follow after the things which make for peace, and things wherewith one may edify another.
- **Romans 16:17** Mark them which cause divisions and offences contrary to the doctrine which ye have learned; and avoid them.
- **1 Corinthians 1:10** Now I beseech you, brethren, by the name of our Lord Jesus Christ, that ye all speak the same thing, and that there be no divisions among you; but that ye be perfectly joined together in the same mind and in the same judgement.
- **Ephesians 4:3** Endeavouring to keep the unity of the Spirit in the bond of peace.

DISCIPLESHIP

- **Matthew 4:19** Follow me, and I will make you fishers of men.
- **Matthew 12:50** Whosoever shall do the will of my Father which is in heaven, the same is my brother, and sister, and mother.
- **Matthew 19:29** Every one that hath forsaken houses, or brethren, or sisters, or father, or mother, or wife, or children, or lands, for my name's sake, shall receive an hundredfold, and shall inherit everlasting life.
- **Luke 9:23–24** If any man will come after me, let him deny himself, and take up his cross daily, and follow me. For whosoever will save his life shall lose it: but whosoever will lose his life for my sake, the same shall save it.

- **John 8:31** If ye continue in my word, then are ye my disciples indeed.
- **John 15:8** Herein is my Father glorified, that ye bear much fruit; so shall ye be my disciples.

THE CHRISTIAN'S RELATIONSHIP TO WORLDLY SOCIETY

- **Matthew 10:16** Behold, I send you forth as sheep in the midst of wolves: be ye therefore wise as serpents, and harmless as doves.
- **John 15:19** If ye were of the world, the world would love his own: but because ye are not of the world, but I have chosen you out of the world, therefore the world hateth you.
- **Romans 12:2** Be not conformed to this world: but be ye transformed by the renewing of your mind, that ye may prove what is that good, and acceptable, and perfect, will of God.
- **2 Corinthians 6:17** Come out from among them, and be ye separate, saith the Lord, and touch not the unclean thing; and I will receive you.
- **1 John 2:15–16** Love not the world, neither the things that are in the world. If any man love the world, the love of the Father is not in him. For all that is in the world, the lust of the flesh, and the lust of the eyes, and the pride of life, is not of the Father, but is of the world.

PERSECUTION

- **Matthew 5:10–12** Blessed are they which are persecuted for righteousness' sake: for theirs is the kingdom of heaven. Blessed are ye, when men shall revile you, and persecute you, and shall say all manner of evil against you falsely, for my sake. Rejoice, and be exceeding glad: for great is your reward in heaven: for so persecuted they the prophets which were before you.
- **John 15:18** If the world hate you, ye know that it hated me before it hated you.
- **John 15:20** Remember the word that I said unto you, The servant is not greater than his Lord. If they have persecuted me, they will also persecute you.
- **John 16:2** The time cometh, that whosoever killeth you will think that he doeth God service.
- **Philippians 1:29** For unto you it is given in the behalf of Christ, not only to believe on him, but also to suffer for his sake.
- **2 Timothy 3:12** Yea, and all that will live godly in Christ Jesus shall suffer persecution.

THE LAW OF CHRIST

- **Matthew 22:37–40** Jesus said unto him, Thou shalt love the Lord thy God with all thy heart, and with all thy soul, and with all thy mind. This is the first and great commandment. And the second is like unto it.
  Thou shalt love thy neighbour as thyself. On these two commandments hang all the law and the prophets.
- **John 1:17** For the law was given by Moses, but grace and truth came by Jesus Christ.
- **Romans 3:28** Therefore we conclude that a man is justified by faith without the deeds of the law.
- **Romans 8:2** The law of the Spirit of life in Christ Jesus hath made me free from the law of sin and death.
- **Romans 10:4** For Christ is the end of the law for righteousness to every one that believeth.
- **Romans 13:8** He that loveth another hath fulfilled the law.
- **Galatians 2:21** I do not frustrate the grace of God: for if righteousness come by the law, then Christ is dead in vain.
- **Galatians 3:13** Christ hath redeemed us from the curse of the law.
- **Galatians 3:24–25** The law was our schoolmaster to bring us unto Christ, that we might be justified by faith. But after that faith is come, we are no longer under a schoolmaster.
- **Galatians 5:1** Stand fast therefore in the liberty wherewith Christ hath made us free, and be not entangled again with the yoke of bondage.
- **Galatians 5:13–14** For, brethren, ye have been called unto liberty; only use not liberty for an occasion to the flesh, but by love serve one another. For all the law is fulfilled in one word, even in this; Thou shalt love thy neighbour as thyself.
- **James 2:10** Whosoever shall keep the whole law, and yet offend in one point, he is guilty of all.

CREATION VS. EVOLUTION

- **Genesis 1:1** In the beginning God created the heaven and the earth.
- **Acts 14:15** Ye should turn from these vanities unto the living God, which made heaven, and earth, and the sea, and all things that are therein.
- **Romans 1:20** For the invisible things of him from the creation of the world are clearly seen, being understood by the things that are made, even his eternal power and Godhead;
- **Hebrews 11:3** Through faith we understand that the worlds were framed by the word of God, so that things which are seen were not made of things which do appear.

references

TO OTHER KEY SCRIPTURES FOR MEMORISATION:

Exodus 15:26

Deuteronomy 31:6
Deuteronomy 33:25

Joshua 23:14

1 Samuel 15:23

2 Kings 20:5

2 Chronicles 20:20

Ezra 8:22

Job 5:17–18

Psalm 1:3
Psalm 27:10
Psalm 34:9
Psalm 37:4–5
Psalm 56:4
Psalm 89:35
Psalm 91:5–7,10
Psalm 106:15
Psalm 118:8
Psalm 119:165
Psalm 127:1
Psalm 127:3

Proverbs 11:14
Proverbs 14:25
Proverbs 14:26
Proverbs 15:32
Proverbs 16:6
Proverbs 22:15
Proverbs 27:5
Proverbs 27:23
Proverbs 28:13

Ecclesiastes 8:11
Ecclesiastes 12:13

Isaiah 43:1
Isaiah 45:11
Isaiah 53:5
Isaiah 55:3–4
Isaiah 59:1
Isaiah 65:24

Jeremiah 1:8

Amos 3:7

Matthew 5:42
Matthew 5:44
Matthew 7:18–20
Matthew 10:1
Matthew 10:8
Matthew 10:20
Matthew 10:28
Matthew 10:36–38
Matthew 17:21
Matthew 18:3
Matthew 18:18
Matthew 18:20
Matthew 22:14
Matthew 23:11
Matthew 25:23
Matthew 25:40
Matthew 28:19–20

Mark 3:33,35
Mark 5:36
Mark 6:4
Mark 8:36–37
Mark 16:17–18

Luke 1:37
Luke 9:2
Luke 10:19
Luke 14:33
Luke 16:10
Luke 17:32
Luke 21:15
Luke 21:17–19
Luke 22:31–32

John 3:30
John 12:24
John 12:32
John 13:34
John 14:14
John 15:2
John 15:4–5
John 15:7
John 15:13
John 15:16
John 15:26
John 16:2

Acts 2:44–45
Acts 4:12
Acts 4:13
Acts 5:38–39
Acts 5:42
Acts 9:34

Romans 6:13
Romans 8:26
Romans 8:31
Romans 8:38–39
Romans 9:20
Romans 10:13
Romans 12:11
Romans 13:8
Romans 14:23

1 Corinthians 2:4–5
1 Corinthians 4:2
1 Corinthians 6:20
1 Corinthians 9:14
1 Corinthians 11:1
1 Corinthians 11:23–26
1 Corinthians 13:4–7
1 Corinthians 13:13

Galatians 5:22–23
Galatians 6:2
Galatians 6:9

Ephesians 3:20–21
Ephesians 5:11
Ephesians 5:20

Philippians 2:13
Philippians 4:8
Philippians 4:9

Colossians 1:13
Colossians 3:13–14

1 Thessalonians.5:17

1 Timothy 5:17
1 Timothy 6:12

2 Timothy 1:12
2 Timothy 2:2
2 Timothy 3:12
2 Timothy 4:18

Titus 1:15
Titus 3:5

Hebrews 4:12
Hebrews 7:25
Hebrews 11:16
Hebrews 12:1
Hebrews 12:6
Hebrews 12:11
Hebrews 12:13
Hebrews 13:8
Hebrews 13:17

James 1:2
James 1:5
James 1:8
James 1:22
James 2:15–17
James 2:26
James 4:3
James 4:7
James 4:17
James 5:16

1 Peter 4:12–13
1 Peter 5:5

2 Peter 1:4

1 John 2:17
1 John 4:4
1 John 4:7
1 John 4:19
1 John 5:4
1 John 5:14
1 John 5:15

Revelation 2:10
Revelation 3:11

index

Familiarising yourself with this index will enable you to quickly and easily find verses on important topics throughout *Bible Basics,* which you may otherwise have difficulty locating.

For example, "Anger" is not a listed topic or subtopic in the Table of Contents, yet some excellent verses on the subject can be found by looking up the references given under this topic in the index.

A typical reference, such as the first one given under "Anger," "pg.205:2l," indicates that you should turn to page 205, topic 2, subtopic l. When a reference has "all" next to it, such as the last reference under "Angels," "pg.169:11all," it indicates that "all" of the subtopics of topic 11 on page 169 pertain to this particular subject.

All references in this index are arranged in consecutive numerical order, except when a major section of *Bible Basics* is devoted to a specific topic—then those references are given first.

Abortion pg.283:3

Action (See Initiative and action.)

Afflictions (See Sickness.)

Alcoholism pg.146:14A

Angels pg.111:7I; pg.114:2D; pg.169:11all

Anger pg.205:2I; pg.209:5I

God's anger (See Punishment of the worldly.)

Anointing of the Holy Spirit (See Baptism of the Holy Spirit.)

Antichrist, the pg.264:2–5; pg.265:6B–D,F; pg.269:12A,B

Apathy (See Lukewarmness.)

Appreciation pg.273:2B

Arguments pg.30:9D; pg.77:7B; pg.78:9C; pg.184:2K; pg.200:11all; pg.204:2C; pg.208:5,K; pg.210:7B,C; pg.211:10; pg.276:6B

Armageddon, Battle of pg.269:12all

Atomic war pg.268:11B

Atonement pg.3:9–10; pg.7:2D,E; pg.69:9B; pg.253:4all; pg.254:5C

B

Babies (See Birth, and Children.)

Backsliding pg.243:1all

Baptism of the Holy Spirit pg.13:10F; pg.19:2all; pg.20:3all; pg.24:10all; pg.80:13A

Baptism, water pg.4:13

Battle of Gog and Magog (See Gog and Magog, Battle of.)

Battles (See Temptation and lust, and Trials and tribulations.)

Beauty pg.185:3A; pg.274:3D

Bible (See Word, the.)

Birth pg.283:4all

Bitterness and grudges pg.35:4E; pg.59:10D; pg.200:10B; pg.206:2K; pg.208:5H; pg.209:6C; pg.238:1M

Boldness/Shyness pg.75:3; pg.81:16A; pg.172:2B,C; pg.200:10E

C

Change pg.216:9D

Chastening pg.2:6B; pg.87:6B; pg.129:3A; pg.130:3C; pg.133:7B; pg.140:2B,C; pg.141:5A; pg.185:3C,4C

Mercy in chastening pg.57:9D; pg.150:3C (See also Forgiveness and mercy.)

Severe chastening pg.145:13; pg.237:1L; pg.290:3F

Children pg.28:8B; pg.284:5–8; pg.297:7

Choice and decision-making pg.96:12all (See also How to find the will of God.)

Christianity pg.70:9F–G

Church (See Christianity, and Fellowship.)

Comfort pg.21:3F; pg.133:7C; pg.144:10; pg.226:2B

Peace of mind and assurance pg.19:1C; pg.20:3D; pg.66:7A,D; pg.171:1D

Commitment (See Dedication and commitment.)

Communism pg.264:2

Competitiveness (See Exaltation, self, and Jealousy.)

Complacency (See Lukewarmness.)

Complaint (See Murmuring, and Thankfulness.)

Compromise pg.88:8B; pg.137:13B; pg.174:4D; pg.221:3G,5all; pg.232:5G; pg.233:8A; pg.247:5D; pg.296:6D

Consideration (See Kindness and courtesy.)

Conviction pg.43:5G; pg.74:2A; pg.126:8G; pg.200:10E; pg.202:11J; pg.211:10all; pg.222:5B; pg.225:9E; pg.228:3C; pg.231:4L; pg.240:7F

Conversation (See Speech, edifying.)

Correction pg.237:1J; pg.240:7G

Counselling tips pg.29:8C,F,G; pg.71:2C; pg.75:4; pg.78:9C; pg.90:3G; pg.93:7A–C; pg.131:3K; pg.134:8all; pg.145:12; pg.152:7all; pg.176:5D; pg.210:7B,C; pg.274:2C

Courage (See Boldness/Shyness, and Fear not.)

Covetousness pg.64:3E; pg.68:8B; pg.123:5D; pg.131:4C; pg.137:13A,B; pg.146:14E; pg.213:3C; pg.218:1E; pg.219:7C,D; pg.230:4J; pg.236:1C,E; pg.246:5A; pg.248:8all

Creation vs. evolution pg.5:1E; pg.17:13A,B; pg.25:3B

Criticism (See Gossip and criticism, and Self-righteousness.)

Cursing and foul speech pg.195:3A,4A–C,E; pg.196:5A

Daydreaming (See Imaginations, vain.)

Death pg.154:8C,D

Decisions (See Choice and decision-making.)

Dedication and commitment pg.29:8D,E; pg.61:1D; pg.63:3A; pg.102:5C; pg.131:4B; pg.135:11A; pg.136:11H; pg.141:4A; pg.213:3all; pg.215:5all; pg.216:7all; pg.241:4J; pg.290:4C; pg.291:5C (See also Renouncing all for Jesus.)

Deliverance (See Exorcism.)

Dependence upon God pg.41:3B; pg.43:5H; pg.105:2,3all; pg.109:6D,E; pg.133:6B; pg.135:11B; pg.143:8B; pg.150:2J; pg.187:6D; pg.188:7C; pg.189:9A; pg.240:7C; pg.256:7B; pg.296:5C

Desires of your heart pg.44:5O; pg.95:9A

Warnings about pg.95:9B; pg.96:12B; pg.102:5B; pg.128:2all; pg.136:11E; pg.236:1B (See also Temptation and lust.)

Devil, the pg.10:6B; pg.13:10D; pg.163:1–8; pg.225:10B

Devil's devices pg.31:11; pg.47:9B; pg.114:3A; pg.134:9B; pg.139:1A,B; pg.160:9D; pg.166:5all; pg.167:6:A,B,7all; pg.174:4I; pg.198:6E; pg.209:6F

Devotion (See Dedication and commitment, and Relationship with God, Renouncing all for Jesus.)

Diligence pg.29:8E; pg.90:3D; pg.124:7C

Discipleship pg.54:6B; pg.63:2E,F; pg.80:14A

Discouragement and despair pg.98:15A; pg.132:5; pg.144:9; pg.154:8E; pg.180:4D–F; pg.181:6B

Disobedience and rebellion pg.102:7,8; pg.140:3B; pg.141:C; pg.174:4E; pg.243:2D; pg.286:6D (See also Stubbornness.)

Punishment for pg.34:4A,D; pg.74:2C; pg.89:3B; pg.97:13A

Disunity and dissension pg.204:1B; pg.208:5–7; pg.244:3B; pg.276:6B

Divorce pg.278:9

Doublemindedness (See Doubt.)

Doubt pg.30:9A; pg.34:4B; pg.49:11all; pg.68:8D; pg.96:10C; pg.172:3A; pg.180:4B,C; pg.237:1G,J; pg.256:6C

Dreams pg.90:4all; pg.289:3D (See also Visions, prophetic.)

Drugs pg.146:14A

Education, Godly pg.284:5A–I

Emergencies pg.36:6B; pg.37:7all; pg.98:15C; pg.112:1E,F; pg.114:3all; pg.117:6B,D; pg.171:2A; pg.263:1C; pg.289:1C; pg.291:6B (See also Protection.)

Employment, secular pg.124:7all; pg.223:7A,B; pg.224:8C,D

Encouragement pg.134:8B; pg.149:2F,G; pg.175:5C; pg.176:5D; pg.192:1E (See also Counselling tips.)

Encouragement through fellowship pg.71:2A

Endtime pg.116:5; pg.121:3A; pg.168:8A,D,E; pg.235:10all; pg.243:1

Enemies pg.116:4; pg.171:1B; pg.234:9A–C; pg.242:5D

Loving enemies pg.56:8D

Entertainment pg.135:10D; pg.220:3D; pg.221:3H,I

Enthusiasm and zeal pg.3:8B; pg.52:4E; pg.89:1C; pg.100:1B

Envy (See Jealousy.)

Evolution, theory of (See Creation vs. evolution.)

Exaltation, self pg.108:5A–C; pg.110:7F; pg.183:2C,F,G; pg.185:3D,4B; pg.208:5F; pg.244:3C (See also Dependence upon God, and Pride.)

Excommunication pg.198:7B; pg.210:8,9; pg.240:4H

Excuses and self-justification pg.214:3G

Exorcism pg.164:3C–E; pg.165:4C–F; pg.169:10A–C; pg.176:5E,G (See also Overcoming the Devil.)

Faith pg.1:4; pg.22:4D; pg.33:2A; pg.94:8E,F; pg.97:12C; pg.116:6A; pg.158:6D–F; pg.256:6C

Faithfulness in little things (See Diligence.)

Faithfulness pg.40:2D; pg.42:4I; pg.43:5I; pg.48:10B; pg.53:5D; pg.100:1C; pg.129:3B; pg.136:11F; pg.138:14; pg.143:8D,G; pg.149:2E; pg.227:3A; pg.228:3D,F; pg.239:4B; pg.268:10C

False doctrine pg.30:9C,10; pg.90:3C; pg.91:4D; pg.92:5D; pg.93:6B; pg.243:2B,C; pg.244:3A,D–G

Fasting pg.38:7G

Fathers pg.124:7A; pg.279:10–13

Fear not pg.48:10B; pg.171:1–5; pg.289:1B

Fear of man pg.63:2G

Not fearing man pg.75:3; pg.110:7D,G; pg.171:1C

Fear of God pg.58:9F; pg.64:4all; pg.117:6C; pg.136:11G; pg.176:6all; pg.183:1B; pg.238:1R

Fellowship pg.56:8B; pg.207:4A,B; pg.245:4all

Fight the good fight of faith pg.25:4; pg.109:7A,C–K; pg.159:8all; pg.165:4A,B; pg.168:9all; pg.266:6I; pg.280:12A,B

Finances (See Prosperity, material, and Giving, and Supply.)

First place (See Relationship with God.)

Fleeces pg.96:10all

Foolishness and shallowness pg.118:6G; pg.194:2H; pg.195:4all; pg.286:6D; pg.296:6C

Forgiveness and mercy pg.57:9–12; pg.140:2D; pg.238:2; pg.242:5A; pg.258:11A; pg.286:7B

Freedom from fear (See Fear not.)

Free will (See Choice and decision-making.)

Fruitfulness pg.79:12; pg.128:2C; pg.130:3D,F; pg.207:3C; pg.212:2A; pg.294:4A

Future (See Endtime.)

Gifts of the Spirit pg.20:3E; pg.21:4all; pg.41:4A; pg.51:4B

Giving pg.214:4C; pg.295:4B (See also Supporters.)

Goals and vision pg.40:1A; pg.64:3E; pg.135:11A,I; pg.236:1C; pg.239:4A,B,F

God pg.5:1A–F,J; pg.6:2A–C; pg.9:5C,E,F; pg.12:10A,E; pg.14:11A–F; pg.15:12A; pg.17:13A,C; pg.45:6C,E; pg.99:16A; pg.104:1all; pg.110:7C; pg.120:1B,C; pg.163:2B; pg.183:2A; pg.186:5B; pg.225:10A; pg.246:4D; pg.261:6,8

God's way vs. man's way pg.6:1G; pg.8:4D; pg.39:9C; pg.45:7; pg.47:9A; pg.93:7D; pg.99:16B; pg.102:7; pg.107:4E; pg.109:6D,E; pg.110:7E,K; pg.139:2A; pg.167:7D; pg.216:6C; pg.227:2D,G; pg.259:11B; pg.289:3B; pg.294:3L; pg.295:4H

Gog and Magog, Battle of pg.271:14

Gossip and criticism pg.195:3all; pg.197:6all; pg.198:7–8; pg.209:5J; pg.231:5A–F; pg.238:1O

Government pg.82:16B; pg.102:6; pg.221:4A; pg.225:9–10

Great tribulation pg.264:6all; pg.235:10B

Great white throne judgement pg.271:15

Happiness and joy pg.44:5J; pg.66:7B; pg.78:9B; pg.86:5A; pg.144:8E; pg.151:6A,B; pg.179:2C; pg.227:3B

Hatred pg.55:7all; pg.59:10D; pg.198:6D; pg.206:2P; pg.208:5C; pg.229:4B

Healing pg.22:4D; pg.44:5N

Heaven pg.2:7all; pg.6:1H; pg.43:5F; pg.133:6D; pg.142:6; pg.154:8D; pg.155:9all; pg.162:12; pg.218:1A; pg.226:2A; pg.265:6H; pg.271:16all

Holy Spirit pg.27:6D; pg.38:8B; pg.43:5D; pg.80:13all; pg.89:2all; pg.108:6A,B; pg.148:1C; pg.245:4A

Honesty pg.87:6D; pg.190:9C; pg.222:6A–D; pg.240:4G (See also Truth, and Lying.)

Hospitality pg.125:8D,E

How to find the will of God pg.28:7D; pg.33:2B,C; pg.38:7E; pg.79:10C

Humility and meekness pg.8:4C; pg.33:2D; pg.65:5E; pg.142:5E; pg.187:7–12; pg.202:11K

Humour pg.193:1H

Husbands pg.273:2all; pg.278:7F (See also Marriage.)

Hypocrisy pg.35:4G,H; pg.52:4F; pg.87:5D,6D; pg.103:8all; pg.186:5D; pg.199:8F; pg.242:5C; pg.243:2D; pg.246:5C; pg.247:6C; pg.248:8B; pg.248:9all

I

Imaginations, vain pg.68:8F; pg.238:1N

Importunity (See Perseverance.)

Industriousness (See Diligence.)

Infidelity pg.278:9

Initiative and action pg.48:10D; pg.49:10E; pg.54:6A; pg.94:8C,D; pg.117:6F; pg.122:4B; pg.158:6G; pg.291:5C (See also Diligence.)

Inspiration (See Enthusiasm and zeal.)

J

Jealousy pg.208:5D; pg.230:4H

Jesus Christ pg.1:3–5; pg.24:9; pg.25:3A; pg.32:1D; pg.38:8A; pg.50:1C; pg.61:1E; pg.62:1F; pg.69:9D–I; pg.101:4; pg.142:7all; pg.156:1,3C; pg.164:3A–C; pg.167:6C; pg.190:10A; pg.200:10D; pg.232:7A,B; pg.253:4C

Joking pg.195:4A–E (See also Humour.)

Joy (See Happiness and joy.)

Judgement seat of Christ pg.16:12F; pg.80:14B; pg.84:3B; pg.133:6D; pg.217:8B,C; pg.239:4B; pg.268:10all

K

Kindness and courtesy pg.53:5E–H; pg.153:7C; pg.205:2E

L

Law of Christ pg.57:9C

Laziness pg.33:1G; pg.123:5C; pg.290:5A,D

Leadership pg.72:2G; pg.131:3H; pg.205:2J; pg.209:6D; pg.210:7B; pg.216:6B; pg.244:3C; pg.247:7all; pg.275:5all

Leadings of God's Spirit pg.21:4A,E; pg.27:6D; pg.62:2D; pg.90:3E; pg.92:6A; pg.95:9A; pg.97:14,15; pg.102:5D

Legalism pg.257:9all; pg.258:10all; pg.258:11A (See also Law of Christ, and Self-righteousness.)

Loneliness pg.71:1D; pg.72:2H; pg.106:3B; pg.131:4D; pg.151:4B; pg.154:8A–C

Love for God (See Relationship with God.)

Love for the lost pg.131:6A; pg.228:3G; pg.247:6B
Love for one another pg.53:5all; pg.56:8all; pg.57:9A; pg.62:2C; pg.97:12D; pg.190:10D; pg.205:2D
Love of God for man pg.6:1J; pg.9:5E; pg.50:1all; pg.67:7E; pg.124:6all
Lukewarmness pg.68:8C; pg.103:8C; pg.236:1A; pg.246:5A; pg.247:6B; pg.291:5E
Lust (See Temptation and lust.)
Lying pg.166:5B; pg.203:12all; pg.231:5A,B (See also Honesty, and Truth.)

Man-pleasing pg.184:2H; pg.206:2L; pg.232:5G (See also Fear of man.)
Marriage pg.63:3C; pg.219:2D; pg.273:1–9
Marriage Supper of the Lamb pg.267:9all
Medicine pg.162:11all
Memorisation pg.29:8D; pg.76:5B; pg.157:6B; pg.240:4D
Mercy (See Forgiveness and mercy.)
Millennium, the pg.269:13all
Miracles pg.22:4D; pg.42:4G; pg.46:8A–C; pg.49:11C; pg.104:1C; pg.116:4; pg.120:2all
Missionaries pg.74:1all; pg.77:8A; pg.125:8C; pg.224:8all (See also Discipleship, and Witnessing.)
Money (See Prosperity, material, and Giving, and Supply.)
Mothers pg.274:3B; pg.279:10A,B,E–J; pg.280:11–13 (See also Parents.)
Moving and travel pg.115:3G; pg.123:5E; pg.226:2C; pg.233:8B (See also Change.)
Murmuring pg.127:11B; pg.144:8F; pg.175:4–6; pg.181:6B; pg.208:5E; pg.238:1P
Music and dancing (See Singing.)

Negative thinking (See Gossip and criticism, and Murmuring.)

Obedience pg.15:11G,H; pg.23:8A,B; pg.26:6A–C; pg.33:2B; pg.89:1D; pg.100:1–8; pg.117:6E,F; pg.122:4A; pg.130:3E; pg.142:5C; pg.149:2D; pg.161:10C; pg.215:6A–C; pg.285:6A; pg.286:6C

Occult, the pg.97:13B

Opportunities pg.93:8all

Overcoming the Devil pg.164:3–4all; pg.168:9–11all (See also Exorcism.)

P

Pacifism pg.110:7B

Parents pg.279:10–12all

Patience pg.37:7C; pg.39:9B; pg.47:8G; pg.131:3I; pg.143:8A; pg.149:2E; pg.193:2B

- **Patience with the errant** pg.58:10B

Peace of mind (See Comfort, and Trust.)

Persecution pg.12:9E; pg.81:16A; pg.141:4B; pg.249:10all; pg.265:6F,G; pg.266:6I

Perseverance pg.36:5C; pg.37:7C–G; pg.47:8F

- **Constantly witness** pg.79:10A
- **Witness despite opposition** pg.81:16A

Personal example pg.78:9all; pg.222:6A,B; pg.101:3A; pg.200:10A–C

Pilgrims and strangers pg.218:1all; pg.220:3B; pg.233:8B (See also Change, and Moving and travel.)

Pioneering (See Initiative and action, and Witnessing.)

Politics (See Government.)

Positive attitude pg.133:7A; pg.151:6all; pg.178:1A,B; pg.181:6A; pg.198:8A; pg.199:8D

Praising God pg.32:1A; pg.107:4C; pg.160:9B; pg.178:2–3; pg.182:6C; pg.183:2B; pg.189:9A; pg.193:1G

Prayer pg.21:3G; pg.46:8B–F; pg.62:2B; pg.72:3D; pg.117:6B; pg.145:11B; pg.148:2A; pg.290:4A,B; pg.291:5B; pg.295:4E

Pregnancy pg.282:1,2

Pride pg.163:1B; pg.183:1–4; pg.186:5C; pg.187:7all; pg.191:11A,B; pg.230:4K (See also Exaltation, self.)

Prodigals (See Repentance.)

Prophecy and direct revelation pg.21:4B; pg.92:6all; pg.153:7F

Prosperity, material pg.28:7C; pg.34:3D, pg.84:2B; pg.85:4D; pg.101:3C; pg.126:10all; pg.133:6C; pg.185:3B; pg.214:4A,B (See also Covetousness.)

Protection pg.44:5L; pg.101:3D; pg.266:6J; pg.280:12all

Punishment of the worldly pg.145:13all; pg.185:4C; pg.234:9C (See also Great white throne judgement.)

R

Rapture, the pg.267:8all

Reading and viewing (See Entertainment.)

Receptivity, spiritual pg.9:5D; pg.42:4E; pg.62:2D; pg.81:15A; pg.89:1D

Redeeming the time (See Diligence.)

Rejection of the truth pg.9:5F,G; pg.10:6B; pg.23:8C,D; pg.30:9E,F; pg.81:15B; pg.93:7C; pg.97:13A; pg.173:3C; pg.237:1F,H,L; pg.246:5B (See also Disobedience and rebellion, and Stubbornness.)

Relations with people pg.30:9D; pg.51:3all,4A,B; pg.52:4E–G; pg.53:5F–H; pg.54:6C; pg.55:6E,F; pg.55:7all; pg.58:10A–D; pg.78:9C; pg.88:8A; pg.97:12D; pg.131:3K; pg.142:5I; pg.145:12all; pg.152:7all; pg.190:10all; pg.204:2all; pg.210:7A,C; pg.221:4A; pg.223:6E; pg.276:6all

Relationship with God pg.20:3C; pg.26:6B; pg.32:1E,F; pg.36:6A,C,D; pg.37:6E; pg.43:5A; pg.50:1D; pg.51:2all; pg.100:2all; pg.101:3B; pg.132:4E; pg.133:7B; pg.188:8B; pg.217:8A; pg.233:7C; pg.288:9B

Relationship to the world pg.56:8A; pg.73:5all; pg.135:10B,D; pg.214:4B; pg.230:4I

Renouncing all for Jesus pg.131:4B; pg.136:11E; pg.213:3all

Repentance pg.35:4C; pg.96:11A; pg.145:11C; pg.145:15all; pg.157:5all; pg.176:5F; pg.189:8G; pg.191:11C; pg.211:9all; pg.238:2all; pg.239:3all

Resentment (See Bitterness and grudges.)

Resting in God (See Trust.)

Resurrection, Jesus' pg.10:7B,C; pg.11:8B,C; pg.12:9F; pg.17:13D

Resurrection, Christians' pg.44:5P; pg.162:12all; pg.267:8all

Rewards (See Judgement seat of Christ.)

Righteousness pg.28:7E; pg.43:5C; pg.159:9A; pg.186:5F

S

Sacrifice (See Dedication and commitment, and Renouncing all for Jesus.)

Safety (See Protection.)

Salvation and eternal life pg.8:5all; pg.19:1all; pg.27:7A; pg.40:2A; pg.69:9B,C,E; pg.70:9I; pg.74:2B; pg.80:13B; pg.99:18A; pg.101:3A; pg.166:5C; pg.169:9E; pg.169:10C,D; pg.244:2E; pg.251:1all; pg.257:9D; pg.285:5G; pg.288:9A

Sample (See Personal example.)

Science pg.260:5all; pg.263:1B

Second coming of Christ pg.266:7all

Secrets, keeping pg.194:2F (See also Silence and guarded speech.)

Selfishness pg.35:4F; pg.39:9D; pg.55:6D; pg.87:6all; pg.146:14E; pg.248:8C; pg.256:8all

Self-righteousness pg.4:12all; pg.35:4G,H; pg.59:10F,G; pg.180:4G; pg.186:5all; pg.187:6all; pg.199:9all; pg.230:4F; pg.249:9B,C; pg.257:9C; pg.258:10A

Service (See Discipleship.)

Sex pg.277:7all

Shyness (See Boldness/Shyness.)

Sickness pg.114:3B,C; pg.159:9all; pg.162:12all; pg.167:7B; pg.174:4G

Signs of the end pg.263:1all

Silence and guarded speech pg.35:4H; pg.193:2all; pg.199:8C; pg.200:10D; pg.201:11B,C; pg.205:2H (See also Secrets, keeping.)

Sin pg.3:9,10all; pg.4:11all; pg.6:1I; pg.35:4C; pg.68:8E; pg.108:5C; pg.123:5A; pg.129:2F; pg.140:3B; pg.157:6A; pg.160:9C; pg.167:6A; pg.173:3D; pg.186:5D,E; pg.237:1K; pg.240:4G; pg.252:2E; pg.253:3B,C

Forgiveness of pg.57:9E; pg.154:8E

Singing pg.72:3C; pg.114:2F; pg.153:7E; pg.159:8A; pg.179:2B

Sorrow pg.131:3J; pg.133:7C; pg.150:3A,B; pg.152:6C; pg.154:8A–C; pg.155:9all; pg.286:6D

Speech, edifying pg.192:1all; pg.196:5B; pg.201:11D (See also Encouragement, and Silence and guarded speech.)

Spirit world (See Angels, and Heaven.)

Steadfastness (See Faithfulness.)

Strength and power pg.13:10F; pg.22:4G; pg.40:2D; pg.42:4I; pg.43:5H; pg.67:7C; pg.71:1C; pg.133:6B; pg.169:10A; pg.206:3B; pg.296:5A

Stubbornness pg.95:9B; pg.129:2K (See also Disobedience and rebellion.)
Submission (See Yieldedness.)
Success and failure pg.28:7C; pg.47:8E,F; pg.49:11B; pg.108:5B; pg.184:2M; pg.188:8D,E; pg.196:4E
Supply pg.44:5M; pg.64:3D; pg.98:15D; pg.266:6J; pg.279:10C; pg.292:1D (See also Supporters.)
Supporters pg.85:4all; pg.125:8A,C,D,F; pg.126:9all; pg.224:8A,C

T

Teaching (See Word, the.)
Teenagers pg.288:8B–D
Temptation and lust pg.95:9B; pg.129:2G; pg.134:9–15
Thankfulness pg.38:8C,E; pg.114:2F; pg.123:4D; pg.127:11A; pg.181:6A; pg.241:4L
Tithing pg.63:2H; pg.88:7all (See also Giving.)
Tongue, the (See Speech, edifying.)
Tongues, the gift of pg.22:4F; pg.32:1B
Trials and tribulations pg.47:9B; pg.48:10A; pg.128:1–8; pg.160:9E; pg.167:7E (See also Temptation and lust.)
Truth pg.7:3A; pg.21:3H (See also Honesty, and Lying.)
Trust pg.41:3B; pg.45:6all; pg.48:10A–E; pg.65:5A,C; pg.105:2A; pg.113:2A; pg.114:2E; pg.140:2E; pg.171:2A; pg.175:5A; pg.285:5F

Unbelief (See Doubt.)
Unity pg.23:6all; pg.36:5B; pg.53:5C; pg.93:7B (See also Disunity and dissension.)
Unselfishness pg.85:4C,D,F; pg.86:5C; pg.88:7D; pg.102:5C; pg.126:8H; pg.213:3B; pg.215:5all; pg.216:7A

Vengeance, God's (See Punishment of the worldly.)

Vision (See Goals and vision.)

Visions, prophetic pg.91:5all (See also Dreams.)

W

War pg.110:7B–K; pg.116:4all; pg.263:1D

Weakness pg.104:1B,D; pg.108:5C; pg.109:6D; pg.133:6B; pg.173:4B; pg.237:1H (See also Dependence upon God.)

Will of God (See How to find the will of God.)

Wisdom, Godly pg.21:4A; pg.27:7B; pg.30:9B; pg.44:5K; pg.64:4C; pg.89:2all; pg.90:3F; pg.142:5G; pg.189:8H; pg.192:1D; pg.193:2B–D; pg.292:1C; pg.296:6A

God's compared to man's pg.5:1F,G; pg.296:6B

Wisdom, ungodly pg.76:6all; pg.184:2I,J

Witnessing pg.29:8F,G; pg.42:4F; pg.73:5; pg.108:6all; pg.219:2C; pg.221:4B,C; pg.226:2C,D,F; pg.266:6K; pg.270:13G; pg.295:4F

Wives pg.274:3all; pg.275:4all; pg.276:5C (See also Marriage, and Women.)

Women pg.275:5all (See also Wives.)

Word, the pg.8:4A; pg.10:7A; pg.32:1F; pg.41:4C–E; pg.45:6E; pg.71:2B; pg.76:5all; pg.81:15A; pg.89:3all; pg.130:3C; pg.136:11D; pg.141:5A; pg.175:5B; pg.190:9B; pg.197:5E; pg.204:2A; pg.255:5H; pg.260:2all; pg.285:5E

Alienation from pg.30:9all; pg.183:2E; pg.244:2A; pg.244:3A,D–G

Disbelief and disobedience to pg.141:3C; pg.173:3C

Work (See Diligence, and Employment, secular.)

Works, good

Commended pg.3:8B; pg.54:6A; pg.59:11; pg.78:9A; pg.81:4; pg.117:6E,F; pg.200:10C; pg.222:6A,B (See also Judgement seat of Christ.)

Warnings pg.1:2all; pg.63:3F; pg.103:8B; pg.251:1all

Worldliness pg.67:8A–C; pg.134:9A; pg.135:10D; pg.219:2B; pg.220:3A,C–H; pg.221:5,5A; pg.236:1E; pg.241:4J
Worry pg.48:10B,C; pg.65:5C; pg.174:4F; pg.175:5C; pg.289:3C; pg.294:3J (See also Faith, and Fear not, and Trust.)
Wrath of God, the pg.268:11all

Y

Yieldedness pg.89:1all; pg.93:7D; pg.96:12B; pg.102:5all; pg.131:4A
Youth pg.287:8all; pg.292:1E

Z

Zeal (See Enthusiasm and zeal.)